THE PROVINCE AND POLITICS OF THE ECONOMIC TORTS

The landmark case of *OBG v Allan* (2008) provided one of the most important decisions in the whole of the law of torts in the last generation, as the House of Lords sought to bring order to an area of the law that has long been beset by doctrinal and theoretical puzzles. Probably the most enduring question of all in this area is whether the economic torts can be unified. This book argues that the search for unity is a will o' the wisp. More particularly, it shows that although some juridical connections exist between some of these torts, there is far more that separates them than unites them. Offering a unique perspective, this is a landmark publication on the law concerning the economic torts.

Volume 40 in the series Hart Studies in Private Law

The Province and Politics of the Economic Torts

John Murphy

• HART •
OXFORD • LONDON • NEW YORK • NEW DELHI • SYDNEY

HART PUBLISHING
Bloomsbury Publishing Plc
Kemp House, Chawley Park, Cumnor Hill, Oxford, OX2 9PH, UK
1385 Broadway, New York, NY 10018, USA
29 Earlsfort Terrace, Dublin 2, Ireland

First published in Great Britain 2022

A catalogue record for this book is available from the British Library.

Library of Congress Cataloging-in-Publication data

Names: Murphy, John, 1965- author.

Title: The province and politics of the economic torts / John Murphy.

Description: Oxford ; New York : Hart, 2022. | Series: Hart studies in private law ; volume 40 | Includes bibliographical references and index.

Identifiers: LCCN 2021042768 (print) | LCCN 2021042769 (ebook) | ISBN 9781509927319 (hardback) | ISBN 9781509955480 (paperback) | ISBN 9781509927333 (pdf) | ISBN 9781509927326 (Epub)

Subjects: LCSH: Torts—Economic aspects—England.

Classification: LCC KD1949 .M87 2021 (print) | LCC KD1949 (ebook) | DDC 346.4203—dc23/eng/20211105

LC record available at https://lccn.loc.gov/2021042768

LC ebook record available at https://lccn.loc.gov/2021042769

ISBN: HB: 978-1-50992-731-9
ePDF: 978-1-50992-733-3
ePub: 978-1-50992-732-6

Typeset by Compuscript Ltd, Shannon

This book is dedicated to my former colleague,
and inspirational friend, Hazel Carty.

FOREWORD

Professor Murphy's book bears witness to the enduring fascination of the so-called 'economic torts', their significance for the theory of tort law and their political and ideological formation. These torts have demonstrated sustained resilience, when so much of tort law has become focused on the advance of negligence. This illustrates the contested nature of the theoretical basis of tort law and the way in which it gives scope for its structures both to be invested with new priorities while others fade, and to be moulded around changing moral and social views across time – what one might call the genealogical aspect of tort law.[1] The history of the tort of conspiracy which the book brings out so clearly is a good example of this. To use the metaphor Professor Murphy borrows, this feature of the area is a vivid illustration of the role of tort law as the common law's Swiss army knife, a tool-kit capable of adjustment to satisfy morally justified claims which do not fit neatly within established liability categories. It is perhaps a consequence of that openness to background moral visions, which are not fixed, that there continues to be 'uncertainty concerning the purposes, scope, unity and future possible uses of these torts', as Professor Murphy notes in chapter one. This is part of what makes these torts so interesting.

It also means that there is lots to argue about regarding how they fit together, what interests they protect and what control mechanisms give them their boundaries. In the leading cases of *Allen v Flood*[2] and *Rookes v Barnard*[3] the House of Lords was forced to grapple with foundational ideas in the law of tort to reason their way through to the result. Lord Watson's speech in the former appears to me to capture an important truth, that there are two basic principles in operation – but this is contested, in debates which Professor Murphy analyses in detail. The first is a principle for the imposition of liability for becoming involved in a wrong committed by another, on the model of *Lumley v Gye*.[4] I think this is capable of generalisation and alignment with ideas of secondary or accessory liability across the law of obligations, though Professor Murphy is not convinced. The second is a principle imposing liability for the intentional infliction of harm by using unlawful means. This principle poses problems about its proper ambit and the conceptual

[1] See, eg, TT Arvind and J Steele, *Tort Law and the Legislature: Common Law, Statute and the Dynamics of Legal Change* (Oxford, Hart Publishing, 2012), Introduction; *cf* R Geuss, *Who Needs a World View?* (Harvard University Press, 2020) Ch 3, 'Enlightenment, Genealogy and the Historicality of Concepts'.

[2] *Allen v Flood* [1898] AC 1.

[3] *Rookes v Barnard* [1964] AC 1129.

[4] *Lumley v Gye* (1853) 2 El & Bl 216.

means by which it may be kept within reasonable bounds. With the decision of the House of Lords in *OBG Ltd v Allan*[5] it appeared that this form of tort had been authoritatively clarified and stabilised, with set limits including in particular that the unlawful means used had to be independently actionable in civil law and did not include criminal actions (however much this conflicted with previous authority, including *Rookes v Barnard*). But within a year, in the *Total Network* case,[6] a different panel of the appellate committee decided that the wider traditional concept of unlawful means was relevant for the cognate tort of conspiracy to injure by unlawful means. This puts pressure on the solution in *OBG Ltd* in both practical and conceptual terms, since it is relatively easy to plead conspiracy in contexts in which the unlawful means tort is in issue. Stability has proved elusive. The economic torts have not settled down into boring orthodoxy.

This book is a deeply thoughtful exploration of the origins, development and conceptual basis for the economic torts. Professor Murphy helpfully casts his net wide to discuss torts (and torts which arguably exist, even if not definitively established) which are within or closely adjacent to the traditionally identified category of the economic torts, to reveal common patterns as well as disjunctures. He presents a powerful argument that these torts are not limited to the protection of trade and business interests, so that it is difficult to regard this as something which gives them coherence. Their grounding has to be fashioned in other ways. This means that there are both centripetal and centrifugal tendencies in the case law and analyses of it, as judges and commentators strive both to identify a unifying principle or principles to make sense of the area but also display sensitivity to variations in the force in different contexts of what may be overlapping, but not fully aligned, sets of reasons or justifications for the imposition of liability. Professor Murphy interrogates the field with intelligence and care to bring this out. He aligns more with the centrifugal tendency in analysis. The book is concerned to build from the ground up, by unearthing the origins and emerging justifications for each strand within this family of liability-imposing rules and treating these seriously on their own terms, rather than dismissing them as flawed or in some way aberrant by reference to some superimposed theory of liability. The various causes of action are thus treated in a more hospitable, less judgmental way than they tend to be by other commentators, myself included.

There is considerable value in this, particularly as an exercise in understanding what has happened and continues to happen in this area. There is also a cost, I think, in terms of a risk to doctrinal coherence. But one ought to make a judgment where the balance between history and doctrine should be struck in relation to these torts on the basis of a thorough understanding of both historical development and tort theory. Professor Murphy provides an informed and helpful

[5] *OBG Ltd v Allan* [2008] 1 AC 1; and see *Secretary of State for Health v Servier Laboratories* [2021] UKSC 24.

[6] *Revenue and Customs Commissioners v Total Network SL* [2008] 1 AC 1174.

discussion of both sides of this debate. He emphasises that two important points in particular emerge: this family of torts is by no means necessarily confined to the protection of economic interests and certain of them are capable of operating for the imposition of liability in two-party contexts. As he says, the torts which he discusses have the potential to 'be put to a range of imaginative and useful future purposes'. There is a lot to play for in thinking carefully about them and how they fit together in the field of tort law.

Philip Sales
United Kingdom Supreme Court
June 2021

PREFACE

This writing of this book, like much of my work on doctrinal tort law over the last 20 years, was inspired by two things: the thought that not nearly enough academic attention has been devoted to the subject, and the belief that, such work as there already is, suffers from serious flaws. This study is an attempt to address both of these matters. The book eschews any commitment to the idea that the torts dealt with are rightly labelled 'the economic torts', and, in fact, advances the idea that (with one exception) it is a mistake to consider them a set of actions whose role is confined to the regulation of trade and business rivalry, or the protection of business interests. It is this central claim that accounts for the reference to *The Province* of the economic torts in the title of this book.

The claim that the scope of these torts is, in reality, much broader than is commonly acknowledged relies primarily – as works of this kind always should do – on what the judges in the leading cases actually said. But it goes further, too. For where ambiguity exists, illuminating the purview of these torts requires that we delve deeply into legal history and that we properly contextualise our analysis of the genesis and subsequent development of the torts in question. Looking to legal history and social context reveals that ideological zeitgeist, and even naked political convictions on the part of certain judges, played an important part in shaping many of these torts. It is this aspect of the study that accounts for the reference to the *Politics* of the economic torts in the title of this book.

There are two further major contentions that are advanced in the chapters that follow. The first is that, despite the prevalence of talk of some of the economic torts being redundant or moribund, all eight of the torts I discuss can properly be regarded as vital in the strict sense of that word. The second is that it is unhelpful to think of these torts as a family of actions with a common basic purpose; for analysis that is attentive to the details of their ingredients and structure reveals that there is more that divides than unites the economic torts. I realise, of course, that in giving this book the title, *The Province and Politics of the Economic Torts* I am helping to perpetuate this misnomer. But in my defence, what else could I have called it that would have alerted potential readers to its contents?

While on the subject of seemingly inappropriate terms that I hope are defensible, I ought also to explain here why I have – in the context of the hypotheticals that I have employed to explain certain points of law – not toed the modern line of using only gender neutral personal and possessive pronouns. The reason for my sticking to 'he', 'she', 'his' and 'her' is simply because it is very helpful to do this when discussing a set of torts that frequently involve three parties. Talking in terms of he and she can help distinguish not just claimant from defendant, but also defendant from intermediary.

Failing to crash test one's work before publishing it is, in my view, a grave error. In relation to three matters, I tested the waters in article form. I did so in relation to intimidation, deceit and injurious falsehood in papers that appeared in the *Modern Law Review*, *Cambridge Law Journal* and *Law Quarterly Review* respectively. None of the text of those articles is directly repeated here, though many of the arguments I advanced in those papers have been foundational to parts of chapters five and six.

I have also turned to many friends and colleagues for advice. Accordingly, I should like now to record my thanks to those who have read, discussed and expressed their disagreements about a good deal of what is to come. All of the following helped in at least one of these ways: Roderick Bagshaw, John Bell, Lionel Bentley, Alan Bogg, Peter Cane, Paul Davies, Neil Duxbury, Matt Dyson, Neil Foster, Sara Fovargue, Jodi Gardner, John Goldberg, Louise Gullifer, David Howarth, David Ibbetson, William Lucy, Nick McBride, Janet O'Sullivan, Jane Stapleton, Andy Summers and Andrew Tettenborn. I would also like to thank the Faculty of Law at the University of Cambridge for awarding me a Herbert Smiths Freehills Visitorship during the first four months of 2019 for it was there and then that the project got underway. I should also like to express my gratitude to the Governing Body of Clare Hall, Cambridge for granting me (simultaneously) a Visiting Fellowship. Daily conversations there with David Ibbetson were invaluable: sometimes because they helped me clarify my thinking on certain matters, and sometimes because they constituted delightful distractions from the project when distractions were most needed. Lizz Edwards-Waller and Kate Faulkner, the librarians at the Squire Law Library, were able to dig out obscure and historical materials that I would never have managed to unearth by myself. I am truly grateful to them for the help that they gave me.

Cambridge provided me with just about the perfect environment to begin work on the book, and the Cambridge Law Faculty's Centre for Private Law (and, in particular, Nick McBride and Sarah Worthington) must be thanked for giving me a platform at the Centre's 2019 Away Day to test drive some of the core ideas contained in it. Lord Sales was enormously kind to agree to write a foreword for this book (and anyone familiar with his own extra-judicial writing on the subject of the economic torts will understand immediately why he was just about the perfect person to have write it). Devon-Jane Airey provided valuable research assistance.

Sinead Moloney at Hart Publishing was prompt, clear, accommodating and helpful in all correspondence between us. In particular, I am indebted to her for allowing me to make a number of brief references throughout the book to *Secretary of State for Health v Servier Laboratories Ltd.* As if to prove the point that one always runs the risk of being overtaken by legal developments when writing about a dynamic area of law, this case was decided between submission of the manuscript and receipt of the proofs.

Last but by no means least I must record my gratitude to my former colleague, Hazel Carty. It was Hazel who first sparked my interest in the economic torts many years ago. In the preface to the 2010 edition of her own monograph on the subject, she thanked me for the 'wise comments (and disagreements)' that I supplied by way of response to the draft chapters that she asked me to read. Hazel has now retired and for this reason I have not asked her to return the favour (despite its being almost certain that her comments would have been a good deal wiser, and her disagreements much more valuable). It follows that I cannot insert a corresponding line of thanks in this preface. There was nothing, however, to stop me dedicating the book to her with enduring gratitude. And that is exactly what I have done.

John Murphy
Manchester
July 2021

TABLE OF CONTENTS

TABLE OF CASES

United Kingdom

Other Jurisdictions

Australia

Canada

Ireland

Malaysia

New Zealand

Singapore

United States of America

TABLE OF LEGISLATION

UK Statutes

UK Secondary Legislation

Overseas Statutes

1

Introduction

Tony Weir, in a series of lectures peppered almost as much with caustic wit as they were with highly perspicacious observations about the array of torts he took as his subject, was assuredly right to observe that the economic torts have been 'generally marginalised' in academic writing.[1] Even now, nearly a quarter of a century after Weir made that claim, Hazel Carty's monograph, *An Analysis of the Economic Torts*,[2] remains the only available book that provides a comprehensive description and analysis of these torts.[3] Furthermore, although it is fair to say that quite a number of journal articles have been written about *some* of the economic torts, this body of scholarship is dwarfed by the number of books, articles and essays that have been written about much more familiar actions, such as negligence, nuisance, defamation and the seldom-invoked rule in *Rylands v Fletcher*.

Possibly, this relative lack of juristic attention is a product of the fact that only a small proportion of torts scholars are especially familiar with the torts in view. It is certainly the case that only a handful of university law schools routinely teach the economic torts.[4] And it is also true that a fair number of the most popular tort textbooks have nothing whatsoever to say about most or all of them.[5] Yet, however much one considers these omissions to be justified – there is, after all, only so much tort that one can teach in a year-long course – it remains true that some of the most important decisions in the whole of the law of torts come from within the economic torts stable. *Allen v Flood*,[6] *Rookes v Barnard*[7] and *OBG Ltd v Allan*[8]

[1] T Weir, *Economic Torts* (Oxford, Clarendon Press, 1997) 5.

[2] H Carty, *An Analysis of the Economic Torts*, 2nd edn (Oxford, Oxford University Press, 2010).

[3] Dyson Heydon's 1978 study of these torts, although it had something to say about all of the torts considered in this book, afforded only scant treatment – a mere eight pages in all – to injurious falsehood and deceit combined: JD Heydon, *Economic Torts*, 2nd edn (London, Sweet and Maxwell, 1978). Weir's own book (n 1) ran to just 77 pages in length.

[4] Even in Oxford, where there is a long tradition of teaching the economic torts, only about half the colleges actually provide tutorials on them in any given year (the rest teach defamation, instead).

[5] There is no discussion whatsoever of the economic torts in any of the following: M Lunney *et al*, *Tort Law: Text and Materials* (Oxford, Oxford University Press, 2017); K Horsey and E Rackley, *Tort Law*, 6th edn (Oxford, Oxford University Press, 2019); R Mulheron, *Principles of Tort Law*, 2nd edn (Cambridge, Cambridge University Press, 2020); K Horsey and E Rackley, *Kidner's Casebook on Torts*, 15th edn (Oxford, Oxford University Press, 2019).

[6] *Allen v Flood* [1898] AC 1 (HL).

[7] *Rookes v Barnard* [1964] AC 1129 (HL).

[8] *OBG Ltd v Allan* [2008] 1 AC 1 (HL).

are prime examples. Writing about the first of these in his Blackstone Lecture, RVF Heuston claimed that *Allen* was 'perhaps the most important [case] in the whole history of the law of torts';[9] while, in a very lengthy case-note concerning *Rookes*, Weir once wrote that 'the central message of *Rookes* ... is an extremely important and beneficial contribution to the development of the law'.[10] Some decades later, in a survey of the way that tort law generally had moved on over the preceding 20 or so years, Rogers suggested that 'the restatement of the economic torts in *OBG v Allan* ... is easily the most important development'.[11]

From a practical perspective, or so it shall be argued in this book, these actions epitomise tort law's capacity to fulfil the role of the common law's Swiss Army Knife.[12] For, with nothing much more than the encouragement of counsel for the claimants, some of these torts were conjured up by judges in order to provide claimants with novel causes of action when they appeared to be clearly morally deserving. Furthermore, as will also be noted at various junctures in this book, these torts have important ramifications for a good deal of contemporary tort theory insofar as most of them depart significantly from what many modern theorists portray as being the structural and juridical hallmarks of tort law.[13]

The very fact that the economic torts have received relatively little juristic attention would probably be reason enough to produce a new book. Add to the mix the fact that they possess considerable theoretical significance, and the case for such an enterprise becomes all the more compelling. But perhaps the most significant reason of all for writing this book is that, for all that the House of Lords may have tried valiantly to bring order to this area of law in recent times, there remains a great deal of uncertainty concerning the purposes, scope, unity and future possible uses of these torts.

This book endeavours to tackle these matters. It is not a treatise. Anyone expecting a fairly routine, textbook-like guide to the essential elements of the various actions discussed in the remaining pages may stop reading now. For, whereas many – perhaps even most – commentators concern themselves primarily with fine-grained analyses (and criticisms) of the particular ingredients of the various economic torts, those matters are largely tangential to what appears in the chapters that follow. Of course, such analyses and criticisms cannot be completely avoided. But it is not my primary objective to suggest how best to construe basic concepts like 'unlawful means', or 'intention' within any given tort. My concern is with much broader matters.

[9] RVF Heuston, 'Judicial Prosopography' (1986) 102 *LQR* 90, 97.

[10] T Weir, 'Chaos or Cosmos? *Rookes, Stratford* and the Economic Torts' [1965] *CLJ* 225, 233.

[11] WVH Rogers, *Winfield and Jolowicz on Tort*, 18th edn (London, Sweet and Maxwell, 2010) *vi*.

[12] The idea is borrowed from A Beever, *Rediscovering the Law of Negligence* (Oxford, Hart Publishing, 2007) 197 where it is used to capture the idea that it is typically tort law (and not other branches of the common law) that is called upon to fashion novel actions in order to provide a remedy to morally worthy claimants who cannot otherwise pursue avenues of civil recourse.

[13] For an introduction to these hallmarks, and for a brief account of the ways in which some of the torts considered in this book belie those putative hallmarks, see J Murphy, 'The Heterogeneity of Tort Law' (2019) 39 *OJLS* 455.

In this chapter, I aim to do four prefatory things. In section I, I begin by demonstrating one fundamental way in which this field is beset by uncertainty. It involves sketching the extent to which there exists profound disagreement about just which causes of action constitute 'the economic torts'. I also include in this section a brief account of the little-noticed fact that the problem of identifying the economic torts is not a new one, but one that can be traced back to the days when jurists took their first, hesitant steps towards thinking in terms of a 'family' of such torts.

In section II, I lay my cards on the table and set out a fairly expansive *dramatis personae* whose features, rationales, domain and vitality will occupy half of the remaining chapters. I fully recognise that a number of distinguished jurists (and probably also some judges) would deny, or at least contest, the independent existence of some of the actions I propose to discuss. But I think it is important to include these putatively 'questionable torts' for reasons that will be given presently. In section III, I introduce the four central claims of the book; and in section IV, I provide a roadmap to the remaining chapters.

I. Identifying 'The Economic Torts'

A. One Major Problem

Though most jurists seem happy enough with using the term 'the economic torts', there is considerable disagreement among them about just which actions ought properly to be regarded as falling within the fold. This is a major problem for anyone intent on theorising or comprehensively analysing the economic torts. Carty adopts the most expansive view of which torts count for these purposes.[14] She places each of the following eight actions on the list: (i) causing loss by unlawful means; (ii) inducing breach of contract (and certain analogous actions); (iii) lawful means conspiracy; (iv) unlawful means conspiracy; (v) intimidation;[15]

[14] It could be argued that she misses one out, namely, bribery. It was certainly suggested in *Mayor of Salford v Lever (No 2)* [1891] 1 QB 168 (CA) that where D bribes C's agent such that C enters into a venture in which C pays an inflated price for whatever is being bought, a special sort of 'fraud' is committed. However, given that the remedy sought in such cases focuses on D's gain rather than any obvious loss to C, it is submitted – in the light of dicta in both *Mahesan S/O Thambiah v Malaysian Government Officers Co-Operative Housing Society* [1979] AC 374 (PC), 448 and *Petrotrade Inc v Smith* [2000] CLC 916, 920 emphasising the money had and received – that such actions are best dealt with on the basis of unjust enrichment. It is certainly hard to see how, in the absence of any untruthful representations by D, the cases can be thought to involve deceit.

[15] Although she devotes an entire chapter to intimidation, Carty's acceptance of the vitality of this tort is far from clear. In her monograph, she explicitly abandons the idea that a discrete three-party version of this tort (ie, one in which D intimidates C through the medium of a third party, T) exists in the wake of *OBG*: Carty (n 2) 115. She also expresses there considerable doubt about the two-party version of this tort, begrudgingly recognising its vitality in the strict sense, but expressing at the same time unease about its merits (*ibid*, 116–17)). By contrast, in a later paper, she stops short of committing herself on

(vi) passing off; (vii) deceit; and (viii) injurious falsehood. Nicholas McBride and Roderick Bagshaw adopt more or less the same list (albeit that they are considerably more hesitant about treating the action for inducing breach of contract as a tort[16]).

By contrast, Allan Beever thinks a much narrower range of actions constitute the economic torts.[17] He clearly regards the torts of deceit, injurious falsehood and passing off as being 'members of the family'.[18] But after that, things become hazy. He considers the existence of inducing breach of contract to be a complete mystery,[19] and suggests (at one point) that it should be permitted 'to die a merciful death'.[20] He doesn't quite say, however, whether he thinks it actually is an economic tort. He reluctantly acknowledges the existence of some sort of cause of action; but he conspicuously stops short of treating it as a thoroughbred tort that is alive and well. On top of this, he is so dismissive about various essential elements in the remaining torts on Carty's list that it is hard to imagine that he recognises their independent existence at all. Instead, he seems to believe that all the so-called 'general economic torts'[21] can be reduced to a single, unifying principle of liability according to which an actionable wrong will be committed where 'one person attempts to control another via the medium of a third party'.[22] If he thinks there is just one tort here, it is a tort with no name.

A different view again is held by Simon Deakin. In an article co-authored with John Randall, Deakin claims that the economic torts are centred on 'the principle that the right to pursue a trade, business or livelihood free of certain forms of interference, deemed to be illegitimate deserves the protection of the law'.[23] Yet, contrary to this conception – which, in fact, is traceable to a nuisance case[24] – his textbook (written with a different co-author) excludes from the list of economic torts the actions for injurious falsehood and passing off. Both of these are dealt with in an entirely separate section of the book devoted to 'the protection of

the existence of this tort: see H Carty, 'The Modern Functions of the Economic Torts: Reviewing the English, Canadian, Australia and New Zealand Positions' [2015] *CLJ* 261.

[16] NJ McBride and R Bagshaw, *Tort Law*, 6th edn (London, Pearson, 2018) 640–41.

[17] And an even shorter list than that – embracing just the unlawful means tort, inducing breach of contract, lawful means conspiracy and unlawful means conspiracy – can be found in P Giliker, *Tort*, 7th edn (London, Sweet and Maxwell, 2020) Ch 12.

[18] A Beever, *A Theory of Tort Liability* (Oxford, Hart Publishing, 2016) 101.

[19] *Ibid*, 114: 'I conclude simply that we do not know why we have a tort of inducing breach of contract'.

[20] *Ibid*, 154.

[21] The economic torts are generally placed into two groups: the misrepresentation economic torts – comprising passing off, injurious falsehood and deceit – and the general economic torts (these being all the remaining ones). The distinction is drawn, inter alia, because the former group has been historically understood as centring on gains that C improperly made at D's expense, while the latter has historically been aligned with various forms of economic or trade losses visited upon D by C (sometimes directly and sometimes indirectly): see Carty (n 2) 3.

[22] Beever (n 18) 154.

[23] S Deakin and J Randall, 'Rethinking the Economic Torts' (2009) 72 *MLR* 519, 534. Elsewhere in the article, the rationale behind these torts is described as being 'to maintain the integrity of the competitive process': *ibid*, 520.

[24] *Keeble v Hickeringill* (1706) 11 East 574, 575–76 (Holt CJ).

human dignity'.[25] And, whereas both Carty, and McBride and Bagshaw recognise two-party intimidation as a freestanding tort (albeit, a tort on stilts), Deakin accepts only the existence of the three-party version of this tort.[26]

Judicial opinions about these torts are equally divided. There is no consensus among the judges now (nor has there ever seemingly been one) about which of the various actions has a discrete existence. In *OBG*, Lord Hoffmann sought to impose order on the general economic torts by simplifying the framework within which they would operate. He wanted to return to the two-tort structure first outlined by Lord Watson in *Allen v Flood*.[27] Indeed, the first 64 paragraphs of his speech in *OBG* were concerned with just this prefatory matter.[28] And yet, despite his efforts, anything but a clear and definitive framework emerged from that case. So apparent was this to Deakin and Randall that they went so far as to contend that 'the analysis in *OBG* raises as many questions as it answers'.[29]

To explain a little here: Lord Hoffmann thought that the vast majority of the previous cases concerning the economic torts could be cashed out either in terms of inducing breach of contract, or the tort of causing loss by unlawful means. *En route* to so saying, his Lordship was keen to tidy things up by expunging from the catalogue of economic torts a number of actions that he considered to be either otiose or ones which had been constructed on unsound foundations. For example, he was dismissive of the idea that *Rookes v Barnard*[30] had formally introduced a free-standing tort of three-party intimidation. This action, he said, was simply one form of the broader tort of causing loss by unlawful means. He acknowledged the fact that the ancient, yet seminal, cases of *Garret v Taylor*[31] and *Tarleton v M'Gawley*[32] had emphasised 'the use of unlawful threats to intimidate potential customers'.[33] And he acknowledged, also, both the fact that '*Salmond on Torts*, 1st ed (1907) [had] classified them under the heading of "Intimidation"' and that 'the existence of a tort of this name was confirmed by the House of Lords in *Rookes v Barnard*'.[34] Yet he insisted, very firmly indeed, that 'Salmond's tort

[25] S Deakin and Z Adams, *Markesinis and Deakin's Tort Law*, 8th edn (Oxford, Oxford University Press, 2019) Part VII. The economic torts, by contrast, are packed into 'Part V: Land, Chattels, and Intentional Interference with Economic Interests'.

[26] But he does so in such a way as to question whether three-party intimidation (as per *Rookes* (n 7)) can properly be viewed as a subset of the unlawful means tort: see Deakin and Randall (n 23) 547–48.

[27] *Allen* (n 6) 96: '[t]here are … two grounds only upon which a person who procures the act of another can be made legally responsible for its consequences … if he knowingly and for his own ends induces that other person to commit an actionable wrong … [and] when the act induced is within the right of the immediate actor … the inducer may be held liable if he can be shewn to have procured his object by the use of illegal means directed against that third party'.

[28] It was only after these prefatory 64 paragraphs that he actually got down to tackling the three appeals before the court.

[29] Deakin and Randall (n 23) 519.

[30] *Rookes* (n 7).

[31] *Garret v Taylor* (1620) Cro Jac 567.

[32] *Tarleton v M'Gawley* (1794) Peake 270.

[33] *OBG* (n 8) [7].

[34] *Ibid.*

of intimidation is … only one variant of a broader tort, usually called for short "causing loss by unlawful means"'.[35]

Two further actions that he laid to rest were both variants of inducing breach of contract. Each of them had emerged during the course of the twentieth century. The first was the action for direct unlawful interference with contractual relations (short of breach),[36] and the second was the action for indirectly inducing breach of contract by unlawful means.[37] For Lord Hoffmann, cases decided on both of these bases presented classic illustrations of 'the muddle' into which the law had descended.[38] In his keenness to do away with that muddle, he set about the task of repackaging the relevant cases as either instances of the tort of causing loss by unlawful means,[39] or as cases that could be overruled on the basis that they had been erroneously decided.[40]

As noted already, despite all this pruning and repackaging, elements of confusion survived the decision in *OBG*. For a start, Lord Hoffmann's preferred two-tort framework was clearly unable to accommodate not only the action known as two-party intimidation, but also numerous cases decided on the basis of the two conspiracy torts. As will be seen in chapter five, the existence of a free-standing tort of two-party intimidation was first judicially floated by Lord Devlin in *Rookes* and subsequently endorsed in later decisions. And as we shall also see there, Lord Hoffmann did not expressly put an end to its existence in *OBG*. Rather, what he had to say on the subject was both opaque and puzzling. He began by announcing the fact that he did 'not intend to say anything about the question of whether a claimant who has been compelled by unlawful intimidation to act to his own detriment, can sue for his loss'.[41] Yet he was not true to his word. For in the very next sentence, he went on to opine, intriguingly, that '[s]uch a case of "two party intimidation" raises altogether different issues'.[42] It was only at that point that he

[35] *Ibid.*

[36] In *Torquay Hotel Co Ltd v Cousins* [1969] 2 Ch 106 (CA) 138, Lord Denning MR declared it to be tortious if 'a third person prevents or hinders one party from performing his contract, even though it be not a breach'. In *The Nadezhda Krupskaya* [1997] 2 Lloyd's Law Reports 35, Rix J stressed the need for unlawful means. He pointed out (at 40) that he was 'far from satisfied that the contractually valid exercise of a right of withdrawal … could ever be tortious, even if done with the intention of destroying some sub-charter'.

[37] See, eg, *DC Thomson & Co Ltd v Deakin* [1952] Ch 646 (CA); *JT Stratford & Son Ltd v Lindley (No 1)* [1965] AC 269 (HL).

[38] *OBG* (n 8) [22].

[39] In *GWK Ltd v Dunlop Rubber Co Ltd* (1926) 42 TLR 376, 377, Lord Hewart CJ had held the defendants liable on the basis that they had 'knowingly committed a violation of the ARM company's legal rights by interfering, without any justification whatever, with the contractual relations existing between them and the GWK company'. By contrast, Lord Hoffmann regarded this case as 'a good example of intentionally causing loss by unlawful means': *OBG* (n 8) [24]. He said much the same (at [44]) about *Dimbleby & Sons Ltd v National Union of Journalists* [1984] 1 WLR 67 (CA).

[40] Lord Hoffmann did not use the exact language of 'overruled', but he did say of *DC Thomson & Co Ltd v Deakin* that 'it would be better … to abandon it': [2008] 1 AC 1 [33]. Equally, the interference short of breach cases cannot stand beside his Lordship's insistence that 'one cannot be liable for inducing a breach unless there has been a breach': *ibid*, [44].

[41] *Ibid*, [61].

[42] *Ibid.*

stopped. He offered precisely no elaboration on what he took those 'altogether different issues' to be.[43] Whilst it is of course possible to speculate on just what matters he might have had in mind here – and I offer some such speculation in chapter four[44] – it is nonetheless the case that his ambivalence in *OBG* about two-party intimidation rendered it a tort with an uncertain future. A similar remark could be made about the two conspiracy torts; for their future was also left in doubt in the immediate wake of *OBG* given that neither of these actions (for reasons that will be explained in chapters four and five) can be slotted comfortably within Lord Hoffmann's preferred two-tort framework.

Lord Hoffmann made no specific mention of unlawful means conspiracy in *OBG*. Nor, for that matter, did any other member of the panel in that case. Whether he (or they) saw it as an entirely redundant cause of action which adds nothing to the principle of joint tortfeasance[45] is simply not discernible from the various speeches in the case. Their Lordships' complete silence on the matter could, perhaps, be interpreted as sounding the death knell for that tort. But on the other hand, it is conceivable that they simply overlooked it.[46] It is impossible to tell.

In relation to its sibling tort – the action for lawful means conspiracy – Lord Hoffmann's dictum was scarcely any clearer. True, he at least proffered a couple of comments in this connection, but neither of them was particularly illuminating. He adverted fleetingly to 'the rarity of [such] actions', adding only that, on those infrequent occasions when this tort is available, 'an improper motive can *anomalously* found a cause of action'.[47] Quite what so saying was intended to achieve is not apparent. And although his Lordship returned to the subject (extra-judicially) just a few years later, he again failed to make clear the lie of the land. He admitted that there had been in *OBG* 'a wish to confine the economic torts as narrowly as possible, on the grounds that they have little rational basis in social or economic policy and that such matters are best left to the legislature'.[48] And he even reiterated his belief that lawful means conspiracy was 'an anomalous cause of action'.[49] Had he said no more, we might reasonably have concluded that *OBG* was intended to signal the demise of this tort. But he did say more. Within just a few pages he recognised that conspiracy in both its forms had survived the decision

[43] For discussion of the possibilities, see chapter five.

[44] I have also considered the matter in, hopefully, exhaustive detail in J Murphy, 'Understanding Intimidation' (2014) 77 *MLR* 33, 50–57.

[45] For an argument along these lines, see R Stevens, *Torts and Rights* (Oxford, Oxford University Press, 2007) 249: 'there is no such independent tort [as unlawful means conspiracy]. Where the "unlawful means" constitute a tort, the principle of attribution of one conspirator's actions to them all means that all will be held liable as joint tortfeasors'.

[46] He later clarified that the silence in relation to conspiracy in *OBG* was due to the fact that it was irrelevant to the instant appeals in that case: L Hoffmann, 'The Rise and Fall of the Economic Torts' in S Degeling *et al* (eds), *Torts in Commercial Law* (Sydney, Thomson Reuters, 2011) 115.

[47] *OBG* (n 8) [14]-[15]. For an argument that malicious motive might be a defensible, if uncommon, basis of tortious liability, see J Murphy, 'Malice as an Ingredient of Tort Liability' [2019] *CLJ* 355.

[48] Hoffmann (n 46) 113.

[49] *Ibid*, 111.

in *OBG*,[50] but then swiftly qualified this statement by observing that conspiracy (in either form) had virtually no practical significance in the modern era. He said of the lawful means variety that it had been rendered all but obsolete by the House of Lords in *Crofter Hand Woven Harris Tweed Co Ltd v Veitch*[51] by 'requiring a motive which was so rare as to be virtually impossible to prove'.[52] And in relation to the unlawful means version, he suggested that it was 'important to realise how limited the application of the [tort] … will be'.[53] In short, in the wake of *OBG*, it was debatable how much life remained in either of these torts. Lord Hoffmann clearly saw them as being more or less moribund *in practice* (though perhaps just clinging to the last vestiges of vitality in strict, juridical terms).

The unresolved state of the law following *OBG* goes a long way towards explaining why the continued existence of unlawful means conspiracy needed to be resolved at the highest judicial level when its vitality was questioned within a year of the decision in *OBG*. In *Revenue and Customs Commissioners v Total Network SL*,[54] a differently constituted House of Lords had to decide whether liability on this basis could be imposed in connection with a series of carousel frauds. The salient facts were as follows. Various companies participated in a circular string of artificial (possibly even bogus) transactions involving certain goods that began and ended with a company based in Spain. By virtue of the operation of a set of VAT laws the details of which need not concern us here, the various transactions resulted in one of the companies fraudulently obtaining a VAT credit to which it was not entitled. The defendant company had a bank account in the United Kingdom, but was registered for VAT in another EC Member State. Because it was registered abroad for such tax, it did not fall within (and therefore could not be pursued in accordance with) the relevant UK tax legislation. Accordingly, the Revenue was forced to rely instead upon the tort of unlawful means conspiracy: the defendant company had conspired with another company that had fraudulently obtained the VAT credit. The Revenue Commissioners claimed damages equivalent to the amount of VAT lost as a result of the carousel fraud in which the defendant company had been a participant.

Although in narrow terms *Total Network* was about the tort of unlawful means conspiracy, the decision turned out to be important also in relation to both two-party intimidation and lawful means conspiracy. Whereas Lord Hoffmann had arguably sought to extirpate the former in *OBG*, it became a critical part of

[50] It is now, lamented Lord Hoffmann, 'too late to do anything about it. The House of Lords in the *Crofter* case affirmed that there was such a tort, which could be committed either by using unlawful means or by having an unlawful motive': Hoffmann (n 46) 115. In saying this there was a distinct echo of Lord Diplock, roughly 30 years earlier, having said that lawful means conspiracy was 'too well-established to be discarded however anomalous it may seem today': *Lonrho Ltd v Shell Petroleum (No 2)* [1982] AC 173 (HL) 189.

[51] *Crofter Hand Woven Harris Tweed Co Ltd v Veitch* [1942] AC 435 (HL).

[52] Hoffmann (n 46) 115.

[53] *Ibid.*

[54] *Revenue and Customs Commissioners v Total Network SL* [2008] 1 AC 1174 (HL).

the means by which their Lordships in *Total Network* sought to breathe new life into both of the conspiracy torts. The details of how they did this are discussed in chapter five. For now, it suffices to note a key feature of *Total Network*: the fact that it was treated as a case in which the conspirators had acted *directly* against the claimant. As Lord Hope put it, 'in this case there was no third party'.[55] Given this conception of *Total Network* as a case involving a two-party tort, it follows that, even if they had wanted to do so, their Lordships would have been unable to explain the liability that was imposed in that case in terms of Lord Hoffmann's two-tort structure. For, according to that two-tort structure, both of the recognised actions – the unlawful means tort and inducing breach of contract – require the defendant to inflict harm on the claimant via a third party.

Perfectly aware of this, Lord Hope specifically revisited the fact that Lord Hoffmann had made the undefended claim in *OBG* that certain 'other considerations' are in play where harm or loss is directly inflicted. He put it this way: '[since] in para 61 of *OBG*, Lord Hoffmann said [a two-party case] raises altogether different issues. One has to ask why, in this situation [*ie*, the one in *Total Network*], the law should not provide a remedy'.[56] In posing the question rhetorically, he was clearly signalling a willingness to accept the prospect of two-party economic tort liability.

Lord Mance was a willing ally. He began by stressing the 'distinction between the infliction of harm through the intermediary of a third party … and the present situation' before proceeding to endorse the imposition of tort liability 'where two wrongdoers join and act together to *inflict injury directly* upon another person or body'.[57] And Lord Neuberger, too, was clearly like-minded. He countenanced the possibility of liability for unlawful means conspiracy in the instant case in stages. First, he noted that, 'the tort is of a two party nature': the conspirators had directly cheated the Revenue. Having drawn this structural distinction between the instant case and those that had been scrutinised by Lord Hoffmann in *OBG*, he ventured to suggest that:

> it may therefore not be inappropriate to hold that the Commissioners have a cause of action in such circumstances, even though they might not have had a claim if they had suffered loss … as a result of a crime directed at a third party.[58]

In reaching their main conclusion that unlawful means conspiracy could be considered an important, free-standing tort (and no mere anomaly that ought properly to be subsumed within the well-established rules on joint tortfeasance), three members of the House of Lords in *Total Network* also thought it appropriate to rescue from widespread condemnation its sister tort of lawful means conspiracy.

[55] *Ibid*, [43].
[56] *Ibid*.
[57] *Ibid*, [124] (emphasis added).
[58] *Ibid*, [223]. In the end, he did not feel able to recognise the claim because he treated the remedial provisions of the Value Added Tax Act 1994 as laying down an exhaustive list of remedies: *ibid*, [227].

Probably the most robust defence of that action was offered by Lord Neuberger. Using it, too, as part of the platform on which unlawful means conspiracy could be resuscitated, he said the following:

> the law of tort takes a particularly censorious view where conspiracy is involved. Thus, a claim based on conspiracy to injure can be established even where no unlawful means, let alone any other actionable tort, is involved … [Although] frequently described as anomalous … its existence is very well established. Its centrally important feature is that the conspiracy must have as its primary purpose injury to the claimant. In my judgment, given the existence of that tort, it would be anomalous if an unlawful means conspiracy could not found a cause of action.[59]

A similar insistence on the significance of combination can be found in the speeches of both Lord Scott[60] and Lord Walker,[61] while Lord Mance made the point that while numbers are not necessarily correlated to the prospect or causing harm, a person who acts on his own 'would be a great deal less likely to try or succeed'.[62] Accordingly, in the wake of *Total Network*, it was clear that Lord Hoffmann's greatly simplified two-tort structure had died in infancy.

Just this brief snapshot of two of the leading cases on economic tort liability reveals amply that judicial views about the vitality and future prospects, of at least three of the general economic torts are as divided as those held by jurists. The Hoffmann approach affords salience and support to only two of them: causing loss by unlawful means and inducing breach of contract. The opposing view – supported by various members of the House of Lords in *Total Network* – tends to confirm, also, the vitality of two-party intimidation as well as both forms of conspiracy.

Given the inconclusive nature of both juristic and judicial views about which actions belong in the box labelled 'extant economic torts', it follows that I will be unlikely to succeed in providing in this book a list of such actions with which no-one will cavil. However, I am also conscious that it would be seriously remiss of me not to state, right from the outset, the various torts that will be discussed in this study. Indeed, the very fact that there exists such profound disagreement about which actions actually qualify as economic torts makes it all the more important that I indicate at this stage the expanse of the terrain that will be traversed in the pages that follow. Accordingly, I provide in the next section a list of the actions that I shall consider.

Before I do that, though, it is worth pointing out that the identification problem is by no means a new one; and this is a point to which I shall return in chapters seven and eight. In those chapters I shall seek to show, respectively, that

[59] *Ibid*, [221].

[60] 'The essential ingredient of this type of action is the combination of people all intent on causing harm to the victim, not on the type of means employed for doing so': *ibid*, [56].

[61] '[T]he fact that claimant's damage is caused by two or more persons acting in concert … identifies what sets conspiracy apart from other torts': *ibid*, [77].

[62] *Ibid*, [122].

there has never been anything that clearly and obviously has bound the economic torts together in juridical terms, and that (partly for this reason) certain novel extensions of some of these torts into previously uncharted territory cannot plausibly be resisted (as some would suggest) on the basis that such developments represent a rejection of a concern that has hitherto linked them together: a concern, that is, to protect trade and business interests.

B. The Major Problem in Historical Perspective

Against the backdrop of such widespread and profound disagreement about something as basic as just which actions comprise the economic torts, it is understandable why (with perhaps a touch of hyperbole) this area of the law is so frequently described as messy, muddled or chaotic.[63] Yet there is, I think, a fairly simple explanation on offer here. It is the fact that there is not now, nor ever has been, an intellectually satisfying, universally accepted, golden, juridical thread that unites these torts and allows us to say confidently which ones belong together, and why.

A trawl through early editions of the leading treatises on tort law tends to confirm this hypothesis. It was not, for example, until 1965 – and the publication of the fourteenth edition of *Salmond on Torts*[64] – that a chapter on 'Injury to Economic Relations' first appeared.[65] And it was in this new chapter that the action for inducing breach of contract was first presented as an economic tort. In previous editions it had been discussed in a chapter concerning 'Injuries to Domestic and Contractual Relations'.[66] It was also in the fourteenth edition of *Salmond* that intimidation, inducing breach of contract, conspiracy and the various misrepresentation torts were, for the first time, dealt with sequentially. Perhaps this novel, grouping together of these actions was intended to reflect a newly formed view on the part of the then editor, Heuston, that they in fact belonged together.[67] But even if it did, he certainly held back (at this stage) from applying the compendious label, 'the economic torts'.

Much the same cautious grouping together of the economic torts is evident in past editions of the textbook originally produced by Percy Winfield. It was not until the eighth edition of *Winfield on Tort*[68] (published in 1967), that there appeared a chapter on 'Interference with Contract or Business'.[69] It contained

[63] See, eg, KW Wedderburn, 'Rocking the Torts' (1983) 46 *MLR* 224, 229; Weir (n 1) 7; Carty (n 2) 23; H Carty, 'The Economic Torts in the 21st Century' (2008) 124 *LQR* 641, 674; Beever (n 18) 154.

[64] RFV Heuston, *Salmond on Torts*, 14th edn (London, Sweet and Maxwell, 1965).

[65] *Ibid*, Ch 17.

[66] See, eg, RFV Heuston, *Salmond on Torts*, 13th edn (London, Sweet and Maxwell, 1961) Ch 16.

[67] It was not, however, until the 16th edition that the conspiracy torts were tucked into the chapter on economic relations (rather than dealt with separately, in an immediately proceeding chapter).

[68] JA Jolowicz and T Ellis Lewis, *Winfield on Tort*, 8th edn (London, Sweet and Maxwell, 1967).

[69] *Ibid*, Ch 21.

descriptions of the actions for inducing breach of contract, intimidation, causing loss by unlawful means, conspiracy and passing off.[70] But only a couple of editions earlier, the treatment of these torts had been much more fragmented and dislocated: deceit occupying Chapter 15, conspiracy being dealt with in Chapter 17 and inducing breach of contract forming part of Chapter 23 alongside causing loss by unlawful means and passing off. In the intervening seventh edition, all but one of the aforementioned torts had been placed into Chapters 24 and 25. Deceit was the exception. It was, at this stage, apparently still viewed as not quite belonging within the economic torts fold, and it was discussed somewhat distantly in Chapter 21.

The very first person to begin concertedly linking the various actions considered in this book was Harold Potter, in *Clerk and Lindsell on Torts* (a book designed for practitioners rather than law students). It is *possible* that what motivated Potter, as editor, to do this was a perception on his part that the relevant torts were linked by a shared capacity to protect trade or business interests;[71] but it is hard to be certain. The 1947 edition of *Clerk and Lindsell* provided, in a single chapter, an exposition of the torts of intimidation, conspiracy and inducing breach of contract.[72] Yet the title given to that chapter – simply, 'Intimidation, Conspiracy and Inducing Breach of Contract' – betrayed nothing of where Potter saw the commonality between the three torts to lie. And nor was the missing link supplied by the text of that chapter. There was simply no positive indication that the perceived connection was thought to inhere in a shared *raison d'être* of protecting trade, business or any other economic interests.

In fact, it was not until almost a decade later that Harry Street became the first author to place most of the then recognised actions in a single chapter *and* give it a title reflecting the idea that they were related via a capacity to protect economic interests. The relevant chapter was entitled 'Trading, Business and Other Economic Interests'.[73] Fleming followed suit with a chapter entitled 'Interference with Economic Relations' just a couple of years later.[74] And so it was that, only around the middle of last century did any notion that there was a distinct group of economic torts begin to form. Not everyone signed up to such language at first;[75]

[70] T Ellis Lewis, *Winfield on Tort*, 6th edn (London, Sweet and Maxwell, 1954).

[71] That these are the widely recognised forms of economic interests protected by these torts is clear, as will be seen in the chapters that follow, from the fact that judges in the leading cases (as well as jurists discussing them) repeatedly refer to defendants who have 'injured a man in his trade', or done harm to his business interests. The term 'economic interest' is *not* used in the sense in which that term is used in P Cane, *Tort Law and Economic Interests*, 2nd edn (Oxford, Oxford University Press, 1996) 5: 'an interest for the invasion of which a finite sum of money can provide complete recompense'.

[72] See H Potter (ed), *Clerk and Lindsell on Torts*, 10th edn (London, Sweet and Maxwell, 1947) Ch XI.

[73] H Street, *The Law of Torts* (London, Butterworths, 1955) Ch 18.

[74] JG Fleming, *The Law of Torts* (Sydney, Law Book Co of Australia, 1957) Ch 27. Whether he saw them as being a family of torts at this stage, may still be doubted, however. In the relevant chapter in his introductory text, he applied the title 'Economic Torts' (no 'the'): see JG Fleming, *An Introduction to the Law of Torts* (Oxford, Oxford University Press, 1967) Ch XI.

[75] Heuston, for example, dealt with the various economic torts across four separate chapters, and the tort of inducing breach of contract was regarded as merely one of several actions dealing with 'wrongful

and even among those who subscribed to this view, there was considerable disagreement about just which torts belonged, and how best to name them.

II. The Actions Dealt with in this Book

The actions considered in this study are as follows: (i) inducing breach of contract; (ii) causing loss by unlawful means; (iii) unlawful means conspiracy; (iv) lawful means conspiracy; (v) two-party intimidation; (vi) passing off; (vii) deceit; and (viii) injurious falsehood. However, the fact that I have enumerated these torts in this very straightforward fashion is not meant to create the impression that the economic torts somehow constitute a straightforward family, still less a family of equals. For one thing, as we have already seen, considerable doubt attaches to the very existence of some of them. And secondly, as chapters three to six will reveal, they do not all possess the same degree of practical significance or future potential in terms of the range of interests they protect (or have the capacity to protect).

I say nothing more at this stage in relation to this second point. For now, it must suffice to explain my including in this book those actions whose vitality is somewhat uncertain, and those actions which are sometimes referred to as the misrepresentation torts. Some authors exclude either or both of these groups from their analyses of the economic torts. For example, there are those who simply say nothing about two-party intimidation even though the decision in *Rookes v Barnard* and its aftermath occupies a sizeable part of their overall discussion.[76] Equally, there are others who view the economic torts as 'a body of law which tries to stipulate what economic behaviour is permissible in the middle ground between too little competition … and too much'[77] – and on this (contestable) basis consider it appropriate to exclude one or more of the misrepresentation torts from their discussion.[78] While I stop short of claiming that there is a definitively right way to construct this group of torts,[79] I nonetheless believe that there is good reason to

interference with a man's relations with others, for example, his wife, his children, or those with whom he holds a contract': see Heuston (n 66) 629.

[76] See, eg, B Simpson, 'Trade Disputes Legislation and the Economic Torts' in TT Arvind and J Steele (eds), *Tort Law and the Legislature* (Oxford, Hart Publishing, 2013) 116–20.

[77] Heydon (n 3) 123.

[78] It is easy to see the reason why this is a deeply contestable basis for excluding the misrepresentation torts from the analysis. For, all cases of passing off, and many cases of injurious falsehood involve actions brought against a rival trader. Beever (although he elsewhere recognises them as economic torts) leaves injurious falsehood and deceit out of the chapter specifically devoted to the economic torts. On top of this, he provides no discussion at all of passing off. The current edition of *Clerk and Lindsell* also omits the misrepresentation torts from the chapter devoted to the economic torts: see, respectively Beever (n 18) and M Jones (ed), *Clerk and Lindsell on Torts*, 23rd edn (London, Sweet and Maxwell, 2020).

[79] Legal categories tend to reflect the aims, aspirations or assumptions of their originators. Thus, the sub-category 'the economic torts' could be constructed by a treatise writer concerned to offer a comprehensive exposition of the field. By contrast, the sub-category must be constructed differently by a tort theorist (such as Beever) who is pre-committed to the idea that economic torts are characterised by

include within this study consideration of not only those of the general economic torts whose vitality is not entirely assured, but also all three of the misrepresentation torts.

I elect to do this because I am conscious of the dangers associated with setting one's radar with too limited a range. If, for example, I were to exclude the misrepresentation torts from my discussion, I might fairly be accused of affording insufficient salience to the idea, advanced by some, that the purpose of the economic torts *as a whole* is to maintain the integrity of the competitive process.[80] Equally, if I failed to include the action for inducing breach of contract by reason of it being possible to argue that this is not a tort of any stripe,[81] that would greatly impoverish this study. For, inducing breach of contract is perhaps the best known (and almost certainly the most widely discussed) of all the economic torts. And in any event, its historical and present-day significance make it one that no serious study of this branch of the law could credibly overlook. If I were to exclude two-party intimidation on the footing that the House of Lords seemed keen to marginalise (if not quite eliminate) it in *OBG*, then I would lose an important strand to two key arguments that will feature at many junctures in this book. They are, first, that these torts are not all logically (or otherwise) confined to the protection of economic interests, and secondly, that some of the economic torts can impose liability in a two-party setting.

Rather than needlessly enfeeble certain of my key theses in these ways, it is imperative that I start with the most inclusive of lists, and then proceed to assess the merits and vitality of each of the torts that appear on it.

III. Aims and Theses

The overall aim of this book is to take a fresh look at the so-called economic torts. It does so, in part, with a view to dispelling a few suppositions for which there is little actual basis, but which have nonetheless closely attended (and to some extent, (mis)directed), the evolution of some of these torts over the last century or so. In addition – via a re-examination of their geneses, and their subsequent development – it also seeks to explore their future potential.

Achieving these two broad aims requires that special attention be paid to a range of factors that have not always been given the prominence they deserve. Proper consideration of this full range of factors allows us to observe just how little genuine unity exists between these torts. And recognising this provides part of the

D's 'indirect control' of C. For any such theorist, two-party economic torts do not warrant inclusion in the account.

[80] See, eg, Deakin and Randall (n 23) 520. Passing off (which almost always involves business rivals) and injurious falsehood (which commonly involves them) are particularly apt to be seen in this way.

[81] For more details concerning the arguments to this effect, see chapter three.

basis for claiming – as I do – that there is no *a priori* reason why they cannot be put to a range of imaginative and useful future purposes, rather than be conceptually marginalised by a set of labour laws that confer immunities on collective action, and a suite of competition law statutes that demarcate the line between aggressive and excessive competition between trade rivals.[82] True: many of the early cases involved litigation between labour and capital, or business rivals. But not so *Allen* or *Rookes* (involving labour *v* labour), or the recent cases which reveal a willingness on the part of the courts to allow them to be used in previously untried ways in order to provide civil law accountability for new, egregious forms of wrongdoing.

Four main arguments – not all of which will be pertinent to each and every chapter – will be advanced. The first is that the province and the potential purposes of these torts stretch (in some cases, considerably) beyond the protection of our economic interests in 'trade, business or employment'.[83] The second argument is closely related, but nonetheless distinct. It is that, once one dispels as misconceived the idea that these torts are bound together by the shared purpose of protecting trade and business interests, or indeed any other purely economic interests, it becomes easy to see that there is often more that divides than unites them.[84] Accordingly, I shall not seek strenuously to unearth (or construct) the elusive golden thread that links them together. Rather, I shall follow the advice of Lord Goff, namely, to resist 'the temptation of elegance'.[85] I shall seek to make plain (principally in chapter 7, but also *ad hoc*, in earlier chapters) the very significant degree to which these torts come apart in structural and juridical terms.

In the course of so doing, I shall also resist the temptation to describe these torts as being linked – either historically or in the current era – by a consistent concern on the part of a creative judiciary to use these torts as a means of imposing liability on especially reprehensible wrongdoers whose activities do not fall within the fold of any other, nominate torts. While I think that such an explanation may plausibly be offered in connection with most if not all of the most recent authorities, I am

[82] *Cf* Deakin and Randall (n 23) 532: '[a]s the statutory immunities were extended and as modern competition law began to develop, the role of the economic torts … became an adjunct one to that of statute'.

[83] Deakin and Randall (n 23) 533 identify these as 'the interests which they [ie, the economic torts] protect'. At various points in time, and across several jurisdictions, these economic interests seem to have been treated by the courts and legal commentators as the ones with which these torts are concerned (hence, eg, the old language of a tort of interfering with trade). For this reason (and to avoid unduly repetitious prose), I treat economic interests as synonymous with trade and business interests *unless* otherwise stated. And sometimes it is necessary to state otherwise, for it is certainly possible to have economic interests that fall beyond the compass of trading or business losses: see, eg, *Secretary of State for the Home Department v Servier Laboratories Ltd* [2021] UKSC 24 (SC) (the Secretary of State who appealed against the decision of the Court of Appeal in this case cannot plausibly be described as a business or trader).

[84] As will be noted in subsequent chapters, although targeted harm is a fairly common element in these torts, it is by no means ubiquitously required. Equally, although these torts are frequently considered to be torts of intention, the concept of intention at play varies among them, as does the meaning of 'unlawful means' (another common, but not universal, element).

[85] *Henderson v Merrett Syndicates Ltd* [1995] 2 AC 145 (HL), 186.

not at all sure that this thesis would hold good for all of the older cases (though it is doubtless true of many). There are many historical examples that could be cited of judges taking a nakedly hostile view towards (despised) collective action; but there is much more to the early development of the economic torts than an overt judicial concern to control organised labour. Any attempt to shoe-horn all of the landmark decisions into this framework would involve intellectual dishonesty on my part. I shall point out several torts in which egregious wrongdoing has always been a concern; but I shall not adopt contrived interpretations of quite a few key cases in order to make all the torts 'fit' this pattern.[86] Artificial interpretations must be resisted if we are to evince a realistic (as opposed to idealistic) image of the actions in view.[87] It is artificial interpretations, as we shall see briefly in a moment, and in more detail in chapter two, that give rise to the quotidian (ungrounded) complaints in this field that certain cases (or torts) are anomalies or aberrations.

Before progressing to my third main claim, I want to make clear that I do not deny that all of the torts examined in this book *have the capacity* to provide a remedy for economic losses. Nor indeed, do I deny that the vast bulk of the decided cases involve such losses. Rather, my claim is merely that it is a mistake to consider all of these torts as being confined to the task of 'policing economic activity'.[88] The various torts are neither linked by their capacity to protect economic interests, nor capable of being rationalised along such lines. They comprise, instead, a fairly disparate bunch of actions. Thus, unlike the corresponding rules found in civil codes – of which Weir wrote '*lex specialis legi generali derogat*'[89] – the position under English law is more accurately captured by the idea that *leges speciales iuxta consistent*. There has never been a single genus tort with several sub-species, all of which, on the whole, fulfil just one remedial purpose. And nor is it likely that they will coalesce around any such purpose in the foreseeable future given the aforementioned inventive ways that some of them have been used in recent years.

The third main argument of this book is that, although the somewhat tortuous history of the economic torts has been trawled over numerous times, this has typically occurred without the holdings in many of the relevant cases being properly contextualised. It is submitted that a richer, more complete understanding of these torts is possible if one is attentive not merely to the various twists and turns that were taken in the leading cases themselves, but also to a variety of other factors that influenced these torts being minted in the first place, and their subsequent

[86] Doing so would, in any event, tend to undermine my central contention that the juridical distinctions between the various torts are more pronounced than their commonalities.

[87] I acknowledge that my 'realistic' image has an inescapable prescriptive dimension to it. But, as I explain in chapter nine, it is an image that is not (unlike the prescriptive claims made by other jurists) contradicted by the case law as it presents itself. To this extent, as I also explain more fully in chapter nine, I think that what I offer can be described as a legitimate interpretation of the existing scope and future potential of these torts.

[88] M Lobban, 'Intentional and Economic Torts' in W Cornish *et al* (eds), *The Oxford History of the Laws of England: Volume XII – Private Law* (Oxford, Oxford University Press, 2010) 1033.

[89] Weir (n 1) 26.

developmental trajectories. As will be seen in most of the following chapters – but especially in chapter seven – social expediency, juristic writing, political predilections on the part of certain judges, and, in some cases, a particular ideological *Zeitgeist* have all exerted an influence, not hitherto explored.[90]

The last main argument of the book is that, although this is often said about some of these torts, there is nothing obviously anomalous about any of them.[91] Recognition of this fact helps reveal their true potential. Those who cry 'anomaly' seldom explain what they mean by this (though of course whatever they mean has clearly pejorative overtones). Various meanings are possible. Yet as we shall see in chapter five – in which lawful means conspiracy and two-party intimidation are considered – none of these meanings seem, on close analysis, an appropriate way to describe the actions concerned. Instead, such utterances are normally reducible to little more than a grumble about the incompatibility of a particular holding here, or a line of authority there, with some or other fairly narrow theoretical understanding of the economic torts.[92] To put it more bluntly: those who voice such complaints about anomalies are typically motivated to do so by a pre-commitment on their part to some theory or agenda concerning tort law generally, or the economic torts in particular.

As against such jurists I shall argue that it is *only because* they are pre-committed in this way that a given cause of action appears to be anomalous. For all that a particular decision may appear anomalous from the perspective of *Theory X*, this need not mean that it is a genuine aberration on the part of the courts. A failure to fit the tenets of a particular theory is no more than that. It is certainly not an indication that the courts have taken a wrong turn at some point. When settled parts of the law clash with putatively explanatory theories, my instinct is to think that the theory is deficient in its explanation of the law rather than to say that the law is deficient by virtue of its non-compliance with the theory.[93]

IV. Structure of the Book

In the next chapter, I examine the various shortcomings in existing scholarship concerning the economic torts (or at least such of that scholarship as is sufficiently

[90] An excellent book that explores the influence of factors such as these on other areas of tort law – but regrettably, not the economic torts – is P Mitchell, *A History of Tort Law 1900–1950* (Cambridge, Cambridge University Press, 2015).

[91] Stevens refuses to single out the much maligned tort of lawful means conspiracy and contends instead that, when the economic torts are '[l]umped together … lawful means conspiracy appears no more anomalous than any of the other economic torts': Stevens (n 45) 298.

[92] I have noted the tendency of certain popular tort theorists to resort to such hollow claims on several previous occasions; but it is a tendency that has been noted by others, too: see, especially J Stapleton, *Three Essays on Torts* (Oxford, Oxford University Press, 2021) 20–25.

[93] Precisely the same instinct is held by Stapleton in her essay 'Taking the Judges Seriously v. Grand Theories': Stapleton (n 92) esp, 25–33.

contemporary to be regarded as offering a credible alternative to my own). I pay especial attention to the work of Hazel Carty, Simon Deakin, Allan Beever and Jason Neyers. All four have very considerable academic pedigrees; and Carty, in particular, has been very influential in both judicial and academic circles when it comes to her analysis of the economic torts. Consequently, any new foray into this area would, I think, be deficient if it were not to engage with the arguments advanced by her or the other three scholars just named. But in any event, some of the claims that I shall seek to defend in this book require that I identify the missteps within, and incompleteness of, others' work.[94]

Chapters three to five will seek to unearth the true gist and province of each of the general economic torts. In chapter three, I shall tackle the hard-to-characterise action for inducing breach of contract. My first and third theses will feature prominently in this chapter since I shall endeavour to show that there is nothing in logic, nor in the historical authorities, which tethers this action to the protection of economic interests. Rather, a trawl of the case law that preceded the landmark decision in *Lumley v Gye*,[95] together with some of the individual judgments in that case, suggest that it is an action that could be applied to contracts of any stripe. A similar exercise will be undertaken in chapter four in relation to the two economic torts that specifically require the claimant to show the use of unlawful means. The scope of these two torts, as well as a properly contextualised account of their development, will be proffered.

In recognition of the fact that they are both highly controversial actions, I shall devote chapter five to a discussion of lawful means conspiracy and two-party intimidation. Here, my main concerns will change. Thus, although I will assuredly show that they are not principally bound up with the protection of trade, business or any other economic interests, I shall concern myself in the main with unearthing a richer understanding of their origins, vitality and future potential than has hitherto been provided. And I shall do this in order to fend off the claim that they are moribund. I cannot, after all, ignore the obvious point that they have both been invoked remarkably infrequently, and then hardly ever successfully.

In chapter six, I shall switch my attention to the various misrepresentation torts. Here, again, I shall seek to show that there is no warrant – in theory or in practice – for thinking that all of these torts are operationally confined to the protection of purely economic interests. Such a limitation applies only to passing off. Also, in relation to injurious falsehood, I shall endeavour to demonstrate that it is by no means a redundant cause of action, one that has been superseded by various statutory actions, the unlawful means tort, passing off or defamation.

The burden of chapter seven will be to defend the claim that there is a good deal more in juridical terms that divides rather than unites the torts in view. In

[94] Of course, it does not necessarily follow from my showing that Beever, Carty and Deakin have supplied incomplete and otherwise flawed analyses that my own is better. But at least my doing this helps to make plausible the claim that I offer a superior view.

[95] *Lumley v Gye* (1853) 2 El & Bl 216.

particular, attention will be paid to the significance we should attach to the fact that they: (1) differ structurally; (2) contain seemingly common ingredients – like intention, and unlawful means – which in fact bear different meanings for the purposes of different causes of action; and (3) cannot all be regarded as responding to the invasion of a right held by the claimant against the defendant.

Chapter eight seeks to explain why – when it is so often supposed that they have a common *raison d'être* – some of the torts considered in this book have developed in various unforeseen ways. It will be argued that there is far more to the story of their evolution than a rather simplistic to-ing and fro-ing on the part of the judiciary with respect to the narrow question of whether the economic torts ought to fulfil an interventionist or abstentionist role with respect to acts done in the name of business or trade rivalry. The chapter, in short, will aim to show that a fairly wide variety of factors have influenced their development.

In chapter nine, I shall bring things to a close with various conclusions about the vitality, province and potential of this rather disparate bunch of torts. Prime among these conclusions will be the claim that it is unhelpful to think of them in terms of 'the economic torts' given that their capacity to protect such interests is only one part of a fascinating and complex story. Seductively simple (and undoubtedly convenient[96]) as that nomenclature may be, it is, to quote Lord Hoffmann in *OBG*, 'a form of seduction which may lure writers onto the rocks'.[97] In recognition that this book aims in significant measure to offer a re-interpretation of the uses to which the various torts considered may be put, I shall also seek to defend in this chapter the (limited) prescriptive dimension to this re-interpretation.

[96] The term is so widely recognised that the use of any other term would *now* probably mystify readers. It is because of its convenient recognisability (but only because of this) that I have persisted with the use of the term in this book.

[97] *OBG* (n 8) [31].

2

The Mistake of Monism

Should we not distrust the jaunty assurance with which every age prides itself that it at last has hit upon the ultimate concepts in which all that happens can be formulated? … We are apt to fall into the error of thinking that the facts are simple because simplicity is the goal of our quest. The guiding motto in the life of every natural philosopher should be, 'Seek simplicity and distrust it' (Alfred North Whitehead, *The Concept of Nature* (1919) 163).

I. Introduction

If on nothing else, there is certainly one matter on which jurists who have written at length about the economic torts seem to agree. It is, as Lord Wedderburn famously put it almost 40 years ago, that the economic torts 'have been at best a ramshackle construction for decades. They have lacked their Atkin'.[1] More or less the same contention was advanced by Dyson Heydon about five years earlier when he wrote: '[t]he generalising tendency of the twentieth century common lawyer has passed the economic torts by'.[2] And this position remained unchanged, even into the twenty-first century. Hazel Carty, writing in 2010, asserted that the law prior to the landmark decision of the House of Lords in *OBG Ltd v Allan*[3] had been a 'mess'.[4] And while she saw the decision in that case as having had the potential to be 'an important stage in clarifying the muddle of the economic torts',[5] she was nonetheless quick to add that the decision in *Revenue and Customs Commissioners v Total Network SL*,[6] handed down within a year of *OBG*, had almost immediately restored the confusion. Her summary of the state of the law by the end of 2008 was as follows:

> the combination of a regrettable concession by Total's counsel, an emphasis on a minor dictum from *OBG* and a knee-jerk response to bad behaviour undermined the good

[1] KW Wedderburn, 'Rocking the Torts' (1983) 46 *MLR* 224, 229.

[2] JD Heydon, *Economic Torts*, 2nd edn (London, Sweet and Maxwell, 1978) 130.

[3] *OBG Ltd v Allan* [2008] 1 AC 1 (HL).

[4] H Carty, *An Analysis of the Economic Torts*, 2nd edn (Oxford, Oxford University Press, 2010) 23. Tony Weir, writing in the years between Heydon and Carty, also spoke of these torts being in a mess: see T Weir, *Economic Torts* (Oxford, Clarendon Press, 1997) 7.

[5] Carty, *ibid*, 28.

[6] *Revenue and Customs Commissioners v Total Network SL* [2008] 1 AC 1174 (HL).

> work of *OBG*, setting the economic torts back on their rocky, chaotic road for the 21st century.[7]

Allan Beever is another prominent jurist who considers the law to be in 'a mess' in the wake of these two landmark decisions.[8] And, like Carty, he not only regards the current law as being an 'area beset with uncertainty',[9] but also envisages 'another century at least of abiding confusion'.[10]

Such laments reveal more than merely a rare instance of agreement between jurists who otherwise disagree markedly about such basic matters as the vitality and proper province of the economic torts. They also betray a shared supposition that there is some fundamental commonality of function which unites them, and which, unfortunately, is obscured by a cluster of interloping, wayward decisions that have emanated from our most senior courts. The supposition which lurks just beneath the surface of remarks about the messiness of the law in this setting, but which is seldom openly articulated, is that the economic torts *can and should* be rationalised. That these authors share this assumption is clear. For, without it, the claim that the law is in a mess tends towards vacuity.[11] Put another way: why would the heterogeneity of these torts be considered a source of regret if it were not for the conviction that such heterogeneity ought not to exist? If the various torts to which they refer had in truth been minted, or subsequently developed, with a view to fulfilling a range of different objectives, then why would the absence of a common purpose around which they coalesce be considered a basis on which to describe them as being chaotic?

Seemingly, it is only among those jurists who have considered the economic torts with comparative brevity that there exists a relative indifference towards the absence of any unity of purpose. For example, in fairly dispassionate terms, Robert Stevens simply proffers the observation that the economic torts 'have no inherent unity',[12] and that, accordingly, so far as the search for a unifying thread is concerned, 'we will be waiting forever'.[13] In similar vein, McBride and Bagshaw note, with no hint of dismay, that there is no golden thread that binds together the various economic torts. They write:

> [T]endencies to mono-mania must be resisted. There is no good reason to think that the torts gathered together [under the banner 'economic torts'] … have anything in common except for the accidental fact of the kind of loss that *normally* tends to be suffered by someone who is a victim of one of these torts.[14]

[7] H Carty, 'The Economic Torts in the 21st Century' (2008) 124 *LQR* 641, 674. For an even more scything condemnation of 'the chaos of *Total*', see *ibid*, 660.

[8] A Beever, *A Theory of Tort Liability* (Oxford, Hart Publishing, 2016) 154.

[9] *Ibid*, 102.

[10] *Ibid*, 145.

[11] The claim need not be absolutely vacuous, however. It is possible for the law to be in a mess where, even accepting that torts A, B and C need not have any common purpose, there exist many conflicting decisions involving just tort A, or just tort B, or just tort C.

[12] R Stevens, *Torts and Rights* (Oxford, Oxford University Press, 2007) 297.

[13] *Ibid*.

[14] NJ McBride and R Bagshaw, *Tort Law*, 6th edn (London, Pearson, 2018) 627.

Jurists who see (or would like to see) unity of purpose in the economic torts will be referred to in this book as monists. And standing in contrast to these authors are the pluralists who (like me) perceive them to be, at most, a loosely affiliated group of actions. Since the monists and pluralists cannot both be right, it is vitally important that I devote a chapter to explaining why it is that the monists do not have the upper hand when it comes to explaining the economic torts.

II. Leading Monistic Accounts

Monistic accounts vary considerably. Although there are several authors who adopt a monistic point of view, they do not generally share the exact same conception of what constitutes the organising principle or purpose that putatively underscores the economic torts. We may conveniently begin with probably the most well-known commentator in the field, Carty. Although Carty thinks 'that there are four main categories of economic tort',[15] it is also clear that she perceives them to have a common purpose. In a section of her book entitled 'The Need to Tackle All the Economic Torts',[16] she notes that '[t]hey are all weapons in the policy to prevent "excessive" competition or economic endeavour. They are all about protecting your competitive edge – whether against lies, confusion or attacks'.[17] Fundamentally, then, at least in Carty's view, 'the economic torts, as their name suggests, have as their primary function the protection of economic interests'.[18] But more precisely than this, given tort law's 'traditional resistance to recovery for pure economic loss',[19] she considers their sphere of operation to be confined to competitive commercial behaviour. Her argument to this effect runs thus:

> [t]he better approach (especially when attempting an overall analysis) is to see all of these torts as protecting against economic harm, against a background of competition … [in which] all of the economic torts set limits on commercial behaviour.[20]

Simon Deakin, holds a similar (but by no means identical) view. He suggests that the 'purpose of the economic torts is to protect a person in relation to his trade, business or livelihood',[21] and that their 'fundamental rationale … is to maintain

[15] Carty (n 4) 318. The four categories represent merely her ideal framework. But she acknowledges that '[t]he decision in *Total Network* demands at the very least that a new category – Category E – be added to the framework to take account of the tort of unlawful means conspiracy': *ibid*, 326.

[16] *Ibid*, 310.

[17] *Ibid*, 311.

[18] Carty (n 4) 1. She acknowledges that some of these torts also allow recovery for other interests – such as physical harm and injury to feelings. See text associated with n 31 below.

[19] *Ibid*, 1.

[20] *Ibid*, 4. Carty expressly extends the idea of commercial competition to 'competition in the industrial relations sphere': *ibid*.

[21] S Deakin and Z Adams, *Markesinis and Deakin's Tort Law*, 8th edn (Oxford, Oxford University Press, 2019) 458.

the integrity of the competitive process'.[22] Jason Neyers, yet another monist, rejects outright such an instrumentalist understanding of these torts. In place of the idea that they are underpinned by, and combine to secure, some such goal, he believes that 'the Anglo-Canadian law on the economic torts is capable of being conceptualised as a manifestation of corrective justice'.[23]

Beever's monism is of yet another variety. Though much of what he argues is clearly influenced by academic sources that are liberally cited in, and perhaps even foundational to, Neyers' work, his ultimate conception of the economic torts is markedly different to that of Neyers. For Beever, the *raison d'être* of the economic torts can be summed up by a simple claim that he makes (albeit one to which he attaches a far from simple meaning). The claim is that we may avail ourselves of:

> an understanding [of these actions] that might be described as a new, though restricted, unified theory [according to which] [t]he so-called economic torts deal with cases in which one person attempts to control another via the medium of a third party.[24]

In Russian-doll-like fashion, Beever's theory of the economic torts needs to be unpacked in stages. When he uses the word 'control', what he means is 'putting the plaintiff or the plaintiff's [property] to one's purposes'.[25] Going back a step further, he also explains that putting another (or their property) to one's own purposes is a form of constraint.[26] And then, going back one final step, he elaborates on what he means by constraint. He says: 'A constrains B if A interferes with B's freedom, as defined in accordance with B's innate and acquired rights'.[27] Thus, in slightly more transparent terms, the economic torts are, for Beever, all about indirect violations of every person's innate right to be free from *unjustified* constraints.[28]

III. The Limitations of Monism

Despite the academic pedigree of the writers who have offered monistic accounts of the economic torts, it seems obvious from the fact that they tether their understandings of these torts to three very different organising principles that at least two of them must be wrong. As it turns out, however – and as I shall explain presently – all of these monistic accounts are vulnerable to very serious objections.

[22] S Deakin and J Randall, 'Rethinking the Economic Torts' (2009) 72 *MLR* 519, 520.

[23] JW Neyers, 'The Economic Torts as Corrective Justice' (2009) *Torts Law Journal* 1, 6.

[24] Beever (n 8) 154.

[25] *Ibid*, 27. The word 'property' is conspicuously absent from Beever's definition of 'control'. However, it is clear from the preceding paragraph that this is the word that is missing.

[26] *Ibid*: 'one constrains another by putting that person to one's purposes' and '[y]ou can constrain me by putting my property to your purposes'.

[27] *Ibid*, 26.

[28] The qualifier is important since, according to Beever, 'constraint is not necessarily wrongful; it is not wrongful when it is necessary to protect equal maximum freedom': *ibid*, 25.

In what follows, I parcel together the broadly similar conceptions of the economic torts espoused by Carty and Deakin. I do so because I regard them as mere variations on what we may call the 'Conventional View'. I label the account proffered by Neyers the 'Rights Based View'.[29] And I dub Beever's approach – assiduously tied, as it is, to the legal philosophy of Immanuel Kant – the 'Kantian View'.

A. The Conventional View

Although I have bracketed Carty and Deakin together as monists who subscribe to a traditional view of the economic torts – one which regards them as being designed to protect economic interests arising within a commercial setting by placing limits on competitive behaviour[30] – it is important to recognise that several significant differences exist between their respective accounts. One in particular needs to be addressed here since it reveals a good deal about the way these authors seek to treat certain authorities that 'inconveniently' clash with their views.

While Carty and Deakin agree on the principal sphere of operation of these torts, they nonetheless disagree in relation to the established *breadth* of their sphere of operation. Carty accepts that some of these torts can occasionally be used in connection with a range of interests besides those of a purely economic nature (even though she clearly views their doing so as very much a secondary – perhaps even accidental – function). In a telling footnote, she notes guardedly that:

> though, eg, the tort of intimidation can also involve physical harm as in *Godwin v Uzoigwe* [and while] compensation for injury to feelings may be recoverable in the torts of inducing breach of contract (*Pratt v BMA*), deceit (*East v Maurer*), malicious falsehood (*Khodaparast v Shad*) and probably also in intimidation and the unlawful means tort, the protection of economic interests is the prime reason for the existence and development of these torts.[31]

Deakin, by contrast, espouses a much more restrictive view. He believes that the economic torts are confined exclusively to the protection of economic interests

[29] Though rights theorists typically point out expressly that their theories differ significantly from corrective justice theories, Neyers states that, for the purposes of his treatment of the economic torts, 'the terms "rights-based" and "corrective justice" can be treated as synonyms': Neyers (n 23) 2, fn 1. His reason for so doing is that both forms of theory belong to 'a legal and philosophical tradition … [concerned with] the rights persons hold against each other … [and how tort law] should respond to violations of those rights': *ibid.* Since he focuses on the source of the injustice (a rights infringement) rather than the corrective element, I prefer to refer to his account as rights-based (something Neyers has himself previously done: see JW Neyers, 'Rights-based Justifications for the Tort of Unlawful Interference with Economic Relations' [2008] *Legal Studies* 215).

[30] I label this the conventional view of the economic torts because it can be traced back to the landmark case of *Mogul Steamship Co Ltd v McGregor Gow & Co* [1892] AC 25 (HL), 43 and 50–51 (Lord Watson and Lord Morris, respectively).

[31] Carty (n 4) 1, fn 2 (citations omitted). Her discomfort with treating the decision in *Godwin v Uzoigwe* as a legitimate use of one of the economic torts is also evident in her writing, 'it is suggested that two-party liability in intimidation is a separate area of tort liability': Carty (n 4) 120.

that arise from, or that are bound up with, the claimant's trade, business or livelihood. '[T]he economic torts', he writes:

> belong to that broad class of civil wrongs in which the gist of the action lies … in an interference with an interest which the law protects. [Thus] *unless a direct interference with trade, business or employment is made out, a vital element of the wrong is missing.*[32]

His failure to entertain the idea that these torts might occasionally provide a remedy in respect of damage to non-economic interests entails the rejection of a range of important developments in case law concerning these torts that cannot be sloughed off as instances of judicial error. Existing authorities – especially when they have been generated by appellate courts such as the House of Lords or Supreme Court – cannot, I would argue, simply be disregarded or implicitly treated as having been erroneously decided.[33] And yet Deakin is guilty of doing one or other of these things when he suggests that

> [a]ll the great cases in the area of the economic torts … have been based on the principle that the right to pursue a trade, business or livelihood free of certain forms of interference … deserves the protection of the law.[34]

Either Deakin overlooks the cases cited by Carty, or – conspicuously, without giving a reason as to why – he rejects the idea that they are among the 'great cases' in this area. If it be the former, then his depiction of the province of the economic torts is an incomplete one. If it be the latter, then everything turns upon his undefended and unelaborated conception of a great case. Either way, his account is obviously inadequate, for – to take but one example – the famous deceit case of *East v Maurer* was one in which general damages of £1000 were awarded in respect of the 'disappointment and inconvenience of the plaintiffs in their attempt to establish this [hairdressing] business'.[35]

On the other hand, Carty's treatment of the various cases she cites does not really provide an accurate reflection of the way that the relevant torts have developed, or of the way that they currently function.[36] The fact that she tucks into

[32] Deakin and Randall (n 22) 533 (emphasis added).

[33] For an especially compelling clarion call to take seriously the judgments of our most senior judges, see J Stapleton, *Three Essays on Torts* (Oxford, Oxford University Press, 2021) Ch 1.

[34] Deakin and Randall (n 22) 534.

[35] There is no first instance report of the case, and this head of loss was not challenged on appeal. However, for confirmation of this award by the Court of Appeal, see *East v Maurer* [1991] 1 WLR 461 (CA), 464 (Beldam LJ).

[36] It is true that in *OBG* Lord Hoffmann said that the unlawful means tort was 'designed only to enforce basic standards of civilised behaviour in economic competition between traders, or between employers and labour': *OBG* (n 3) [56]. But what a tort has been *designed* to do, and the range of uses to which it may be put need not necessarily be the same thing. A suit of clothes originally *designed* to be worn by a person, may nonetheless be legitimately used (usually after some years) to make a scarecrow; a dessert spoon may legitimately be used to remove a bicycle tyre in order to repair a puncture. It is certainly noteworthy that in *Secretary of State for Health v Servier Laboratories Ltd* [2021] UKSC 24 (SC), [85], Lord Hamblen seemed to acknowledge (though he did not interrogate closely) the possibility that the unlawful means tort might develop into an action that protects interests other than those associated with trade or business.

a single footnote her admission that several economic torts can be invoked in connection with the protection of certain non-economic interests is highly suggestive. So, too, is the fact that she attaches to this admission an insistence that the 'prime reason' for the existence of these torts remains the protection of economic interests. In short, she remains, at heart, a monist. She sticks firmly to the notion that (even if certain terminological inconsistencies exist between them) the torts in view share a common *raison d'être*, namely, the protection against business losses. Her somewhat grudging acceptance that there is, here and there, a secondary role for these torts does not cause her to deviate from her belief about what constitutes their fundamental purpose.

In my view, any such unshakeable commitment to the idea that these torts were at their inception, and remain even now, overwhelmingly, about the provision of remedies for economic losses caused by excessive competitive behaviour obstructs our gaining a true understanding of what animates these actions, particularly in the modern era.[37] In addition to the handful of cases cited by Carty in which non-economic interests were protected by the torts she mentioned, several others could have been mentioned in which the economic torts have been used to protect non-financial interests. For example, the tort of deceit has been successfully used to recover damages for physical injury to the person caused by a defective chattel that was falsely represented to be safe[38] (and it seems probable that damage caused to chattels in like fashion would also be recoverable[39]). That the tort of deceit can be used in this way is, I think, not in the least bit problematic. It has been held by the Court of Appeal that reliance upon a negligent misstatement will ground an action for damages when such reliance results in physical injury.[40] It would, in my view, be extremely odd if no remedy were available in similar circumstances but in which the false statement in question had been made deliberately or recklessly.

Equally, one version of the action of trespass *per quod servitium amisit* (which, as we will see in detail in chapter three, formed an important part of the basis for the initial formulation of the modern tort of inducing breach of contract) specifically allowed damages to be claimed for the distress of a parent caused by the defendant depriving that parent of his or her daughter's services by seducing and

[37] For an account of the way in which 'the law moves with changes in social facts, values, and expectations providing people with appropriately adjusted entitlements and responsibilities', see Stapleton (n 33) 10.

[38] *Langridge v Levy* (1837) 2 M & W 519. In another case, Mummery LJ said that '[k]nowledge of a dangerous defect in a product may provide a foundation for a case of fraud': see *Hamble Fisheries Ltd v L Gardner & Sons Ltd* [1999] 2 Lloyd's Rep 1 (CA), 9.

[39] *Ward v Hobbs* (1878) 4 App Cas 13 (HL): D sold pigs to C that he knew to be diseased and therefore a risk to C's existing pigs; but on the facts D had expressly stated that he did not warrant that they were disease-free.

[40] *Perrett v Collins* [1998] 2 Lloyd's Rep 255 (CA). In similar vein, see *Hedley Byrne & Co Ltd v Heller & Partners Ltd* [1964] AC 465 (HL), 517 (Lord Devlin): '[i]f irrespective of contract, a doctor negligently advises a patient that he can safely pursue his occupation and he cannot and the patient's health suffers … the patient has a remedy'.

debauching her and leaving her pregnant.[41] One would have thought – bearing in mind the weight afforded to this line of authority in *Lumley*[42] – that there is no *a priori* reason why a present-day action for inducing breach of contract should be confined to protection against financial losses.[43]

Cumulatively, this fairly significant array of cases serves to falsify the forceful assertion made by Carty and Deakin that the protection of economic interests in a business setting is the only (or at least only proper) purpose of the so-called economic torts and therefore the key to understanding them. Whether tested against historical or current usage, their position can be seen to be untenable, at least so long as one affords proper respect to decisions made by our most senior judges. It is certainly difficult to see how the milestone case of *Total Network*[44] – considered at length in chapter four – can be interpreted as a case about excessive competitive behaviour in the commercial setting. The case involved a cartel fraud that was designed to cheat the Revenue out of certain VAT payments. Being cheated in this way cannot plausibly be cashed out in terms of the Revenue suffering losses caused by excessive competitive behaviour on the part of one commercial rival towards another. And, indeed, Lord Walker specifically stated in that case that '[t]he gist of conspiracy is damage intentionally inflicted by persons who combine for that purpose … and the claimant *need not be a trader who is injured in his trade*'.[45] Writing together with John Randall, Deakin freely admits that this dictum is 'plainly at odds with our analysis'.[46] Yet he nonetheless attempts to accommodate that case within his vision of the economic torts by arguing that allowing

> HMRC's claim … can be seen as helping to bring to an end a situation in which illegal trading harmed the integrity of the market and imposed losses on third parties, including competitors, who would not themselves have been in a position to sue because they were not the intended victims of the conspiracy.[47]

However, even if this were not a particularly tenuous explanation of the case, and even if it were not a direct contradiction of what Lord Walker specifically

[41] In *Dodd v Norris* (1814) 3 Camp 519, Lord Ellenborough ruled (*ibid*) that 'the law considered this an action of trespass for assaulting the daughter, whereby the parent lost her service' but added that 'a further compensation was allowed for the injury to the parental feelings'. Similarly, in *Andrews v Askey* 173 ER 376, Tindal CJ directed the jury (*ibid*, 377) as follows: '[y]ou are not confined to the consideration of the mere loss of service, but may give some damages for the distress and anxiety of mind which the mother has felt'. *Cf* the version of the tort concerned purely with enticing a servant away from his master where compensation was limited purely to the financial loss suffered: see, eg, *Hart v Aldridge* (1774) 1 Cowp 54. And for discussion of both versions, see M Lobban, 'Intentional and Economic Torts' in W Cornish *et al* (eds), *The Oxford History of The Laws of England – Vol XII: 1820-1914* (Oxford, Oxford University Press, 2010) 1041–43.

[42] Today, a court would doubtless distinguish cases in which a person is (1) *prevented from doing X* from those in which she is (2) *persuaded not to do X*. But these matters go the meaning of procurement, and not what is compensable.

[43] For other types of loss that should, in principle, be recoverable under the auspices of inducing breach of contract, see the various examples supplied in chapter three, p 70.

[44] *Total Network* (n 6).

[45] *Ibid*, 100 (emphasis added).

[46] Deakin and Randall (n 22) 534.

[47] *Ibid*.

said, it would still be an unconvincing attempt to square *Total Network* with their more general claim that the economic torts protect business competitors' trade or business interests by giving those competitors a right of action when their trade or business interests are wrongfully interfered with. This is because Deakin and Randall's attempted rationalisation of the case seems to suggest that the decision in *Total Network* can be tolerated because it *indirectly* protects competitors' trade or business interests by granting a right of action to *someone other than those competitors*. When the Revenue Commissioners sued for conspiracy, in other words, their doing so (apparently) helped restore the integrity of the market to which the defendant's business competitors belonged: granting C a right of action against D meant that an indirect economic benefit could be secured for D's competitors E, F and G. But notice how far this is from their commitment to the idea that:

> the general requirement for liability in tort for interfering with trade or business, including in the conspiracy torts, should be restated in terms of the defendant 'aiming at' or 'targeting' his conduct at the claimant in such a way as to bring about a direct interference with his interests.[48]

In contrast to this, Deakin and Randall's attempted accommodation of the decision in *Total Network* emphasises the *indirect* effects of the conspiracy on the economic interests of the defendant's business rivals, and it ignores the fact that the last thing that those involved in the carousel fraud were attempting to do was target traders in the market.

I would suggest that a much more plausible, and far less convoluted justification for the decision in that case is available, namely that unlawful means conspiracy cannot be understood as being confined to the protection of business competitors' trading interests. *Total Network* stands on the highest judicial authority and supports the contention that economic losses caused otherwise than through 'excessive rivalrous behaviour … in the context of trade competition'[49] may be recovered.

This altogether simpler explanation reflects the idea at the heart of tort law that C's right to sue D ordinarily stems, not from the fact that tort law fulfils a 'market-protecting role',[50] but from the fact that D has wronged or harmed C. And this interpretation of *Total Network* can also be endorsed by reference to the more recent Supreme Court decision in *JSC BTA Bank v Khrapunov*.[51] In that case, a bank brought a claim based on unlawful means conspiracy against the son-in-law of a former chairman of the bank. The latter had allegedly embezzled US$6 billion of the bank's funds and, in an attempt to recoup the money, the bank had obtained an order compelling the former chairman to disclose the whereabouts of those funds together with a worldwide freezing order that prevented him

[48] Deakin and Randall (n 22) 541.

[49] H Carty, 'The Tort of Conspiracy as a Can of Worms' in SGA Pitel *et al* (eds), *Tort Law: Challenging Orthodoxy* (Oxford, Hart Publishing, 2013) 391.

[50] Deakin and Randall (n 22) 534.

[51] *JSC BTA Bank v Khrapunov* [2020] AC 717 (SC).

from dealing with them. However, the son-in-law and former chairman entered into an arrangement whereby the former would assist the latter in dissipating and concealing those assets. His actions were held to amount to a conspiracy to cause financial loss to the bank by unlawful means (ie, via a breach of the freezing order in contempt of court).

Naturally, there is no plausible way that the bank on the one hand, and either the son-in-law or the former chairman on the other, could be described as business rivals. Accordingly, the case cannot be slotted into the narrow tramlines set for the economic torts by Deakin and Carty. Yet – for all its novelty in treating contempt of court as sufficient unlawful means[52] – *Khrapunov* can very easily be regarded as a case involving the especially reprehensible causing of economic loss outside the context of 'trade competition' (with the especial reprehensibility located in the contempt of court). And here, it will be recalled from chapter one that one of my main claims in this book is that the recent development of the economic torts has been driven in large part by a judicial willingness to hold that certain forms of egregious wrongdoing (that fall beyond the clutches of more familiar torts), may nonetheless be regarded as falling within the compass of the torts considered in this book.

Yet another development that is worthy of note here – albeit one that has hitherto only occurred concretely in other common law jurisdictions – concerns unlawful means conspiracy being used to extend liability from insolvent companies to those who stand behind them, *qua* conspirators. At bottom, this usage treats unlawful means conspiracy as a device for circumventing the 'problem' of limited corporate liability. In so doing, it further weakens the monists' claim that the central function of the economic torts is to police excessive competitive behaviour between trade or business rivals. In *Taylor v Smythe*,[53] for example, the Irish Supreme Court held that a controlling shareholder and the company in which those shares are held may be treated as parties to a conspiracy. And McCarthy J could see:

> no reason why the mere fact that one individual controls the company of limited liability should give immunity from suit to both that company and that individual in the case of an established arrangement for the benefit of both company and that individual to the detriment of others.[54]

Just the same conclusion – that a controlling shareholder and his company may be regarded as conspirators for the purposes of the civil law – was reached by the Singapore Court of Appeal in *Chew Kong Huat v Ricwil (Singapore) Pte Ltd*.[55]

In England, it has been held for the purposes of the criminal law that a company and its directors can conspire with one another.[56] And although, to date, it is only

[52] For more details, see chapter four.
[53] *Taylor v Smythe* [1991] 1 IR 142.
[54] *Ibid*, 163.
[55] *Chew Kong Huat v Ricwil (Singapore) Pte Ltd* [1999] 3 SLR (R) 1167. For discussion, see C Witting, 'Intra-Corporate Conspiracy: An Intriguing Prospect' [2013] *CLJ* 178, 197.
[56] *R v Blamires Transport Services Ltd* [1964] 1 QB 278 (CA).

at first instance that it has been held possible to treat those who stand behind a company as a party to a *civil* conspiracy with the company itself,[57] two members of the Court of Appeal also accepted this possibility in principle in *Gulf Oil (Great Britain) Ltd v Page*.[58] Parker LJ – who provided the leading judgment in that case of lawful means conspiracy – made clear that the issue did not strictly need to be decided, but nonetheless signalled his willingness to treat two directors of a garage business as having conspired with the garage itself on the strength of the defendants having conceded as much in various bits of correspondence.[59] Equally, making no attempt to discriminate between the two directors and the garage itself, Ralph Gibson LJ stated also that there was 'an arguable case' that could be advanced based on the fact that the act in question 'was carried out by the defendants as part of a concerted plan to inflict deliberate damage'.[60]

Admittedly, some of the developments in the cases mentioned in the preceding paragraphs could not possibly have found their way into either Carty's or Deakin's discussion of these torts since they were decided after the publication of the works in question. However, they might both reasonably have envisaged (and dealt with) at least two further matters that test the forcefulness with which they advance their respective monistic accounts. They centre on the purview of inducing breach of contract and injurious falsehood, respectively.

As far as inducing breach of contract is concerned, I made the point in chapter one that not all contracts have a commercial dimension to them, and that an induced breach of contract could well result in compensable mental distress. But it is perfectly possible to add here that another well-known class of contracts, namely, those designed to provide enjoyment rather than economic enrichment, could also result in compensable damage in the form of disappointment. Contracts for holidays are the best known example;[61] and it is hard to think why inducing a breach of a contract to provide, say, high quality holiday accommodation would not be actionable. Similarly, inducing the breach of a contract to provide some form of health care could easily result in a loss that would fall outside the narrow tramlines of economic loss, yet be regarded as compensable (*pace* Deakin and Carty). Quite why contracts of both these types were not considered by these authors is unclear. They are, after all, very well-known types of contract.

In relation to injurious falsehood, too, it is notable that in *Joyce v Sengupta* the then Vice-Chancellor, Sir Donald Nicholls, specifically countenanced the possibility of this tort being used to recover for any mental distress caused by the falsehood. And he was happy to recognise the possibility of such a claim regardless of whether the claimant also suffered some form of pecuniary loss.[62] Full details

[57] *Raja v McMillan* [2020] EWHC 951 (Ch).
[58] *Gulf Oil (Great Britain) Ltd v Page* [1987] Ch 327 (CA).
[59] *Ibid*, 334.
[60] *Ibid*.
[61] See, eg, *Jarvis v Swan Tours Ltd* [1972] 3 WLR 954 (CA); *Jackson v Horizon Holidays Ltd* [1975] 1 WLR 1468 (CA).
[62] *Joyce v Sengupta* [1993] 1 WLR 337 (CA), 348–49.

of the case are provided in chapter six; but for present purposes we need only note that it was decided before Carty and Deakin produced the work referred to in the preceding paragraphs.

What the foregoing paragraphs reveal is that monists who subscribe to the Conventional View are far too forceful in their insistence that the economic torts ought properly to apply only to the protection of economic interests arising in the arena of trade competition. They are too forceful in advancing this line of argument because their approach leads inescapably to the conclusion that the various novel uses of the economic torts adverted to above should be regarded as unprincipled departures from the straight and narrow rather than as welcome judicial innovations that can deal commendably with certain *ad hoc* injustices brought about by especially reprehensible defendants. Carty's inability to see these developments in this light is linked directly to her monistic commitments, as the following passage from one of her later articles reveals:

> the conspiracy tort has been handed a wider function: the control of intentional harm caused by commercial misbehaviour – which concept as yet has not been adequately defined or delimited but clearly extends beyond the presence of civil wrongs … [The] courts have failed to justify the acceptance of this new function for the conspiracy tort and … the ripples of uncertainty that flow from the revitalised tort of conspiracy will ultimately call into question the future function of the unlawful means tort.[63]

Unpacked, her reluctance to accept innovative developments in the use of the economic torts is rooted in a worry that they will undermine the fact that the 'traditional function of the economic torts was to protect against excessive trade competition'.[64] They should not, she maintains, be used as gap-fillers providing civil recourse in circumstances characterised by non-economic losses inflicted otherwise than by excessive competitive behaviour in an industrial or trade setting.[65] Likewise, Deakin is of the view that limits should be placed on the ways in which these torts are used; and, again, the claim seems to rest ultimately on the value he ascribes to conceptual neatness. Wishing to turn back the clock, he argues that 'a narrower conception of the economic torts could … become a more coherent one. [Hence] [t]he way forward is to refocus on their fundamental rationale, which is to maintain the integrity of the competitive process'.[66]

Such thinking is doubtless well-intended: it aims to ensure (or make achievable) unity of purpose among these notoriously fragmented torts. Both Carty and

[63] H Carty, 'The Modern Functions of the Economic Torts: Reviewing the English, Canadian, and New Zealand Positions' [2015] *CLJ* 261, 265.

[64] *Ibid*, 277.

[65] I provide a *positive* defence of these torts fulfilling a gap-filling role in chapter nine. For present purposes, though, it is enough to note only that monists oppose their doing so not on jurisprudential grounds but because gap-filling creates a risk that these torts will become uncoupled from their traditional moorings.

[66] Deakin and Randall (n 22) 520.

Deakin seek to achieve such unity via a brand of juridical conservatism which suffers from the following flaw. It is founded upon the mistaken supposition that there ever was a common purpose shared by the various economic torts. We saw in chapter one how quotidian talk of 'the economic torts' emerged only very gradually via the leading torts treatises, and even then without any uniformly held view by the various authors about which torts made up this putative family of wrongs. Indeed, as has been observed by numerous authors, the absence of a clear organising principle is exactly what has *always* dogged the economic torts. As is very well known, the job of reconciling the early landmark cases of *Allen v Flood*[67] and *Quinn v Leathem*[68] has been one of the most obdurately difficult tasks facing tort lawyers ever since they were decided over a century ago.

In my view, the keenness of authors such as Carty and Deakin for conceptual unity and normative elegance is misguided. They have, I think, been in pursuit of a will o' the wisp, rather than a genuinely discoverable Holy Grail.[69] For the overwhelming majority of its history, this area of the law has eluded such neatness and tidiness for the simple reason that its development is not guided by rigid theoretical precepts, but instead by a combination of (often ad hoc) factors.[70] It is slightly puzzling, then, that Carty should express concern about the future creative uses of the economic torts on the basis that they 'can only lead to further chaos in this area – where litigation often starts and ends at the interim stage – unless the courts clarify and adhere to a clear rationale for economic tort liability generally'.[71] Tort law as a whole is not elegant and coherent and it never has been.[72] The same is true of the economic torts as a microcosm of that whole. Thus, it is by no means inapt, despite its being oxymoronic, to talk in terms of the 'normal chaos' of the economic torts.[73]

A slight variation – or perhaps, elaboration – of the argument advanced by these monists has been supplied by Roderick Bagshaw. Although he is receptive to the idea that these torts cannot logically be confined to the protection of economic interests, he nonetheless argues that they do:

> restrict the liberty of competitors, employees, suppliers and protesters … [and that] [s]uch restrictions can be beneficial in that they can provide welcome protection for the valuable expectations of individuals, businesses and other enterprises against

[67] *Allen v Flood* [1898] AC 1 (HL).

[68] *Quinn v Leathem* [1901] AC 495 (HL).

[69] This is not to say that it is completely without merit. One thing that can certainly be said for the identification of a clear organising principle is that it promotes clarity in the law and thus better allows the law's addressees to conduct themselves within the bounds of legality.

[70] Some of these are discussed (in relation to tort law generally) in J Murphy, 'Contemporary Tort Theory and Tort Law's Evolution' (2019) 32 *Canadian Journal of Law and Jurisprudence* 413. And in relation to the economic torts in particular, see chapter seven.

[71] Carty (n 4) 15.

[72] See J Murphy, 'The Heterogeneity of Tort Law' (2019) 39 *OJLS* 455.

[73] The idea of normal chaos is borrowed from U Beck and E Beck-Gernsheim, *The Normal Chaos of Love* (Cambridge, Polity Press, 1995).

> disruption by unfair and egregious methods, such as the use of lies, threats, theft and violence against customers, suppliers or employees.[74]

Implicit in his claim is a different reason why the economic torts ought not to be used as gap-fillers, namely, that fairly rigid, clear rules are beneficial to the commercial actors whose activities these torts principally serve to regulate. But this, I suggest, is to presuppose the very thing that really ought to be shown in order to make trumpeting the virtue of nice, clear rules a valid reason to object to judges using these torts as gap-fillers. The value of certainty for commercial addressees of these torts plainly assumes that their chief function is to impose suitable restrictions on the liberty of competitors, suppliers and other businesses. If other interests underscore these torts – and this, I shall argue, is certainly the case with some of them – then they may well be used as gap-fillers without there being a departure from their *raison d'être*.

Because monists who sign up to the Conventional View are pre-committed to a relatively narrow conception of what these torts are (or should be) about, their work has a tendency to obstruct an objective assessment of their true purview and purposes. We shall have occasion in subsequent chapters to unearth the actual protective range of the torts in view, as well as what underscores the avowedly hard-to-explain cases dealt with in the preceding pages. For now, though, there are two further types of monistic explanation that need to be assessed. They are Jason Neyers' rights-based account, and Allan Beever's Kantian account.

B. The Rights-Based View

Jason Neyers has supplied a highly original, and in places ingenious, account of most of the general economic torts.[75] But as with Carty's and Deakin's analyses, it paints an incomplete picture: it makes no mention of the misrepresentation torts.[76] It also presents what I think is, ultimately, a misleading theoretical account of the torts that it does treat.

Neyers makes it his goal to offer 'the best interpretive theory'[77] of each of: (1) inducing breach of contract; (2) the unlawful means tort; and (3) conspiracy in both its forms. By his own admission, any theory of this kind will be more compelling if, 'it fits the cases .... [and] less persuasive if it radically departs from the cases'.[78] It is partly because I think that his account fails in terms of fit, and partly

[74] R Bagshaw, 'Lord Hoffmann and the Economic Torts' in PS Davies and J Pila (eds), *The Jurisprudence of Lord Hoffmann: A Festschrift in Honour of Lord Hoffmann* (Oxford, Hart Publishing, 2015) 60.

[75] Neyers (n 23).

[76] It also eschews discussion of intimidation because, Neyers says, the three-party version 'has largely become absorbed into the tort of unlawful interference with economic relations ... [while] in its two-party version it does not seem to raise any particular challenges to a rights-based view of tort law': *ibid*, 7.

[77] *Ibid*, 6.

[78] *Ibid*.

because he strays from the interpretive agenda into *purely* prescriptive writing,[79] that I would suggest that his particular monistic theory must also be rejected.

We can conveniently start with his analysis of inducing breach of contract. In Neyers' view, this action relies on the idea that 'a contractual right to performance is quasi-property in the sense that it may be transferred consensually from the parties in privity to someone outside the relationship'.[80] More fully, and unpacked in stages, his argument runs thus:

(1) the contractual right to performance is a form of quasi-property because it can be voluntarily transferred in much the same way that chattels and real property can be transferred; and
(2) it follows from the fact that the transfer of the right to contractual performance can be voluntary that it can also be involuntary, that is 'when a defendant … treats the right as a valuable asset which he can use, appropriate or injure without the right-holder's consent';[81] but crucially
(3) 'it is the intention to appropriate which creates the protected interest (the quasi-property) and the actual appropriation which constitutes the violation of that right'.[82]

Such thinking is, in my view, unconvincing for two main reasons. First, there is an obvious internal tension in what Neyers argues. We are told (in (1)) that rights to contractual performance constitute a form of quasi-property *by virtue* of their transferability; but we are also told (in (3)) that it is 'the intention to appropriate [them] which creates the quasi-property'.[83] So which factor is it that generates the property-like quality: the fact that a contractual right is transferable, or the intention to appropriate it on the part of the wrongdoer? Secondly, even if we put to one side the internal tension in what he says, there are fundamental problems with both of the possible sources of the property-like quality that Neyers identifies.

[79] There is, I freely admit, an inescapable prescriptive dimension to interpretive theories insofar as they aim to present a body of law in its best possible light. But pure prescription is different. Accordingly, interpretive theories – in the Dworkinian sense, at least – can be distinguished from the type of writing I criticise here. To explain: purely prescriptive writing prescinds with no compunction from the holdings of the past. By contrast, the idealised claims about the nature and functions of the law found in genuinely interpretive theories – 'combine [both] backward- and forward-looking elements': R Dworkin, *Law's Empire* (Cambridge, Massachusetts, Belknap Press, 1996) 255. I shall have more to say about the legitimate extent to which my own interpretative endeavour bears a limited prescriptive dimension in the final chapter of this book.

[80] *Ibid.* The argument relies heavily on arguments made in P Benson, 'The Basis for Excluding Liability for Economic Loss in Tort Law' in DG Owen (ed), *Philosophical Foundations of Tort Law* (Oxford, Clarendon Press, 1993).

[81] Benson, *ibid*, 456–57.

[82] Neyers (n 23) 14.

[83] In saying this, Neyers appears to have misinterpreted what Benson – upon whom he relies – says in this regard. For Benson, it is the wrongfulness of D's actions (rather than the quasi-property status of the right to performance) that is anchored to D's having acted intentionally. In his words: '[w]hether there has been a wrongful taking or injury to the contract right viewed as a quasi-property interest will crucially depend on the defendant having the necessary intention': Benson (n 80) 457.

The idea that the source of the property-like interest might be the wrongdoer's intention to appropriate the contractual right to performance seems obviously flawed because it is hard to see how A's property rights can depend on what is in B's mind. At the same time, however, it is equally implausible to suggest that the source of the interest can be identified in the transferability of rights to contractual performance. For one thing, it is clear that a case of inducing breach of contract need not involve, as Neyers puts it, an 'appropriation [by the defendant] of the plaintiff's contractual right to performance'.[84] True, in the seminal case of *Lumley v Gye*[85] the defendant induced the famous opera singer, Johanna Wagner, to break her contract with the claimant and sing for him instead at his own, rival opera house. But it is perfectly possible for A to invoke this action where B persuades C to break her contract with A without B simultaneously acquiring for himself what C had promised to do for A. There is, in short, no requirement in this tort that B should take for herself the contractual performance that was due to A. B may simply want C to break her contract with A because B wants A to suffer loss. It cannot, therefore, be true that it is 'the actual appropriation which constitutes the violation' for which the claimant is entitled to sue because this would render inexplicable any case in which no appropriation for the defendant's own ends occurs.

Secondly, if we accept that the transferability of a right to contractual performance gives that right a property-like quality, it is nonetheless property-like in an irrelevant sense. The key question is not whether contract rights are transferable. It is whether they share with real and personal property the quality of generating rights of action against a third party (whether or not the third party is seeking to appropriate those rights for himself). This is the analogy with real and personal property that could conceivably work; but it is not the one that Neyers proffers. His insistence upon emphasising the transferability of rights to contractual performance is in truth a red herring. And it fails to ground his claim that 'an *in personam* right created by the law of contract can be treated, in limited circumstances, as a right *in rem* by the law of tort'.[86] There is nothing in what Neyers says – or, more importantly, in the case law – that explains why such a right *in rem* should somehow arise out of (or attach itself to) the established *in personam* right to contractual performance. Simply saying that such a right *in rem* exists does not make it so. That is mere affirmation. So, for all that it may be true that his preferred explanation is not inconsistent with the decided cases, nor is it an interpretation of inducing breach of contract that can be drawn from what was actually said in the relevant authorities.[87] It is at this point that Neyers can be observed to have

[84] Neyers (n 23) 15.

[85] *Lumley v Gye* (1853) 2 El & Bl 216.

[86] Neyers (n 23) 15.

[87] At one point in his speech in the now leading case, Lord Hoffmann does say of inducing breach of contract that '[i]t treats contractual rights as a species of property which deserve special protection, not only by giving a right of action against the party who breaks his contract but by imposing secondary liability on a person who procures him to do so': *OBG* (n 3) [32]. But his saying this is confused.

abandoned his interpretive promise. His account of inducing breach of contract is based ultimately on ideas that are conspicuous by their absence in the law as it presents itself.

As regards the capacity of his preferred framework to accommodate the tort of causing loss by unlawful means, Neyers begins by identifying the most obvious problem for a rights-based account of this tort. This is that 'the tort of unlawful interference with economic relations seemingly allows a plaintiff to sue a defendant for losses caused by the violation of *another's* rights rather than for losses occasioned by violation of the plaintiff's own rights'.[88] He nonetheless contends that there are two possible solutions to this problem. The first of these is premised upon an 'abuse of rights theory' while the second relies upon what he calls a 'public right theory'.[89] According to the first solution, the relevant right held by the claimant is said to be a 'universal right in everyone' that others do not exercise abusively their own rights to purposive activity by acting maliciously. The argument is elegantly expressed, and Neyers unpacks it with considerable sophistication. But it is ultimately a failure *qua* interpretive theory. For, as Neyers concedes, it relies on the existence of a doctrine that clashes fundamentally with established authority in that it 'contradicts well-accepted and defining principles of Anglo-Canadian common law relating to the relevance of motive'.[90] True: the abuse of rights idea has some traction in the USA in the form of the *prima facie* tort doctrine which underpins the famous case of *Tuttle v Buck*.[91] Yet, as Lord Nicholls made clear in *OBG*: '*Tuttle v Buck* is not the law in England. In this country intentionally causing damage without using unlawful means is not of itself actionable'.[92]

His alternative, rights-based conception of this tort – based on what he calls 'public right theory' – suffers from precisely the same problem. At the heart of this theoretical explanation are two key propositions. The first is 'that the criminal law creates rights that are actionable in the private law'.[93] The second is that, on this footing, '"unlawful means" should be limited to crimes (and other actionable breaches of statute) and should not include torts, breaches of contract or other actions that one is "not at liberty to commit"'.[94]

The first of these propositions is hard to accept given that in *Lonrho Ltd v Shell Petroleum (No 2)* Lord Diplock reiterated the well-established rule that, ordinarily,

If A infringes B's property right, good against the world, then this involves primary (not secondary) liability. And here it is worth noting that Lord Hoffmann repeatedly insisted that inducing breach of contract is a form of secondary liability: see, eg, *ibid*: [3], [5], [8], [20], [21], [29], [32], [67] and [69]. It seems, therefore, that this isolated and almost immediately contradicted claim that inducing breach of contract involves primary liability for the infringement of a (quasi-) property right was no more than a slip of the pen.

88 Neyers (n 23) 18.

89 *Ibid*, 21–34.

90 *Ibid*, 24. And despite his saying that fit is an important marker of the success of an interpretive theory, he admits that his abuse of rights theory 'fails to fit the Anglo-Canadian' law: *ibid*, 25.

91 *Tuttle v Buck* 119 NW 946 (1909).

92 *OBG* (n 3) [145].

93 Neyers (n 23) 26.

94 *Ibid*, 29.

'where an Act creates an obligation, and enforces the performance in a specified manner … that performance cannot be enforced in any other manner'.[95] Thus, if a statute creates an offence that is punishable under the criminal law, there was, in his Lordship's view, something akin to a presumption against that offence also being actionable as a tort. Admittedly, his Lordship set out two exceptions to this general rule, but neither was very wide.[96] Accordingly, Neyers' suggestion that the unlawful means tort can *interpretively* be understood in terms of actionable rights created by the criminal law is simply implausible. If his general proposition about crimes generating actionable rights for the purposes of tort law were true, then all of their Lordships' hard work to resuscitate and revitalise unlawful means conspiracy in the *Total Network* case would seem to have been pointless. Why would they have gone to such extreme lengths to establish both the ingredients, and potential reach, of that tort if the mere fact of the conspirators having combined to commit the crime of cheating the Revenue were, in its own right, a perfectly good basis for allowing the latter to sue in tort? The availability of an action for unlawful means conspiracy would add nothing of value to the existing avenue of civil recourse that was already open to the claimant by virtue of the criminal law having automatically generated a civil right of action. However, once one accepts that Lord Diplock was right, and that the crime alone was not enough to invest the Revenue with a right of action in tort, the reason that so much trouble was taken in *Total Network* to establish a claim for unlawful means conspiracy becomes obvious.

In my view, Neyers' contention that the unlawful means tort can be accommodated within a rights-based framework on the basis of a public right theory is an even less plausible exercise in interpretivism than his abuse of rights suggestion. This is because it is flatly contradicted by *OBG*, which is, of course, the leading case on the very tort that he seeks to explain.[97] Lord Hoffmann could scarcely have been clearer when he said, 'it is not for the courts to create a cause of action out of a regulatory or criminal statute which Parliament did not intend to be actionable in private law'.[98] Rather, 'subject to one qualification, acts against a third party count as unlawful means only if they are actionable by that third party';[99] and the only 'qualification is that they will also be unlawful means if the only reason why they are not actionable is because the third party has suffered no loss'.[100] It is only in the dissenting speech of Lord Nicholls in that case that one can find any support for the idea that criminal offences might count as unlawful means for the purposes of this tort. Yet even Lord Nicholls, in contrast to Neyers, was clear that civil wrongs

[95] *Lonrho Ltd v Shell Petroleum (No 2)* [1982] AC 173 (HL), 185.

[96] The first applies where the Act, properly construed, could be taken to have imposed the relevant duty for the benefit of a particular class of persons; and the second applies where the statute created a public right the violation of which resulted in special damage for the claimant: *ibid.*

[97] On the limited extent to which interpretivist theories may legitimately overlook or side-line existing precedents, see chapter nine pp 273–74.

[98] *OBG* (n 3) [57].

[99] *Ibid*, [49].

[100] *Ibid.*

would count, too.[101] Faced with this wall of opposing authority, Neyers admits that his preferred understanding 'would mean jettisoning portions of several decisions of the House of Lords'.[102] He nonetheless contents himself with the observation that those in the majority in *OBG* showed themselves 'in the pursuit of a sensible law' from which he concludes that the 'English courts are willing to reshape the law if such molding [*sic*] is necessary to have a coherent and workable interpretative theory of the tort'.[103]

It is true that the House of Lords was keen to restore order to the economic torts in *OBG*. But none of the Law Lords said, or even hinted, that they were trying to do this in the interests of *theoretical* neatness. Furthermore, Neyers' stating that changes to the existing law are needed in order for us 'to have a coherent and workable interpretative theory of the tort' can be taken as an admission by Neyers that, as they presently stand, the existing authorities do not support an interpretive theory of the kind that he favours.[104]

Lastly, his treatment of the two conspiracy torts is just as hard to reconcile with the case law. So far as lawful means conspiracy is concerned, he believes that the self-same abuse of rights and public right theories that he invokes to explain the unlawful means tort can be used in connection with this tort.[105] In my view, his public right theory is just as implausible here as it is in relation to the unlawful means tort. As already observed, it is simply not the case – though Neyers would have us believe otherwise – 'that the criminal law creates rights that are actionable in the private law';[106] and the fact that frackers are forced to rely on complex tort claims for an injunction *quia timet* rather than a ready-made, right of action deriving from the criminality of their conduct, is good evidence of this.[107]

At the same time, the idea that lawful means conspiracy can be cashed out in terms of an abuse of *rights*, is also untenable so long as one adopts (as Neyers does) a Hohfeldian conception of rights. The truth is that, in Hohfeldian terms,

[101] '[T]he concept of "unlawful means" stretches far and wide. It covers common law torts, statutory torts, crimes, breaches of contract, breaches of trust and equitable obligations, breaches of confidence, and so on': *ibid*, [150].

[102] Neyers (n 23) 32. He suggests (*ibid*) that 'removing torts from the unlawful means equation does not really affect the law since most if not all crimes have tortious counterparts'. This is irrelevant, because the key question is not whether his theory would require changes in the law in order for it to be plausible but, rather, whether it represents an appealing interpretation of the body of case law it addresses.

[103] *Ibid*, 32–33.

[104] Neyers does not say that there must be a perfect fit between an interpretive theory and the decided cases. He argues merely that such a theory will not be compelling if it departs significantly from the cases, is incoherent, or in direct conflict with other private law principles': Neyers (n 23) 6. Even so, it is clear that Stephen Smith's criteria for measuring the success of an interpretive theory (which Neyers expressly adopts, *ibid*) require a certain minimal level of fit. Thus, '[a] theory of contract fails the fit criterion if it rejects … so much of contract law that those familiar with the law would not recognize what remains as "contract law"': SA Smith, *Contract Theory* (Oxford, Oxford University Press, 2004) 10. *Mutatis mutandis* Neyers cannot hope to meet the fit criterion laid down by Smith if he is required to jettison the leading cases in this setting in order to produce his theory.

[105] Neyers (n 23) 40.

[106] *Ibid*, 26.

[107] See, eg, *Ineos Upstream Ltd v Persons Unknown* [2019] 4 WLR 100 (CA).

the individual's freedom to perform a certain act – the very thing at the heart of lawful means conspiracy – cannot be explained in terms of *rights*. The freedom to do *X* for Hohfeld would have been a *liberty*.[108] As such, any attempt to explain this tort in terms of an abuse of rights must fail (even though, as will be seen in chapter five, something along the lines of an abuse of a *public power* idea may be invoked to explain it).

In relation to unlawful means conspiracy, Neyers takes a different approach. He opts in this connection for an understanding popularised by others,[109] namely, that the tort is in essence an application of the rules on joint tortfeasance.[110] Yet, once again, his preferred understanding – for all that it is supposed to be an interpretive one – flies in the face of established authority. The House of Lords said explicitly in *Total Network* that '[t]he conspirators cannot … be sued as joint tortfeasors because there was no independent tort actionable by the commissioners'.[111] In order to meet this objection, Neyers attempts to argue that there was conceivably a tort in play. It was, he asserts, merely 'due to the artificiality of the pleadings, [that] their Lordships did not canvass whether the commissioners had a separate action in tort against at least one of the conspirators'.[112] But notice what happens here: the commission of a crime – the very thing that was made central to Neyers' putative explanation of the unlawful means tort (along the lines of what he calls 'public right theory') – becomes suddenly an instance of artificial pleading in the context of unlawful means conspiracy. In order to accept his analysis of unlawful means conspiracy, we would have to reject his explanation of the unlawful means tort. In my view, the preferable take-away point from *Total Network* is not that the pleadings in that case were artificial, but that quite simply, as Neyers freely admits, the joint tortfeasance explanation was 'expressly rejected by the House of Lords'.[113]

As with Carty's and Deakin's endeavours, Neyers' monistic account of the general economic torts fails to fit or capture the true state of the law and is therefore apt to mislead us in our search for juridical truths in this setting. In order to understand why this is so, it is important to be clear about the sense in which Neyers' account of these torts may be described as monistic. Unlike Carty and Deakin who both regard the economic torts as being linked by a common function or purpose, Neyers believes, instead, that their commonality exists in terms of their bilateral structure. He thinks that the key to understanding these torts inheres in their conformity with a structural norm found right throughout tort

[108] WN Hohfeld, 'Some Fundamental Legal Conceptions as Applied in Judicial Reasoning' (1913) 23 *Yale Law Journal* 16, 36. And Neyers recognises this! When Hohfeld considered the landmark case of *Quinn v Leathem* (n 68), Neyers rightly observes that '[t]he right to trade theory was found wanting since, as Hohfeld noted, there is no right to trade which correlates with a duty not to compete, but merely a liberty to trade which correlates with a 'no right'': Neyers (n 23) 19.

[109] See Stevens (n 12) 249–50 and Carty (n 4) 131.

[110] Neyers (n 23) 36.

[111] *Total Network* (n 6) [44] (Lord Hope). See also *ibid*, [225]–[226] (Lord Neuberger).

[112] Neyers (n 23) 39.

[113] *Ibid*, 37.

law, one which views all torts as being centred on defendants infringing *ex-ante* rights held by claimants against those defendants. And it is precisely because he is so insistent that the economic torts can be seen as conforming to this structural norm that he is apt to mislead.

He suggests that there is structural simplicity where no such simplicity exists. Furthermore, we are likely to get led even further astray if we accept his claims about these torts being animated by rights, the existence of which is frequently denied by the courts and nowhere in evidence in the leading cases. Indeed, Neyers openly invites us to reject certain House of Lords authorities, not because they were bad decisions, or poorly reasoned, but purely because they obstruct the formulation of a neat and tidy rights-based theory.

C. The Kantian View

Beever, like Neyers, purports to offer an interpretive account of the economic torts. Accordingly, one prefatory question that must be answered is why I label his approach 'the Kantian view' and examine it in a separate section from Neyers. The question is all the more pressing given that both authors insist that rights violations are central to the operation of the economic torts. Nonetheless, I think that there are three significant differences between their respective accounts which require them to be examined separately.

Unlike Neyers, who maintains that the economic torts can be conceptualised according to the familiar bipolar structure of tort law, Beever is clear from the outset that the economic torts are characterised by a three-party structure: one in which A wrongs C via an intermediary, B. He even gives the section of his book dealing with the economic torts the title 'Indirect Control'.[114] Secondly, although Neyers signs up to an avowedly corrective justice based view of the economic torts, it is not one that places Kantian legal philosophy at its core. Accordingly, unlike Beever's theory, Neyers' account is not anchored to the concept of 'innate right'. Thirdly, because they disagree about these structural and conceptual matters, Beever and Neyers also disagree markedly over which of the extant torts and leading cases should be regarded as meritorious and which should be seen as anomalous.

Against the background of such differences, two things are clear: (1) Beever's quintessentially Kantian theory deserves separate treatment; and (2) given the nature and extent of the disagreement between these rival rights-based accounts, it must be the case that at least one of them is wrong in some major respect. I have already explained what I think are the main inadequacies of Neyers' account. But this, for those attracted by rights-based theories, gives no warrant for thinking

[114] This is intended to capture the fact that, in the economic torts, the defendant will 'exert control over a person by acting on a third party': see Beever (n 8) 99.

that Beever's treatment of the economic torts will fare any better when subjected to scrutiny. Thinking that way would be to fall prey to the fallacy of the excluded middle. It simply does not follow from the fact that *x* is bad that *not-x* is good. It is perfectly possible that *not-x* is equally bad, albeit for a different set of reasons.

Before getting down to an analysis of what Beever has to say about the economic torts, it is important to appreciate that his interpretation of them forms but one part of an overall endeavour to supply a grand theory of the whole of tort law. Put another way: his monistic account of the economic torts is merely one strand to that broader project. In his view, tort law is best explained in terms of Kantian legal philosophy for which reason, Kant's fundamental principle of law occupies centre stage in his theory. In Kant's original text, this fundamental principle is expressed somewhat wordily.[115] At its heart, however, is the fairly simple idea that a person is entitled to the maximum possible freedom of choice and action insofar as that freedom of choice and action is consistent with equivalent freedoms in everyone else. Having established this as his central, animating idea, Beever goes on to make three key observations.

The first of these is that, each of us enjoys a single, innate right to freedom. The second is that, for these purposes, freedom is 'defined as independence from constraint imposed by others' choices'.[116] The third is that, as a corollary to the innate right just sketched, 'one is free to do anything that does not violate a right in another'.[117] He labels this freedom the 'principle of innocence'.[118] And it follows from this innocence principle, says Beever, that for one person to wrong another (ie, commit a tort against them), he must unjustifiably constrain that other by performing an action which interferes with her freedom. In his exact words: 'action must violate another's innate or acquired rights' in order for it to constitute a tort.[119] So what, in the light of these central propositions, are the weaknesses of Beever's avowedly Kantian approach to the economic torts?

To begin with, his insistence that '[t]he so-called economic torts deal with cases in which one person seeks to control another *via the medium of a third party*'[120] is confounded by both the landmark case of *Total Network*, and by what was said in *Rookes v Barnard*.[121] In the former, Lord Mance was crystal clear that the case before him involved a two-party economic tort. He said:

> I accept that conspiracy can be categorised as a three- rather than two-party tort, in that liability depends on at least two persons joining together to injure another … Nevertheless, there is in my view a distinction between the infliction of harm through

[115] 'Any action is *lawful* if it can co-exist with everyone's freedom in accordance with a universal law, or if on its maxim the freedom of choice of each can coexist with everyone's freedom in accordance with a universal law': I Kant, *The Metaphysics of Morals* (translated by M Gregor) (Cambridge, Cambridge University Press, 1996) 6:230.

[116] Beever (n 8) 19.

[117] *Ibid*, 20.

[118] *Ibid*.

[119] *Ibid*, 24.

[120] *Ibid*, 154 (emphasis added).

[121] *Rookes v Barnard* [1964] AC 1129 (HL).

> the intermediary of a third party (as in the case of the tort of causing harm by unlawful means under consideration in *OBG Ltd v Allan*) and the present situation where two wrongdoers join and act together to inflict injury directly upon another person or body.[122]

He was not alone in thinking this. Lord Hope agreed that 'in this case there was no third party';[123] while Lord Neuberger also expressed the view that 'the tort is of a two-party nature'.[124] Importantly, these proclamations did not come out of the blue. Both Lord Hope and Lord Neuberger picked up on something that had been conceded in *OBG* by Lord Hoffmann, namely, the possibility (considered in chapter one) of a two-party version of intimidation. After stating that liability within the economic torts will *ordinarily* arise within a three-party framework, Lord Hoffmann left open the question of whether there might be liability for intimidation in a two-party framework.[125] It was precisely the mention of this potential liability for two-party intimidation in *OBG* that was used in constructing the platform on which the tort of unlawful means conspiracy was resuscitated in *Total Network*.[126]

But their Lordships could have looked elsewhere for support. The idea that there might be a two-party tort of this stripe was first floated by Sir John Salmond in his textbook on torts;[127] and its existence as an independent cause of action was whole-heartedly supported by Lord Devlin in *Rookes v Barnard*. He said: 'there is a tort of intimidation … [which] can take one of two forms … [the first of which is] [i]ntimidation of the plaintiff himself'.[128] His Lordship then went on, quoting directly from the then latest edition of Salmond's textbook, to give an example. He said, 'an action will doubtless lie at the suit of a trader who has been compelled to discontinue his business by means of threats of personal violence made against him by the defendant with that intention'.[129] More concretely still, the action for two-party intimidation was actually invoked, successfully, in both *Newsgroup Newspapers Ltd v SOGAT '82*[130] and *Godwin v Uzoigwe*.[131]

[122] *Total Network* (n 6) [124].
[123] *Ibid*, [43].
[124] *Ibid*, [223].
[125] He insisted that 'the tort of causing loss by unlawful means … requires interference with the actions of a third party in relation to the plaintiff' yet went on to add 'I do not intend to say anything about the question of whether a claimant who has been compelled by unlawful intimidation to act to his own detriment, can sue for his loss. Such a case of "two party intimidation" raises altogether different issues': *OBG* (n 3) [61].
[126] *Total Network* (n 6) [43] (Lord Hope), [99] (Lord Walker), [124] (Lord Mance) and [223] (Lord Neuberger).
[127] J Salmond, *The Law of Torts* (London, Stevens and Haynes, 1907) 439: 'This wrong is of two distinct kinds, for the liberty of action so interfered with may be either that of the plaintiff himself, or that of other persons with resulting damage to the plaintiff'.
[128] *Rookes v Barnard* (n 121) 1205.
[129] *Ibid*.
[130] *Newsgroup Newspapers Ltd v SOGAT '82* [1987] ICR 181, 205 (Stuart-Smith J).
[131] *Godwin v Uzoigwe* [1992] TLR 300 (CA).

None of the cases mentioned in the previous few paragraphs can be cashed out in terms of Beever's necessarily tripartite conception of the economic torts: that is, as a group of actions which have in common the characteristic that one person controls another *via an intermediary*. And the same two-party structure is an inescapable feature of deceit (a tort which Beever accepts is one of the economic torts[132]). Liability will only arise in deceit where A has intentionally or recklessly made a false representation to B, and B has relied upon that representation and thereby suffered loss.[133] It is the fact that B *himself* must have relied on the statement made by A that guarantees the tort its two-party structure. The tort of deceit certainly cannot be invoked where a false representation is made to a third party (who is not an agent of the claimant) and it is the third party who acts in reliance on what is said with the end result being loss suffered by the claimant.[134] As Lord Clarke recently confirmed, in deceit, the claimant personally must have been influenced by the misrepresentation.[135] The short point, then, is that, for all that Beever is content to criticise the theories of others on the basis that they do not reflect the law as it stands,[136] his own suffers from precisely that flaw so far as it makes a structural claim.

The second major weakness in Beever's depiction of the economic torts inheres in his insistence that they are concerned with violations of the putative innate right that he draws from Kant (ie, the right to be free from unlawful constraints imposed by others). In order to see where the weakness lies, here, it is important to realise that Kant's innate right was reserved only for purposive beings. He said:

> The concept of Right … [concerns] the external and indeed the practical relation of one person to another, insofar as their actions, as facts, can have (direct or indirect) influence on each other … All that is in question is the *form* of the relationship of choice on the part of both, insofar as choice is regarded merely as *free*, and whether the action of one of the two parties can be united with the freedom of the other in accordance with a universal law.[137]

Because Kant described the innate right in terms of 'the practical relation of one person to another', it is clear that it was intended as a right to equal maximum freedom that could be claimed *only* by, or on behalf of, human addressees of the law. It is, after all, only such persons who have the capacity to exercise free will in the requisite sense; and Kant was certainly keen to make clear that it was only the free will of those who are able to pursue pre-conceived projects of their own to whom his universal law applied. He said: '[a] will which can be determined

[132] Beever (n 8) 101.
[133] In *Bradford Third Equitable Building Society v Borders* [1941] 2 All ER 205 (HL), 211 (Viscount Maugham).
[134] See, eg, *Gross v Lewis Hillman Ltd* [1970] Ch 445 (CA).
[135] *Hayward v Zurich Insurance Co Plc* [2017] AC 142 (SC), [15]: '[T]he ingredients of a claim for deceit … are not in dispute. It must be shown that the defendant made a materially false representation which was intended to, and did, induce the representee to act to its detriment'.
[136] He criticises both Stevens and Carty on this basis: see Beever (n 8) 115 and 117, respectively.
[137] Kant (n 115) 6:230.

independently of sensuous impulses, and therefore through motives which are represented only by reason, is entitled freewill'[138] whereas this is not the case when '[a] will is purely *animal* (*arbitrium brutum*) … [and] cannot be determined save through sensuous impulses'.[139] More simply, since animals act out of instinct – 'sensuous impulses' to use Kant's phrase – they are not holders of the innate right that is acquired at birth by humans *purely by virtue of their being humans.*

The significance of this for Beever's account is as follows. If the economic torts are to be understood in terms of the innate right found in Kantian legal philosophy, then there arises an obvious problem for him in explaining those cases in which non-human litigants have successfully relied on the economic torts. After all, they are self-evidently litigants that do not possess the innate right which Beever treats as foundational to his analysis. It makes no sense to speak of innate rights where the litigation in question involves rival companies, or a company and a trade union. Yet, of course, many of the early, landmark authorities are cases of this kind. And there is no easy way for Beever to wriggle out of this when one bears in mind the fact that his intellectual mentor, Ernest Weinrib, explains, Kantian right is an innate right that applies to human addressees of the law only. According to Weinrib, animals cannot be holders of Kantian right on account of their inability to reason. If animals can be excluded on this footing, then so too must companies be excluded on the basis of their being equally unable to reason.[140]

The third major shortcoming in Beever's treatment of the economic torts is the fact that there exist numerous decisions (or aspects thereof[141]) which are hard to reconcile with his theory. Quite apart from the telling fact that none of the leading (or lesser) cases refer to Kantian right (the putative underpinning principle), there are entire torts that are, by Beever's own admission, incompatible with what he says. For example, he concedes that the whole of the law concerning inducing breach of contract is inexplicable from the Kantian perspective.[142] Equally, he finds conspiracy – in both its forms – unintelligible; and he concedes with an air of resignation that, frankly, 'we do not know why we have this tort'.[143] Between them, these torts comprise a very significant part of the economic torts canon. So, even though I would accept that an interpretive theory may be considered respectable even if it cannot account satisfactorily for every single decision,[144] there is

[138] I Kant, *Critique of Pure Reason* (translated by NK Smith) (London, Macmillan & Co, 1929) 633.

[139] *Ibid.*

[140] Note, however, that it does not follow that it is inappropriate to think of companies as having autonomy rights *for the purposes of the law*. The autonomy rights of companies are enshrined in legislation, and the innate rights with which Kant was concerned are very different beasts.

[141] For example, he makes the staggering claim that 'it is wrong to state that liability in causing loss by unlawful means requires unlawful means': Beever (n 8) 121.

[142] He says variously, 'we do not know why we have the tort of inducing breach of contract' (*ibid*, 114), that 'it is impossible to support the existence of a tort of inducing breach of contract' (*ibid*, 153) and that 'the tort of inducing breach of contract must be rejected' (*ibid*, 154).

[143] *Ibid*, 122.

[144] For an argument to this effect, see chapter nine.

undoubtedly a problem for Beever's theory when *so much of the law* falls beyond its explanatory compass.[145] By his own admission, '[a]n understanding that presents a principle with so vast a list of exceptions is no understanding at all'.[146]

The fact that Beever portrays cases and torts that clash with his theory as wrongly decided or anomalous involves a sleight of hand. Without ever admitting to this, what he is in fact doing when he makes such claims, is abandoning a core theoretical commitment *of his own making*, namely, the commitment to provide an avowedly interpretive theory of the economic torts. Such theories – taking as they typically do an unacknowledged steer from Dworkin's 'Law as Integrity' idea[147] – are intended to present *the law as we encounter it* in its best possible light.[148] But in saying that very large chunks of the case law have been wrongly decided, or that they are anomalous, Beever is not explaining or interpreting the law; he is making instead a normative claim *about what the law should say*.[149] If one claims that an entire line of authority concerning tort X is groundless in theoretical terms, one is ultimately suggesting that the tort should be abandoned or modified simply because it does not fit the theory to which one subscribes. But in what sense is Beever's *suggestion* that the law ought to change, a suggestion that is consistent with his stated project of *explaining* the law as it stands and showing how his theory fits the law? I would submit that there is no sense in which it does this. Any claim along the lines that the law ought to change in some significant respect is not merely an admission that the theory does not fit the law, it is also a barely concealed lapse into *purely* prescriptive (as opposed to explanatory) theory.[150]

Finally, Beever's slide into prescription is apt, just like the other monistic accounts I have considered, to place a serious impediment in the way of our unearthing the true rationales behind the economic torts. It has the capacity to do this because, if Beever succeeds in masking the fact that a great deal of what he

[145] Peter Cane once captured the point this way: 'there must come a point where gaps between the *explanandum* and the *explanans* cast doubt on the value of the explanation': P Cane, 'The Anatomy of Private Law Theory: A 25th Anniversary Essay' (2005) 25 *OJLS* 203, 207.

[146] Beever (n 8) 15.

[147] Dworkin (n 79) Ch 7.

[148] Beever says that his aim 'is to provide the best account of the normative structure of the law as that law is found in the actual jurisdictions in which we live': Beever (n 8) 5.

[149] For example, Beever says of inducing breach of contract that: '[t]he tort of inducing breach of contract is a mistake … Its modern form was invented out of nothing and to nothing it must return': *ibid*, 151.

[150] To repeat a point made earlier – because, frankly, it bears repetition – I do not deny that any interpretive account of the law has an inescapable prescriptive dimension to it. My treatment of the torts considered in this book is therefore vulnerable to the criticism that it, too, possesses a prescriptive dimension. It is not the case, however, as I shall seek to show in chapter nine, that all prescriptive claims are alike. Any attempt to describe the nature and contours of the law, when its nature and contours are fuzzy, means that authors seeking to explain the law must inevitably make choices of the kind 'understanding X is preferable to understanding Y'. But at least any expression of a preference for X (or Y) is supportable by reference to the some or other plainly extant feature of the thing being discussed. Simply saying 'Z is best' when there is nothing to ground Z is prescriptive writing of a different order.

has to say about the economic torts is normative in nature – that his claims about the gist, structure and uses of some of these torts is contradicted by cases decided at the highest judicial level – then he is liable to persuade readers to consider as wrongheaded, errant or anomalous a number of important authorities that have every right to be considered orthodox.

IV. Conclusion

All monistic accounts of the economic torts are undermined by being partial in both senses of that word. Taking partial to mean incomplete, the various authors considered in this chapter simply do not acknowledge (or in some cases, accept) that certain well-established torts have a strong claim to be regarded as actions that are alive and well. Taking partial to mean biased, the various monists all register complaints about certain torts or cases that do not conform with their pre-conceived ideas of what the 'family' of economic torts should look like. Occasionally, their criticisms seem reasonable. It is certainly fair that interpretive accounts should point out – as they sometimes do – various stylistic infelicities or inconsistencies in judicial reasoning. However, caution should be exercised before sizeable parts of the law, which stand on repeated House of Lords or Supreme Court authority, are described by jurists as anomalous.[151] The monists never explain what they mean by 'anomaly'; and yet they frequently invoke this term in order to disparage certain cases or torts that do not fit their respective (pre)conceptions about this area of the law.

In the case of Carty and Deakin, it is their fundamental commitment to the idea that the primary function of the economic torts is (or should be) the protection of trade or business interests that leads them to regard various cases as aberrant. If we scratch beneath the surface, however, it soon becomes apparent that the only reason they have for portraying these cases in this way is that they do not fit within the tramlines of their pre-conceived idea of what these torts are designed to achieve. The same is true of Neyers' and Beever's respective rights-based and Kantian accounts. They applaud only those cases that fit comfortably with their theories, and they seek to undermine, marginalise or reject out of hand those parts of the law that clash with their theories.

All of the monistic accounts considered in this chapter purport to identify a unifying feature or purpose for the economic torts. The bases for these competing organising ideas vary from the historical foundations of these torts (in the case of Carty and Deakin), to contemporary tort theory (in the case of Neyers), to abstract ideas drawn from Kantian legal philosophy (in the case of Beever). In each case, though – as I shall demonstrate fully in chapter eight – there is

[151] For a staunch defence of presumptive respect for the decisions of our most senior courts, see Stapleton (n 33).

insufficient attention paid by all these scholars to a miscellany of other factors that have helped to shape (and therefore provide the key to a deeper understanding of), the economic torts. But this is to get ahead of ourselves. For now, it suffices to note that the currently dominant, monistic accounts are inadequate. The remainder of this book is devoted to providing a fuller, better, pluralistic understanding of the various torts enumerated in chapter one.

3

Inducing Breach of Contract

Although the action for inducing breach of contract is well-established, its rationale and scope have never been identified conclusively.[1] Thus, although the vitality of this *action* cannot be doubted, the confusion that surrounds these two matters remains considerable; and it is confusion that is caused by a combination of factors. To begin with, there has been the persistent – some would say intractable – question of whether inducing breach of contract is best seen as a form of 'accessory liability',[2] a freestanding tort,[3] or, fairly implausibly, neither of these things.[4] Even in the seminal case of *Lumley v Gye*,[5] there were marked differences of opinion between the various judges about just why and when inducing a breach of contract should be regarded as tortious.[6] Secondly, although it clearly owes a good deal to the ancient action *per quod servitium amisit* (as numerous jurists have pointed out over the years[7]), it has never been made clear just which of the *three*

[1] Unearthing what is required for two key ingredients of the action – ie, 'inducement' and 'knowledge of the contract' – can also prove tricky. But these matters are of no concern here, since they do not impinge on the four central theses of this study. Excellent analysis of them can, however, be found in PS Davies, *Accessory Liability* (Oxford, Hart Publishing, 2015) 158–60, and in H Carty, *An Analysis of the Economic Torts*, 2nd edn (Oxford, Oxford University Press, 2010) 36–43.

[2] For support of this interpretation, see Davies, *ibid*, Ch 5 and *OBG Ltd v Allan* [2008] 1 AC 1 (HL), [8], [172], [320] (Lords Hoffmann, Nicholls and Brown respectively).

[3] For the view that, because D suborns an intermediary, it is a freestanding tort: see AP Simester and W Chan, 'Inducing Breach of Contract: One Tort or Two?' [2004] *CLJ* 132. And for the novel, yet unsupported, claim that the defendant is liable for breach of a 'secondary right [that] is accessory to the primary right … [the infringement of which] is a freestanding tort', see R Stevens, *Torts and Rights* (Oxford, Oxford University Press, 2007) 281.

[4] For this view, see A Beever, *A Theory of Tort Liability* (Oxford, Hart Publishing, 2016) 114.

[5] *Lumley v Gye* (1853) 2 El & Bl 216.

[6] Only three members of the Court of Queen's Bench held that an action may lie in respect of inducing breach of contract: Coleridge J dissented. For Crompton J, the action was available wherever there had been an 'enticing away of any person employed to give his personal labour or service' (*ibid*, 227, 231). Wightman J thought likewise (*ibid*, 240). Erle J, however, took a broader view. He thought *generally* that the 'procurement of a breach of contract … [is] a wrong' and specifically countenanced an 'action for this wrong, in respect of other contracts than those of hiring' (*ibid*, 232).

[7] See, eg, Beever (n 4) 147; S Deakin and J Randall, 'Rethinking the Economic Torts' (2009) 72 *MLR* 519, 535; J Danforth, 'Tortious Interference with Contract: A Reassertion of Society's Interest in Commercial Stability and Contractual Integrity' (1981) 81 *Columbia Law Review* 1491, 1494; JH Baker, *Introduction to English Legal History*, 5th edn (Oxford, Oxford University Press, 2019) 491–92; W Cornish *et al* (eds), *Law and Society in England 1750–1950*, 2nd edn (Oxford, Hart Publishing, 2019) 467; FB Sayre, 'Inducing Breach of Contract' (1923) 36 *Harvard Law Review* 663, 665–66.

different versions of that *per quod* action[8] should be regarded as having been the most influential in *Lumley*. Nor, so far as I am aware, has there been any scholarly attention directed towards the possibility that the decision in *Lumley* may, in fact, owe more to the similarly antiquated action *per quod consortium amisit*.[9]

A third source of the confusion surrounding inducing breach of contract can be traced to the fact that, during the course of the twentieth century, its development was both influenced by, and tightly bound up with, the parallel development of the tort of causing loss by unlawful means. By virtue of this, English law housed, for quite some time, what Bagshaw colourfully describes as 'the misbegotten chimera of direct interference with contractual relations'.[10]

Against the background of such considerable confusion, this chapter has two main aims. The first is to provide an answer to the enduring question of whether inducing breach of contract is better seen as a freestanding tort or as a form of accessory liability. I do this in section I where the argument will be that, despite an obvious effort to resolve this matter in *OBG Ltd v Allan*,[11] their Lordships did not conclusively establish that it is something other than a tort. There was certainly an effort made to show that it involved a rule of accessory liability; but the idea that it may nonetheless be regarded as a tort is present not just within *OBG* but also within a significant amount of post-*OBG* case law. I conclude this section with the suggestion that inducing breach of contract is best seen as a freestanding tort, albeit one with very pronounced juridical peculiarities.[12] I fortify the claim by reference to a range of considerations that, in my view, make this the least unpalatable conception of the action.

My conclusion on this matter will doubtless attract its critics. Prime among them, I suspect, will be certain contemporary tort theorists who will resist my characterisation by reference to the various juridical oddities that I freely accept it possesses. But I take comfort in the fact their probable objections will also rely in significant measure on their own, equally hard to ground, conceptions about what a tort is and (according to them, but not the courts) must be.

[8] One version involved D debauching C's daughter and leaving her pregnant: see, eg, *Grinnell v Wells* (1844) 7 M & G 1033. A second version involved D depriving C of the value of his servant's services by means of an incapacitating tortious act committed against the servant: see, eg, *Hodsoll v Stallebrass* (1840) Ad & El 301. The third version involved D enticing a servant away from his present job with C: see, eg, *Hart v Aldridge* (1774) 1 Cowp 54. For discussion of the three different versions, see M Lobban, 'Intentional and Economic Torts' in W Cornish *et al* (eds), *The Oxford History of the Laws of England: Volume XII – Private Law* (Oxford, Oxford University Press, 2010) 1041.

[9] For details, see below (n 94) and associated text.

[10] R Bagshaw, 'Lord Hoffmann and the Economic Torts' in PS Davies and J Pila (eds), *The Jurisprudence of Lord Hoffmann* (Oxford, Hart Publishing, 2015) 59.

[11] *OBG* (n 2).

[12] I have elsewhere dealt with these juridical oddities at length, arguing that, because of them, this action might fairly be *labelled* a 'hybrid tort', but *formally treated* as a thoroughbred tort: see J Murphy, 'Hybrid Torts and Explanatory Tort Theory' (2018) 64 *McGill Law Journal* 1, 12–15. For the related view that notions of contract, wrongdoing unjust enrichment, property rights and public policy are *all* discernible in *Lumley*, see SM Waddams, 'Johanna Wagner and the Rival Opera Houses' (2001) 117 *LQR* 431, 448.

Having established its credentials as a tort – albeit a strange one – section II is devoted to the second main aim of this chapter: to explain why the *Lumley* action should be regarded as one that stretches beyond the protection of trade or business interests *despite the fact* that many commentators assert vigorously that its operation is confined to such a role.[13] I take further comfort here in the thought that even if various tort theorists remain sceptical about the claim made in section I, their objections on that front will in no way undermine the arguments advanced in section II.

In section III, I conclude. Partly, I do this by drawing together the major arguments of the previous two sections. But I also advance in this section for the sake of completeness certain normative reasons why I think it would be objectionable for inducing breach of contract to be confined to the protection of trade or business interests.

I. An Inexplicable Action?

Many jurists have tried to unearth a theoretically satisfying rationale for inducing breach of contract. None of them, however, has managed to produce an account that has escaped the powerful objections of other leading scholars. After briefly outlining the main strands (and objections) to the most prominent theories, Beever resigns himself to the view 'that we do not know why we have a tort of inducing breach of contract'.[14] He concludes that it should be permitted 'to die a merciful death'.[15] Other commentators are markedly less defeatist; and it is worth, briefly, revisiting some of the arguments that they have advanced in an attempt to rationalise the liability instantiated in *Lumley*.

A. Attempted Rationales

One popular answer to the question concerning the rationale behind *Lumley* liability involves what we might loosely call the 'property thesis'. The qualifier 'loosely' is required because there is no single property thesis to which all proponents of this line of thought subscribe. Rather, there are numerous variations on a theme that have been advanced by a range of jurists over the years.[16] But for reasons that will

[13] See, eg, T Weir, *Economic Torts* (Oxford, Clarendon Press, 1997) 18; P Cane, *The Anatomy of Tort Law* (Oxford, Hart Publishing, 1997) 151; Danforth (n 7) 1500. Notably, Deakin and Randall (n 7) 536 recognise the *potential* for the *Lumley* action to be used in connection with *any* contract, but they nonetheless conclude that: 'convenience and a recognition that most *Lumley v Gye* cases have arisen, and will continue to arise, from competition in trade or business suggest that it should continue to be treated as one of the economic torts'.

[14] Beever (n 4) 114.

[15] *Ibid*, 154.

[16] See, eg, PW Lee, 'Inducing Breach of Contract, Conversion and Contract as Property' (2009) 29 *OJLS* 511, 524; R Bagshaw, 'Inducing Breach of Contract' in J Horder (ed), *Oxford Essays in*

become apparent presently, we need not tease out here the subtle differences that exist between them. It is enough to note that, in all versions, there is a common, general idea in play. It is that D is liable for inducing breach of contract, not because he himself breaches a duty imposed upon him by a term of the contract between C and the party induced to break that contract, but because the contractual rights with which D interferes can be considered a species of (quasi) property. And it is D's interference with C's supposed property right that explains D's liability in *tort*. More fully, the idea is that C's proprietary interest in the contractual obligation explains why that right holds good against the world at large (just as do, absent any immunities, all such rights protected by tort law). It is in this way that the property thesis speaks directly to the question of how and why inducing breach of contract may properly be considered a tort.

One thing that can certainly be said for this understanding of *Lumley* liability is that weighty judicial statements can be cited in support of it. For example, in *OBG*, Lord Hoffmann opined as follows:

> *Lumley v Gye* … treats contractual rights as a species of property which deserve special protection, not only by giving a right of action against the party who breaks his contract but by imposing secondary liability on a person who procures him to do so.[17]

Leaving to one side the fact that his Lordship's saying this bears an element of self-contradiction,[18] it is important to get straight just why the property thesis *in all its guises* fails. And it fails for three main reasons: it rings hollow when one considers that D must know he is inducing a breach of contract;[19] it is based on circular reasoning; and the limited analogy that can be drawn between property (on the one hand) and the right to contractual performance (on the other) is unhelpful insofar as it emphasises a characteristic of private property that is irrelevant to the question of why inducing breach of contract is tortious. Each of these matters requires some explanation.

To begin with, the fact that D must know (1) that C has a contract with the third party *and* (2) that he is inducing a breach of this contract is hard to reconcile with the idea that a property right is at stake. This is because my entitlement to something – the essence of a property right – does not turn on your knowing that it is mine.[20] No such knowledge of C's ownership is required in either the tort of trespass to land, or the tort of conversion. If I walk onto your land in the mistaken belief that the land belongs to me, I am just as much a trespasser as if I did so knowing the land was yours.[21] Neither a property right in the strict sense, nor any

Jurisprudence, 4th edn (Oxford, Oxford University Press, 2000) 133–37; R Epstein, 'Inducement of Breach of Contract as a Problem of Ostensible Ownership' (1987) *Journal of Legal Studies* 1, 19–20; Waddams (n 12) 444; W Anson, *Principles of the Law of Contract* (Oxford, Clarendon Press, 1879) 199.

[17] *OBG* (n 2) [32].

[18] D's acting in violation of C's property right would be a form of primary (not secondary) liability. So having established that there is a property right at stake, it seems odd to suggest (as his Lordship does in the last clause of that sentence) that D's liability is secondary in nature.

[19] *OBG* (n 2) 39 (Lord Hoffmann).

[20] See further Cane (n 13) 84.

[21] *Basely v Clarkson* (1682) 3 Lev 37.

close approximation of a property right, can plausibly be contingent upon what a particular defendant happens to know.

The second reason for rejecting the property thesis – its circularity – is rather more complex and must be unpacked carefully. The first point to note is that the property thesis is firmly anchored to the observation that *Lumley* liability protects contractual rights *against third party interference*. In this regard, so the argument goes, these contractual rights can be said to possess a proprietary (or property-like) quality, given that property rights are quintessentially good against the world. However, the ostensible appeal of such thinking ought not to mislead us. If we want to know why contractual rights enjoy a property-like quality for the purposes of *Lumley* liability, it is no use answering, 'Because they offer protection against third party interference'. For if we then ask the obvious question about the basis on which they enjoy such protection, the only answer available is: 'Because they are a form of property'. The circularity of the argument and the absence of any compelling, independent reason to regard contractual rights as a species of property are both patent.[22]

The third reason for rejecting the property thesis inheres in the inadequacy of a putative prop for that thesis supplied by Benson. In his view, 'since a contract right can be deemed to be a property interest when it is the object of a voluntary transaction of assignment, it must also be the case that it can function in this way in an involuntary transaction'?[23] Now, it is absolutely true, as Benson notes, that the transferability of contract rights (via assignment) does supply a basis on which to see a parallel between contract rights and private property. But the snag is that this commonality is of no relevance for present purposes.[24] It is not a shared feature that explains why procuring a breach by a third party is tortious.[25] Look again. Benson's remark is tied firmly to the matter of transferability *and in particular* to involuntary transfers of contractual obligations. Because of this, what he says has no purchase in relation to inducing breach of contract. It is where D coerces (rather than persuades) the intermediary to do for him what she was originally contractually bound to do for C that the transfer can be described as involuntary.

[22] *Cf* Waddams (n 12), 449 who attaches great significance to the fact that inducing breach of contract affords extensive protection against third party interference. He stresses: (1) the fact that injunctions are available to restrain D from inducing a breach of contract; and (2) the observation that injunctions are typically available to protect proprietary interests; as well as (3) the fact that damages are available against the procurer in order to make the argument that, in *Lumley v Gye*, 'the willingness of the one court to grant an injunction … and the willingness of the other to hold Gye liable in tort, can be described as a recognition of something like a proprietary interest in Wagner's services': *ibid*, 449.

[23] P Benson, 'The Basis of Excluding Liability for Economic Loss in Tort Law' in DG Owen (ed), *Philosophical Foundations of Tort Law* (Oxford, Clarendon Press, 1995) 456.

[24] See also chapter two at pp 34–35.

[25] Another alleged guide is the fact that tortious invasions of proprietary interests are often actionable *per se*, and yet another, the fact that they often involve strict liability: see P Cane, *Tort Law and Economic Interests*, 2nd edn (Oxford, Clarendon Press, 1996) 124. If this be the yardstick against which to measure the presence of property, then property-based explanations of inducing breach of contract look decidedly weak.

But in any such case – because of the absence of persuasion or seduction – there is no prospect of liability for inducing breach of contract.

Put shortly: telling us that contract rights are like property in as much as they are capable of being transferred voluntarily tells us nothing about why D is liable in tort for procuring a breach of contract. And the hint of wrongdoing conveyed by the mention of 'an involuntary transaction' is a red herring, for that too – just like transferability – has nothing to do with an archetypal inducing breach of contract case, like *Lumley*.

The other popular rationalisations of *Lumley* liability can be dealt with a little more swiftly. We can conveniently begin with those jurists who believe that inducing breach of contract could be (or already is) subsumed within the tort of causing loss by unlawful means.[26] Such writers freely admit that, in order for this to be so, a markedly different conception of the mental element currently in operation in inducing breach of contract would be needed: 'it would have to be shown' write Deakin and Randall, 'that the defendant aimed at or targeted the claimant's trade, business or livelihood'.[27] But this is not what orthodoxy posits. According to *OBG*, the defendant in a case of inducing breach of contract must, with knowledge of the relevant term of the claimant's contract,[28] have intended that the contract be broken.[29] And as these authors freely admit, an alignment of these two different tests of intention is most unlikely to occur.[30] In the absence of any such probable change in the law, and bearing in mind the absence of the need to show unlawful means in inducing breach of contract, we can safely dismiss this understanding of *Lumley* liability. True: an early, scholarly defence of the decisions in *Lumley* and *Bowen v Hall*[31] proffered by Sir Frederick Pollock did rely heavily on the claim that the action was justified on the basis of a defendant's acting maliciously.[32] But as is very well known, the need to show malice was short-lived;[33] and *OBG* stands firmly in the way of its reinstatement as an element of the tort.

[26] '[A]t least in the context of trade or business, the *Lumley v Gye* tort could be folded into the wider tort of interference with trade or business, without sacrificing the unity of purpose and structural logic of the economic torts': Deakin and Randall (n 7) 537. See also Weir (n 13) 28.

[27] Deakin and Randall (n 7) 552. This is a huge understatement on their part given the very considerable efforts made in *OBG* to distinguish *Lumley* liability from that imposed under the unlawful means tort.

[28] *OBG* (n 2) [39]-[41] and [202] (Lords Hoffmann and Nicholls respectively); and for an excellent analysis of this requirement, see Davies (n 1) 158–60.

[29] *Ibid*, [42]-[43], [191] (Lords Hoffmann and Nicholls).

[30] Deakin and Randall (n 7) 552: 'it seems unlikely that the *Lumley v Gye* tort will now be overruled'.

[31] *Bowen v Hall* (1881) 6 QBD 333 (CA).

[32] F Pollock, *The Law of Torts: A Treatise on the Principles of Obligations Arising From Civil Wrongs in the Common Law*, 4th edn (London, Stevens & Sons, 1886) 227: '[Although] [t]he precise extent and bearing of the doctrine … [is surrounded by] difficulties … [t]hose difficulties … either disappear or are greatly reduced when the cause of action is considered as belonging to the class in which malice, in the sense of actual ill-will, is a necessary element'.

[33] In *Quinn v Leathem* [1901] AC 495 (HL), 510, Lord Macnaghten said: 'I have no hesitation in saying that I think the decision [in *Lumley*] was right, [but] not on the ground of malicious intention – that was not, I think, the gist of the action'.

An altogether more inventive explanation of *Lumley* liability has been proffered by Robert Stevens. In his view, 'all contracts carry with them a right good against everyone else that they do not induce the infringement of the contractual right'.[34] But this explanation founders, too, because there is no support for the existence of any such a right in the case law. Stevens' attempt to rationalise inducing breach of contract in this way is just one among several of his departures from what he promises his readers, namely, an account of tortious liability that reflects faithfully the law as we find it.[35]

Yet another way in which jurists have commonly tried to rationalise inducing breach of contract relies on treating it as a form of accessory (or secondary) liability. But there are problems with this explanation, too. In particular, although many have made essentially the same point, it is hard to improve on the way that Deakin and Randall capture the chief difficulty here:

> Accessories are persons who aid and abet the principal offender in the commission of an offence. There is only one crime, although there may be more than one person criminally liable for it. The same is true of the liability of joint tortfeasors, in respect of the same tort, of one who commits a tort and one who procures him to do so, and of the so-called 'accessory liability' for dishonestly assisting in a breach of trust which puts the defendant in the same position as if he was himself in breach of trust.[36]

In response to this, Paul Davies – probably the most prominent and zealous defender of the accessory liability interpretation – asserts bluntly that '[a] "secondary liability" approach which insists that the liability of the accessory replicates that of the primary wrongdoer distorts the law and is inconsistent with principle'.[37] Yet he cites no relevant authorities in support of his claim; and nor does he explain the way in which the law is supposedly being distorted. Simply saying that 'the nature of the accessory's wrong is distinct from that of the primary wrongdoer'[38] does not make it so. The weight of the law is assuredly against Davies in this respect. For, as Deakin and Randall accurately observe in the passage just quoted, accessory liability usually does involve joint liability. Thus, although various other problems can be identified with an understanding of inducing breach of contract based on accessory liability,[39] the most fundamental

[34] Stevens (n 3) 281.

[35] *Ibid*, 306. For other such departures, see J Murphy, 'Rights, Reductionism and Tort Law' (2008) 28 *OJLS* 393; J Murphy, 'The Heterogeneity of Tort Law' (2019) 39 *OJLS* 455.

[36] Deakin and Randall (n 7) 543 (footnotes omitted). Others who have made this point include Beever (n 4) 108–109 and 146–47; and Stevens (n 3) 276–77.

[37] Davies (n 1) 284–85. Notably, although he devotes an entire section of the chapter dealing with inducing breach of contract to major arguments against liability for inducing breach of contract (*ibid*, 166–72), he does not deal *there* with the complaint that inducing breach of contract does not mirror other forms of accessory liability.

[38] *Ibid*, 284.

[39] See, eg, Stevens (n 3) 276–78; Carty (n 1) 62; Beever (n 4) 108–109; J Neyers, 'The Economic Torts as Corrective Justice' (2009) 17 *Torts Law Journal* 1, 9; A Botterell *et al* (eds), *Fridman's The Law of Torts in Canada*, 4th edn (Toronto, Carswell, 2020) 944–46.

one remains: the 'party who induces another to breach a contract is *not held* jointly liable with the party in breach of contract for the same wrong'.[40]

B. An Alternative View

The fact that many previous attempts to rationalise *Lumley* liability have failed is not, I think, a reason to adopt Beever's approach and advocate its being allowed to lapse into desuetude. This is because a plausible, alternative account of this form of liability is available, even though it is one that will doubtless attract the opposition of many contemporary tort theorists. This alternative approach to explaining *Lumley* liability suggests that, regardless of the fact that a given action displays certain juridical oddities, it nonetheless deserves to be regarded as *a tort* by Bench, Bar and Academy alike, *so long as* the claim that it *is a tort* rests on suitable judicial authority.

Given the equivocation in *OBG* – at many points it was described as a form of secondary liability, while at others it was labelled a tort[41] – I think that turning to cases decided both before and after that landmark decision can be helpful here. And in turning to such cases, what we discover is fairly consistent judicial support for the claim that inducing breach of contract is a tort. I accept that, in the absence of a fully developed (and widely accepted) theory of exactly what constitutes a tort, this claim is likely to engender opposition. But I nonetheless think – especially bearing in mind the problems that beset its being treated as a form of accessory liability – that there exist several reasons for treating as highly persuasive the fact that the courts have repeatedly referred to the *Lumley* action as a tort. They occupy the remainder of this section.

i. Respecting our Most Senior Courts' Decisions

As Scott Hershovitz observes, 'judges sometimes grasp for principles they can't quite articulate. But for the most part, they are pretty good at saying what they mean'.[42] This, I think, creates a very strong prima facie case for taking seriously the

[40] Stevens (n 3) 276.

[41] Lord Hoffmann, who delivered the leading speech in *OBG*, was for the most part concerned to show that *Lumley* liability is accessory in nature. But he still referred to it as either 'the tort of inducing breaches of contract' or 'the *Lumley v Gye* tort' no fewer than ten times: see *OBG* (n 2) [17], [25], [27], [32], [33], [38], [44], [62], [62] and [69]. In addition – and perhaps more fundamentally – he was (as noted already) also committed to the idea that contractual rights comprise a 'species of property which deserve special protection' (*ibid*, [32]). So saying strongly supports the contention that the *Lumley* action may be considered a freestanding tort. On top of this, there was equivocation in what was said by his fellow Law Lords in that case. At various points, agreement was expressed with Lord Hoffmann's reference to a primary/secondary liability dichotomy. But there was also continued reference among the other judges to either 'the tort of inducing breach of contract' or 'the *Lumley v Gye* tort': see, *ibid*, [139] and [175] (Lord Nicholls) and [264] (Lord Walker).

[42] S Hershovitz, 'The Search for a Grand Theory of Tort Law' (2017) 130 *Harvard Law Review* 942, 969.

fact that, *even after OBG*, the senior courts have continued to refer to the action in view as either 'the tort of inducing breach of contract'[43] or 'the *Lumley v Gye* tort'.[44] Indeed, I would submit that *precisely because the courts* continue to refer to this action as a freestanding tort, there is (in the absence of a better explanation) good reason for us to do likewise.

Herbert Hart was famously of the view that any satisfactory account or explanation of the law should begin with the way that it is understood and deployed by those who work with it. He labelled this the 'internal point of view'.[45] It is a starting point for theorisation that has been accepted by many scholars over the years.[46] According to one commentator, starting with the internal point of view is more or less a 'methodological injunction'[47] in the realm of legal theory. Put more simply: it is generally taken as read that we must begin with the participants' view or understanding of a law or institution if we are to succeed in theorising or explaining it.

On top of accepting the point made by Hershowitz – that the judges are ordinarily good at saying what they mean – there is also a closely related, second reason for taking seriously things said by our most senior courts: the very fact that the thing in question has been said by our most senior courts! Of course, in so saying, I do not mean to suggest that the most highly elevated members of the judiciary are in some way infallible. They, naturally, like everyone else, make mistakes from time to time. As Stapleton rightly points out, their decisions can be 'poorly reasoned, perhaps even incoherently reasoned or indeed *per incuriam* by a failure to advert to an applicable statute'.[48] But for all this, there is no escaping the fact that what they say constitutes the law unless and until it is overruled by a superior court or superseded by legislation. A convenient Latin phrase captures this well: *declarant ergo est.* As Hart put it over 50 years ago, when writing about decisions of the House of Lords (prior to the well-known Practice Statement of 1966[49]):

> A supreme tribunal has the last word in saying what the law is and … [although] [t]he decision may, of course, be deprived of legal effect by legislation … the very fact that resort to this [legislation] is necessary demonstrates the empty character, so far as the law is concerned, of the statement that the court's decision was wrong.[50]

[43] See, *inter multos alios*, *Kawasaki Kisen Kaisha Ltd v James Kemball Ltd* [2021] EWCA Civ 33 (CA), [6] (Popplewell LJ); *Racing Partnership Ltd v Sports Information Services Ltd* [2021] 2 WLR 469 (CA), [142] (Arnold LJ); *Allen v Dodd & Co Ltd* [2020] 2 WLR 1070 (CA), [21] (Lewison LJ); *Eurasia Sports Ltd v Aguad* [2018] 1 WLR 6089 (CA), [23] (Floyd LJ).

[44] *Secretary of State for Health v Servier Laboratories Ltd* [2020] Ch 717 (CA), [55], [68] and [84] (Sir Terence Etherton MR, Longmore LJ and McCombe LJ). The same phrase was used by Lord Hamblen when the case was appealed to the Supreme Court: see [2021] UKSC 24 (SC), [27].

[45] HLA Hart, *The Concept of Law*, 2nd edn (Oxford, Clarendon Press, 1994) 89.

[46] See, eg, Ronald Dworkin, *Law's Empire* (Oxford, Hart Publishing, 1998) 11–15; E Weinrib, *The Idea of Private Law* (Cambridge, Harvard University Press, 1995) 2–3.

[47] W Lucy, 'Method and Fit: Two Problems for Contemporary Philosophies of Tort Law' (2007) 52 *McGill Law Journal* 606, 616.

[48] J Stapleton, *Three Essays on Torts* (Oxford, Oxford University Press, 2021) 18.

[49] Practice Statement [1966] 3 All ER 77.

[50] Hart (n 45) 141. Note that this was said prior to the Practice Statement, *ibid*, which allowed the House of Lords to overrule its own, previous decisions.

Concerned to emphasise the immateriality of judicial errors, he drew an analogy with mistakes made by an umpire in a game of cricket. He said: 'the fact that some rulings given by a scorer are plainly wrong is not inconsistent with the game continuing: they count as much as rulings which are obviously correct'.[51] In like fashion, even the poorly reasoned decisions of our most senior courts count as authoritative statements of the law; and this is so whether contemporary tort theorists like it or not. So, the fact that in *OBG*, as well as in many cases since then, the appellate courts have spoken in terms of the *tort* of inducing breach of contract must, I think, count for a great deal.[52]

ii. Tort Rules that Lack a Clear Rationale

A rather different reason for persisting with the hard-to-explain notion that inducing breach of contract is a tort is this: we need not be troubled by the fact that it lacks any clear rationale. In this respect, it is just one among several examples of tort doctrines that lack any clear rationale. The vicarious liability principle is probably the best known. A great many attempts have been made to justify vicarious liability over the years. They include theories based on notions of control, compensation guarantees, deterrence, loss-spreading, enterprise liability and 'mixed policies'; but they can all be shown to fail to a greater or lesser extent.[53] In a recent study that traces the doctrine back centuries, Swain demonstrates that it has never been a very satisfactory doctrine in theoretical terms. He asserts that 'few legal doctrines can be as difficult to pin down as vicarious liability',[54] and he cites in support of this claim a host of scholars (going back to the time of Frederick Pollock and beyond) who have struggled to rationalise the principle.

Judges, too, have been similarly confounded. For example, in one recent High Court of Australia case, in a judgment delivered on behalf of the majority, it was acknowledged that '[c]ommon law courts have struggled to identify a coherent basis for identifying the circumstances in which an employer should be held vicariously liable for negligent acts of an employee, let alone for intentional, criminal acts'.[55] And yet, despite all these failures in theorisation, no judge or jurist (so far as I am aware) has even come close to suggesting that vicarious liability is

[51] Hart, *ibid*, 144.

[52] I would suggest that this is so *despite the fact* that strenuous efforts were made in the opening paragraphs of Lord Hoffmann's speech in *OBG* to portray inducing breach of contract as a form of secondary liability. The truth is that the case sends out mixed messages. For example, once he got past his path-clearing and began to address in earnest one of the three appeals before him, Lord Hoffmann employed the following heading in his speech: 'Inducing breach of contract: elements of the *Lumley v Gye* tort': see *OBG* (n 2) [39].

[53] For an exposure of the various ways in which these competing theories all fail, see JW Neyers, 'A Theory of Vicarious Liability' (2005) 43 *Alberta Law Review* 287.

[54] W Swain, 'A Historical Examination of Vicarious Liability: A "Veritable Upas Tree"' [2019] *CLJ* 640, 661.

[55] *Prince Alfred College v ADC* (2016) 258 CLR 134, 148.

an anomaly or that it must be abandoned. The short point is this: the fact that an entrenched principle is hard to rationalise is not, *ipso facto*, a reason for rejecting its established status.

The now discredited doctrine of common employment never had a satisfactory rationale, either.[56] But when it came to the question of why, ultimately, it had to be abandoned, it was not the fact that it lacked a clear and defensible *raison d'être* that was key. It was the fact that it could not be reconciled with the doctrine of vicarious liability.[57] As Lord Macmillan put it: '[i]f a servant is injured by the negligence of a fellow-servant acting within the scope of their common employment, the former doctrine would impose liability on the master, while the latter doctrine would exculpate him'.[58] Such incoherence in the law could not be tolerated, and the doctrine of common employment gave way.

Now, of course, neither the vicarious liability principle nor the doctrine of common employment have any obvious connection with inducing breach of contract. But they do at least illustrate the durability of hard-to-fathom principles of tort law that stand on appellate court authority. So, however much Beever may think that the lack of a clear rationale for inducing breach of contract provides a good reason for letting it 'die a merciful death', the traditional approach of the common law to such rules would suggest we do otherwise.

iii. Contemporary Theories and the Problem of Fit

As I have argued at some length elsewhere, the single biggest criticism that can be levelled at contemporary, explanatory theories of tort law is the fact that they are unable to supply a plausible account of a very significant amount of established tort law.[59] Often, the problem of fit arises because a particular tort or doctrine conflicts with claims that are central to those theories. Two such claims – especially closely associated with both rights-based and Kantian theories of tort law – are that (1) torts are characterised by infringements *ex-ante* private rights, and (2) torts involve a purely bilateral relationship between the tortfeasor and the claimant. Both of these putatively classic characteristics are conspicuously absent in the context of inducing breach of contract. But the fact that the *Lumley* action does not conform to these supposedly quintessential features of torts is no basis

[56] In *Radcliffe v Ribble Motor Services Ltd* [1939] AC 215 (HL), 245, Lord Wright described it as 'an arbitrary departure from the rules of the common law … sanctioned by no previous authority'. See also RW Kostal, *Law and English Railway Capitalism 1825–1875* (Oxford, Clarendon Press, 1994) 263 *et seq*; AWB Simpson, *Leading Cases in the Common Law* (Oxford, Oxford University Press, 1995) 100–34.

[57] See Swain (n 54) 654.

[58] *Wilson & Clyde Coal Company Ltd v English* [1938] AC 57 (HL), 74.

[59] For details of the ways in which I have, over the years, defended the various claims made in this paragraph and the next one, see Murphy, 'Heterogeneity' (n 35); Murphy (n 12); J Murphy, 'Misfeasance in a Public Office: A Tort Law Misfit' (2012) 32 *OJLS* 51; Murphy, 'Rights, Reductionism and Tort Law' (n 35); J Goudkamp and J Murphy, 'The Failure of Universal Theories of Tort Law' (2015) 21 *Legal Theory* 47.

on which to claim that it is an anomaly without which we (and tort law) would be better off.

The simple fact that a given case, principle or tort does not fit a particular theoretical understanding provides no licence for declaring that that case, principle or tort is something that ought to be abandoned. A moment's reflection reveals why: it is clearly the task of theories which purport to explain the law to fit the law, to respect the precedents as they stand. It is not the job of tort law to conform to the tenets of those theories. The argument for abandonment based on non-conformity therefore gets things the wrong way round. And the very fact that non-conformity exists – at least, as long as we can describe the case, principle or tort in question as significant[60] – indicates a weakness in the theory, not an anomaly within the law.

Lord Reid famously wrote that 'common sense, legal principle and public policy' all have a role to play (and in that order) in the resolution of hard cases.[61] He also remarked that, 'we [the judiciary] are here to serve the public, the common ordinary reasonable man [who] has no great faith in theories and he is quite right'.[62] It should therefore be unsurprising that parts of the common law – minted in this way – sometimes defy theoretical neatness; especially when one bears in mind another of Lord Reid's points, namely, the fact that '[w]hat passed for common sense three hundred or even one hundred years ago sometimes seems nonsense today … *Communis error facit jus* may seem a paradox but it is a fact'.[63] If a rule of law here, or an ancient tort there, looks odd from the perspective of some or other grand theory, this is no guarantee that there was a slip of the judicial pen. It is much more indicative of business as usual.

iv. *The Weight of History*

A final reason for accepting that the *Lumley* action has a respectable claim to be recognised as a free-standing tort draws on the fact that rules of law with a considerable historical pedigree cannot easily be dismissed just because the rule in question does not reflect modern expectations or understandings of what the law is or should be seeking to do.[64]

Most accounts of inducing breach of contract start in earnest with *Lumley v Gye*. Some of these, it is true, do make fleeting reference to various, much older *per quod* actions. But none of them, in my view, attends properly to the *significance*

[60] For a suggestion of what may be the desiderata governing significance, see J Goudkamp and J Murphy, 'Tort Statutes and Tort Theories' (2015) 131 *LQR* 133, 137.

[61] Lord Reid, 'The Judge and Law-Maker' (1972) 12 *Journal of the Society of Public Teachers of Law* 22, 25.

[62] *Ibid.*

[63] *Ibid.*

[64] It took, for example, until almost the end of the twentieth century, and then a decision of the House of Lords, to make clear that the ancient rule that a man could not be convicted of raping his wife must be overturned: see *R v R* [1992] 1 AC 599 (HL).

of these older actions when it comes to trying to rationalise the *Lumley* tort. That the influence of the *per quod* actions should not be given a light touch, comes through loud and clear in the cautionary note sounded by David Ibbetson: 'the modern law is too heavily dependent on the past for it to be marginalized as something of purely antiquarian interest. If we are to make sense of today's law we have to understand its history'.[65]

Put more expansively: we should not be too hasty in saying that a branch of the law – such as inducing breach of contract – is irrational *simply because* it makes little or no sense when viewed through twenty-first century eyes. The declaratory theory of the common law has long since been abandoned and no-one these days denies that the judiciary plays a key role in developing the common law.[66] Yet, as the common law moves incrementally forwards, it is nonetheless the case that 'the inventing of the new is rarely combined with the discarding of the old'.[67] Accordingly, we ought not to be surprised to find that, sometimes, 'inconvenient or inconsistent, centuries-old rules, principles and doctrines can remain in place'[68] even if the circumstances that warranted their creation in the first place have long since ceased to exist. In other words, it is sometimes possible to identify torts or other rules of law that were formulated in line with the social concerns, values or expectations of the day, but which have subsequently reached the point where they look either antiquated or redundant. The rule in *Rylands v Fletcher* is a prime example.[69] In the days before a fully developed law of negligence, a tort that could be used in connection with the then pressing problem of bursting dams was clearly called for. *Rylands* provided the solution. As Brian Simpson's classic treatment of that case ably shows, the rule that was promulgated can best be understood in terms of the then contemporary issue of 'bursting reservoirs and [the question of] what, if anything, the common law should do about them'.[70] But as the problem of bursting dams abated, and as the law of negligence began to burgeon, it appeared to some that the *Rylands* rule had become 'moribund'.[71] Contradicting that view, the important decision in *Cambridge Water Co v Eastern Counties Leather Plc* made clear that the tort was far from dead (even if, henceforth, it was to be seen as a sub-branch of the law of private nuisance).[72]

[65] D Ibbetson, *A Historical Introduction to the Law of Obligations* (Oxford, Oxford University Press, 1999) *v–vi*.

[66] Whether they do this as judicial legislators, or as mere mirrors on what has been called the 'Living Common Law' (which is thought to develop autonomously) is a moot point. For an account of the 'Living Common Law', see Stapleton (n 48) 4–10.

[67] Ibbetson (n 65) 294.

[68] *Ibid.*

[69] The rule derives from *Rylands v Fletcher* (1868) LR 3 HL 330 (HL).

[70] Simpson (n 56) 199.

[71] P Cane, 'The Changing Fortunes of *Rylands v Fletcher*' (1994) 24 *University of Western Australia Law Review* 237, 237.

[72] *Cambridge Water Co v Eastern Counties Leather Plc* [1994] 2 AC (HL), 264.

A similar story can be told of the rule in *Wilkinson v Downton*[73] which, as is well known, was formulated at a time when no liability for illness triggered by nervous shock could then be imposed by reference to the defendant's negligence. One Court of Appeal judge, perplexed as to the rule's rationale, suggested that it should now be brought within the fold of negligence. He said: '[i]t seems preferable for the law to develop along conventional modern lines rather than through recourse to this obscure tort, whose jurisprudential basis remains unclear'.[74] But against this, not very many years later, the Supreme Court reasserted (albeit with some reformulation) the independent existence of this action in *O (a child) v Rhodes*.[75]

And so it goes with inducing breach of contract. The various *per quod* actions which were influential in *Lumley* all made sense at the time they were first formulated. The rule regarding the seduction of servants can be traced to the Statute of Labourers 1349 which was passed against a background of an exceptional labour shortage caused by the Black Death. And equally antiquated ideas – such as the notion that a ward or wife might be regarded as the property of a father or husband – explain the *per quod* actions associated with their seduction. Of course, such archaic concerns have not survived the effluxion of time, but this does not mean that the cause of action to which they gave birth must likewise be treated as part of legal history. Any given tort – just like the reformulated rule in *Wilkinson v Downton* – may undergo a certain amount of (precedent-respecting) reconfiguration in order to preserve its vitality. Indeed, this is the norm, for as Ibbetson observes, '[l]egal change occurs through … twisting existing rules, or rediscovering old ones, to give the impression that a change in the law is no more than the application of the law that was already in place'.[76] And thus it is that judges, charged with the task of delivering a just result in any given case, are conspicuously more attentive to precedent (and its possibilities) than they are to the tenets of whatever overarching theory of the law of torts happens to be in vogue at the time.[77]

If one combines what was said in the ancient antecedents of inducing breach of contract with (1) the judges' acknowledged willingness in *Lumley* to do common-sense justice, and (2) their reluctance to disregard those earlier cases, it becomes understandable how it should be that we find ourselves with a *tort* of inducing breach of contract that cannot, to modern eyes, be cashed out in theoretically satisfying terms. *Lumley* did not replicate in precise terms anything said in the early authorities; but nor did it wholly come apart from them. It added (and now constitutes) a bricoleur's incremental twist on those early cases.

To expect that tort law should be neatly reducible to some simple, unifying principle or norm is a bit like crying for the moon. As was pithily observed over

[73] *Wilkinson v Downton* [1897] 2 QB 57.
[74] *A v Hoare* [2006] 1 WLR 2320 (CA), [136] (Sir Anthony Clarke MR).
[75] *O (a child) v Rhodes* [2016] AC 219 (SC).
[76] Ibbetson (n 65) 294. See also Stapleton (n 48) 4–10.
[77] See further chapter nine.

20 years ago: '[t]he common law has many virtues, [but] tidiness is not among them'.[78] Nothing has changed since those words were written. Furthermore, we ought also to bear in mind (even though the point was made with a heavy dose of cynicism) Weir's comment that we have 'a system powered by advocates who would rather win than be right, even if their winning makes the law wrong'.[79]

Lord Hoffmann acknowledged in *OBG* that inducing breach of contract is only a tort 'because the court in *Lumley v Gye* said that inducing a breach of contract was tortious'.[80] His saying this seems to me to be both true and unobjectionable from a practical point of view.

II. An Action Protecting Purely Economic Interests?

The landmark decision in *Lumley v Gye* has been analysed by many jurists over the years; and various propositions concerning the interests it protects can be found within the relevant literature.[81] Close engagement with the debate about whether inducing breach of contract is better viewed as an action that protects certain status-based relationships (such as that of master and servant), or one that treats contractual rights as though they possess some kind of proprietary (or quasi-proprietary) quality,[82] is not crucial when it comes to identifying the scope of the action. However, as we shall see, certain arguments from within this debate are relevant, albeit indirectly, to the scope of *Lumley* liability.

Similarly, the hotly contested issue of whether inducing breach of contract is better seen as a free-standing tort or simply part of a general private law rule about the liability of accessories[83] is, again, not something we need analyse closely. But from within this debate, too, there are points that have been made that are pertinent to the issue that occupies this section of the chapter, namely, whether the action minted in *Lumley* is, according to the authorities, confined to the protection of purely economic interests.

A. A Lesson from 'Status-Based' Theory

Quite a lot of what was said by the majority in *Lumley* harked back to the action *per quod servitium amisit*: an action afforded to those who suffer harm by virtue

[78] Ibbetson (n 65) 294.

[79] Weir (n 13) 3.

[80] *OBG* (n 2) [18].

[81] See, eg, from the last 20 years alone, Bagshaw (n 16); Danforth (n 7); Davies (n 1); Deakin and Randall (n 7) 535–36; D Howarth, 'Against *Lumley v Gye*' (2005) 68 *MLR* 195; Simester and Chan (n 3); Waddams (n 12). The idea that contract rights carry with them some sort of (ill-defined) proprietary quality can be traced to cases decided in the early part of the twentieth century: see CE Carpenter, 'Interference with Contract Relations' (1928) 41 *Harvard Law Review* 728, 732–34.

[82] See, eg, Benson (n 23) 456; Bagshaw (n 16) 131 ('quasi-property'), 143 ('an interest … akin to a property interest').

[83] For a thoroughgoing defence of this contention, see Davies (n 1).

of their having had a servant either enticed away from them, or otherwise prevented from working for them.[84] On this footing, John Danforth suggests that a fair interpretation of what was decided in *Lumley* would be the following:

> because it was explicitly based on the enticement-of-servant action, and because two of the majority judges took care to note the details of Lumley's relation with Wagner, *Lumley v Gye's* holding strongly suggested that the character of the relationship disrupted would determine whether one could be liable in tort for interfering with another's contract.[85]

Alan Beever is another scholar who regards *Lumley* as having been decided on narrow grounds related to the particular relationship that existed between the contract breaker and the claimant. He argues that, '[t]he case is about status, not contract',[86] and adds the fairly startling claim that there is nothing in *Lumley* that could be said to ground *a tort* of inducing breach of contract.[87] In relation to the second point, Beever is clearly wrong. Erle J was emphatically of the view that, 'in a case of the procurement of a breach of contract the action is *for a wrong*'.[88] But what is there to ground Beever's claim in relation to the action being confined to cases in which the claimant held a particular status *vis à vis* the contract breaker? Erle J's judgment does not supply a definitive answer. For, although he recognised the tort's role outside the realm of master-servant contracts – he acknowledged there could be an 'action for this wrong, *in respect of other contracts than those of hiring*'[89] – he gave no indication whether he intended it to be confined to other status-based relationships. That matter was only resolved later, though Beever omits to mention this.

Although he devotes some space to considering the 'subsequent history'[90] of the action, conspicuous by its absence in Beever's analysis is any mention of *Temperton v Russell (No 2)*.[91] In that case, Lord Esher put beyond doubt the fact that inducing breach of contract could be invoked in connection with a contract for the supply of goods rather than one for the supply of labour.[92] Thus, Beever is not just wrong to say that *Lumley* did not give rise to an action in tort, he is also remiss not to point out in his discussion of the way the tort developed, that *Temperton* made clear that it was not an action confined to situations in which the claimant held a particular status *vis-à-vis* the contract breaker.

Notwithstanding these errors, however, there is still something of value to be drawn from Beever's account of *Lumley*. For, unlike Danforth (who commits himself to seeing the decision in *Lumley* as intimately tethered to contracts of

[84] *Lumley* (n 5) 229, 231 and 240 (Crompton, Erle and Wightman JJ, respectively).
[85] Danforth (n 7) 1496.
[86] Beever (n 4) 149.
[87] *Ibid*: '[t]here is no support for that tort in any of the judgments in *Lumley v Gye*'.
[88] *Lumley* (n 5) 232.
[89] *Ibid*, (emphasis added). Notably, a court in an American case decided not long after *Lumley* applied what was perceived to be the doctrine in *Lumley* to all contracts and not just those involving a contract for personal services: see *Walker v Cronin*, 107 Mass 555 (1871).
[90] Beever (n 4) 150–54.
[91] *Temperton v Russell (No 2)* [1893] 1 QB 715 (CA).
[92] *Ibid*, 727.

the master-servant variety), Beever rightly alights upon the fact that, the action *per quod consortium amisit* – an action concerned with depriving a husband of the society and support of his wife – also played a very important role in the decision that was reached.[93]

Winsmore v Greenbank[94] was a case of this type. In it, the defendant persuaded the claimant's wife to remain absent from her husband in breach of the marriage contract. In *Lumley*, both Erle and Wightman JJ placed significant weight on what was held in *Winsmore*. Indeed, Wightman J even went so far as to describe it as 'an exceedingly strong authority in the plaintiff's favour in the present case'.[95]

Crucial for our purposes is the fact that the husband in *Winsmore* recovered damages for loss of what Wightman J called the 'comfort and society of the wife and her aid in his domestic affairs'.[96] In *Philp v Squire*, too, Lord Kenyon stated that: '[t]he ground of this action is that the defendant retains the plaintiff's wife against the inclination of her husband', adding shortly thereafter that 'this kind of action materially differs from that for harbouring an apprentice, the ground of the action in that case being the loss of the apprentice's service'.[97] In other words, a distinction was being drawn between loss of wifely company (recognised in *Winsmore*) and the loss of an employee. The critical point, then, is that, right from the outset, the action that was articulated in *Lumley* was not one that was anchored to antecedents concerned purely with protection of trade or business interests. The loss of a wife's companionship is simply not capable of being cashed out in any such terms. And yet Wightman J could not have been clearer in saying that 'upon the authority of … *Winsmore v Greenhank*, as well as upon general principle … an action on the case is maintainable [in the present case]'.[98] Erle J also noted that marital (not commercial) rights were what lay at the heart of *Winsmore*. And he, too, was emphatically of the view that 'procuring a violation of the plaintiffs *right under the marriage contract* is … an actionable wrong'.[99]

Now, a possible response to the argument of the last few paragraphs may be as follows. The action *per quod servitium amisit* – the *per quod* action that involved enticement of a menial servant away from his master – was also referred to in *Lumley*. This *per quod* action, objectors might persist, was emphatically an action that allowed damages only up to the value, and in respect of, the services lost.[100] But even so, this line of authority must be placed in context. For a start, it was only Crompton J who seemed impressed by these cases. Coleridge J (dissenting)

[93] Beever (n 4) 147.
[94] *Winsmore v Greenbank* (1745) Willes 577.
[95] *Lumley* (n 5) 238.
[96] *Ibid.*
[97] *Philp v Squire* (1791) Peake 114, 115. See also *Berthon v Cartwright* (1796) 2 Esp 480 in which the very brief report of the case records that the action in that case was purely for 'seducing the plaintiff's wife, detaining her, and thereby depriving him of her society': *ibid*, 480.
[98] *Lumley* (n 5) 238.
[99] *Ibid*, 232 (emphasis added).
[100] See *Hart* (n 8).

showed meticulously how this line of authority had originated in the cause of action created by the Statute of Labourers.[101] His pointing this out is important because, unlike the other *per quod* actions, the statutory action required no enticement on the part of the defendant. Take, for example, the case of *Blake v Lanyon*.[102] There, the defendant had simply continued to employ a man who had left his previous employer, but without the second employer knowing this. As the brief report of that case makes clear:

> '[a]n action will lie for … continuing to employ the servant of another after notice, without enticing him away. Here no fault could be imputed to the defendant, for taking Hobbs into his service in the first instance, because then he had no notice of Hobbs's prior engagement with the plaintiff: but as soon as he had notice of that fact, he ought to have discharged him.[103]

Thus, given the centrality of *inducement* to the action formulated in *Lumley*, it is hard to regard its *principal roots* as lying in this particular line of cases. Erle and Wightman JJ (the other members of the majority) clearly afforded much greater significance to the action *per quod consortium amisit*.[104] Thus, even though certain types of cases involving servants did attend only to economic losses, they were the *per quod* cases that exerted the least influence over the majority in *Lumley*. My central point, then, remains more or less unscathed. Although the court in *Lumley* did indeed consider various different *per quod* actions, it is wrong to conclude from this, as Beever does, that the operation of inducing breach of contract is best seen as an action confined to the *inter partes* rights that exist in certain types of relationships. The value in his analysis is that it draws helpful attention to a line of early cases, treated as influential in *Lumley*, in which damages were not confined to the reparation of harm caused to purely economic interests.

Just a moment's reflection reveals that the protection of marital promises is about as far removed as one can get from the purely commercial. And even some of the early *per quod servitium amisit* cases – ie, those involving the debauching of a daughter (rather than the poaching of a servant) – were not truly concerned with harm caused to the claimant's economic interests. As Lobban explains, any case of this kind was one designed 'to compensate parents for the corruption of their daughters, masquerading as an economic tort'.[105] His claim is readily borne out by reference to *Andrews v Askey* where Tindal CJ specifically directed the jury in the following terms: '[y]ou are not confined to the consideration of the mere loss of service, but may give some damages for the distress and anxiety of mind which the mother has felt'.[106] Likewise, in the case of *Dodd v Norris*,

[101] *Lumley* (n 5) 252.
[102] *Blake v Lanyon* (1795) 6 Term Rep 221.
[103] *Ibid*, 222.
[104] See text associated with (n 95).
[105] Lobban (n 8) 1041.
[106] *Andrews v Askey* (1837) 8 Car & P 7, 9.

Lord Ellenborough made clear that, 'compensation … [is] allowed for the injury to the parental feelings'.[107]

The conclusion to which we are impelled, then, is that the action formulated in *Lumley* was not quite so novel as is sometimes suggested.[108] Its principal origins can be found in two ancient *per quod* actions in neither of which do we find, when we dig deeply enough, a particular focus on the protection of the claimant's trade or business interests. If we take this point in conjunction with the fact that several important cases have subsequently made clear that the action should be available in connection with procured breaches of *any contracts*,[109] it is hard to see why the tort established in *Lumley v Gye* should be viewed as a specifically *economic* tort.

B. A Lesson from the 'Property Thesis'

As we have seen already, one fundamental question concerning inducing breach of contract is why, when the breach of contract is committed by C's contracting partner, X, the claimant, C, should have a right of action against D who 'merely' induced X to break his contract with C. As Neyers puts it, the problem here is that of 'explaining how a right that is personal as between the [contracting] parties can give rise to liability to parties not bound by these rights and how the liability is not a violation of privity of contract'.[110]

At this juncture we need not delve deeply into the various versions of the property thesis. It suffices to note one particular point that is relevant to the scope of *Lumley* liability that has been made by Roderick Bagshaw, who is just one among numerous scholars to have elaborated (albeit tentatively) a version of the property thesis. In the course of his account of what can be said in favour of affording the right to contractual performance a proprietary (or, more accurately, a quasi-proprietary) status, Bagshaw makes an important observation. It is that, '[a] breach of contract can be procured by whispering an offer in a soprano's ear' though this is 'not in itself an unlawful act … [which in turn means that] "unlawful means" is not a necessary condition [of liability]'.[111] The significance of this observation inheres in the fact that it comprehensively undermines the contention made by Weir that inducing breach of contract is, *pace* what was said in *OBG*, a sub-branch of the

[107] *Dodd v Norris* (1814) 3 Camp 519, 520.

[108] See, eg, Waddams (n 12) 447: 'This was a novel claim in relation to professional services, and Gye demurred. This procedure (demurrer) enabled the Court of Queen's Bench to determine … whether, assuming the facts alleged in the declaration to be proved, Lumley would be entitled to succeed'. In similar vein, see Carty (n 1) 30.

[109] As noted already, this point was made in *Temperton* (n 91). But dicta to similar effect can also be found in *Allen v Flood* [1898] AC 1 (HL), 67 and 113 (Lords Halsbury and Ashbourne respectively) and *Quinn* (n 33), 510 (Lord Macnaghten).

[110] Neyers (n 39) 8.

[111] Bagshaw (n 16) 145.

broader tort of causing loss by unlawful means.[112] But since the value of Bagshaw's observation may not be obvious, some unpacking of the relevant points is perhaps called for.

For Weir, the simple fact that D induced X to break his contract with C would amount to unlawful means. On that basis, just like any other case involving the unlawful means tort, D could be said to have caused loss to C via unlawful means employed against a third party. For Weir, the inherent wrongfulness of inducement was captured in the following, typically colourful, way: '[t]he serpent was worse than Eve. So, too, the person who bribes … another into breaking his contract is a primary wrongdoer'.[113] But this cannot be right. If uttering an inducement to break a contract were inherently wrongful – a tort in itself – it would be hard to explain the need to satisfy various other requirements that must be shown before an action for this tort may be brought, namely, knowledge, intention and damage.

It follows from this that there exists a very significant gap between inducing breach of contract and the unlawful means tort. And the very fact that the two actions are so distinct in juridical terms removes any plausible licence for thinking that inducing breach of contract is restricted to the protection of purely economic interests, *even if it were true that* this restriction applies to the unlawful means tort. Bagshaw's point, in short, can helpfully be added to the juridical distinction between inducing breach of contract and the tort of causing loss by unlawful means that the House of Lords was so clearly at pains to draw in *OBG*.

C. A Lesson from 'Accessory (or Secondary) Liability Theory'

As noted already, some useful light may be shed on the scope of inducing breach of contract by consulting arguments marshalled in support of the property and status-based theses. The same is true of the (not quite settled) debate about whether it is better to regard *Lumley* as having introduced a free-standing tort or a rule of accessory liability. This is because, in this context, too, there are certain arguments raised that are incidentally relevant to the scope of the action in view. To explain: some of those who argue that inducing breach of contract is best seen as rule of accessory (or secondary[114]) liability have put forward arguments that

[112] He said not only that 'to induce an employee to break his contract of employment is in itself a wrong', but also that 'inducing breach of contract has now been absorbed into the general tort of causing harm by unlawful means': Weir (n 13) 41 and 28 respectively.

[113] Weir (n 13) 35.

[114] Carty and Sales both prefer the language of 'secondary liability', while Deakin and Randall prefer the notion of parasitic liability. For Carty, there was, in *OBG*, a 'regrettable use of the term "accessory" liability' which simply provides 'ammunition for the argument that facilitation [as opposed to active inducement] should suffice for liability': see Carty (n 1) 62. Sales offers no reason for preferring to speak of secondary liability: see P Sales, 'The Tort of Conspiracy and Civil Secondary Liability' [1990] *CLJ* 491, 502–503; but Deakin and Randall (above (n 7) 543) think that 'parasitic liability' works

also undermine Weir's claim that this action forms a mere sub-branch of the tort of causing loss by unlawful means.[115] They have done this, once again, by adverting to various pronounced differences between the unlawful means tort and inducing breach of contract. Some of these – including the different intentionality requirements of the two torts – were, of course, noted in what their Lordships had to say on the matter in *OBG*.[116] But subsequent scholarship has also drawn out the important ramifications of this distinction. Paul Davies' work is especially relevant here. But before turning to that, it is important to be clear about just where the difference lies.

In contrast to the torts of causing loss by unlawful means and unlawful means conspiracy in both which *intention to injure the claimant* is a key ingredient, in *Lumley v Gye*, liability did not require that Gye set out to injure Lumley. As was confirmed in *OBG*, it is enough for the purposes of inducing breach of contract that the defendant, with knowledge of the relevant term of the claimant's contract, must have intended that the contract be broken. The mention of the need for malice in *Lumley*[117] was, admittedly, treated as central to the imposition of this form of liability in *Bowen*.[118] But, as we also noted earlier, the idea that the defendant must have been actuated by malice was later forcefully quashed by the House of Lords in *Quinn v Leathem*.[119] It is therefore now beyond doubt that malice is irrelevant, and that intention to procure a breach of contract is enough, there being no need to show an intention to cause loss to the claimant.[120]

It is the ramifications of this absence of the need to prove an intention to cause loss that Davies has helpfully illuminated. His analysis begins with one case decided by the House of Lords in which the defendant union called a strike of coal miners. The strike would inevitably lead to a reduction in the supply of coal, which in turn could foreseeably lead to an increase in its price. Such an increase in price, if it occurred, would be financially beneficial for the claimant. It was therefore possible to argue that the striking miners in that case did not intend to inflict a loss on the claimant.[121] But this made no difference to the outcome. Davies is therefore right to point out that this case – endorsed as having been correctly

because 'such tortious liability is dependent on, and cannot exist without, the liability of another for breach of contract'. Beever (like the Law Lords in *OBG*) simply uses the terms interchangeably: Beever (n 4) 108 *et seq*.

[115] See above (n 112).

[116] In *OBG* (n 2) the idea of accessorial liability was invoked numerous times: see *ibid*, [3] and [20], [21] (Lord Hoffmann), [172] (Lord Nicholls) and [320] (Lord Brown). Yet the alternative language of 'secondary liability' was also used as if it were somehow an interchangeable concept: see *ibid*, [32] (Lord Hoffmann), [172] (Lord Nicholls) and [320] (Lord Brown). In *Lumley* itself, things were much hazier. Some of the dicta suggested a freestanding tort: see *Lumley* (n 5) 232 and 238 (Erle and Wightman JJ respectively: see also section I, above.

[117] *Lumley* (n 5) 224, 233 and 238 (Crompton, Erle and Wightman JJ, respectively).

[118] *Bowen* (n 31) 338 (Brett LJ).

[119] *Quinn* (n 33).

[120] '[T]he pleader in *Lumley v Gye* used the word "maliciously", but the court construed this as meaning only that the defendant intended to procure a breach of contract': *OBG* (n 2) [8] (Lord Hoffmann).

[121] *South Wales Miners' Federation v Glamorgan Coal Co Ltd* [1905] AC 239 (HL).

decided in *OBG*[122] – shows that 'the contention that the economic torts all operate to protect economic interests is not entirely persuasive'.[123] And this ability to distance inducing breach of contract from the unlawful means tort (as well as the other economic torts) helps ground his conclusion that '*Lumley* liability can arise in relation to any breach of contract, and is not limited to protecting, economic, trade or business interests'.[124]

At the very least, Davies' analysis of this important juridical difference means that anyone wishing to treat inducing breach of contract as an *economic* tort must now show on independent grounds why it is worthy of that appellation. Deakin and Randall effectively concede this point[125] before offering a pretty thin justification for continuing to do just that. They write:

> Whilst a purist might conclude that it [ie, inducing breach of contract] ought … to be categorised separately, both convenience and a recognition that most *Lumley v Gye* cases have arisen, and will continue to arise, from competition in trade or business suggest that it should continue to be treated as one of the economic torts.[126]

There are several flaws here. The argument from convenience is obviously weak because it presupposes the very thing that needs to be shown: ie, that it is appropriate to consider inducing breach of contract an *economic* tort. And the argument based on the preponderance of reported cases is also fairly feeble because it does not follow from the fact that most cases within a certain tort involve damage of kind X, that those which involve damage of kind Y are somehow unimportant. The vast preponderance of negligence cases concern claims for various forms of personal injury and property damage;[127] but this does not render anomalous or worthy of disregard those (admittedly less numerous) cases involving pure economic loss, especially where ruinous amounts are involved.

A comparable absence of any sound reason to treat inducing breach of contract as a specifically *economic* tort besets the treatment of it in Carty's principal work, *An Analysis of the Economic Torts*. There, in contradistinction to Deakin and Randall, she claims in relation to the requirement that damage be shown (in order to secure compensatory damages), that 'it is likely that injury to reputation is not compensatable [*sic*] under this tort, *in line with decisions in conspiracy and malicious falsehood*'.[128] But, just like Deakin and Randall, she

[122] '*South Wales Miners' Federation v Glamorgan Coal Co Ltd* [1905] AC 239 shows that one may intend to procure a breach of contract without intending to cause loss': *OBG* (n 2) [62] (Lord Hoffmann).

[123] Davies (n 1) 139.

[124] *Ibid.*

[125] '*Lumley v Gye* [is] in a distinct position as compared to the other economic torts: its ambit may on occasion extend beyond their core function of protecting trade or business interests': Deakin and Randall (n 7) 536.

[126] *Ibid.*

[127] See P Cane and J Goudkamp, *Atiyah's Accidents, Compensation and the Law*, 9th edn (Cambridge, Cambridge University Press 2018) 187–94.

[128] Carty (n 1) 45 (emphasis added).

simply assumes (rather than shows) the existence of a juridical link between inducing breach of contract and the torts on which her claim relies.

It is, of course, perfectly true that most contracts have a commercial purpose and will naturally result, if breached, in economic loss. But not all contracts are of this kind. In just the same way that some of *Lumley*'s antecedents allowed a claimant to sue in respect of various forms of distress, it seems perfectly apt that someone should be able to sue for such loss in the present era (as well as for other forms of personal injury). Imagine, for example, a patient who has made a contract for the surgical removal of a cancerous tumour in an awkward position. Imagine, too, that her doctor – the only private one around with the relevant skills – is then induced to breach his contract to perform that surgery with the result that a considerable delay is incurred in finding an alternative private surgeon. In such a case, I would submit that it is entirely foreseeable and appropriate that the claimant be compensated for the mental distress (or other discernible harm) associated with the delay in receiving treatment.[129] It would be just the same in terms of distress, if D persuaded a photographer to break a contract to take wedding photographs at the eleventh hour, leaving no time for a replacement photographer to be found.[130]

And there is no basis for thinking that the action should extend only to the protection of personal interests. There is no *a priori* reason to rule out property damage. So, if D induced T to break her contract with C for the removal of Japanese knotweed – a weed that grows so quickly that damage to C's property will occur before C can find someone else to remove it – that property damage ought to be recoverable. And as Paul Davies has argued,[131] where D induces T to break a contract for the provision of enjoyment or pleasure – damages for the disappointment thereby caused ought to be available for inducing the breach, just as they would for the breach itself.[132] In this connection, the wedding photograph example might again be usefully invoked.

III. Conclusion

In this chapter, I have given a relatively light touch to various questions that have dogged the *Lumley* action for years, the principal one being whether it should be seen as a property-protecting tort. My limited engagement with some of these familiar questions was in large part driven by the fact that their resolution was not central to the two principal contentions of this chapter. These, it will be recalled

[129] For a similar example, in which a patient is in a remote location, and suffers a deterioration in health that may be compensable if a doctor is induced not to visit the patient with the result that the patient's health suffers, see NJ McBride and R Bagshaw, *Tort Law*, 6th edn (London, Pearson, 2018) 668.
[130] I am grateful to Roderick Bagshaw for suggesting this example to me.
[131] See Davies (n 1) 143.
[132] See, eg, *Jackson v Horizon Holidays* [1975] 1 WLR 1468 (CA).

were, first, that, for all its oddities and historical baggage, inducing breach of contract has a respectable claim to be treated as a freestanding tort; and secondly, that *Lumley* liability cannot – either in theory, or on the basis of established authority – be confined to the protection of trade and business interests.

As regards the first of these claims, I argued that there are numerous reasons which combine to fortify the case for treating the *Lumley* action as a tort. Prime among these is the fact that it has repeatedly been referred to as a tort by our most senior courts. True: it has also been said by some important judges that it is a rule of accessory (or secondary) liability; but the self-same judges who have said this have also called it a tort. It may be theoretically unsatisfying to think of a form of accessory (or secondary) liability as a tort, but torts are occasionally characterised by juridical oddities. For example, some tort actions may be brought in the absence of any rights infringement,[133] while others are enlivened by infringements of public (not private rights).[134] Juridical peculiarities inevitably irritate purists who crave theoretical neatness, but they are an entirely quotidian feature of tort law.

My other main claim occupied the second section of this chapter. My reason for devoting so much space to identifying the scope of this tort was simply that no-one to date has tackled this question with anything approaching the rigour it deserves. A few commentators – as noted – have recognised the absence of any obvious constraints on the breadth of the action in the leading cases. But they have not sedulously defended the proposition. Worse still, Carty – by any measure one of the leading commentators in the field – has actively misled her readers in relation to the purview of this tort. She wrote: '*its scope* is limited to where the defendant has intentionally procured a breach of contract by the claimant's partner'.[135] But this, of course, says nothing at all about *the scope* of the action: it is proposition that concerns the required mental element in the tort.

In order to make good my claim about *Lumley* liability stretching further than many jurists seem to suppose, I made much of the several important ways in which the action comes apart from the tort of causing loss by unlawful means. The point of making this distinction was to facilitate my arguing that, however much one may find appealing the idea that the unlawful means tort is confined to the protection of trade and business interests, this should have no bearing on the scope of inducing breach of contract. But I went further, too, and sought to evince some *positive support* for the claim that it is not a tort confined to the protection of purely economic interests. To do this, I drew upon some of the ancient *per quod* actions to which the decision in *Lumley v Gye* was expressly anchored.

[133] The tort of causing loss by unlawful means fits this description; so too does the dependency action under the Fatal Accidents Act 1976 and the rule in *Rylands v Fletcher* (n 69). See further, Murphy, 'Rights, Reductionism and Tort Law' (n 35).

[134] The torts of public nuisance and misfeasance in a public office both meet this description.

[135] H Carty, 'The Modern Functions of the Economic Torts: Reviewing the English, Canadian, Australian, and New Zealand Positions' [2015] *CLJ* 261, 262 (emphasis added).

My discussion of inducing breach of contract in no way exhausted the array of awkward legal questions that continue to surround it. I dealt briefly with the unique notion of intention that features in this tort; but there are other ways, too, in which it conspicuously comes apart from the other general economic torts. Discussion of these, however, is postponed until chapter seven where my principal concern is to show that the so-called economic torts have a great deal more that divides than unites them.

4

Torts Requiring Unlawful Means

I. Introduction

Unlike some of the torts dealt with in this book, there is no serious doubt that can now be cast over the vitality of the two torts considered in this chapter.[1] The first of them – causing loss by unlawful means – was given very firm judicial endorsement by the Law Lords in *OBG Ltd v Allan*.[2] The second – unlawful means conspiracy – was possibly imperilled in the immediate wake of *OBG*. But its imperilment did not last long; for the tort was fully resuscitated within a year by a differently constituted House of Lords in *Revenue and Customs Commissioners v Total Network SL*.[3] Accordingly, even though both these torts remain controversial by virtue of their possessing certain juridical peculiarities (discussed fully in chapter seven), the focus of this chapter lies elsewhere than with the question of whether they can be said to be alive and well. It is instead directed towards their scope, their rationales and their potential uses.

Thus, in just the same way that I was concerned in chapter three to show that, properly understood, the tort of inducing breach of contract is not confined to the protection of economic interests (by which I mean trade and business interests[4]), so shall I do likewise here. And as will be seen in due course, this claim can be defended with relative ease in relation to unlawful means conspiracy, chiefly thanks to two recent decisions of our most senior court. The same, however, cannot be said of causing loss by unlawful means. The obstacles that stand in the way of regarding this tort as one that stretches beyond the protection of economic interests are not insurmountable, but they are considerable.

[1] There can, of course, still be normative quibbles raised in connection with these torts. And as regards unlawful means conspiracy, such normative arguments have indeed been made: see, in particular, PS Davies and P Sales, 'Intentional Harm, Accessories and Conspiracies' (2018) 134 *LQR* 69; H Carty, 'The Modern Functions of the Economic Torts: Reviewing the English, Canadian, Australian, and New Zealand Positions' [2015] *CLJ* 261.

[2] *OBG Ltd v Allan* [2008] 1 AC 1 (HL).

[3] *Revenue and Customs Commissioners v Total Network SL* [2008] 1 AC 1174 (HL).

[4] Rather than use the rather wordy phrase, 'trade, business and employment interests' favoured by Deakin (see, eg, S Deakin and J Randall, 'Rethinking the Economic Torts' (2009) 72 *MLR* 519, 533), I mention only trade and business interests. To my mind, employment interests are a mere sub-set of trade interests: after all, employees trade their labour for salaries or wages. As noted in chapter two, Carty also thinks that the proper purview of the economic torts is set according to these interests.

II. Causing Loss by Unlawful Means

This tort is committed where a claimant suffers loss caused by unlawful conduct on the part of the defendant that has been threatened or taken against a third party with the intention of harming the claimant in circumstances where the claimant has some form of economic relationship with the third party. Its three central elements are unlawful means,[5] intention and harm. So much was laid down in the seminal case of *Allen v Flood*,[6] even though none of these ingredients received the same depth of consideration in that case as was afforded to the question of whether ostensibly lawful acts could be transformed into actionable wrongs purely on the basis that they were performed maliciously.[7]

In fact, the question concerning the role of malice so dominated *Allen v Flood*, that juristic writing that followed on its heels often concentrated on only that issue.[8] Other, 'subordinate questions', such as the types of loss covered by this tort – on which the various members of the House of Lords expressed mixed views – were largely overlooked. Scholars ever since seem largely to have assumed that the unlawful means tort is confined to the protection of trade or business interests. But this is not a proposition that can safely be anchored to what the House of Lords actually decided in *Allen v Flood*. And nor is it a view that can be firmly defended by reference to *OBG*. Indeed, as I demonstrate in the remainder of this section of the chapter, the view that this tort is (or should be) confined to such interests persists despite the absence of any secure historical or present-day foundations for that view. There is, as I shall also seek to show, a hefty cost associated with thinking this way. It is that the full potential of this tort is likely to be obscured from view.

A. The Conventional View on Scope

Jurists and judges often assert – although they seldom attempt to demonstrate this point rigorously – that the tort of causing loss by unlawful means protects only economic interests. Particularly popular, as noted already, is the view that it is tied to the protection of trade or business interests. There is certainly overwhelming support among academic commentators for the notion that, in order for there to

[5] For the maverick view that unlawful means are not required in the commission of this tort, see A Beever, *A Theory of Tort Liability* (Oxford, Hart Publishing, 2016) 135: 'despite official doctrine, unlawful means are not necessary for liability'.

[6] *Allen v Flood* [1898] AC 1 (HL).

[7] By a majority of 6:3 their Lordships decided that an act which is otherwise lawful cannot be rendered unlawful just because the actor was actuated by malice.

[8] See, eg, JB Ames, 'How Far an Act May be a Tort Because of the Wrongful Motive of the Actor' (1905) 18 *Harvard Law Review* 411; L Krauthoff, 'Malice as an Ingredient of a Civil Cause of Action' (1898) 21 *Annual Report of the American Bar Association* 335.

be a remedy, the harm suffered must be of the economic variety. Simon Deakin and John Randall, for example, have claimed that 'unless a direct interference with trade, business or employment is made out, a vital element of the wrong is missing, even if loss or damage is also present'.[9] Likewise, Jason Neyers insists that, in an action of this kind, the claimant must show that 'she suffered resultant economic loss'.[10] In a putative justification of this view, to which she also subscribes, Hazel Carty offers the following explanation: '[t]he unlawful means tort remains linked to its history and to the prevention of excessive competitive conflict', for which reason it is best understood as a tort 'that helps claimants who are intentionally economically harmed'.[11]

Judicial figures who have also portrayed the tort in this way include Lord Diplock (who described it as the tort of 'interference with business by the use of unlawful means'[12]), as well as numerous Court of Appeal judges who have referred to it as an action based on 'wrongful interference with trade or business'.[13] But arguably the most significant judicial voice in this respect is that of Lord Hoffmann. In his leading speech in *OBG*, he averred that the unlawful means tort is 'designed *only* to enforce basic standards of civilised behaviour in economic competition between traders or between or employers and labour'.[14] Also, in the course of his setting out the ingredients of the tort, he insisted that there must be 'a wrongful interference with the actions of a third party *in which the claimant has an economic interest*' in order for this tort to be available.[15] No doubt influenced by this, courts in the post-*OBG* era have routinely referred to this tort in terms that suggest that it is confined to unlawful interferences with economic interests.[16] And the very fact that they have done this, as noted in the previous chapter, is not a matter to be taken lightly.

[9] Deakin and Randall (n 4) 533.

[10] J Neyers, 'Rights-based Justifications for the Tort of Unlawful Interference with Economic Relations' [2008] *Legal Studies* 215, 219.

[11] Carty (n 1) 277.

[12] *Hadmor Productions Ltd v Hamilton* [1983] 1 AC 191 (HL), 223. A little later in his speech, his Lordship defined the tort's scope slightly more expansively in terms of interference with 'trade or business': *ibid*, 229.

[13] See, eg, *Lonrho Plc v Fayed (No 1)* [1989] 2 QB 479 (CA), 487 (Dillon LJ); *Merkur Island Shipping Corporation v Laughton* [1983] 2 AC 570 (HL), 609 (Lord Diplock); *Millar v Bassey* [1994] EMLR 44 (CA), 66 (Ralph Gibson LJ).

[14] *OBG* (n 2) [56] (emphasis added). Even the powerful dissentient in that case, Lord Nicholls, labelled it the tort of 'interference with a business by unlawful means': *ibid*, [139]. Both of these characterisations, however, seem to overlook the fact that the classic case of *Allen v Flood* was one involving, as it were, labour versus labour.

[15] *Ibid*, [47] (emphasis added). The status of this 'dealing requirement' was examined in *Secretary of State for Health v Servier Laboratories Ltd* [2021] UKSC 24 (SC), and it was specifically confirmed to be an essential element of the unlawful means tort: see *ibid*, [63] (Lord Hamblen). *Cf* Beever (n 5) 137 who interprets this requirement in terms of D's exercising indirect control over C.

[16] See, eg, *Merricks v Mastercard* [2019] Bus LR 3025 (CA), [41] (Patten LJ) (affd [2020] UKSC 51 (SC)); *Servier* (n 15); *JSC BTA Bank v Khrapunov* [2020] AC 717 (SC), [6] (Lords Sumption and Lloyd-Jones); *Holyoake v Candy* [2017] EWHC 3397 (Ch), [7] (Nugee J); *Erste Group Bank AG (London) v JSC (VMZ Red October)* [2015] EWCA Civ 379 (CA), [10] (Gloster LJ).

Particularly noteworthy in this context is the decision in *Chalfont St Peter Parish Council v Holy Cross Sisters Trustees Inc.*[17] This was a case in which what was at stake were the aspirations of a parish council that opposed the development of a former catholic school at location A (ie, in the heart of the village). The council wanted the premises to be taken over by an Anglican school so that the premises currently occupied by the Anglican school (at location B) could be developed instead. The council preferred the idea of location B (which lay outside the village) being developed because this would allow the character of the village to be preserved. The allegation made by the council was that the planning permission to develop location A had been obtained fraudulently and that it was via these unlawful means, directed at a third party, that its own interests (in preserving the character of the village) were being harmed. Swift J rejected the council's claim. He held that no action would lie because the parish council had no economic interests that were at stake. In his view, this was critical because 'the clear inference in the speeches in *OBG v Allan* is that the tort is aimed only at the protection of forms of economic interest'.[18]

With respect, however – and mindful of my commitment to taking seriously what the courts say – I would suggest that Swift J misinterpreted what was said in *OBG*. And I would argue, too, that a careful reading of the early cases reveals no such constraint, either. These two claims require some defending.

B. Challenges to the Conventional View on Scope

Overt judicial talk of trade and business interests in this sphere first appeared in *Keeble v Hickeringill*, where it was said that 'he that hinders another in his trade or livelihood is liable to an action for so doing'.[19] But even so, the case cannot be taken as a reliable guide to the interests protected by the unlawful means tort for the simple reason, given by Lord Watson in *Allen v Flood*, that '[t]he act complained of [in *Keeble*] was, in substance, the making of a noise so close to the lands of the plaintiff as to be *a nuisance*'.[20] In other words, it was a nuisance case and not one involving the unlawful means tort. The defendant was being sued in relation to his firing guns on his own land, not in order to kill game or wild fowl, but simply to frighten birds that would otherwise have been attracted to the claimant's decoy pond where they would have been caught and subsequently sold by the claimant.[21]

The key point here is that, for the purposes of understanding the scope of the tort of causing loss by unlawful means, nothing conclusive can be read into what

[17] *Chalfont St Peter Parish Council v Holy Cross Sisters Trustees Inc* [2019] EWHC 1128 (QB).

[18] *Ibid*, [99].

[19] *Keeble v Hickeringill* (1706) 11 East 574, 575–76 (Holt CJ).

[20] *Allen* (n 6) 101 (emphasis added). Lord Davey offered a more or less identical interpretation of the case: *ibid*, 174.

[21] Trading interests do not enjoy independent juridical significance even in the nuisance context. Rather, injury to them is a mere indication of the negative impact upon the amenity interest (which is what really lies at the heart of most nuisance cases).

was said in *Keeble*. Lord Herschell was clear about this in *Allen v Flood*. In the course of his addressing the question of whether there exists the 'principle that intentional interference with the trade of another is wrongful'[22] he proffered the following observation:

> if the defendant merely fired on his own land in the ordinary use of it, his neighbour could make no complaint, whilst, if he was not firing for any legitimate purpose, connected with the ordinary use of land, he might be held to commit a nuisance ... [But] *Keeble v Hickeringill* has, of course, no bearing on the present case [ie, *Allen v Flood*].[23]

Equally, even though there was an intense focus on traders' rights in *Mogul Steamship Co Ltd v McGregor Gow & Co*,[24] there was nothing said there about the tort of causing loss by unlawful means being confined to the protection of economic interests. Indeed, the only tort involving unlawful means considered in the case was that of unlawful means conspiracy. And, likewise, although in *Quinn v Leathem* Lord Shand addressed his mind to 'the question whether the intention of the defendants was to injure the plaintiff in his trade',[25] that case was one of lawful means conspiracy.

Allen v Flood, however, cannot be put to one side. But nor can it be taken as conclusive of the need to show harm to trade or business interests in order to invoke the unlawful means tort. For a start, as noted already, the significance of malice was what dominated the decision in that case, not the question of what interests were protected by the unlawful means tort. Furthermore, among those of their Lordships who did express an opinion on the matter, there was clear opposition to the idea that it was a tort of narrow compass. Lord Herschell, for example, was dismissive of the idea that there was anything special about trade or employment interests in this context. He said: 'a man cannot be called upon to justify either act or word merely because it interferes with another's trade or calling' since 'the notion that there may be a difference in this respect between acts affecting trade or employment and other acts seems to be largely founded on certain dicta of Bowen LJ in the case of the Mogul Steamship Company'.[26] Indeed, he was adamant that it 'be remembered that these [words of Bowen LJ] were [just] obiter dicta'.[27] And lest there be any doubt about how expansive he considered the unlawful means tort to be, he said, just a few pages later (in a passage that, conspicuously, was never cited in *OBG*):

> It is suggested that it is difficult to explain this decision [in *Garret v Taylor*[28]] except on the ground that the law recognises in every man a right to carry on his trade without disturbance. I am unable to see ... that the case rests on any principle specially relating

[22] *Allen* (n 6) 133.
[23] *Ibid.*
[24] *Mogul Steamship Co Ltd v McGregor Gow & Co* [1892] AC 25 (HL).
[25] *Quinn v Leathem* [1901] AC 495 (HL), 512.
[26] *Allen* (n 6) 133.
[27] *Ibid.*
[28] *Garret v Taylor* (1620) Cro Jac 367.

> to trade. If the plaintiff had not been a tradesman, but the owner of a house, and the same menaces had been uttered to those who came from time to time to visit him, I cannot but think that he would equally have had a cause of action.[29]

A similar reluctance to confine the tort to the protection of trade or business interests is evident in Lord Davey's speech. He considered it 'strange that if there be any such right of action *for interference with trade*, there is not to be found some clear authority in the law books in its favour'.[30] And he also observed – in the course of assessing various earlier cases in which people's livelihoods (like those of Flood and Taylor) had been affected – that '[a] man has no right to be employed by any particular employer, and has no right to any particular employment' before adding, '[n]or does it appear to me that the gist of the action in those cases was that the plaintiff was a trader or exercised a profitable calling'.[31] These remarks, too, went uncited in *OBG*.

Lord James, also, could 'see no ground for saying that any different rule should be applied to cases of interference with a man when carrying on his trade or business, or when he is engaged in any other pursuit';[32] while Lord Watson, in laying out his (classic) two-tort structure, made no reference to any need to show economic harm.[33] Even Lord Halsbury, the most powerful of the three dissentients in that case, seemed unprepared to confine actionable loss to trade and business interests.[34] Woolf LJ captured the true state of affairs in *Lonrho Plc v Fayed (No 1)* when he said that 'the tort relied upon by Lonrho of unlawful interference is still, in my view, of uncertain ambit'.[35] So how, if at all, did things change with the decision in *OBG*?

Lord Hoffmann, as we have already noted, was clearly of the view that the tort was of limited scope, one that required 'a wrongful interference with the actions of a third party in which the claimant has an economic interest'. However – and this is crucial – there is no insistence here that D should have targeted that particular economic interest (ie, the one that C has with the intermediary). All that Lord Hoffmann said was that there should be some kind of economic relation between C and the intermediary. Indeed, elsewhere in his speech he suggested the possibility of the tort's being used to protect non-economic interests. He said: '[i]t is sufficient that the intended consequence of the wrongful act is *damage in any form*; for example, to the claimant's economic expectations'.[36]

Arguably then, the need for an economic relationship between the third party and the claimant – the dealing requirement which has subsequently been

[29] *Allen* (n 6) 136.
[30] *Ibid*, 174.
[31] *Ibid*, 173.
[32] *Ibid*, 180.
[33] *Ibid*, 96.
[34] 'The right invaded', he opined, was 'freedom from restraint, that liberty of action, which, in my view, may be found running through the principles of our law': *ibid*, 72.
[35] *Lonrho* (n 13) 493.
[36] *OBG* (n 2) [8].

confirmed to be an essential element of the tort[37] – is better seen as a *locus standi* rule[38] than as one that serves to delimit the kinds of losses that are recoverable.[39] Of course, there is a strong indication from the general tenor of his speech that Lord Hoffmann may have favoured restricting the protection of this tort to economic losses; and it is true that the loss he referred to as a mere example – that of economic expectations – does not exhaust the category of economic losses. But he never actually said that recoverable losses were confined to those of a economic kind.[40] And the fact that he never quite said this has been regarded as salient by Deakin and Randall *even though* they support the idea that the tort's scope *should be* narrowly confined to the protection of trade and business interests. With more than just a hint of regret, they write:

> [Although] Lord Hoffmann came close to adopting this approach … [a] more straightforward approach would have been to stress the need for the claimant to show that he had an economic interest not in the specific relation with the third party that was being interfered with, but, more generally, in a trade business, or employment which was the subject or target of the defendant's action.[41]

Thus, given that Lord Hoffmann stopped short of stating unambiguously that the unlawful means tort is confined to the protection of trade and business interests, and given that many of the judgments in the milestone case of *Allen v Flood* clearly countenance an expansive role for this tort, is there any good reason for considering its scope to be restricted in the way that many commentators and courts (conspicuously below House of Lords level) have since suggested? I do not think that there is. Instead, we may advert to six reasons which I think combine to fortify my suggestion that the remit of this tort should not be so confined.

To begin with, Philip Sales and Daniel Stilitz have made a compelling case in favour of allowing the tort to be invoked by claimants who suffer mental distress or inconvenience. Their argument can be reduced to the following proposition: it is nonsensical to treat differently two claimants, who were identically positioned in relation to the third party, but who happened to suffer different types of harm. Their analysis takes as its starting point the decision in *Falconer v ASLEF and NUR*.[42]

[37] *Servier* (n 15) [63].

[38] Note: saying that it functions as a *locus standi* rule is not the same as saying that it was *designed* as a *locus standi* rule. It is, after all, far from obvious that there is a potential floodgates problem here.

[39] It is certainly notable that in the most recent consideration of the matter, their Lordships regarded it conceivable that the unlawful means tort could in future be argued to be available in connection with losses of a non-economic variety: see *Servier* (n 15) [85] (Lord Hamblen).

[40] The closest that he got to this was when he said that '[u]nlawful means … consists of acts intended to cause loss to the claimant by interfering with the freedom of a third party in a way which is unlawful as against that third party and which is intended to cause loss to the claimant. It does not in my opinion include acts which may be unlawful against a third party but which do not affect his freedom to deal with the claimant': *OBG* (n 2) [51].

[41] Deakin and Randall (n 4) 533–34.

[42] *Falconer v ASLEF and NUR* [1986] IRLR 331.

In that case, the claimant bought a ticket from British Rail to travel by train to a business appointment. Trade union action caused certain British Rail employees to withdraw their labour and the claimant was unable to travel on the planned date, but he was still liable to pay his hotel expenses. The industrial action was unlawful (because the defendants had failed to call a ballot of its members in accordance with the relevant legislation). The defendants were held liable to pay damages to the would-be traveller. Mindful of this decision, Sales and Stilitz put forward a hypothetical in which a similar disruption is caused by D which affects not just business passengers, but also those travelling for recreational purposes. In their view, 'it would be invidious indeed if business passengers could recover, but those out on a day trip could not'.[43] What makes this argument a particularly compelling rejoinder to what was said in *OBG* by Lord Hoffmann is that, in *Hunter v Canary Wharf Ltd*, Lord Hoffmann himself opined that there is 'no reason why a tort of intention should be subject to the rule which excludes compensation for mere distress, inconvenience or discomfort in actions based on negligence'.[44] With that dictum in mind, it is – as Sales and Stilitz observe – 'difficult to see why those who suffer loss as a result of a defendant's deliberate wrongdoing aimed at them should not be able to recover damages merely because they suffer no damage to any trade, profession or business'.[45]

Of course, Sales and Stilitz were writing before the House of Lords decided *OBG*. So, their argument *of principle* – however appealing it may appear – will count for nothing if the day-tripper cannot be said to meet Lord Hoffmann's requirement that there be 'a wrongful interference with the actions of a third party in which the claimant has an economic interest'. But in fact the day-tripper can do this. For as Nicholas McBride and Roderick Bagshaw point out in their endorsement of the Sales and Stilitz argument:

> A passenger who was planning to spend the day at the seaside with his family but whose journey was ruined by the defendant's actions could bring himself within Lord Hoffmann's definition of … the intentional harm tort, as the defendant's actions have interfered with the train company's freedom to provide its services to the passenger.[46]

The claimant, in other words, does indeed possess the requisite economic link with the third party. It is simply that the harm that he suffers as a consequence of the defendant's wrongdoing is harm of a non-economic kind.[47]

[43] P Sales and D Stilitz, 'Intentional Infliction of Harm by Unlawful Means' (1999) 115 *LQR* 411, 431. I think, though the authors do not spell this out, that there is an assumption here that a day-tripper's contract is of a kind the breach of which would ordinarily justify damages in respect of disappointment or distress.

[44] *Hunter v Canary Wharf Ltd* [1997] AC 655 (HL), 707.

[45] Sales and Stilitz (n 43) 431.

[46] NJ McBride and R Bagshaw, *Tort Law*, 6th edn (London, Pearson, 2018) 671.

[47] Deakin and Randall seem to recognise this possibility when they write that Lord Hoffmann's test is one 'which might have been satisfied on the facts of *Falconer v Aslef* … [since the Union] interfered with BR's freedom to deal with its passengers, including the claimant': Deakin and Randall (n 4) 549.

A second reason to reject the idea that Lord Hoffmann should be read as having confined the scope of the unlawful means tort to business and trade interests is the fact that, on close inspection, even those cases that are sometimes cited as offering obiter support for this approach, in fact do nothing of the sort. Take for example, the dictum of Bowen LJ in the *Mogul Steamship* case. This, as was noted earlier, was considered by Lord Herschell (in *Allen v Flood*) to be supportive of the view that the tort of causing loss by unlawful means is specifically an *economic* tort. Yet this is not what Bowen LJ actually said. True, he certainly did provide a fairly comprehensive list of the instances in which a trader might claim in respect of an interference with his 'right' to trade. But his doing so ought not to be confused with his suggesting that the various torts he mentioned were all specifically limited to the protection of trade or business interests. Saying that a given tort *can protect* trade and business interests is not the same as saying that it *can only protect* trade and business interests. Importantly, in the passage (which Deakin and Randall describe as being 'canonical'[48]), Bowen LJ was not actually seeking to delimit the domain of the unlawful means tort. He was merely trying to sketch the extent to which the 'right' to trade is protected by the law of torts. The question that Bowen LJ set himself was this: 'What, then, are the limitations which the law imposes on a trader in the conduct of his business as between himself and other traders?'.[49] He then proceeded to illustrate the fact that those limits could be found in a host of places, including the torts of deceit, intimidation, inducing breach of contract and nuisance.[50]

In the course of doing just this, he did not single out the unlawful means tort, nor did he define it by reference to the protection of such interests, and nor did he suggest that any of the torts that he mentioned were limited to the protection of trade or business interests. They were identified by him as mere examples of torts in which harm to such interests might be compensated. The two enterprises are very different and must not be confused. To take a parallel example: most textbooks on the law of torts devote space to sketching the extent to which pure economic loss is protected by the tort of negligence; but in doing so, the relevant authors are not attempting to show that the tort of negligence may be defined (or confined) by reference to its limited capacity to provide a remedy in relation to pure economic loss.

Third, we should not overlook the obiter comments of Lord Evershed in *Rookes v Barnard*. For while, here and there in *Rookes*, one may certainly find remarks supportive of the idea that the unlawful means tort is confined specifically to the protection of economic interests, this is not a case of one-way traffic. According to Lord Evershed, a claimant, A,

> might well, as a consequence of B's intimidation, suffer in many ways including health, and, if he did, then, as I conceive, his cause of action against B would be founded on the

[48] *Ibid*, 534.
[49] (1889) LR 23 QBD 598, 614.
[50] *Ibid*.

> tort of intimidation and would not be confined, by reference to the damage suffered, to interference with his business.[51]

Admittedly, this hypothetical was strictly speaking one that concerned two-party intimidation. But even so, I think it is highly unlikely that his Lordship considered the two-party version of the tort of intimidation to be protective of a wider array of interests than its three-party sibling. Indeed, in *Rookes*, two- and three-party intimidation were not considered separate torts, but as structurally different branches of the same tort. It is only in the wake of *OBG* that we have had cause to think of the latter as a mere sub-branch of the unlawful means tort. Accordingly, it is not unreasonable to assume that Lord Evershed was also of the view that health was compensable under the auspices of three-party intimidation.

Fourth, it is hard to accept the idea sometimes impliedly advanced, that the original conception of the unlawful means tort is of an action that is specifically concerned with the protection of trade or business interests.[52] The reason this is hard to accept is that the very idea of economic torts did not exist at this time. As we saw in chapter one, the entry into the legal lexicon of the phrase 'economic torts' did not occur until the second half of the twentieth century. Accordingly, in the absence of any *a priori* commitment to the idea that the cases they were deciding were specifically 'economic tort' cases, it seems presumptuous to cite cases, like *Mogul*, *Allen* and *Quinn*, in support of the contention that the judges who decided them were seeking to elaborate the ingredients of torts whose specific function was to protect economic interests against certain types of invasion.

Fifth, despite Lord Hoffmann's obvious attraction to the idea that the tort of causing loss by unlawful means is best conceived as an 'economic tort', it remains demonstrably the case (as noted) that the relevant authorities do not unequivocally establish that harm to one's trade or business interests is an essential ingredient of this tort. Neyers, for example, rightly observes that, 'little was said in the recent decision in *OBG* [about whether economic loss is an essential ingredient] since it was evident that all the plaintiffs had suffered economic losses'.[53] And Robert Stevens, too, submits that, '[i]n principle, there is no reason why the relevant harm unlawfully inflicted needs to be economic: it could be distress or physical discomfort'.[54] This lack of finality in *OBG* is important to note,[55] for it is by no means clear that when, ultimately, the matter falls to be resolved – and the

[51] *Rookes v Barnard* [1964] AC 1129 (HL), 1194.

[52] Carty, for example, states that 'the House of Lords' decision in *Allen v Flood* … set the agenda for … the economic torts': see H Carty, *An Analysis of the Economic Torts*, 2nd edn (Oxford, Oxford University Press, 2010) 17. She also makes an almost identical claim slightly earlier in the book: see *ibid*, 6.

[53] Neyers (n 10) 219.

[54] R Stevens, *Torts and Rights* (Oxford, Oxford University Press, 2007) 189. For an essentially similar view, see McBride and Bagshaw (n 46) 671; and Beever (n 5) 135.

[55] The idea that the unlawful means used against the intermediary must affect the trading relations between the claimant and that intermediary was applied by the Supreme Court in its recent decision in *Servier* (n 15).

Supreme Court specifically declined to resolve it in *Secretary of State for Health v Servier Laboratories Ltd*[56] – it will be resolved in favour of a tort concerned exclusively with economic losses. It is certainly noteworthy that other commentators remain unconvinced that this tort is, or should be, limited to the protection of trade or business interests. The train passengers hypothetical supplied by Sales and Stilitz constitutes one excellent example of where C may have the requisite economic relationship with the intermediary, and yet suffer non-economic loss. But other such hypotheticals are not difficult to construct.[57]

Imagine – in an adaptation of a scenario suggested by Tony Weir[58] – that there were a kidney patient, C, who had a contract for the provision of regular dialysis by a private doctor. Suppose, also, that C's sworn enemy and next-door neighbour, D, kidnaps the doctor (thus preventing her from treating C). In such a case, C ought to be able to recover damages when alternative treatment cannot be arranged at short notice and her health deteriorates as a result of this. Any such remedy would be granted in connection with C's personal injury (and not for an economic loss). But, just as with the train passenger whose plans for a day trip are thwarted, C would here be able to demonstrate Lord Hoffmann's required economic link with the intermediary. Furthermore, it seems deeply counterintuitive to suppose that C's loss would or should be ruled out simply because it took the form of personal injury rather than economic loss.

To take another example, if D were to kidnap, say, a puppeteer hired by C to put on a show at C's daughter's birthday party, it is hard to see why a claim based on C's disappointment should not succeed.[59] It would be just the same – but perhaps more obvious – if D kidnapped a chef hired to provide a special dinner for C and her guests just an hour before the dinner preparations were due to begin.

What makes the idea that the claims in these hypotheticals should fail so repugnant is the fact that, as one commentator put it: 'in the hierarchy of protected values wealth, especially corporate wealth is simply not as important as the well-being of the individual and does not deserve equal protection'.[60] This particular

[56] *Servier* (n 15) [85] (Lord Hamblen). Here, his Lordship acknowledged the possibility that non-economic losses might plausibly be argued to fall within the remit of this tort even though the existing authorities have not yet gone this far. He refrained from offering his own view on the matter on the footing that it was not in issue in the case before him. He noted that, '[h]istorically the tort has been so confined [to the protection of economic interests] but acknowledged immediately thereafter that '[i]t may be that in an appropriate case a challenge is made to the established position': *ibid.*

[57] For examples based on personal injury and property damage being caused by unlawfully preventing a third party performing their contract with C, see R Bagshaw, 'Lord Hoffmann and the Economic Torts' in PS Davies and J Pila (eds), *The Jurisprudence of Lord Hoffmann* (Oxford, Hart Publishing, 2015) 61.

[58] T Weir, 'Chaos or Cosmos: *Rookes*, *Stratford* and the Economic Torts' [1964] *CLJ* 225, 228 (Weir envisaged the kidnap of a prima donna who would thus be prevented from performing for C).

[59] In the previous chapter, it was argued that D should in principle be liable for *inducing breach* of such a contract. That being so, D ought to be liable for unlawfully *preventing performance* of such a contract.

[60] T Weir, *Economic Torts* (Oxford, Clarendon Press, 1997) 9–10. For an expression of this hierarchy in terms of the relative weight of different rights, see R Stevens, 'The Conflict of Rights' in A Robertson

prioritisation of personal well-being over economic welfare was openly acknowledged in *Allen v Flood*.[61] And Lord Herschell, as noted above, was certainly prepared to countenance other forms of loss than those of an economic variety caused by an interference in the trading relations that existed between the claimant and the intermediary. Also, the idea that the tort should be limited to the protection of trade or other economic interests (and not include physical well-being) is hard to square with the hierarchy of protected interests that is sometimes acknowledged by judges[62] and jurists[63] to exist within tort law.

The sixth, but by no means the least important reason for regarding the unlawful means tort as protective of interests other than those of an economic variety, can be unearthed from the fact that, in *OBG*, it was held that cases that had formerly been regarded as falling under the banner of three-party intimidation should now be seen as mere instances of the unlawful means tort. Drawing upon *Garret v Taylor*[64] and *Tarleton v M'Gawley*,[65] Lord Hoffmann was keen to point out that in both of these early cases – which John Salmond dubbed cases of 'intimidation' – D's threatening a third party (with the ultimate intention of causing loss to C) was an unlawful act.[66] This meant, he said, that 'Salmond's tort of intimidation is … only one variant of a broader tort, usually called "causing loss by unlawful means"'.[67] His Lordship's treatment of these cases in this way is important because, as McBride and Bagshaw correctly point out, 'the tort of *three-party intimidation* put no limit on the way in which a claimant might

and HW Tang, *The Goals of Private Law* (Oxford, Hart Publishing, 2009). For an examination of derogations from this hierarchy – none of which is relevant here – see J Murphy, 'Tort's Hierarchy of Protected Interests' [2022] *CLJ* (forthcoming).

[61] *Allen* (n 6) 72 (Lord Halsbury): 'there was no right in this country under our laws so sacred as the right of personal liberty. No right of property or capital … was so sacred or so carefully guarded by the law'.

[62] See, eg, Davies and Sales (n 1) 84: 'the usual priority in the law of tort is for protection of individuals' physical integrity and property'.

[63] Peter Cane suggests the existence of such a hierarchy that takes in: (1) personal interests; (2) property interests; (3) contractual rights; (4) non-contractual expectancies; (5) trade values; and (6) purely financial interests: see P Cane, *The Anatomy of Tort Law* (Oxford, Hart Publishing, 1997) 90. Nicholas McBride (dealing with private law generally) proffers a scheme of primary, secondary and tertiary goods: see NJ McBride, *The Humanity of Private Law* (Oxford, Hart Publishing, 2019) 125: 'a private law [concerned with promoting human flourishing] … could be expected … to place the highest value on people's enjoying the primary goods … and the next highest value on people's enjoying the secondary goods … and the next highest value after that on people's enjoying tertiary goods'. See also *Murphy v Brentwood DC* [1990] 1 AC 398 (HL), 487 (Lord Oliver): '[t]he infliction of physical injury to the person or property of another universally requires to be justified. The causing of economic loss does not'. For others who note the existence of such a hierarchy, see Carty (n 52) 4–5; H Carpenter, 'Interference with Contractual Relations' (1928) 41 *Harvard Law Review* 728, 746.

[64] *Garret v Taylor* (n 28).

[65] *Tarleton v M'Gawley* (1794) Peake 270.

[66] On the independent juridical significance attached to *illegitimate threats*, see, eg, *Rookes* (n 51) 1200–1201 (Lord Hodson): 'the vice of the respondents' action is the threat to break and not the breach itself'. *Cf* the position with respect to lawful threats set out in *Allen* (n 6) 165 (Lord Shand): 'A master who warns his servant that a repetition of certain faults will result in dismissal may be said to use a threat; but he is not only acting lawfully, but in most cases is to be commended for so doing in place of giving an instant dismissal'. On the way in which legitimate and illegitimate threats can be distinguished, see J Murphy, 'Understanding Intimidation' (2014) 77 *MLR* 33, 38–44.

[67] *OBG* (n 2) [7]. See also, in similar vein, *ibid*, [150] (Lord Nicholls).

suffer loss'.[68] Certainly, as we have seen, the talk in *Rookes*, as well as in a number of subsequent cases, was of harm generally, and not economic loss in particular.[69] Accordingly, it is particularly noteworthy that the very judge whose dictum is inconclusive in *OBG* on which losses are recoverable should be the one to have subsumed within the unlawful means tort those cases that suggest protection of interests other than those of a purely economic variety.

One possible rejoinder here is that it is not so easy to describe the tort of three-party intimidation established in *Rookes* as being a mere subspecies of the unlawful means tort. Deakin and Randall certainly think that 'it is very difficult to see how *OBG* can stand alongside the House's decision in *Rookes v Barnard*'.[70] And their reason for so thinking is that, in *Rookes*, there was no independently actionable wrong committed against the recipients of the threat *so long as* one discounts the jurisdiction in equity to issue an injunction *quia timet* against the threatened strike action.[71] But discounting the possibility of injunctive relief in this context is prevented by Court of Appeal authority.

Just because a wrong can furnish only injunctive relief does not mean that it is *not an actionable tort*. Just this point was made in *Torquay Hotel Co Ltd v Cousins*.[72] A key question there was whether an action for an injunction *quia timet* against a trade union was barred by the tortious immunity granted to such bodies under the Trade Disputes Act 1906. The claimant argued that, while actions for damages were certainly barred (on the basis that 'the intention of Parliament in passing the Act was to protect trade union funds'[73]), no such immunity existed in respect of actions for an injunction. More specifically, asserted the claimant, although the statute afforded immunity in tort, '[a]n injunction can be granted against a trade union because *quia timet* proceedings are not founded in tort [but in equity]'.[74] Lord Denning MR flatly rejected this submission, holding that such actions were indeed *actions in tort* (and that they were, moreover, actions to which the statutory immunity extended). He said:

> [The statute] clearly prohibits an action for damages. But does it prevent an action for an injunction? The words are a 'tortious act *alleged to have been committed*' … It would be strange if a trade union could *not* be sued for the wrong [already] done … but *could* be sued for the self-same wrong to be done in the future.[75]

In the light of this authority, it is implausible to argue (as Deakin and Randall seek to do) that threats which are not by themselves enough to ground an award

[68] McBride and Bagshaw (n 46) 645.

[69] See, eg, *Rookes* (n 51) 1202 (Lord Hodson): 'reasonably foreseeable damage'; *Newsgroup Newspapers Ltd v SOGAT ('82)* [1987] ICR 181 (CA), 204 (Stuart-Smith J): '[C] must be a person whom [D] intended to injure'; *Morgan v Fry* [1968] 2 QB 710 (CA), 724 (Lord Denning): 'the person damnified … can sue for intimidation' (endorsed in *Berezovsky v Abramovich* [2011] 1 WLR 2290 (CA), [5] (Longmore LJ).

[70] Deakin and Randall (n 4) 546.

[71] *Ibid*, 547.

[72] *Torquay Hotel Co Ltd v Cousins* [1969] 2 Ch 106 (CA).

[73] *Ibid*, 130.

[74] *Ibid*.

[75] *Ibid*, 140 (italics in the original).

of damages are not independently actionable civil wrongs because the most that a claimant can hope to obtain is an injunction *quia timet*.

C. The Rationale of the Unlawful Means Tort

One of the central claims of this book is that the so-called economic torts are not concerned exclusively with the protection of economic interests. Accordingly, the preceding pages have gone to considerable lengths to show that, neither as a matter of established law nor as a matter of principle can it be said that the tort of causing loss by unlawful means does and should fulfil this role.[76] As was noted with some care, no such claim was ever made to this effect in the landmark decision in *Allen v Flood*. The significance of malice was what dominated that case and – insofar as judicial opinions were expressed about the types of harm protected by the unlawful means tort – they were uniformly expressed *obiter*, and in any event went both ways. *Rookes* gave no *firm* indication about the purview of three-party intimidation, though there was undoubtedly a willingness in that case to countenance recovery for losses of a non-economic kind. Also, there are statements in various cases decided after *Rookes* which suggest that *any* form of harm recognised by tort law generally is recoverable on facts that fit the three-party intimidation mould. And any such case would, of course, nowadays be treated as one involving the unlawful means tort given the way that three-party intimidation cases were treated in *OBG*.

For quite some time, scholars have been just as divided as the judges on the question of whether the operation of the unlawful means tort is confined to the protection of trade and business interests. As noted, a fair number of commentators – including Sales and Stilitz, McBride and Bagshaw, and Stevens – have proffered compelling arguments *of principle* as to why the tort should *not* be limited in this way. Mindful that nothing conclusive was said on the matter in *OBG*, I added to that list of reasons. And yet, the idea that this is aptly considered a tort whose rationale is the protection of economic interests persists. I would suggest that the explanation as to why this is so was well captured by Sales and Stilitz when they wrote:

> It may be that the label of 'interference with business' has retained its currency largely as a description of the tort's typical application. However, the correct view, in the light of *Allen v Flood*, is that an action founded on the intentional harm tort is a simple action on the case, which will lie whenever a plaintiff can demonstrate that he has suffered damage.[77]

[76] One caveat here is that in *Mbasogo v Logo Ltd* [2007] QB 846 (CA) it was held by Sir Anthony Clarke MR that mental distress short of a recognised psychiatric condition was not recoverable. His reason for so saying (*ibid*, [99]) was tethered to the fact that the Protection from Harassment Act 1997 requires acts inflicting such harm on at least two occasions: '[since] Parliament has chosen not to provide for compensation arising out of a single action … it seems to us impossible for the court to recognise such a right by development of the common law'.

[77] Sales and Stilitz (n 43) 431.

It is probably stretching things a little to say, as they do, that damages are available 'whenever' a claimant suffers damage since some losses might still conceivably be regarded as too remote;[78] and a defence of justification may perhaps also be available here and there.[79] But these exceptions aside, the general point that causing loss by unlawful means is best seen as a tort that is capable of being invoked in connection with a broader range of interests than is commonly supposed or suggested seems sound enough. Implicitly sympathetic to such thinking, Neyers predicts that, so far as this tort is concerned, the matter that will vex the courts going forward is just where the outer bounds of recoverable loss lie.[80]

At all events, we would do well to abandon certain alternative names for this action that are sometimes used. I have in mind here 'unlawful interference with business' and 'unlawful interference with economic interests'. The use of such labels runs the risk of embedding the belief that it can *only* be invoked in connection with specific forms of economic loss. Indeed, as we saw in chapter two, Carty is among those who resist the idea that it has (or has the potential to fulfil) an expansive role providing remedies for various forms of loss. In her view, recognising or attributing such a role to this tort would render it a largely incoherent, gap-filler. Instead, she is adamant that:

> The unlawful means tort remains linked to its history and to the prevention of excessive competitive conflict … As a result, this is not a gap-filler. It is a liability stretcher that helps claimants who are intentionally economically harmed by a civil wrong but who are one step beyond the normal privity rules of tort law.[81]

Carty's resistance to its performing a gap-filling role rests upon two concerns: a perceived 'need for certainty in the legality of commercial activity and judicial reluctance to assess fairness in competition'.[82] But both the desirability of legal certainty and the need for judges not to meddle in matters of fair competition have their limits as reasons for confining the unlawful means tort within its supposedly

[78] The question of whether remoteness applies to this tort is moot. On the one hand, it was said (obiter) by Lord Lindley in *Quinn* (n 25) 537 that '[t]he intention to injure the plaintiff negatives all excuses and disposes of any question of remoteness of damage'. But on the other hand, there are cases which suggest that a remoteness test *is* applied in torts that involve the intentional infliction of harm. The rule in question is that D will be liable for all losses caused as a *direct consequence* of D's tort. A test of this kind has, for example, been said to apply in cases of deceit (see, eg, *Smith New Court v Scrimgeour Vickers (Asset Management) Ltd* [1997] AC 254 (HL)).

[79] Whether such a defence may be invoked in relation to this tort is moot: see Carty (n 52) 100–101. Supporters include Deakin and Randall (n 4) 551; Weir (n 60) 76 and *Morgan* (n 69) 729. Opposition can be found in B Ong, 'Two Tripartite Economic Torts' (2008) 8 *Journal of Business Law* 723, 744–45 and Sales and Stilitz (n 43) 418 ('[this defence] cannot apply where D's actions are unlawful in themselves'). But such opposition is wrongheaded. No defence would ever succeed if D's acting unlawfully constituted a bar since D must always have done something wrong in order to need a defence in the first place. As one commentator once put it: '[o]ne must … take care of the question-begging phrase … "you cannot justify a wrongful act" … [since this] would kill the defence right away': Weir (n 58) 230.

[80] Neyers (n 10) 219.

[81] Carty (n 1) 277.

[82] *Ibid.*

traditional limits. To take her second worry first, the reason why the desire to keep judges away from matters of fair competition enjoys limited purchase in this context is because an expansion in the remit of this tort need not carry with it the danger of this occurring. In none of the hypotheticals suggested earlier was there any risk of this happening for the very simple reason that no issue of fair competition arose. In the example involving the interrupted medical services, the patient and his sworn enemy next door were not business rivals. So not even at a stretch could that case be conceptualised in terms of 'excessive competitive conflict'. In similar vein, those who kidnap puppeteers or chefs need not be business rivals of those who host events for children or dinner parties.

As regards Carty's first concern – the loss of commercial certainty if this tort were to be afforded a gap-filling role – there is, admittedly, *some risk*. But the danger is not, I think, of sufficient magnitude to warrant confining the operation of the action to the protection of trade and business interests. My reason for saying this stems from a common thread that links all the actions dealt with in this book. In chapter one, I made clear that one of my four main arguments would be that the torts in view are, in the modern era (but only in the modern era), broadly speaking linked by a discernible concern to make especially reprehensible wrongdoers tortiously accountable. The importance of that shared characteristic for present purposes is as follows.

The unlawful means tort always requires that D should have struck at C via an intermediary using means that constitute a civil wrong in order to do so. In other words, the tort will always turn on D's *intentional* wrongdoing and, on top of that, involve wrongs against *two* people. In all such cases, the intermediary will have been used as a mere means to inflict harm or loss on the claimant. A key characteristic of cases involving this tort, in other words, is the presence of especially egregious wrongdoing:[83] the fact that one abuses a middle-man, T, in order to inflict harm on C.[84] It is a feature which persuades Robert Stevens that its departure from what he calls 'the privity of torts' is justified, *even though* he otherwise considers tort law's bilateral structure to be a structural imperative. Yes: this tort fails to comply with that structural imperative, but at least 'it prevents D from using others for his own ends'.[85] The critical point here is that, by definition, cases of this kind have very little to do with *ordinary* commercial activity; yet it is only in relation to *ordinary* commercial activity that legal certainty is desirable.

[83] It is markedly more egregious in nature than is required for other intentional torts. If D intentionally steps onto land that he believes to be his own land, but which belongs to C, D may be liable for trespass (*Basely v Clarkson* (1682) 3 Lev 37). If a prison governor, in good faith (but without justification) deprives C of his liberty, he may still be held liable for false imprisonment (*R v Governor of Brockhill Prison Ex p Evans (No 2)* [2001] 2 AC 19 (HL)).

[84] It is of course entirely normal to seek to win over another person's customers, suppliers and employees *by accepted means*. Better products, better prices and better wages are all par for the course in this respect. But prying away another's customers, suppliers and employees by unlawful methods that a make a third party a means to an end is behaviour of an appreciably different order.

[85] Stevens (n 54) 188. For a similar observation, see Beever (n 5) 135.

On top of this it is important to realise that straying into territory where commercial certainty is put at risk has never been a red line for the judiciary in its development of the common law. Rather, as I have argued at length elsewhere, judicial legislation in the field of tort law is frequently driven, not so much by an overriding concern for internal coherence, as by a deep-seated concern to move with the times and do 'justice' *in novel scenarios* as and when the need arises.[86] The law of torts has a long track record of being the 'Swiss army knife of the common law'.[87] If a concern to achieve commercial certainty were of paramount importance, there presumably would not be – as Stapleton has ably shown that there is – such inconsistency in the way that the law of negligence has developed in relation to what she calls 'complex commercial arrangements'.[88]

III. Unlawful Means Conspiracy

For many years, it has been questioned in both judicial and academic circles whether the tort of unlawful means conspiracy adds anything distinctive to tort law. The various arguments proceed along four broad lines. First, there are those who believe that this action is really only an instance of joint tortfeasance. Next, there are those who consider it a mere subset of the tort of causing loss by unlawful means (the only distinguishing feature being that, in the case of unlawful means conspiracy, there will, or may, be multiple defendants). Third, there are those who doubt whether it can meaningfully be separated from lawful means conspiracy: it is, they argue, simply one part of a single, general tort of conspiracy. Finally, there are those who think that the tort is redundant and that the various cases decided according to this rubric could either be recast as instances of the unlawful means tort, or brought within a general principle of accessory liability for torts.[89] An important prefatory question, then, is whether there is anything of substance in these claims, whether there is nothing that is genuinely distinctive about unlawful means conspiracy.

[86] J Murphy, 'Contemporary Tort Theory and Tort Law's Evolution' (2019) 32 *Canadian Journal of Law and Jurisprudence* 413.

[87] A Beever, *Rediscovering the Law of Negligence* (Oxford, Hart Publishing, 2007) 197. See also, Murphy, *ibid*, 413.

[88] J Stapleton, *Three Essays on Torts* (Oxford, Oxford University Press, 2021) Ch 2.

[89] This last argument belongs to Davies and Sales. Their argument is overwhelmingly normative (as opposed to descriptive). As regards the broad suggestion, that conspiracy might in large part be subsumed within a broad principle of accessory liability that applies right across private law, they freely admit that '[t]he law has not (yet) explicitly recognised such a general principle': Davies and Sales (n 1) 79. They also admit, mindful of the decision in *Total Network* that for this case to be presented as a case involving the unlawful means tort, the concept of unlawful means for the purposes of the latter would need to include crimes as unlawful means: *ibid*, 87–88. Put another way, they do not contend that *on the law as it currently stands* unlawful means conspiracy is redundant, merely that it should be.

A. Distinctiveness of the Tort

As to the first contention just sketched, the argument, more fully expressed, runs as follows. If X has acted in combination with Y in Y's commission of a tort against Z, then Z need not establish conspiracy in order to sue X. Simple reliance on the well-established rules concerning joint tortfeasance will suffice.[90] In one case, Lord Denning put it thus: 'when a tort has been committed by two or more persons, an allegation of a prior conspiracy to commit the tort adds nothing'.[91] And Lord Dunedin said much the same thing in another one.[92] However, in two relatively recent cases, both decided at the highest judicial level, the falsity of such thinking was exposed.

In *Total Network*, the defendant had acted in combination with others in committing the common law crime of cheating the Revenue. Unlike very many crimes, however, this is not an offence that has a tort law equivalent. Accordingly, there was simply no prospect of alleging that the defendant was a joint tortfeasor. But the House of Lords held that an action could nonetheless be brought on the basis of unlawful means conspiracy.[93] There had been a combination to which the defendant was party, *and* the intended loss that was suffered by the Revenue had been brought about by the use of unlawful means. Moreover, just a few years later, in a case that reached the Supreme Court, Lords Sumption and Lloyd-Jones (in a joint speech with which Lords Mance, Hodge and Briggs agreed) could scarcely have been clearer in declaring that 'the tort of conspiracy is not simply a particular form of joint tortfeasance',[94] that 'it is not a form of secondary liability, but a primary liability'.[95] Thereafter, the independence of unlawful means conspiracy from joint tortfeasance could not seriously be doubted.

Their Lordships also made plain in *Total Network* the various ways in which unlawful means conspiracy comes apart from both lawful means conspiracy and the tort of causing loss by unlawful means. But since chapter seven is devoted to defending the contention that there is more that divides than unites the economic torts, detailed discussion of these differences is postponed until then. That said, I am conscious that my discussion of lawful means conspiracy is located in the next chapter, and that I split my discussion of the two torts that require unlawful means into separate sections in this chapter. So, in order to explain in a rudimentary way

[90] For academic support of this view, see Stevens (n 54) 249. *Cf* P Sales, 'The Tort of Conspiracy and Civil Secondary Liability' [1990] *CLJ* 491, 511 arguing that joint tortfeasance is not always a substitute for conspiracy given that 'one can imagine a case in which loss has been suffered by the plaintiff as a result of the co-ordinated activities of two defendants, but where the loss suffered by the plaintiff has resulted only from a combination of the wrongful acts of the first defendant and of the second defendant'.

[91] *Ward v Lewis* [1955] 1 WLR 9 (CA), 11.

[92] *Sorrell v Smith* [1925] AC 700 (HL), 716: 'if a combination of persons do what if done by one would be a tort, an averment of conspiracy so far as founding a civil action is mere surplusage'.

[93] Lords Walker, Mance and Neuberger were crystal clear in stating that unlawful means conspiracy was not a form of secondary liability: see *Total Network* (n 3) [104], [125] and [225] respectively.

[94] *Khrapunov* (n 16) [9].

[95] *Ibid.*

the reasons behind my making these divisions, I say a little here about the two sets of differences that exist before proceeding to my main concern in this chapter, namely, the scope and potential uses of unlawful means conspiracy.

i. Lawful Means Conspiracy Distinguished

It is by no means unknown for there to be two versions of a single tort. For example, libel and slander constitute two branches of the tort of defamation; and there are also two versions of the tort of misfeasance a public office.[96] It is therefore, perhaps, not surprising that one commentator should contend that lawful means conspiracy and unlawful means conspiracy are mere 'variants of a single species of primary liability',[97] while another should suggest that there is a single tort that simply 'comes in two flavours'.[98] Such thinking has occasionally been echoed in judicial quarters, though not in any case in which anything material was thought to hang on the question of whether they are two separate torts or merely two subspecies of a single tort.[99]

Even so, I think the better view is that the two conspiracy actions are sufficiently different to be regarded as separate torts in the same way that, say, private and public nuisance are very different torts in juridical terms (even though they, like the conspiracy torts, share a common element in terms of nomenclature). In addition to the important and obvious distinction that one of these actions turns on the use of lawful means while the other requires unlawful means, it is also noteworthy that the need for a predominant malicious purpose in the former tort sets a much more stringent test for liability than does the requirement of intentional injury in the latter.[100] As Lords Sumption and Lloyd-Jones recognised in *JSC BTA Bank v Khrapunov*, 'both lawful means and unlawful means conspiracies are torts of intent. But the nature of the intent required differs as between the two'.[101]

The differences in the means used and mental elements required are, I think, significant juridical distinctions. The depth of these divisions are not, in my view, matched when one considers either the two limbs of the misfeasance tort, or the two varieties of defamation. With the misfeasance tort, the so-called 'targeted malice' limb and the 'illegality' limb are *both* capable of being cashed out in terms of the infliction of harm via acts undertaken in bad faith.[102] Likewise, regardless of whether one is dealing with libel or slander, it is always injury to the claimant's

[96] See *Three Rivers DC v Governor and Company of the Bank of England (No 3)* [2003] 2 AC 1 (HL), 190.

[97] Ong (n 79) 723, 746.

[98] J O'Sullivan, 'Unlawful Means Conspiracy in the House of Lords' [2008] *CLJ* 459, 459.

[99] See, eg, *Khrapunov* (n 16) [8]: (Lords Sumption and Lloyd Jones): 'the tort takes two forms'; *Total Network* (n 3) [44] (Lord Hope): 'the [present] case is virtually indistinguishable from the tort of conspiracy to injure'.

[100] *Total Network* (n 3) [82] (Lord Walker).

[101] *Khrapunov* (n 16) [13].

[102] The intricacies of this tort are beyond the remit of this study, but for an excellent account of the juridical commonalities shared by the two versions of this tort, see D Nolan, 'Tort and Public Law: Overlapping Categories' (2019) 135 *LQR* 272, 276–77.

reputation that forms the gist of the action. The chief difference between the two forms of defamation is a mere *factual* one concerning the form in which the relevant statement about the claimant appears.[103]

To reiterate, the *juridical* differences that exist between the two conspiracy torts are altogether more significant. The fact that one version requires the use of unlawful means, while the other does not, is plainly very important. And as to the mental elements of these torts, it is noteworthy that Lord Walker said in *Total Network* that there is a 'clear distinction between the requirement of predominant purpose under one variety of the tort of conspiracy and the *lower requirement of intentional injury* needed for the other variety'.[104]

ii. Causing Loss by Unlawful Means Distinguished

Just as there is a significant juridical distinction between the two conspiracy torts, so is there also a considerable juridical gap between unlawful means conspiracy and the tort of causing loss by unlawful means. This difference, too, must be laid bare if we are to dispel the notion – put forward by some scholars – that unlawful means conspiracy is 'essentially an extension of the tort clarified in *Rookes*',[105] or that it 'is simply causing loss by unlawful means by multiple persons'.[106] Rebuttal of such contentions can be achieved in part by adverting to the fact that, while the tort of causing loss by unlawful means necessarily involves the infliction of harm or loss via an intermediary (the person with whom the claimant has the requisite economic link), the tort of unlawful means conspiracy can be committed directly. Lord Mance highlighted just this point in *Total Network*. He said:

> I accept that conspiracy can be categorised as a three- rather than two-party tort, in that liability depends on at least two persons joining together to injure another … Nevertheless there is in my view a distinction between the infliction of harm through the intermediary of a third party (as in the case of the tort of causing harm by unlawful means under consideration in *OBG Ltd v Allan*) and the present situation where two wrongdoers join and act together to inflict injury directly upon another person or body.[107]

On top of this, unlawful means conspiracy and the tort of causing loss by unlawful means can equally well be distinguished along the lines that, although only

[103] Loosely, libel involves defamation in permanent form, whereas slander involves defamation in impermanent form. It is true that in *some cases of slander* there may also be a need to prove loss caused by D's statement; but this is not universally true and therefore not an infallible means of distinguishing libel from slander.

[104] *Total Network* (n 3) [82].

[105] Deakin and Randall (n 4) 523.

[106] Beever (n 5) 104.

[107] *Total Network* (n 3) [124]. Others of their Lordships also stressed the fact that *Total Network* was a two-party case: see *ibid*, [43] and [223] (Lords Hope and Neuberger, respectively). But note, too, that unlawful means conspiracy can still operate in a three-party setting: see, eg, *Racing Partnership Ltd v Sports Information Services Ltd* [2021] 2 WLR 469 (CA).

actionable civil wrongs will constitute unlawful means for the purposes of the latter, the concept bears a much broader meaning in the context of unlawful means conspiracy. As the decisions in *Total Network* and *Khrapunov* have respectively made clear, common law crimes and acts amounting to a contempt of court will suffice in this setting. It is clear, then, given the stature of the courts that decided these two cases, that unlawful means conspiracy cannot plausibly be regarded as a mere sub-branch of the tort of causing loss by unlawful means.

B. Scope and Potential of Unlawful Means Conspiracy

Having established that unlawful means conspiracy deserves to be seen as a freestanding tort, I turn now to two important questions that arise in relation to its scope and potential uses. The first is whether it is a tort that can plausibly be thought to be limited to the protection of purely economic interests, and the second is whether – at least in the modern era – it can best be seen or used as a gap-filler whose role is to render liable in tort those who engage in especially egregious forms of collective wrongdoing that would otherwise not be tortious.

i. A Tort Confined to Economic Interests?

Writing about the modern function of unlawful means conspiracy, Carty has suggested that this tort serves to impose tortious liability for 'commercial misbehaviour that intentionally causes economic harm to the claimant'.[108] But few others who have contributed to the relevant literature – at least as far as I can see – have stated outright that its role is confined to the protection of such economic interests. Nonetheless, this is the impression that they inadvertently run the risk of conveying when they routinely refer to it as an *economic* tort.[109] For example, Lord Hope's dissenting speech in *Total Network* was clearly affected by such thinking. In his view, a critical feature of the case was that the Revenue Commissioners had no commercial interests of their own at stake. Because '[t]he commissioners are not authorised by the statute to carry on a business for profit', he began, '[t]hey have no commercial interests that need to be protected by the tort of conspiracy … Their only function is to gather in and account to the Crown for VAT charged'.[110] For Lord Hope, then, no action based on unlawful means conspiracy was available.

[108] Carty (n 1) 277. For a slight reformulation of the focus, see H Carty, 'The Tort of Conspiracy as a Can of Worms' in SGA Pitel *et al* (eds), *Tort Law: Challenging Orthodoxy* (Oxford, Hart Publishing, 2013): 'commercial or economic misbehaviour causing harm'.

[109] See, eg, McBride and Bagshaw (n 46) Ch 20; M Jones (ed), *Clerk and Lindsell on Torts*, 23rd edn (London, Sweet & Maxwell, 2020) Ch 23; C Witting, *Street on Torts*, 15th edn (Oxford, Oxford University Press, 2018) Ch 15; Deakin and Randall (n 4); Beever (n 5) Ch 8.

[110] *Total Network* (n 3) [28].

Lord Walker (who delivered the leading speech) was having none of this. He was firmly of the view that a personal economic loss is not required in order for a claimant to be able to sue on the basis of unlawful means conspiracy. Thus, he said, although '[t]he gist of the intentional harm tort [in *OBG*] … is striking at the claimant through, a third party, and doing so by interfering with his freedom of economic activity' a contrast can be made with unlawful means conspiracy since '[t]he gist … [of this tort] is damage intentionally inflicted by persons who combine for that purpose … and the claimant need not be a trader who is injured in his trade'.[111]

Furthermore, there is no intimation that economic loss was regarded as key in the early, landmark cases that either involved, or simply offered discussion of, unlawful means conspiracy. Indeed, the only conspiracy cases in which there is any trace of the idea that damage to trade or business interests is key are those concerning *lawful means* conspiracy.[112] In his study of the way that unlawful means conspiracy took shape in the minds of the late nineteenth and early twentieth century judges, Michael Lobban highlights the fact that the main debate centred around the question of whether it was malice, coercion, or simply the fact of combination that was the most salient element in this tort.[113] The infliction of economic loss was simply not a contender. In an attempt to 'remedy' this and place such loss at the heart of this tort, Deakin and Randall offer a highly creative interpretation of the decision in *Total Network*. They acknowledge that Lord Walker's analysis confounds their preferred understanding of its scope[114] – ie, the protection of trade and business interests – yet they seek to overcome that hurdle in the following way. They write:

> the result in *Total* is not necessarily incompatible with our approach. Market outcomes in which some actors thrive at the expense of others by committing crimes (as in *Total*) should in principle attract economic tort liability … [for] this is the very kind of situation in which the residual market-protecting role which we are suggesting for the economic torts comes into play … HMRC's claim, if it succeeds, can be seen as helping to bring to an end a situation in which illegal trading *harmed the integrity of the market* and *imposed losses on third parties*, including competitors, who would not themselves have been in a position to sue because they were not the intended victims of the conspiracy.[115]

The trouble with this approach, however, is that it is incompatible with the view (expressed elsewhere in the same article) that the economic torts are best seen as

[111] *Ibid*, [100].

[112] See *Quinn* (n 25) 512: 'the question [is] whether the intention of the defendants was to injure the plaintiff in his trade' (Lord Shand); and *ibid*, 526: 'the acts complained of [amount] to a serious and wrongful invasion of the plaintiff's trade rights' (Lord Brampton).

[113] See M Lobban, 'Intentional and Economic Torts' in W Cornish *et al* (eds), *The Oxford History of the Laws of England: Volume XII – Private Law* (Oxford, Oxford University Press, 2010) 1060–67.

[114] Deakin and Randall (n 4) 534.

[115] *Ibid*, (emphasis added).

addressing economic harm that was 'direct and targeted' against the claimant.[116] The attention in their attempt to explain *Total Network* focuses not on D's having targeted C and harmed C directly, but on D's having disturbed the 'integrity of the market' in such a way as to cause loss to 'third parties'. It is trite to state that tort law does not typically grant a remedy in favour of C in connection with harm visited by D upon society as a whole, or upon some third party who is himself unable to sue.[117] But in any case, the subsequent decision in *Khrapunov* is equally incapable of being regarded as one involving rival traders or harm to the market. The defendant in that case had conspired to conceal and dissipate assets allegedly stolen from the claimant bank by his co-conspirator, a former chairman of that bank. There was no market that was being affected here: the interests of those who could claim to be the bank's competitors were in no way impacted.

ii. A Tort to Address Especially Egregious Wrongdoing

For all that the tort of unlawful means conspiracy is not confined to cases involving the infliction of trade or business losses, it is still not a tort of widespread application. In large part, the reason for this is that, in the majority of cases in which it could be invoked – that is, where the unlawful means complained of constitute free-standing torts – it is also possible to eschew its use and rely instead on the established principles of joint-tortfeasance in holding liable those who assist the immediate wrongdoer in their commission of a tort. But its limited practical application should not be mistaken for redundancy. Indeed, one of the virtues of unlawful means conspiracy is that, in exceptional circumstances – by which I mean circumstances that would not fall within the compass of the joint commission of some other tort – unlawful means conspiracy can be invoked to provide a remedy for those who are victims of especially egregious, collaborative wrongdoing.

Total Network itself provides an excellent example of its being used to such effect. The common law crime of cheating the Revenue has no tort law equivalent, and there was insufficient evidence in that case to ground an action for deceit against either Total Network, or any of its co-conspirators.[118] But rather than allow the defendant to escape liability for cheating the Revenue, Lord Mance took the view that unlawful means conspiracy could be pressed into service as a gap-filler. He said: 'I think that there would be an evident lacuna if the law did not respond to this situation by recognising a civil liability'.[119]

[116] *Ibid*, 553.

[117] There are, however, certain (mainly statutory) exceptions such as the dependency action under the Fatal Accidents Act 1976, and the action conferred on a child born with disabilities under the Congenital Disabilities (Civil Liability) Act 1976.

[118] See *Total Network* (n 3) [10] (Lord Hope).

[119] *Ibid*, [120].

But there was plainly more to it than the fact that existing torts did not cover the situation at bar. What clearly vexed their Lordships in *Total Network* was the fact that the defendants had engaged in *especially egregious* conduct. For Lord Scott, the fact that the wrong in question did not occur within the usual paradigm setting of commercial rivalry was unimportant. What was key for him was that 'the harm had been caused in circumstances where the conduct of the authors of the harm had been sufficiently reprehensible to require the conclusion that they ought to be held responsible for the harm'.[120] And as Lord Neuberger pointed out, 'the law of tort takes a particularly censorious view where conspiracy is involved'.[121]

That especially reprehensible conduct – or, at least, conduct perceived to meet this description – has always been important in the context of this tort is something that was expressly recognised by Lord Walker in *Total Network*. He noted that,

> judges at the end of the 19th century … [subscribed to] the deep suspicion which the governing class had, in Georgian and Victorian England, of collective action in the political and economic spheres, as potential threats to the constitution and the framework of society.[122]

It was an observation endorsed by Lords Sumption and Lloyd-Jones in their jointly written speech in *Khrapunov* just shy of a decade later.[123] Of course, there are very good reasons to reject the depiction of Trade Unions as a special kind of social evil. But that is not the point. Rather, what is important – as will be seen at length in chapter eight – is that, when this tort was in its infancy, *certain* judges (and in particular, certain House of Lords judges), took such a dim, personal view of trade unions that they allowed their aversion to them to insinuate itself into their decision making.[124]

Recognising the long-standing preparedness of the courts to employ unlawful means conspiracy in connection with those perceived to be combining to do something especially reprehensible is helpful. For, it renders intelligible what some scholars consider to be the missteps of *Total Network* and *Khrapunov*. Carty, for example, objects to their Lordships treating a common law crime as unlawful means in the former. She thinks that their doing this threatened to 're-muddle the economic torts, taking them back to the twentieth-century' and that, potentially, it would unsettle various other areas of tort law.[125] As we have seen, however, it is easy enough to identify significant ways in which unlawful means conspiracy

[120] *Ibid*, [56].
[121] *Ibid*, [222].
[122] *Ibid*, [78].
[123] *Khrapunov* (n 16) [7].
[124] Other judges simply took a dim view of ganging up. See, eg, *Pratt v British Medical Association* [1919] 1 KB 244, 263 (McCardie J); and see also the various other judges cited therein who adopted a similar view.
[125] Carty, 'The Tort of Conspiracy' (n 108) 407.

can be distinguished from the other torts with which it has been confused in the past. Accordingly, so long as these differences are appreciated, it is not true that *Total Network* poses a risk of the economic torts getting muddled up again.[126] Also, treating a crime as unlawful means does not – as Carty presumably feared – threaten to unsettle the rules on tort liability for breach of a statutory duty. The fact that C, in showing D's unlawful means, may be permitted to advert to D's breach of a penal statute that has previously been held not to support an action in tort does not undermine that previous holding. This is because, in order to sue for unlawful means conspiracy, C must also show D's combination with another and that D intended to harm her. In other words, the extra ingredients of the tort prevent there being a situation in which C's showing D's breach of a penal statute will allow her to sue if she calls it conspiracy but not if she calls it breach of statutory duty.[127]

Beyond helping to render intelligible the cases of *Total Network* and *Khrapunov* (in both of which the claimant and defendant were *not* business rivals[128]), the courts' attentiveness to the presence of egregious wrongdoing also provides a means by which certain otherwise hard-to-reach defendants may be held to account within the civil law. For example, one possible use of unlawful means conspiracy involves its being employed to circumvent the 'problem' of corporate limited liability and make liable in damages the directors of a company who have committed acts that otherwise would not provide the claimant with a remedy in tort. Typical obstacles to obtaining damages from the company itself include its being under-capitalised, insolvent or simply otherwise unable to pay the cost of a successful claim for damages. Another, more remote, obstacle is that the company in question is responsible for a corporate crime for which there is no tort law counterpart. In any such case, the victim would ordinarily go without tortious redress. But if the directors can be treated as co-conspirators along with the company, then following the use of a crime as unlawful means in *Total Network*, an action in tort could well be made available.[129]

[126] It might be argued that if a two-party tort case can be founded on D's intentionally causing C loss by the use of criminal means used *directly* against C, it would only be a short step to say that a two-party version of the unlawful means tort could easily exist. This would require D having the requisite intention, and using criminal means and these means restricting C's freedom to trade. But this misapplies Lord Hoffmann's freedom to deal rule. His Lordship was crystal clear in *OBG* that the person whose freedom to deal with another must be affected is the third party (and not C): *OBG* (n 2) [51]: '[u]nlawful means therefore consists of acts intended to cause loss to the claimant by interfering with the freedom of a third party'.

[127] Also, the statute only sets limits on what sanctions may be brought to bear on the person who infringes its terms. So, even if the statute is a comprehensive guide to the sanctions that may be imposed on *conspirator No 1* (who commits the offence), that has no bearing on an action brought against *conspirator No 2* (who does not commit the offence).

[128] The Revenue Commissioners have no business rivals; and, equally, a bank's former chairman's son-in-law (as in *Khrapunov*) cannot be deemed a business rival of the bank.

[129] A possible objection here may run thus: since Parliament created a specific criminal offence, it is fair to assume that the creation of that crime was the only change to the law that it intended to make, and that it did not thereby authorise the courts to use the statute to extend civil liability. The point has *some* force. Yet it is difficult to square with the approach taken in *Total Network* and *Khrapunov*; and

The possibility of using this tort in the corporate context has been recognised by others. Writing proleptically in the immediate wake of *Total Network*, O'Sullivan suggested that there arises in relation to companies, 'the possibility that a director, being a separate person from the company, might incur tort liability for … conspiring with the company' which prospect would be 'particularly significant if the company is insolvent and no personal guarantee is in place from the director'.[130] And the point has been echoed in the work of other jurists,[131] as well as in the courts in a number of jurisdictions,[132] including England and Wales.

In *Palmer Birch v Lloyd*,[133] the facts were very complicated. But simplified, they involved two brothers who had arranged via two closely-linked companies for certain refurbishment work to be done on a particular property. The contract for this work was with a company (HHL) which was directed, *effectively*,[134] by the brothers. HHL, was an undercapitalised limited liability company with no guarantees for the payment of its debts by either of the brothers. It became insolvent before the invoices for the building work were paid. Thus, in the absence of a right to sue the brothers who stood behind the company, its insolvency represented a major obstacle to the claimant's obtaining compensation for the breach of contract. However, while it was not specifically argued by the claimant that either of the brothers had conspired with HHL, the judge nonetheless observed that they 'did collude to bring about the repudiatory breach';[135] and that 'it is clear that liability on the part of a director for the tort of conspiracy can arise where the company itself is also a wrongdoer'.[136]

On the other hand, HH Judge Russen QC did not commit himself to the proposition that it is possible for a conspiracy to occur between a director and a company where the company in question is a one-person company.[137] He simply

nor does it undermine the rule about civil actions for breach of statutory duty (because the director is not the one who has acted in breach of the statute). If the judicial will to take this step existed, it could certainly be taken without offending against established authority.

[130] J O'Sullivan, 'Intentional economic torts, commercial transactions and professional liability' (2008) 24 *Professional Negligence* 164, 175.

[131] See PW Lee, 'Civil Conspiracy in the Corporate Context' (2016) 23 *Torts Law Journal* 257, 259: 'the tort's potency as a liability-extending mechanism far exceeds that of the [existing] veil-piercing doctrine'; Carty (n 1) 281: 'a company having a separate legal status can conspire with its directors'.

[132] *Raja v McMillan* [2020] EWHC 951 (Ch) [England and Wales]; *Barclay Pharmaceuticals Limited v Waypharm LP* [2012] EWHC 306 (Comm), 225–26 [England and Wales]; *Total English Learning Global Pte Ltd v Kids Counsel Pte Ltd* [2014] SGHC 258 [Singapore]; *Wagner v Gill* [2015] 3 NZLR 157 [New Zealand].

[133] *Palmer Birch v Lloyd* [2018] 4 WLR 164.

[134] Only one of the brothers was technically a director; but they were equally behind the scam. As the judge – who, like me, opted for simplicity of exposition – put it (*ibid*, [7]): 'Expressing myself in necessarily vague terms at this stage, Christopher and Michael therefore each stood behind HHL (Christopher as its shareholder and director and Michael … as both its direct and indirect funder).

[135] *Ibid*, [369].

[136] *Ibid*, [215].

[137] Despite there being technically more than one shareholder in most cases, the term 'one-person company' is nonetheless used either where one person owns all, or practically all, the shares. In the famous case of *Salomon v Salomon* [1897] AC 22 (HL), the company in question was described by

said, in line with a previous, equally non-committal first instance decision,[138] that 'there may well be difficulties in the way of establishing, for the purposes of a civil law conspiracy, that a "one-man company" under the sole control of that individual can be party to a conspiracy with him'.[139] The main perceived difficulty here is one long recognised by criminal law,[140] namely, that (as would be required for a conspiracy) the director and company 'cannot, in such circumstances, be attributed with separate minds'.[141] With respect, however, this need not be considered an obstacle within the civil law. This is because it is well established that, for the purposes of civil liability, the acts of a sole director can be regarded as separate from those of the company he or she directs.[142]

Nor, for the sake of completeness, need we afford salience to a second possible objection drawn from the criminal law: the so-called 'double jeopardy' concern. This is based on the idea that both the sole director *and his or her company* would be at risk of being punished as conspirators. If both were in fact punished, then the effect would (inappropriately) be to punish a single person twice over. However, this concern is equally without traction in the context of the civil law. For, as Lee rightly observes, the only sanction in issue in a tort case is that of compensation, which will never have to be paid twice.[143]

A further prospective use of unlawful means conspiracy in the corporate context has been highlighted by O'Sullivan: 'if X (a wholly-owned subsidiary of D) breaches its contract with C then … where D has … conspired with X, it will be directly liable to C in damages … [regardless] of whether or not X is solvent'.[144] Such an occurrence is far from fanciful since it is fairly common for corporate transactions 'to be structured using a special purpose vehicle company, whose actions are entirely controlled by its parent company'.[145] Indeed, in *Palmer Birch*, HHL was just such a special vehicle company. As the judge in that case noted:

> HHL never came close to running any business and it can in hindsight be seen to have been nothing more than a conduit for the receipt of funding provided or arranged by

Lord Herschell (at 44) as a '"one man" company', even though six members of Mr Salomon's family held one share each in it.

[138] *Fiona Trust & Holding Corpn v Privalov* [2010] EWHC 3199 (Comm), [1521].

[139] *Palmer Birch* (n 133) [211].

[140] *R v McDonnell* (1966) 50 Cr App Rep 5.

[141] *Palmer Birch* (n 133) [211].

[142] *Standard Chartered Bank v Pakistan National Shipping Corp (No 2)* [2003] 1 AC 959 (HL). The idea, once put forward in *Stone & Rolls Ltd v Moore Stephens* [2009] 1 AC 1391 (HL) that such attribution should automatically occur in the case of one-person companies has been effectively laid to rest by two subsequent decisions of the Supreme Court: *Bilta (UK) Ltd v Nazir* [2016] AC 1 (SC) and *Singularis Holdings Ltd (In Liquidation) v Daiwa Capital Markets Europe Ltd* [2020] AC 1189 (SC), [34] ('*Stone & Rolls* can finally be laid to rest'). For a trenchant academic criticism of *Stone & Rolls*, see E Lim, 'A Critique of Corporate Attribution: "Directing Mind and Will" and Corporate Objectives' [2013] *Journal of Business Law* 333 and E Ferran, 'Corporate Attribution and the Directing Mind and Will' (2011) 127 *LQR* 239.

[143] Lee (n 131) 265.

[144] O'Sullivan (n 130) 174–75. The point is also echoed in Lee (n 131) 273: '[o]nce it is accepted that a company is a juristic person capable of tortiously "conspiring" with another, there is, in principle, no reason why it cannot be liable for conspiring with a company within the same corporate group'.

[145] O'Sullivan (n 130) 175.

> Michael [ie, one of the brothers] … With no significant assets of its own to be lost in any insolvency, the liquidation of HHL would come at the cost of any third party creditors but not … at any real price to SHL or Michael as its funders.[146]

Presumably, the two possible uses of unlawful means conspiracy just sketched will be applied cautiously. The worry will doubtless be that an easily available device to circumvent the prospect of corporate limited liability might deter would-be entrepreneurs from going into business on the basis that the guarantee of limited liability may be considered vital when it comes to their taking the plunge. But such a worry must be seen in context. So long as a director acts in good faith, her acts will be attributed to the company, and thus no prospect of arguing that A conspired with B will exist.[147] Accordingly, recognising the potential role of unlawful means conspiracy in the corporate context, and in particular in the context of the one-person company, need not be interpreted as an unwelcome threat to the sanctity of corporate limited liability. In order for a director to incur *personal* liability, he or she must be shown to have acted in bad faith.[148] And here, it will be noted, that the potential uses of unlawful means conspiracy just sketched become easy to reconcile with that tort's history. For, the requirement of bad faith on the part of the director places us squarely back in the realm of egregious collective wrong-doing which has always been a hallmark of this tort. As Lewison LJ concluded in *Racing Partnership Ltd v Sports Information Services Ltd*, having trawled through the previous holdings: 'the cases stress the need for blameworthiness on the part of the conspirators … conduct "sufficiently reprehensible" to justify imposing on those who have brought about the harm liability in damages'.[149]

IV. Conclusion

Mindful of the four main theses of this book,[150] this chapter has for the most part eschewed discussion of the knotty, interpretive problems associated with certain ingredients of the two torts discussed. For example, no attempt has been made to state definitively what counts as unlawful means for the purposes of these actions. Nor has there been any engagement with the question of whether knowledge of the unlawfulness of the means used to target the claimant is required where the unlawful means in issue constitute a crime.[151] Instead, it has been argued that both the *OBG* tort and unlawful means conspiracy have a clear role to play beyond the

[146] *Palmer Birch* (n 133) [124].

[147] *Said v Butt* [1920] 3 KB 497.

[148] See, eg, *Antuzis v DJ Houghton Catching Services Ltd* [2019] Bus LR 1532, [125] (Lane J) (liability imposed jointly on company's sole director and its secretary for inducing breach of contract).

[149] *Racing Partnership* (n 107) [247].

[150] See chapter one.

[151] The Court of Appeal has carefully gone no further than saying that knowledge that a given act constitutes a *private wrong* is required by this tort: see *Racing Partnership* (n 107), [265] (Lewison LJ).

paradigm setting of economic losses inflicted by one trade or business entity upon its rival.

In relation to the former, there is little if anything in the leading cases to suggest that the tort is confined to the protection of economic interests. And although it is true – as Lord Hoffmann made clear in *OBG* – that in order for a claimant to sue, he must have held an economic link with the third party through whom the defendant struck at him, it was also noted that there was no accompanying insistence by his Lordship that the harm of which the claimant complains must be economic in nature. At the same time, I noted that *every case* involving the unlawful means tort may be portrayed as one involving egregious wrongdoing. This is because, in every such case, the defendant will have struck at the claimant via a third party, that third party being someone who necessarily did not deserve to be made the victim of a wrong and thus used as a means to an end.[152] For D intentionally to harm C is morally wrong; but for D to commit a wrong against a third party, T, just so that harm will then result for C is plainly worse: there are (of necessity) two intentional wrongs wrapped up in the one of which C complains.

Very similar observations were made in relation to the tort of unlawful means conspiracy. *Total Network* and *Khrapunov* made clear that recoverable losses were not confined to those inflicted by one business rival upon the other, and in both of those cases, D's conduct was highly reprehensible. On top of this, the decision in *Palmer Birch* helps to reveal the considerable, yet largely untapped potential of this tort in the corporate context. There is value yet in an independent tort of unlawful means conspiracy.

[152] The idea that the intermediary does not deserve to be used in this way should not be taken to mean that the intermediary will always be entirely innocent. Sometimes – *Rookes* would be a good example – employers who have been unwilling to abide by closed shop agreements and had their hands forced could scarcely claim to be entirely innocent. I am grateful to Roderick Bagshaw for alerting me to this point.

5

Lawful Means Conspiracy and Intimidation

The principal aim of this chapter is to explore the vitality and the merits of two causes of action that most jurists portray as enjoying a doubtful (or, at least, controversial) existence. The torts in question are lawful means conspiracy (sometimes referred to in the relevant case law as conspiracy to injure[1]) and two-party intimidation. The vitality of lawful means conspiracy is typically called into question via the claim that it is an anomalous tort. By contrast, the equivalent doubts concerning two-party intimidation can be traced to what was said about it by Lord Hoffmann in the landmark case of *OBG Ltd v Allan*.[2] As regards the merits of these two torts, it seems generally to be thought that neither action has very much going for it. They are both typically considered largely superfluous: either because they are seldom used, or because they overlap to a significant degree with various other civil actions which render them more or less otiose.

In this chapter, I shall seek to counter this image of lawful means conspiracy and two-party intimidation. I shall suggest instead that, despite the doubts that have been expressed, they both deserve to be regarded as vital (in the strict sense), and as torts that possess genuine juridical significance. I shall also attempt to show that each of them has considerable untapped practical potential, once we unearth their true rationales. Doing this requires a rejection of the artificial and inappropriate confinement of these torts to the protection of trade and business interests.

[1] See, eg, *Crofter Handwoven Harris Tweed Co Ltd v Veitch* [1942] AC 435 (HL), 448 (Lord Wright); *Lonrho Ltd v Shell Petroleum Co Ltd (No 2)* [1982] AC 173 (HL), 189 (Lord Diplock); *Lonrho v Fayed (No 1)* [1992] 1 AC 448 (HL), 463 (Lord Bridge); *Revenue and Customs Commissioners v Total Network SL* [2008] 1 AC 1174 (HL), [44] and [230] (Lords Hope and Neuberger, respectively); J Thomson, 'An Island Legacy – The Delict of Conspiracy' in DL Carey Miller and DW Meyers (eds), *Comparative and Historical Essays in Scots Law* (Edinburgh, Butterworths, 1992) 148.

[2] *OBG Ltd v Allan* [2008] 1 AC 1 (HL).

I. Lawful Means Conspiracy

A. Vitality

It is hard to think of a cause of action that has been described as 'an anomaly' quite so often as lawful means conspiracy. Occasionally, this is said of public nuisance,[3] malicious prosecution[4] and misfeasance in a public office.[5] But even then, the academic community – including those who make these remarks – seems to accept that all these actions are alive and well (even if their status as *torts* is sometimes doubted). With lawful means conspiracy, however, things are very different.

Somewhat oddly, there are both judges and jurists who have simply asserted, without offering any elaboration, that lawful means conspiracy is an anomaly. The problem with such remarks is that they neither reveal the sense in which the word 'anomaly' is being used,[6] nor provide any indication of the benchmark against which this claim is to be measured. Typical is Lord Herschell's remark in *Allen v Flood* that 'conspiracy … is anomalous in more than one respect'.[7] In just which ways he thought it was anomalous, he conspicuously failed to state. Similarly, Janet O'Sullivan speaks cryptically of 'the somewhat anomalous "conspiracy to injure"';[8] but she provides no clue as to why that description is warranted. Because of their opacity, it is simply not possible to say whether claims such as these are intended to reflect a doubt about the vitality of this tort.

Happily, others who are sceptical about lawful means conspiracy have been considerably clearer in what they mean when describing the tort as an anomaly. And there seem to be no fewer than four particular senses in which the term has been used, sometimes by scholars, sometimes by judges. As we shall see, the first two of these usages offer no real challenge to the vitality of lawful means conspiracy. By contrast, the third and fourth do ostensibly strike at the vitality of the tort, but as we shall also see, these claims are made without firm foundations.

The first clear sense in which lawful means conspiracy has been described as an anomaly draws on its most obvious peculiarity: the fact that 'a plaintiff may have an action against each of two or more parties [actuated by malice] where their actions, if performed by one party alone, would not give rise to a remedy'.[9]

[3] JR Spencer, 'Public Nuisance: A Critical Examination' (1989) 48 *CLJ* 55, 83.
[4] See, eg, *Crawford Adjusters Ltd v Sagicor Insurance Ltd* [2014] AC 366 (PC), [145]: 'malicious prosecution is in modern conditions an anomalous tort' (Lord Sumption).
[5] E Chamberlain, 'Misfeasance in a Public Office: A Justifiable Anomaly within the Rights-Based Approach?' in D Nolan and A Robertson (eds), *Rights and Private Law* (Oxford, Hart Publishing, 2012); R Stevens, *Torts and Rights* (Oxford, Oxford University Press, 2007) 113.
[6] On the various meanings that are sometimes applied to the word 'anomaly' when it is used to describe torts, see J Murphy, 'Malice as an Ingredient of Tort Liability' [2019] *CLJ* 355, 356–57.
[7] *Allen v Flood* [1898] AC 1 (HL), 124.
[8] J O'Sullivan, 'Unlawful Means Conspiracy in the House of Lords' [2008] *CLJ* 459, 459.
[9] P Edmundson, 'Conspiracy by Unlawful Means: Keeping the Tort Untangled' (2008) 16 *Torts Law Journal* 189, 191. The claim has its origins in *Lonrho v Shell* (n 1) 189 (Lord Diplock) and *Lonrho v*

One example of the term 'anomaly' being used in this way can be seen in *OBG v Allan* where Lord Hoffmann declared that '*Quinn v Leathem* … [was] a case on lawful means conspiracy, which established that an improper motive can anomalously found a cause of action'.[10] A substantively identical claim was made in the speeches of Lord Walker and Lord Neuberger in *Total Network*,[11] and the joint speech of Lords Sumption and Lloyd-Jones in *JSC BTA Bank v Khrapunov*.[12] But there is no suggestion in such proclamations that the tort has lost its vitality. Those, like Lord Hoffmann, who consider lawful means conspiracy to be an anomaly by virtue of the fact that it allows the presence of malice to transform what would ordinarily be a lawful act into a tort actionable against several parties who have combined together, does nothing to deny the existence of the action.[13]

The second discernible sense in which lawful means conspiracy is sometimes described as an anomaly draws on the idea that, in one way or another, the tort is a juridical misfit. Some take this view because they consider it an oddity when measured against the yardstick of certain juridical features that typically characterise tort law as a whole. Others, more narrowly, simply think that it is a misfit when it is compared to the other economic torts. Robert Stevens is firmly of the broader view. As the author of a rights-based theory of the whole of tort law, he states unequivocally that, '[t]his tort is anomalous'.[14] His reason for so saying is that the tort does not require the infringement of an ex-ante right held against the defendant. He asserts: '[u]nless a right of the claimant is infringed, it is difficult to see why … the mere fact that the loss is inflicted because of a combination of persons should make any difference'.[15] But notice: all that he objects to, here, is the fact that lawful means conspiracy responds to the infliction of a loss in the absence of a rights infringement. He does not seek to deny the tort's vitality. It is only anomalous, in his view, insofar as it clashes with the core claim of his theory.

Hazel Carty is typical of those who hold the narrower view. She regards lawful means conspiracy as a cuckoo in the nest inasmuch as it fails to fit her conception of the way the economic torts are structured. It will be recalled from chapter two that Carty is firmly wedded to a narrow understanding of the economic torts. Part of the narrowness of her conception of their role derives from her commitment to

Fayed (n 1) 463 (Lord Bridge). The exact same point is made in P Sales, 'The Tort of Conspiracy and Civil Secondary Liability' [1990] *CLJ* 491, 501.

[10] *OBG* (n 2) [15].

[11] *Total Network* (n 1) [67] and [221] respectively.

[12] *JSC BTA Bank v Khrapunov* [2020] AC 727 (SC), [7]: 'It is an anomalous tort because it may make actionable acts which would be lawful apart from the element of combination'.

[13] This has long been the case. Charlesworth made effectively the same observation as long ago as 1920, yet concluded that the tort was alive and well. He wrote that '*Allen v Flood* decided that a particular act done by one person was not actionable, while *Temperton v Russell* [[1893] 1 QB 715 (CA)] decided that the same act done in pursuance of a conspiracy was actionable': J Charlesworth, 'Conspiracy as a Ground of Liability in Tort' (1920) 36 *LQR* 38, 41.

[14] Stevens (n 5) 251.

[15] *Ibid.*

the idea that 'intermediary-use liability is the paradigm setting for the economic torts'.[16] Thus, insofar as lawful means conspiracy can be used in a two-party setting, it is, in her view, best seen (along with its sibling, unlawful means conspiracy) as a 'can of worms' that 'unsettles the other economic torts'.[17] Note, however, that, just like Stevens, she stops short of denying the vitality of the tort. Indeed, as an empirical (not theoretical) matter, Carty begrudgingly concedes that there have been certain recent 'developments … [which] appear to accept that the tort of conspiracy has its own vitality'.[18] The simple truth is that, both these scholars base their claims about the anomalous status of this tort on the fact that it clashes with normative, theoretical precommitments that they each hold.

Thirdly, lawful means conspiracy is said to be an anomaly in the sense that it is something of an outlier, an action that somehow manages to linger in a state of near-desuetude at the fringes of tort law. Lord Hoffmann espoused such a view in *OBG* in the course of his extensive examination of the muddle into which the economic torts had lapsed during the course of the twentieth century. He opined that it would be 'better to abandon it and return to the two torts identified by Lord Watson in *Allen v Flood*'.[19] True, he did not specifically invoke Lord Diplock's earlier proclamation that 'the civil tort of conspiracy to injure … must I think be accepted by this House as too well-established to be discarded however anomalous it may seem today',[20] but it seems fairly clear that he sympathised with that view. For, just a few years later, writing extra-judicially, he clarified what had been his goal in *OBG*. He put it this way: '[t]he message intended to be conveyed by *OBG* was that in regulating industrial relations, the economic torts have run their course'.[21] The idea that he specifically had conspiracy (in both its forms) in mind when he spoke of actions that had run their course seems clear enough once one realises that the 'tort of conspiracy was developed in the late nineteenth and early twentieth century, as a device for imposing civil liability on the organisers of strikes and other industrial action'.[22] The fact that disruptive industrial action is more or less a thing of the past seems patently to be what drove him to think of the conspiracy torts as having gone past their sell-by date. He seemed prepared only to afford

[16] *Ibid*, 393.

[17] H Carty, 'The Tort of Conspiracy as a Can of Worms' in SGA Pitel *et al* (eds), *Tort Law: Challenging Orthodoxy* (London, Hart Publishing, 2013) 391, 404.

[18] *Ibid*, 392.

[19] *OBG* (n 2) [33].

[20] *Lonrho v Shell* (n 1) 189. Note, too, that just one year later Estey J said: '[t]he tort of conspiracy to injure … is indeed a commercial anachronism … [that] … may have lost much of its usefulness in our commercial world': *Canada Cement LaFarge Ltd v British Columbia Lightweight Aggregate Ltd* [1983] 1 SCR 452, 473.

[21] Lord Hoffmann, 'The Rise and Fall of the Economic Torts' in J Edelman *et al* (eds), *Torts in Commercial Law* (Sydney, LBC, 2011) 114.

[22] *Khrapunov* (n 12) [7].

modern-day salience to the torts of causing loss by unlawful means and inducing breach of contract. As Burton Ong puts it:

> [t]he single most important observation to emerge from Lord Hoffmann's historical overview of the decided cases is that there were two distinct bases of tortious liability … the tort of inducing breach of contract and the tort of causing loss by unlawful means.[23]

Carty, too, reads the case that way: '[w]hat *OBG v Allan* offered as a framework for the general economic torts was a two-tort paradigm, based on a three-party scenario.'[24] There was no future role for conspiracy envisaged; and hence Lord Hoffmann's speech would appear to have cast doubt over the future vitality of lawful means conspiracy. It was, therefore, in the wake of *OBG*, a tort that had been left hanging by a thread, somewhere at the margins of tort law.

Fourthly, in saying that lawful means conspiracy is an anomaly, some of its detractors mean to convey that the original justification for the tort no longer exists with the necessary implication being that, without sound foundations, we should consider the superstructure doomed: *cessante ratione legis, cessat lex ipsa*. This conception of the action's anomalous status draws upon the fact that the early cases of lawful means conspiracy seemed to make the mere fact of combination the tort's *raison d'être*. The classic statement to this effect was enunciated by Bowen LJ in *Mogul Steamship Co Ltd v McGregor Gow & Co*. He said, 'a combination may make oppressive or dangerous that which if it proceeded only from a single person would be otherwise.'[25] But the suggestion that there is any magic in mere numbers in the modern era was laid to rest by Lord Diplock in *Lonrho Ltd v Shell Petroleum Co Ltd (No 2)*. He said:

> to suggest today that acts done by one street-corner grocer in concert with a second are more oppressive and dangerous to a competitor than the same acts done by a string of supermarkets under a single ownership or that a multi-national conglomerate … does not exercise greater power today than any combination of small businesses, is to shut one's eyes to what has been happening in the business and industrial world since the turn of the century and in particular since the end of World War II.[26]

On this view also, then, the vitality of lawful means conspiracy is doubted, not because it has lapsed into desuetude, but because its putative moorings have been removed. Add to this the fact that not all torts last forever – the seduction of a woman, and slander in the form of an allegation that a woman is unchaste are just two examples of actions that no longer exist – and the idea that lawful means conspiracy may have 'run its course', as Lord Hoffmann suggested, seems plausible enough.

[23] B Ong, 'Two Tripartite Economic Torts' [2008] *Journal of Business Law* 723, 724.
[24] H Carty, *An Analysis of the Economic Torts*, 2nd edn (Oxford, Oxford University Press, 2010) 25.
[25] *Mogul Steamship Co Ltd v McGregor Gow & Co* (1889) 23 QBD 598 (CA), 616.
[26] *Lonrho v Shell* (n 1) 189. See also *OBG* (n 2) [72] (Lord Walker).

But, for all that there have been certain judges who have *suggested* that this tort has either lapsed into desuetude or had its foundations withdrawn, there is also evidence that points the other way. Importantly, in the two most recent relevant cases to have been decided by our most senior judges, there was sympathy for the view that – although it was not directly in issue in either of them – the tort of lawful means conspiracy remains vital. The first of those cases was *Total Network*, and the tort in issue there, as we saw in chapter four, was *unlawful* means conspiracy. Nonetheless, there was considerable support expressed *obiter* for the idea that lawful means conspiracy continues to exist. Lord Hope, for example, said that '[i]f the predominant intention of the combination is to injure, what is done is actionable even though the means used were lawful';[27] and he even used lawful means conspiracy as part of the basis for his resuscitating the tort of unlawful means conspiracy,[28] as did Lord Neuberger.[29] In addition, Lord Scott also considered lawful means conspiracy to be 'a highly relevant … judicial development of the action on the case',[30] while Lord Neuberger observed that 'a claim based on conspiracy to injure can be established even where no unlawful means, let alone any other actionable tort, is involved'.[31] Indeed, the latter even thought that the lawsuit in *Total Network* could conceivably have been based on lawful means conspiracy. He said:

> in this case, there is little, if any, difference between the conspirators' intention to make money and their intention to deprive the commissioners of money: each is the obverse of the other. On that basis, it may well be that it could be said that the predominant purpose of Total and the other conspirators was indeed to inflict loss on the commissioners just as much as it was to profit the conspirators, and hence the claim in tort is made out in conspiracy to injure.[32]

The second case that can be understood as having kept alive the tort of lawful means conspiracy is *Khrapunov*.[33] In that case, the speech prepared jointly by Lords Sumption and Lloyd-Jones (and with which all the remaining members of the Supreme Court agreed), contained a clear enunciation of the following points: (1) 'conspiracy has an established place in the law of tort';[34] (2) it is one of 'four

[27] *Total Network* (n 1) [41].

[28] He saw the potential actionability of the conspiracy in that case to reside in the fact that, '[a]s a subspecies of the tort of unlawful means conspiracy, the case is virtually indistinguishable from the tort of conspiracy to injure': *ibid*, [44].

[29] *Ibid*, [224].

[30] *Ibid*, [56].

[31] *Ibid*, [221].

[32] *Ibid*, [228]. Whether this view is grounded is a moot point. Arguably, the fraudsters' predominant purpose was to make a gain for themselves and not to cause loss to the Revenue. But as against that is the idea, captured in this excerpt from Lord Neuberger's dictum, that causing loss and making a gain are merely opposite sides of the same coin. To like effect, see *Mogul Steamship Co Ltd v McGregor Gow & Co* [1892] AC 25 (HL), 36 and 42 (Lord Halsbury and Lord Watson respectively); Edmundson (n 9) 198.

[33] *Khrapunov* (n 12).

[34] *Ibid*, [7].

established economic torts';[35] and (3) 'it is actionable as a distinct tort'.[36] On top of this, however, there was also what appears to have been a conscious effort to downplay Lord Hoffmann's obvious attempt to undermine the vitality of conspiracy in *OBG*, for their Lordships stressed the fact that, in *OBG*, 'Lord Hoffmann was not directly concerned with the tort of conspiracy'.[37]

To sum up: many commentators – including scholars and some of our most senior judges – have labelled lawful means conspiracy an anomalous tort; but relatively few have done so in such a way as to convincingly call into question its continued vitality. There are of course those (including most prominently Lord Hoffmann), who have strongly intimated, if not quite overtly said, that the action is best seen as a thing of the past. But crucially, they have not done so with the force of law. Indeed, as we have seen, some of the tort's staunchest critics begrudgingly accept that it is too well entrenched, standing on the most solid of foundations, to be abolished or treated as having lapsed into desuetude. It is even the case, as was noted, that one of the panel in *Total Network* was prepared to suggest that that case would have been much simpler to decide had counsel for the claimant pursued the possibility of lawful means conspiracy.

Given such weighty dicta, it seems best to regard lawful means conspiracy as an extant tort, albeit one that is only invoked infrequently in modern-day tort litigation. But this is of no real moment. For, the fact that a particular tort is engaged only rarely is no basis on which to downplay its significance or its potential. No-one would say, for example, that treason or arson are unimportant crimes simply on the basis that they are, by comparison with other crimes, only infrequently committed. Also, closer to home, few would say that the torts of misfeasance in a public office, abuse of process or malicious prosecution can be ignored or marginalised on the basis that there is only a handful of successful reported cases.[38] In law, as in life, it is a mistake to consider something that we rarely use as pointless or redundant. A more considered conclusion on the value of lawful means conspiracy ought, accordingly, to be suspended until its rationale and untapped potential have been unearthed. Only once we are clear about these matters can we properly evaluate its merits.

B. Rationale

When lawful means conspiracy was in its infancy, the courts stressed, and attached juridical significance to, the fact that this tort is committed by those who act in combination. No clearer example of the supposed significance of combination

[35] *Ibid*, [6].
[36] *Ibid*, [9].
[37] *Ibid*.
[38] For a defence of these torts, see Murphy (n 6) 374–81.

may be given than what was said by Lord Lindley in the seminal case of *Quinn*, namely, that 'numbers may annoy and coerce where one may not'.[39] Elaborating upon this claim, he said:

> an organized body of men working together can produce results very different from those which can be produced by an individual without assistance. Moreover, laws adapted to individuals not acting in concert with others require modification and extension if they are to be applied with effect to large bodies of persons acting in concert. The English law of conspiracy is based upon and is justified by this undeniable truth.[40]

Several other such proclamations were subsequently made at the highest judicial level. In *Crofter Handwoven Harris Tweed Co Ltd v Veitch*, for example, Lord Wright opined that, 'it is in the fact of conspiracy that the unlawfulness resides',[41] while Viscount Simon stated forthrightly that, 'the gist of the action is that damage was inflicted by defendants who combined together for the purpose of inflicting it'.[42] Later still, in *Lonrho v Fayed (No 1)*, Lord Bridge opined: 'it is in the fact of their concerted action … that the law, however anomalous it may now seem, finds a sufficient ground to condemn that action as illegal and tortious'.[43] And even more recently, Lord Hope employed very similar language in *Total Network* to emphasise the importance of combination (albeit that he was dealing with unlawful means conspiracy in that case). He stressed the fact that the combination in the instant case made it possible 'to secure that result which could not have been secured by either of [the defendants] … acting alone'.[44] Likewise, in the same case, Lord Walker drew attention to the fact that 'the fraud … could not have been carried out otherwise than by a number of persons acting in concert';[45] while, more broadly, Lord Mance observed that an 'individual or entity might – possibly – achieve the same result by himself or itself, but would be a great deal less likely to try or succeed'.[46]

Such dicta, as O'Sullivan has pointed out, certainly appear to reflect the belief that '[t]he gist seems to be that it is the combination, the conspiracy itself, that makes the difference'.[47] And the difference, supposedly, inheres in the idea

[39] *Quinn v Leathem* [1901] AC 495, 538. Lord Macnaghten made an essentially similar claim: *ibid*, 511.

[40] *South Wales Miners' Federation v Glamorgan Coal Co Ltd* [1905] AC 239 (HL), 252.

[41] *Crofter* (n 1) 445 and 462 (Lord Wright). This understanding was cited with approval by Lord Walker in *Total Network* (n 1) [41] and [75]. See also *Mogul Steamship* (n 32) 45 (Lord Bramwell): 'a man may encounter the acts of a single person, yet not be fairly matched against several'; *Crofter* (n 1) 448 (Viscount Maugham): 'I have never myself felt any difficulty in seeing the great difference between the acts of one person and the acts in combination of two or of a multitude'.

[42] *Crofter* (n 1) 444.

[43] *Lonrho v Fayed* (n 1) 465.

[44] *Total Network* (n 1) [42].

[45] *Ibid*, [77].

[46] *Ibid*, [122]. See, too, the rather vague suggestion that the law takes a 'particularly censorious view where conspiracy is concerned': *ibid*, [222] (Lord Neuberger).

[47] O'Sullivan (n 8) 460. It certainly seems to be the belief held by at least one academic, too: see Thomson (n 1) 148.

that '[g]anging up on someone is much more serious than going it alone'.[48] But, as we have already noted, such thinking does not necessarily hold in the modern era. As Allan Beever puts it: there is no reason to assume that 'two or more people have greater power' than their victim.[49] O'Sullivan agrees, and concludes that:

> [i]t is not clear that this is an entirely convincing justification; after all, it is frequently pointed out (in relation to conspiracy to injure) how absurd it is for the law to imagine that two shopkeepers combining to injure a competitor are more oppressive and dangerous than one huge international conglomerate doing the same alone.[50]

So what is it, if not the fact of combination, that undergirds lawful means conspiracy? In *Total Network*, Lord Walker alighted upon an alternative rationale. After rejecting as 'not very satisfactory' the notion that mere numbers were significant,[51] he identified a different possible *raison d'être* in something Bowen LJ said in the *Mogul Steamship* case,[52] namely, that 'the object is simply to do harm, and not to exercise one's own just rights'.[53] What, in other words, triggers liability for this tort is a 'combination for an unlawful object'.[54] More specifically, what was seen as crucial was the requirement that the conspirators' predominant purpose was to cause loss to the claimant.[55] I have elsewhere argued that combining in this way, in order to inflict loss for no good reason, is best understood in terms of an abuse of the freedom of association.[56] Such an understanding helps makes sense of Bowen LJ's talk of the defendant not exercising his or her 'own just rights'. And although the power of association is not strictly a right in the Hohfeldian sense, it is nonetheless a 'right' guaranteed by Article 11 of the European Convention on Human Rights. And even before the European Convention was given the force of law,

[48] A Beever, *A Theory of Tort Liability* (Oxford, Hart Publishing, 2016) 138.

[49] *Ibid.*

[50] *Ibid.* In similar vein, see PG Heffey, 'The Survival of Civil Conspiracy: A Question of Magic or Logic' (1975) 1 *Monash University Law Review* 136, 136: '[t]he modern tort of conspiracy … rests rather shakily on a notion of plurality which derives more from magic than reason'.

[51] *Total Network* (n 1) [77].

[52] *Mogul Steamship* (n 25) 616.

[53] *Total Network* (n 1) [78].

[54] *Ibid*, [68]. Note that *unilaterally* pursuing an illegitimate purpose would suffice for liability in the United States of America: *Tuttle v Buck* 119 NW 946 (Minn 1909). And for a defence of such an approach, see JD Heydon, *Economic Torts*, 2nd edn (London, Sweet and Maxwell, 1978) 28.

[55] *Crofter* (n 1) 445 (Viscount Simon LC): '[L]iability must depend on ascertaining the predominant purpose. If that predominant purpose is to damage another person and damage results, that is tortious conspiracy'.

[56] See Murphy (n 6) 374–75. I there elaborate on the point in the text, being careful to distinguish public powers from private powers and the abuse of the former from the abuse of rights. For misguided accounts that see lawful means conspiracy as an abuse of rights *strictu sensu*, see JW Neyers, 'Explaining the Inexplicable? Four Manifestations of Abuse of Rights in English Law' in Nolan and Robertson (n 5) and N Tamblyn, 'Lawful Act Conspiracy: Malice and Abuse of Rights' [2013] *Singapore Journal of Legal Studies* 158.

a roughly corresponding power to associate and form trade unions was granted by statute.[57] It was to the abuse of this early power that Fridman, writing over half a century ago, correctly attached juridical significance. He observed: although 'men have the legal power to combine, such power may only be exercised with a rightful and justified intention'.[58]

Further support for this interpretation may also be drawn from *Khrapunov* even though, strictly, that was a case of unlawful means conspiracy. For there, it was observed that, 'it cannot be an answer to say that he [ie, the conspirator] was simply exercising a legal right', for such a person will have had 'no interest recognised by the law in exercising his legal right for the predominant purpose not of advancing his own interests but of injuring the claimant'.[59] In other words, the freedom of association is restricted to associations for legitimate purposes.

Altogether the clearest endorsement of the interpretation of the tort's rationale being an abuse of the power to associate freely can be gleaned from the *Crofter* case. The claimants in that case were able to cut costs of production by importing yarn to the island of Lewis from the mainland that was later woven on the island. The defendants, who were trade union officials, were told by the mill owners on the island that the pay claims made by spinners employed by them were unmanageable. The spinners were members of the union, and their pay demands were unmanageable because the mill owners would not then be able to compete on price with the claimants (who could produce cloth more cheaply thanks to the lower cost of the imported yarn). The defendants then instructed dockers (who were also members of the same union) not to handle the claimants' yarn, and their refusal to do so involved no breach of contract. If there were to be liability, it would have to lie in tort. Critically, it was held that no liability for lawful means conspiracy could be imposed in the absence of an *abuse of the power to combine*. As Lord Wright explained:

> In the report of *Reg v Rowlands*[60] (a criminal case, but the same principles apply in a civil suit), Erle J directed the jury: 'The law is clear, that workmen have a right to combine for their own protection, and to obtain such wages as they choose to agree to demand' … He added that while the law allowed them to combine for the purpose of obtaining a lawful benefit for themselves, it gave no sanction to combinations which had for their immediate purpose the hurt of another.[61]

[57] Trade union powers to associate for various purposes were introduced piecemeal during the nineteenth century via the Combinations of Workmen Act 1825, the Trade Union Act 1871 and the Conspiracy and Protection of Property Act 1875. See further MJ Klarman, 'The Judges versus the Unions: The Development of British Labour Law, 1867–1913' (1989) 75 *Virginia Law Review* 1487.

[58] G Fridman, 'Malice in the Law of Torts' (1958) 21 *MLR* 484, 497. See also P Elias and K Ewing, 'Economic Torts and Labour Law: Old Principles and New Liabilities' [1982] *CLJ* 321, 325.

[59] *Khrapunov* (n 12), [10] (Lord Sumption and Lord Lloyd-Jones, joint speech).

[60] *Reg v Rowlands* (1851) 17 QB 671.

[61] *Crofter* (n 1) 464.

It is, of course, logically impossible for there to be an abuse of the power to combine in the absence of an actual combination. For this reason, a combination – like damage[62] – must be shown in a case of lawful means conspiracy. But it is a mistake to treat either the combination or the infliction of loss as if it were the gist of this tort. That honour, as Lord Wright made clear, goes squarely to an abuse of the power to combine.

Critically, the question of whether there has been such an abuse will turn on whether the defendant was actuated by malice: true: this malice requirement is sometimes referred to as an improper motive or purpose (which, incidentally, must be the defendant's sole or predominant purpose[63]). But I nonetheless think it is preferable to stick to the language of malice here, since this is how it was originally expressed in *Quinn*.[64] That the two concepts are interchangeable for present purposes is clear enough. In *Quinn* itself, Lord Shand said that a 'combination … in pursuit merely of a malicious purpose to injure another, would be clearly unlawful',[65] but he was keen to explain that such malice was to be discovered in defendants' improper motives.[66] Equally, in that case, Lord Lindley spoke of the need to act 'maliciously in the sense of proceeding from a bad motive';[67] while in *Crofter*, roughly half a century later, Lord Porter also aligned malice with motive. He said there could be liability 'if one of the parties had no purpose but to vent his own vindictive spite and if the other [conspirator] knew of and countenanced that purpose by giving his assistance to the malicious acts of the first'.[68] Addressing the side-issue of what must be shown where a defendant has mixed motives, Viscount Maugham opined that the court must discover the predominant purpose by weighing the fact that 'what the defendants had done was *done with malice*' against the fact that 'one at least of the motives actuating the defendant was the benefit [to himself or to others]'.[69]

[62] Although conspiracy in the criminal law setting is an inchoate offence, it has been made clear that, in tort, no action will lie in the absence of tangible loss: see, eg, *Crofter* (n 1) 439: 'The crime consists in the agreement. But the tort of conspiracy is constituted only if the agreed combination is carried into effect in a greater or lesser degree and damage to the plaintiff is thereby produced' (Lord Simon); *Sorrell v Smith* [1925] AC 700 (HL), 712 (Lord Cave): 'A combination of two or more persons wilfully to injure a man in his trade is unlawful and, if it results in damage to him, is actionable'.

[63] See, eg, *Crofter* (n 1) 445. It has been argued that malice and bad motive should be understood as interchangeable terms *generally* in tort law: see P Cane, '*Mens Rea* in Tort Law' (2000) 20 *OJLS* 533, 539; Murphy (n 6) 366–70.

[64] Sales has reached a similar conclusion: see Sales (n 9) 492: 'in effect [the tort's] … scope was limited to conspiracy to injure others out of spite, where no commercial purpose of the conspirators was furthered thereby'. Another reason for thinking in terms of malice is that so doing allows the connection between this tort and three others in which malice is a central requirement to be seen (and thus rebut the suggestion that this tort is unique and thus an anomaly): see Murphy (n 6).

[65] *Quinn* (n 39) 512.

[66] *Ibid*, 515: 'Their acts were wrongful and malicious … [since] they acted … for the sole purpose of injuring the plaintiff in his trade'.

[67] *Ibid*, 533.

[68] *Crofter* (n 1) 495. Note, however, that the second conspirator need not share that improper purpose: *Huntley v Thornton* [1957] 1 All ER 234 (two defendants were not liable on account of their not having the requisite improper purpose).

[69] *Crofter* (n 1) 452.

C. Merits

There can be no doubt that lawful means conspiracy, for all that it remains vital in the strict sense, is a tort that is seldom successfully invoked. As Lord Diplock put it, 'the civil tort of conspiracy attracted more controversy among academic writers than success in practical application'.[70] To a large extent, this history of having had very limited practical importance can be attributed to the need for a claimant to show that the defendant was preponderantly actuated by malice, a problem that may be especially pronounced where the defendant had mixed motives.[71] It is generally thought that this requirement ought not to be relaxed, since it serves 'to hold the balance between the defendant's right to exercise his lawful rights and the plaintiff's right not to be injured by an injurious conspiracy'.[72] But equally, its retention should not be taken as a basis for thinking that this tort has neither present day significance, nor any future potential.

In practical terms, as noted briefly already, its existence was treated by four members of the panel in *Total Network* as an important part of the platform on which its sister tort – unlawful means conspiracy – could be reconstructed. Lord Neuberger was especially clear in this regard. He said:

> given the existence of that [lawful means] tort, it would be anomalous if an unlawful means conspiracy could not found a cause of action where, as here, the means 'merely' involved a crime, where the loss to the claimant was the obvious and inevitable … result.[73]

And as Carty subsequently explained:

> though [in *Total Network*] the claimant pleaded unlawful means conspiracy, the main discussion is in fact on the lawful means form of the tort (with key House of Lords decisions on that form of the tort analysed). Thus, the lawful means form of the tort, far from being dismissed as anomalous and practically useless, is in fact presented as a template for conspiracy liability generally.[74]

The second way in which lawful means conspiracy possesses practical significance can be observed in relation to the limits of competition law. It is true that, historically, lawful means conspiracy has been used to address the 'oppressive abuse of economic power'.[75] And it is true, too, that the line between fair and unfair competition is nowadays drawn principally by statute, specifically by the Competition Act 1998. But even so, the statute does not catch all possible cases. One of the

[70] *Lonrho v Shell* (n 1) 188.
[71] For details see Carty (n 24) 143–44; NJ McBride and R Bagshaw, *Tort Law*, 6th edn (London, Pearson, 2018) 657.
[72] *Crofter* (n 1) 462 (Lord Wright).
[73] See *Total Network* (n 1) [221]. See also *ibid*, [41], [56] and [68] (Lords Hope, Scott and Walker respectively).
[74] Carty (n 17) 402.
[75] Carty (n 24) 147. For doubts about whether the tort can be so confined, see below.

key features of *Total Network*, it will be recalled from chapter four, was the fact that it involved conspirators domiciled abroad. They were beyond the reach of the relevant taxation legislation. Overseas conspirators will ordinarily also fall beyond the compass of the Competition Act.[76] But, via use of the rules of private international law, it might still be possible to rely on the common law tort of lawful means conspiracy in any such situation. Indeed, as we observed earlier, Lord Neuberger expressly admitted that he thought the claim in *Total Network* could conceivably have been pursued along these lines.[77]

Even if the defendant is not domiciled abroad, it is perfectly possible that an individual's ostensibly lawful acts might nonetheless fall within the compass of lawful means conspiracy (even if they do not fall within the terms of the statutory regime).[78] The short point is this: the introduction of the Competition Act 1998 cannot be understood to have completely eclipsed the traditional role of this much maligned tort.

A third practical virtue of lawful means conspiracy is that it can be used to extend the reach of tort law to those who can fairly be regarded as having behaved in an especially reprehensible fashion, but not in such a way that their actions would be caught by another tort. A central issue in *Total Network* was whether there was a tort law counterpart to the crime of cheating the Revenue. There was not. And the fact that there was no such tort was a clear concern to the majority of their Lordships. Lord Scott, for example, made the following very general point:

> We were taught at law school that the action on the case was the means whereby our judicial forbears allowed tortious remedies in damages where harm had been caused in circumstances *where the conduct of the authors of the harm had been sufficiently reprehensible* to require the conclusion that they ought to be held responsible for the harm.[79]

There was nothing in his saying this that can be regarded as a justification for extending the reach of *only* unlawful means conspiracy. His thinking could just as readily be adopted in order to justify an extension of its lawful means sibling. It is equally clear that Lord Mance took an especially dim view of cheats in that case: he acknowledged openly that there was 'force in the point' that there should be liability for cheating in its own right.[80]

[76] It can of course be applied in a foreign court in a case with a private international law dimension wherein the relevant choice of law rules direct the foreign court to the law applicable in this country.

[77] *Total Network* (n 1) [228].

[78] See, eg, *Eastham v Newcastle United FC* [1964] Ch 413. (Claimant was successful in securing a declaration that a particular system employed in relation to the transfer of professional footballers was in restraint of trade.).

[79] *Total Network* (n 1) [56] (emphasis added). This was no careless use of words, for just a few lines later he reiterated the point saying that, '[t]his difference between the torts of lawful means conspiracy and unlawful means conspiracy is sometimes described as anomalous. In my opinion it is not. The difference reflects and demonstrates the essential flexibility of the action on the case. It is not all conduct foreseeably likely to cause, and that does cause, economic harm to another that is tortious … The circumstances must be such as to make the conduct sufficiently reprehensible to justify imposing on those who have brought about the harm liability in damages for having done so': *ibid*, [56].

[80] *Ibid*, [121].

The idea that lawful means conspiracy may be available in order to impose liability for particularly egregious conduct can be traced at least as far back as *Quinn* where Lord Halsbury expressed the view that the tort could be justified in terms of the 'jurisprudence of a civilised community'.[81] Lord Lindley, too, was attentive to just how reprehensible the defendants' conduct was in that case.[82] For both of these judges, one might say, there was a hole in the web of protection offered by tort law that needed to be plugged. Lord Hope was completely open about this kind of concern in *Total Network*, noting that '[t]he conspirators … cannot be sued as joint tortfeasors because there was no independent tort [of cheating the Revenue] … This is a gap that needs to be filled'.[83] Likewise, Lord Mance was of the view that 'there would be an evident lacuna if the law did not respond to this situation'.[84]

A fourth thing that can be said on behalf of lawful means conspiracy stems from the fact that it need not be thought of as a tort that is confined to the protection of trade and business interests. In *Scala Ballroom (Wolverhampton) Ltd v Ratcliffe*, for example, Hodson LJ remarked: '[a]lthough most of the cases have dealt with trade rivalry in some form or other, I do not see why the proposition as to the conditions under which conspiracy becomes a tort should be limited to trade competition'.[85] If this be so, the fact that its traditional role has largely been eclipsed by the 1998 Act must not be trumpeted too loudly.

The burden of this section has been to show that lawful means conspiracy – though by no means invoked on a day-to-day basis – can nonetheless be seen to possess a fair amount of (potential) practical significance, and in four clear ways. It helps anchor the modern tort of unlawful means conspiracy (as *Total Network* makes clear); it provides remedies in situations not covered by statutory competition law; it stands ready to provide a remedy against those who behave in an especially egregious way; and it may, in principle, be used beyond the confines of purely economic interests. These last two points concerning its largely unexplored potential, require some elaboration; and the next section of this chapter aims to provide just that.

D. Potential

On the back of an assessment of twenty-first century case law from Australia, Canada and England, Carty concludes that there is a marked 'revitalisation of

[81] *Quinn* (n 39) 506.
[82] *Ibid*, 536: 'The defendants' conduct was the more reprehensible because the plaintiff offered to pay the fees necessary to enable his non-union men to become members of the defendants' union; but this would not satisfy the defendants'.
[83] *Total Network* (n 1) [44].
[84] *Ibid*, [120] (Lord Mance). The idea of conspiracy being a gap-filler was also floated by Hodge J at first instance: 'a claim in conspiracy … may be used to bring to account those against whom the claimants might have no direct redress': [2005] EWHC 1 (QB) [21].
[85] *Scala Ballroom (Wolverhampton) Ltd v Ratcliffe* [1958] 1 WLR 1057 (CA), 1061.

judicial interest in conspiracy' which now 'signals to claimants that the conspiracy tort has a dynamic role to play'.[86] Equally, in *Lawrence v Peel Regional Police Force*, it was noted by the Ontario Court of Appeal that the respondent had engaged in intentional and malicious conduct which was 'at least arguably capable of implicating the respondent in … civil conspiracy'.[87] The court then made the point that 'the tort of … conspiracy [was] still developing and [that its] outer limits have not been defined'.[88] Such observations naturally prompt enquiry into the potential uses to which this tort could yet be put.

One important possibility is that, just like unlawful means conspiracy, it may conceivably be used as a device for circumventing the 'problem' posed by corporate limited liability where existing methods for so doing would be of no avail. The malicious purpose necessary for this tort would, I think, be evidence enough of the fact that a director could not plausibly claim to have acted with the good faith that would ensure the shield of limited corporate liability.[89] A number of scholars have certainly noted this possibility;[90] and so, too – perhaps more importantly – have a number of courts in several common law jurisdictions. The Irish Supreme Court held in *Taylor v Smyth* that a controlling shareholder and the company in which the shares are held may be treated as parties to a conspiracy. McCarthy J observed that 'it would seem invidious … that the assets of a limited company should not be liable to answer for conspiracy where its assets had been augmented as a result of the action alleged to constitute the conspiracy'.[91] He also concluded that what underpinned the decision in *Belmont Finance (No 1) v Williams Furniture*[92] was the principle that 'the separate legal entity of the company may, in law, conspire with those directors who, in effect, control it'.[93] In *Barclay Pharmaceuticals Ltd v Waypharm LP*,[94] Gloster J made clear that he, too, found this reasoning persuasive. He duly applied it in the case before him,[95] and the Singapore Court of Appeal took much the same approach in *Chew Kong Huat v Ricwil (Singapore) Pte Ltd*.[96]

Secondly, it is conceivable that lawful means conspiracy could be used in connection with losses other than those associated with trade or business.[97] It might, for example, be used in connection with damage to one's reputation in a

[86] Carty (n 17) 392.
[87] *Lawrence v Peel Regional Police Force* (2005) 250 DLR (4th) 287 (ONCA), [6].
[88] *Ibid*, [8].
[89] *Said v Butt* [1920] 3 KB 497.
[90] See, eg, C Witting, 'Intra-Corporate Conspiracy: An Intriguing Prospect' [2013] *CLJ* 178, 197; J O'Sullivan, 'Intentional Economic Torts, Commercial Transactions and Professional Liability' (2008) 24 *Professional Negligence* 164, 175–78.
[91] *Taylor v Smyth* [1991] 1 IR 142, 165.
[92] *Belmont Finance (No 1) v Williams Furniture* [1979] Ch 25 (CA).
[93] *Taylor v Smyth* (n 91) 166 (McCarthy J).
[94] *Barclay Pharmaceuticals Ltd v Waypharm LP* [2012] EWHC 306 (Comm).
[95] *Ibid*, [229].
[96] *Chew Kong Huat v Ricwil (Singapore) Pte Ltd* [1999] 3 SLR (R) 1167.
[97] Contrast the view of Deakin and Randall that '[t]he essence of the tort … [is] unjustified combination leading to economic pressure or harm': S Deakin and J Randall, 'Rethinking the Economic Torts' (2009) 72 *MLR* 519, 523.

case in which conspirators, actuated by malice, combine to spread damaging truths about an individual that would fall beyond the reach of defamation law. In *Gulf Oil (GB) Ltd v Page*,[98] the defendants conspired to fly a light aircraft over a race-course at which the claimant was entertaining a number of customers. Attached to the aircraft was a banner saying: 'Gulf exposed in fundamental breach' (which was perfectly true). The claimant sought an injunction to restrain the defendants from displaying the sign on the basis of lawful means conspiracy (it having been held at first instance that an injunction based on libel was unavailable because of the truth of what had been said[99]). Parker LJ noted the potential overlap between lawful means conspiracy and libel (which latter necessarily protects reputation).[100] And he noted, also, that in the instant case, the defendants had 'no immediate interest of their own to protect against Gulf and no interest of their own to further as against Gulf' for which reason there was, he said, 'a strong inference that the purpose of the display was simply to inflict upon Gulf the maximum possible damage … [and thus] a strong prima facie case in conspiracy to injure'.[101] A few years later, however, a differently constituted Court of Appeal held that *damages* for loss of reputation should never be available under the auspices of lawful means conspiracy.[102] Given, however, that injunctive relief would appear to be available, the question of whether there should be a blanket prohibition on the recovery of *damages* for lawful means conspiracy is perhaps best seen as a moot point. Chan, for example, argues powerfully that 'the ratio in *Lonrho* that non-pecuniary loss of reputation is not recoverable in the tort of conspiracy should be restricted to its particular facts' and that '[t]he case should not serve as a precedent to support a general blanket prohibition against loss of reputation claims in the tort of simple conspiracy'.[103]

These arguments cannot be dismissed lightly. For one thing, it is arguable that, in this respect, *Lonrho v Fayed* was decided *per incuriam*. There was a gap of only six years between the two cases, yet *Gulf Oil* was not cited once in *Lonrho*. Had it just been overlooked? More substantively, the argument that defamation law would be undermined by granting damages in lawful means conspiracy for loss of reputation is by no means watertight.[104] The fact that truth would comprise a complete

[98] *Gulf Oil (GB) Ltd v Page* [1987] Ch 327.

[99] There is no report of the first instance decision, but that this is why an action in defamation had been refused by Warner J was recorded in the Court of Appeal by Parker LJ: *ibid*, 332.

[100] *Ibid*, 333–34: '[a] plaintiff in an action against the author and publisher of a newspaper article, for example, might well establish a combination … [but given the predominant purpose requirement in the latter] the court would scrutinise with the greatest care any case where a cause of action in conspiracy was joined to a cause of action in defamation'.

[101] *Ibid*, 332–33.

[102] *Lonrho Plc v Fayed (No 5)* [1994] 1 All ER 188 (CA), 195–96, 202–203 and 210–11 (Dillon, Stuart-Smith and Evans LJJ, respectively).

[103] G Chan, 'Never say "Never" for the Truth Can Hurt: Defamatory but True Statements in the Tort of Simple Conspiracy' (2007) 31 *Melbourne University Law Review* 321, 342.

[104] This argument appears in the judgment of Dillon LJ in the *Lonrho* case. He said: 'it would, in my judgment, be lamentable if a plaintiff could recover damages against defendants who had combined to tell the truth about the plaintiff and so had destroyed his unwarranted reputation': *Lonrho* (n 102) 195.

defence in defamation cannot be translated into the claim that saying something truthful is an *absolute* freedom that we all possess. Clearly, modern developments in the law concerning the misuse of private information[105] would have no basis if there were always immunity granted to those who disclose certain truthful, confidential facts about someone else. Furthermore, the House of Lords in *Spring v Guardian Assurance Plc*[106] has since made clear that, just because the facts of a case might support a defence under the law of defamation, does not preclude the possibility of liability under a different tort. In that case, the claimant successfully sued a former employer in connection with a negligently prepared reference written by the latter about the claimant which falsely stated that the claimant was dishonest and not to be trusted. According to their Lordships, the fact that a defence of qualified privilege would have been available had the action been framed in defamation made no difference to liability under the tort of negligence.

E. Reservations

As against the idea that lawful means conspiracy has the potential to operate more broadly than it presently does, there are those who would (at most) wish to keep it confined to its established functions which are limited both in number and in scope. Carty, for example, thinks that the economic torts ought only to apply in three-party cases. In her view, the recognition in *Total Network* of conspiracy's capacity to operate in a purely two-party setting 'takes the tort out of obscurity, unsettles the other economic torts and places it centre-stage in controlling commercial practice'.[107] But it is difficult to agree with this claim. Allowing claims for lawful means conspiracy in two-party cases does not, *ipso facto*, unsettle the other economic torts. Indeed, it is arguable that the nineteenth century case of *Gregory v Duke of Brunswick*[108] was an early two-party conspiracy case. If that be right, then it is especially notable: for it has never been overruled, and it has never exerted any unsettling effect on the development of the three-party economic torts.

Equally, it is hard to see why Carty should suppose that rescuing conspiracy from a slide into post-*OBG* redundancy will or could lead to its being placed 'centre-stage in controlling commercial practice'. The rule in *Rylands v Fletcher* was similarly rescued from near desuetude in the mid-1990s in *Cambridge Water Co Ltd v Eastern Counties Leather Plc*,[109] but this did not affect the infrequency with which this action has been invoked by tort claimants ever since. There are, when it

[105] See, eg, *Campbell v MGN Ltd* [2004] 2 AC 457 (HL).
[106] *Spring v Guardian Assurance Plc* [1995] 2 AC 296 (HL).
[107] *Ibid*, 404.
[108] *Gregory v Duke of Brunswick* (1843) 6 Man & G 205 (defendants conspired to hiss the claimant in a theatre, force him off the stage, and prevent him from earning a living). For analysis, see J Charlesworth, 'Conspiracy as a Ground of Civil Liability' (1920) 36 *LQR* 38, 40–41.
[109] *Cambridge Water Co Ltd v Eastern Counties Leather Plc* [1994] AC 264.

comes to controlling commercial practices, far more reported cases based on causing loss by unlawful means, inducing breach of contract and the Competition Act 1998, than there are cases concerning lawful means conspiracy. That this should be so seems unsurprising given that none of these wrongs, unlike conspiracy, requires a combination of multiple wrongdoers. But by the same token, as noted earlier, it does not follow that, just because lawful means conspiracy cases are thin on the ground, they deserve to be regarded as unimportant.

A second reservation concerning the indirect resuscitation of lawful means conspiracy in *Total Network* strikes directly at my suggestion that this tort could play an important potential role in circumventing corporate limited liability in certain cases. Once again, it is Carty who has registered the objection. She puts it this way:

> In recent English cases where claimants have complained that the defendant has used complex commercial arrangements to facilitate a gain or avoid financial obligations at the claimant's expense, other established civil liability was in fact available … [For example] the use of complex company structures involved breaches of contract and the tort of causing loss by unlawful means in *Barclay*; [and] the use of asset transfer arrangements to defeat the claimant's financial stake involved a breach of contract in *Meretz Investments NV v ACP Ltd*.[110] And of course the use of a transaction chain in *Total Network* was at one point alleged to have involved fraudulent misrepresentation.[111]

In essence, the argument here can be reduced to the following proposition: there is no need to extend the reach of conspiracy liability since so doing will needlessly replicate the protection already afforded by other branches of the civil law. The argument, however, is flawed because, although causes of action do sometimes overlap, it does not follow that any given one of them can be regarded as superfluous. So, for example, where tort liability runs concurrently with liability for breach of contract – one of the overlaps specifically mentioned by Carty – the limitation periods will not be the same and the claimant may well benefit from being able to sue in tort even though the contract limitation period has expired given that, for torts in which damage must be shown (including those in this book), the tort limitation period does not begin to run until damage occurs.[112] Equally, if the case were to possess an international dimension, it would attract the application of a different set of choice of jurisdiction and choice of law rules depending on whether it was pursued in contract or tort. These different rules could well make a significant difference to the claimant's case.

[110] *Meretz Investments NV v ACP Ltd* [2007] EWCA Civ 1303.
[111] Carty (n 17) 410.
[112] *Roberts v Read* (1812) 16 East 215. By contrast, the limitation period in contract begins on the date of the breach, regardless of whether loss occurs at that stage. For an example of this difference making it advantageous to pursue an action in tort in a case of concurrent liability, see *Henderson v Merrett Syndicates Ltd* [1995] 2 AC 145 (HL). For analysis of further ways in which these overlapping actions come apart, see J Gardner and J Murphy, 'Concurrent Liability in Contract and Tort: A Separation Thesis' (2021) 137 *LQR* 77.

Leaving the overlap with contract to one side, it may be argued that there is no reason to consider it a problem that two or more of the economic torts overlap. For one thing, not all torts share the same remoteness of damage rules; and it is not clear that there are any at all in relation to lawful means conspiracy bearing in mind that Lord Lindley said in *Quinn* that 'intention to injure the plaintiff negatives all excuses and disposes of any question of remoteness of damage'.[113] In any event, it has been judicially accepted that various economic torts may overlap. In *OBG*, Lord Walker said: '[t]he tort of intentionally inducing a breach of contract is essentially different from inflicting harm by unlawful means, although in some factual situations they may overlap'.[114] But there is no need to stop at just two torts. If D_1 and D_2 were to combine and make a joint threat against intermediary X, saying: 'we will beat you up unless you break your contract with C', they might conceivably be liable for inducing breaching contract, or the unlawful means tort, or unlawful means conspiracy.

What is vital here is not the fact that overlap can occur but the point that there is no reason to suppose that any two overlapping torts will furnish identical remedies. The malice element in lawful means conspiracy, for example, could well pave the way to an award of aggravated damages,[115] depending on whether the claimant is a corporate entity or a real person.[116] And even if one thinks that such damages should be available in all the economic torts (by virtue of their requiring intentional wrongdoing), it is noteworthy that Woolf J once stated that they would be 'wholly inappropriate' in relation to a breach of contract.[117]

F. Final Remarks

The first part of this chapter has attempted to demonstrate that, far from being an anomaly whose days are numbered, lawful means conspiracy remains a vital tort that fulfils (or has the capacity to fulfil) a number of roles which, for all that they are rather esoteric, are nonetheless important. To Carty's claim that this tort offers 'protection only in the most extreme cases of hostility and vendetta'[118] may be added the observation that it can also be used to impose liability for the underhand

[113] *Quinn* (n 39) 537.

[114] *OBG* (n 2) [264]. Similarly, Lord Hoffmann noted (*ibid*, [21]): 'there is no reason why the same facts should not give rise to both accessory liability under *Lumley v Gye* and primary liability for using unlawful means'.

[115] For example, in *Thompson v Commissioner of Police for the Metropolis* [1998] QB 498 (CA), 516, Woolf MR specifically recognised that '[a]ggravating features can include … [behaving] in a high-handed, insulting, malicious or oppressive manner'.

[116] For the argument that it is hard to see how a corporation can have the necessary dignitary interest to be awarded aggravated damages, see J Murphy, 'The Nature and Domain of Aggravated Damages' [2010] *CLJ* 353, 369.

[117] *Kralj v McGrath* [1986] 1 All ER 54, 61 (Woolf J).

[118] Carty (n 24) 149.

use – by individuals and parent companies – of various corporate devices designed to secure for the unscrupulous businessman an immunity from liability that few would consider just.

Nor must the rarity with which this tort is used in practice be mistaken for its redundancy. The fact, noted by Tony Weir, that '[d]isinterested malevolence is so rare'[119] in no way undermines the observation, also made by Weir, that without this tort 'some deplorable conduct escapes sanction because no law or contract was broken'.[120]

Certainly, some eyebrows will always be raised at the fact that this tort renders ostensibly lawful acts unlawful when they are performed by (or on behalf of) two or more conspirators. But, as noted, this aspect of the tort is readily explained in terms of an abuse of the power to combine. And equally, although malice – the factor that illuminates that abuse of power – is a fairly unusual touchstone of liability in tort, it is by no means unique to this tort.[121] Furthermore, although tethering liability to a malice requirement makes the judicial task of deciding lawful means conspiracy cases a difficult one, it is a long way from being an impossible one. After all, 'the state of a man's mind is as much a fact as the state of his digestion';[122] and though establishing what a person may have been thinking is always likely to be at least tricky, this does not license the claim that the need to prove malice 'plunges the courts into all sorts of difficulty … ascertaining people's motives'.[123] Such alarmist concerns must be dismissed for at least four reasons.

First, the criminal law almost invariably requires proof of intent; so it might well be asked why proof of malice (on the balance of probabilities) in a civil law case is likely to create any such problem when proof of intent (beyond all reasonable doubt) in criminal law does not do so. Secondly, the very fact that this tort is only infrequently invoked helps put into perspective the true amount of time-consuming work for the courts that it is capable of generating. Thirdly, in other tort cases in which malice may figure – such as cases in which aggravated damages are sought, or defamation cases in which the facility to plead qualified privilege is in question – it seems fairly clear that the courts do not consider themselves to be placed under unmanageable strain because they are forced to grapple with the question of malice. Fourthly, even if the need to prove malice does produce more work for the courts, it remains true (as Lord Toulson pointed out in *Willers v Joyce*) that '[e]xpenditure of court time is sometimes the public price of justice'.[124]

A final thought is this. Even if one remains unconvinced by the merits and largely untapped potential of this tort, it remains true to say that providing a compelling reason as to why it should be abandoned is a good deal harder. Our

[119] T Weir, *Economic Torts* (Oxford, Clarendon Press, 1997) 73.
[120] *Ibid.*
[121] See Murphy (n 6).
[122] *Edgington v Fitzmaurice* (1885) 29 Ch 459 (CA), 483.
[123] McBride and Bagshaw (n 71) 659.
[124] *Willers v Joyce* [2018] AC 779 (SC), [58].

most senior courts often supplement, distinguish, modify, reinterpret or extend to new spheres of operation existing rules of law. But rare is the day when they conjure up convincing reasons to abandon them. The idea that the recently revitalised law of conspiracy threatens to unsettle the other economic torts was shown to be wrongheaded. And the fact that this tort may overlap with other causes of action was shown also not to warrant the conclusion that it is superfluous, a fifth wheel on the coach.

I would suggest, in fact, that the only plausible basis for abandoning this tort would be that is clashes irreconcilably with some other established tort or rule of law. Some, of course, suggest that this is exactly what it does. For them, the decision in *Quinn* is seen as incompatible with the perceived orthodoxy of *Allen*.[125] Yet that argument, too, is ultimately unconvincing. Not only was there a different majority view on the presence of threats in the two cases,[126] there was also, in *Allen*, the express reservation that, 'this case can have no bearing on any case which involves the element of oppressive combination' since '[t]he vice of that form of terrorism … and other forms of oppressive combination, seem to me to depend on considerations which are … in the present case conspicuously absent'.[127]

II. Two-Party Intimidation

A. Introduction

The tort of intimidation is of very considerable vintage.[128] Yet, so sparse were the reported cases during the three centuries that followed its first application that, in the landmark case of *Rookes v Barnard*, one Court of Appeal judge described it as an 'obscure, unfamiliar and peculiar cause of action'.[129] The tort had certainly eluded anything approaching rigorous judicial analysis or exposition until the House of Lords had occasion to examine it thoroughly in that case.[130] So it was

[125] See, eg, P Elias and K Ewing, 'Economic Torts and Labour Law: Old Principles and New Liabilities' [1982] *CLJ* 321, 324: 'The immediate problem with *Quinn v Leathem* was how to reconcile it with *Allen v Flood* … [since] [m]any statements in *Quinn v Leathem* are simply irreconcilable with *Allen*'.

[126] For a useful summary of these, see Beever (n 48) 125–28.

[127] *Allen* (n 7) 153 (Lord Macnaghten). Lord Wright, roughly half a century later, agreed that the presence of a combination in the latter case made all the difference in *Crofter* (n 1) 467.

[128] One very early case is *Garrett v Taylor* (1620) Cro Jac 567 (the claimant, a quarryman, could sue the defendant who had threatened would-be purchasers of quarried stone with 'mayhem' if they continued to buy from the claimant). A more doubtful antecedent, though one which is regularly cited, is *Tarleton v M'Gawley* (1793) Peake NP 270. There was an unlawful act, rather than an unlawful threat, on the part of the defendant in that case. He fired a ship's canon at a canoe containing Cameroonian natives to prevent the natives from trading with the defendant's rival whose vessel was moored just off the coast. Making a distinction between unlawful threats and unlawful acts is crucial in understanding intimidation properly: see below pp 129–30.

[129] *Rookes v Barnard* [1963] 1 QB 623 (CA), 694 (Pearson LJ).

[130] *Rookes v Barnard* [1964] AC 1129 (HL). The case in which the tort had most rigorously been examined prior to *Rookes* was *Allen* (n 7).

perhaps unsurprising that one stand-out feature of *Rookes* should have been that the defendant persisted throughout the litigation in denying the existence of any such tort.[131] No doubt with this persistent denial in mind, academic commentary at the time suggested that, 'in *Rookes v Barnard*, the House of Lords has invented a new extension of civil liability',[132] and that the case involved 'a bold instance of judicial lawmaking'.[133]

Rookes involved a claimant who successfully invoked intimidation as an independent cause of action when he was lawfully dismissed, with proper notice, from his job. His dismissal was brought about when various colleagues threatened to break their own contracts of employment with their common employer unless the latter dismissed the claimant. More important than the bare recognition by the House of Lords of this tort's existence is the fact that Lord Devlin maintained that 'the tort can take one of two forms':[134] the first involving two parties; the second involving three.[135] It is only the two-party version that concerns us in this chapter. According to Lord Devlin, it entails A threatening B and thereby coercing B into acting to his detriment. The existence of such a version – though not the variety actually invoked by the claimant in *Rookes* – was accepted by jurists and judges alike in the decades that followed;[136] and this represented the orthodox view of the law for a little over 40 years.[137]

Then, quite momentously, Lord Hoffmann painted a very different picture of the legal landscape in *OBG*. Among other things, he specifically called into question the continued vitality of *both* versions of the tort. He said, first, that any case of three-party intimidation ought henceforth to be seen as a mere example, or subspecies, of the unlawful means tort whereby A uses unlawful means – whether they be threats or acts – against B with the intention of thereby causing loss to C.[138] On this account, an act of intimidation would in future count as no more than one among several possible forms of the requisite 'unlawful means'. Such an approach to the three-party version of intimidation seems perfectly sensible; but his Lordship's

[131] No less remarkable is the fact that, when he subsequently wrote a book about the case, the claimant gave it the title 'Conspiracy': see D Rookes, *Conspiracy* (London, Johnson Publications, 1966).

[132] KW Wedderburn, 'Intimidation and the Right to Strike' (1964) 27 *MLR* 257, 257.

[133] L Hoffmann, '*Rookes v Barnard*' (1965) 81 *LQR* 116, 116.

[134] *Rookes* (n 130) 1205. A similar point was made by Lord Watson in *Allen* (n 7) 98: '[i]f coercion … was employed, it was a wrong done as much to the Glengall Iron Company, who are the parties said to have been coerced, as to the respondents'.

[135] In this there was nothing genuinely new: two-party intimidation was clearly recognised in *Gilbert v Stone* (1641) Aleyn 35; whereas the three-party version of the tort had its origins in *Garrett v Taylor* (n 128).

[136] As to jurists, see, eg, Heydon (n 54) 64; M Jones (ed), *Clerk and Lindsell on Torts*, 23rd edn (London, Sweet & Maxwell, 2020) 1770; BA Hepple *et al*, *Tort – Cases and Materials*, 5th edn (London, Butterworths, 2000) 99. As to the judges, there were no reported cases before *OBG* that cast the slightest doubt on Lord Devlin's taxonomy.

[137] Without questioning what had been said in *Rookes*, Stuart Smith J, in the middle of this 40-year period, said no more than that, '[t]he tort is one of intention and the plaintiff … must be a person whom A intended to injure': *Newsgroup Newspapers Ltd v SOGAT '82* [1987] ICR 181 (CA), 204.

[138] *OBG* (n 2) [6]–[7] and [47].

view of two-party intimidation was much less commendable because, ultimately, he was entirely cryptic in dealing with it.

Insofar as he can be said to have dealt with it at all, Lord Hoffmann said all that he had to say about two-party intimidation in roughly the first third of his speech in *OBG*. This was the part of his judgment devoted to the 'clearing of the ground'.[139] In it, he was at pains to distil from the confused state of the relevant case law concerning the economic torts just two main causes of action: causing loss by unlawful means and inducing breach of contract. His assiduous attempt to repackage the various cases into either one or other of these actions could arguably be interpreted as an implicit rejection of two-party intimidation since both causing loss by unlawful means and inducing breach of contract operate *necessarily* in a three-party framework.

Even if this is not right, Lord Hoffmann certainly raised doubts about the future role of two-party intimidation in this setting when he said that it raised 'altogether different issues'[140] than those at play in the actions for causing loss by unlawful means and inducing breach of contract. The suggestion that there was an important distinction between two-party intimidation, on the one hand, and the other two causes of action (which he readily endorsed) on the other, was plain enough, even though he failed to elaborate on what exactly was meant by 'altogether different issues'. Did he mean to suggest that it was a recognised cause of action, but not one that had anything to do with the two economic torts he so sedulously described? Or was his point, rather, that two-party intimidation was not a recognised part of tort law, but something else, such as – for example – another way of referring to economic duress in the sphere of contract law?[141] In the remainder of this chapter, I seek to show that, notwithstanding Lord Hoffmann's hostility towards two-party intimidation, it remains a vital tort and one that, like lawful means conspiracy, cannot simply or sensibly be labelled an anomaly.

B. Vitality

The very fact that Lord Hoffmann suggested that a different set of considerations were applicable in cases of two-party intimidation naturally invited conjecture as to just what those considerations might be. And a number of commentators have since duly speculated in this respect. The plausibility of their suggestions will be examined in due course. But for now it is important to establish just why, despite the cloud of doubt that was cast over its existence in *OBG*, the tort of two-party intimidation must still be regarded as alive and well.

[139] *Ibid*, [65].

[140] *Ibid*, [61].

[141] There is clearly some overlap (explored below); and the Court of Appeal certainly said in *Dawson v Bell* [2016] EWCA Civ 96 (CA) that pressure of a kind that would not amount to economic duress would also not be enough to ground an action for two-party intimidation.

Within a year of *OBG* being decided, *Total Network* provided weighty support for the idea that two-party intimidation should be regarded as an extant tort. Indeed, as we have noted already, the differently constituted panel in that case specifically used its existence as part of the platform upon which they felt able to reconstruct the tort of unlawful means conspiracy. Lord Hope was keen to draw a distinction between the three-party cases that occupied their Lordships' thoughts in *OBG* and the two-party cases of intimidation and conspiracy. This second class of case, he opined, was characterised by 'loss caused by an unlawful act directed at the claimants themselves'.[142] It was, therefore, agreed Lord Mance, a very different type of tort.[143]

A second, no less compelling, reason for regarding as vital the tort of two-party intimidation comes into view once we recognise an obvious oversight on the part of Lord Hoffmann in *OBG* when he reconceptualised three-party intimidation as merely one way in which the broader tort of causing loss by unlawful means could be committed. The thing that he seemed not to notice is that it is impossible to treat three-party cases as mere instances of the more general tort without first accepting the juridical vitality of two-party intimidation. This claim requires some unpacking.

Lord Hoffmann treated the now rather ancient cases of *Garrett v Taylor*[144] and *Tarleton v M'Gawley*[145] as the starting point for understanding the modern tort of causing loss by unlawful means.[146] He explained that, '[because these cases] involved the use of unlawful threats to intimidate potential customers, *Salmond on Torts* had classified them as "intimidation" cases'.[147] He then pointed out that judicial confirmation of this tort's existence was supplied by the House of Lords in *Rookes v Barnard*. However, in the very next sentence of his speech he suggested that, since 'an interference with the liberty of others by unlawful means does not require threats', it must follow that 'Salmond's tort of intimidation is therefore only one variant of a broader tort, usually called for short "causing loss by unlawful means"'.[148]

Although there is nothing objectionable about the reasoning here, what is questionable is his Lordship's attempt, somewhat later in the speech, to side-line (perhaps even undermine) the independent tort of two-party intimidation by suggesting, as we have already seen, that it (along with lawful means conspiracy) raised 'altogether different issues'. But how true can this really be?

[142] *Total Network* (n 1) [43]–[44].

[143] After making specific reference to the fact that Lord Hoffmann had said that two-party intimidation raised 'altogether different issues', his Lordship went on (effectively) to restate Lord Hope's point that 'there is … a distinction between the infliction of harm through the intermediary of a third party (as in the case of the tort of causing harm by unlawful means under consideration in *OBG Ltd v Allan*) and [cases of two-party intimidation as well as] the present situation [involving unlawful means conspiracy]': *ibid*, [124]. Lord Walker agreed: *ibid*, [99].

[144] *Garrett v Taylor* (n 128).

[145] *Ibid.*

[146] *OBG* (n 2) [6].

[147] *Ibid*, [7].

[148] *Ibid.*

The presence of unlawful means is central to the operation of the 'broader tort'. Thus, in the examples he considered, such unlawful means could only be the illegitimate threat that was made by the defendant to the intermediary (for this is all that the defendant will have done). If A's threatening B so as to compel B into a course of conduct that B would not otherwise have chosen to pursue is not independently actionable (or at least potentially so[149]), there would never be, according to Lord Hoffmann's conception of the 'broader tort', any prospect of a third party, C, invoking the unlawful means tort against A. Put bluntly, a case of three-party intimidation cannot logically be treated as an example of the broader tort without first acknowledging the independent tortious quality of two-party intimidation.[150] It is the commission of the two-party tort that supplies the requisite unlawful means in a three-party case.

Also, although as a general matter Lord Hoffmann seemed keen to cast doubt over the existence of two-party intimidation, he also implicitly acknowledged its vitality at one point in his speech. When explaining his exception to the rule that the unlawful means must be actionable by the intermediary in a case involving the unlawful means tort, he noted specifically that, '[i]n the case of intimidation … the threat will usually give rise to no cause of action by the [threatened] third party because he will have suffered no loss'.[151] But in so saying, he was as good as acknowledging that the threatened intermediary would be able to sue if she herself had also suffered loss. The implied acceptance of two-party intimidation as an independent tort is inescapable, here.

A third and final reason for thinking that two-party intimidation is alive and well stems from the fact that there are a number of cases which have been decided on this exact basis (or at least expressly recognised its existence). *Godwin v Uzoigwe*,[152] *Kolmar Group AG v Traxpo Enterprises Pvt Ltd*,[153] *Gilbert v Stone*,[154] *Newsgroup Newspapers Ltd v SOGAT '82*,[155] *AS v Murray*[156] and *Al Nehayan v Kent*[157] all provide concrete evidence of the existence of the tort.

[149] Lord Hoffmann was insistent that unlawful means must be a civil wrong against the intermediary that is (or would be, but for the absence of loss) independently actionable by that intermediary: *OBG* (n 2) [49].

[150] For other academic recognition of this point, see A Botterell *et al* (eds), *Fridman's The Law of Torts in Canada*, 4th edn (Toronto, Carswell, 2020) 918–19.

[151] *OBG* (n 2) [49].

[152] *Godwin v Uzoigwe* [1993] *Fam Law* 65 (CA).

[153] *Kolmar Group AG v Traxpo Enterprises Pvt Ltd* [2010] 1 CLC 256.

[154] *Gilbert* (n 135), and see especially the dictum reproduced there.

[155] *Newsgroup Newspapers* (n 137). Only the action against the seventh defendant turned on two-party intimidation.

[156] *AS v Murray* [2013] NSWSC 733. In this case, the claimant had been using an internet dating service but did not want his wife and family to know about this. The defendant, however, threatened to tell the claimant's family unless he paid the defendant a large amount of money. Although the claimant did not plead intimidation, the trial judge found for him on this basis (at [14]), relying on the crime of extortion which is defined under the Crimes Act (NSW) 1900, ss 249K and 249M in terms of making menacing (illegal) threats with the intention of obtaining a gain.

[157] *Al Nehayan v Kent* [2018] EWHC 333 (Comm). Two-party intimidation was just one of three alternative reasons given for saying that the claimant could claim damages in this case.

True, some of these cases pre-date Lord Hoffmann's scepticism in *OBG*. But while that may be so, it is equally true that none of them was held to have been wrongly decided in *OBG*. Indeed, *Gilbert v Stone* was specifically relied upon in his Lordship's construction of the unlawful means tort.

C. Gist

It is generally accepted that in order for an action for intimidation to succeed, three things must be shown: intention to cause harm, an illegitimate threat and resulting harm.

It may reasonably be supposed that intention bears the same meaning in the context of two-party intimidation as it does in the three-party intimidation cases to which Lord Hoffmann referred in sketching the origins of the unlawful means tort. After all, it is perfectly possible that in a three-party case, both the threatened intermediary and the targeted victim may wish to pursue a claim. In a scenario such as the one in *Rookes* itself, both the employer who loses an employee, and the employee who loses his job may consider themselves to have suffered a loss as a result of the defendant's intimidation. The test of intention adopted in *OBG*[158] in relation to the three-party tort, can therefore be said with some confidence to be the applicable test of intention here.

Nor is it necessary to describe here the fine-grained distinctions that can be made between threats, on the one hand, and mere warnings or advice, on the other.[159] This is because these matters have no bearing on the twin aims of this chapter: that is, to demonstrate that the tort is vital and to show that it has considerable potential *so long as* it is accepted that it has nothing specifically to do with the protection of economic interests. That said, it is worth saying a little about what is required in order for a threat to be regarded as an illegitimate one and also, considerably more about what constitutes the crux of actionability, since these matters are central to our grasping the true potential of this tort.

i. Illegitimate Threats

Although it is trite to say that the tort of intimidation requires the defendant to have made an unlawful threat (or at least one that is illegitimate[160]), it is not quite

[158] 'In the unlawful means tort, there must be an intention to cause loss … [and] [o]ne intends to cause loss even though it is the means by which one achieved the end of enriching oneself': *OBG* (n 2) [62].

[159] For the difference between threats and advice, see *JT Stratford & Son Ltd v Lindley* [1965] AC 269 (HL), 340 (Lord Donovan); and for the difference between threats and inducements and warnings, see *Conway v Wade* [1909] AC 506 (HL), 510 (Lord Loreburn).

[160] For the suggestion that two-party intimidation is a distinct tort but that it requires illegitimate (as opposed to unlawful) threats, see J Edelman, 'A Historical Essay on Duress, Intimidation and Menaces' [2011] *Journal of Corporate Affairs and Corporate Crimes* 1. For Edelman, the requirement of illegitimacy is seemingly a mere control device used to limit 'the indirect and potentially expansive liability which can arise in those cases': *ibid*, 9.

so obvious just what such threats consist of. And yet, for all that I shall argue in due course that this tort possesses considerable untapped potential, it is important to appreciate the limits on its usefulness imposed by this requirement.

We can work towards an understanding of what is involved here by use of a hypothetical. Suppose a mother were to cajole her child into action saying, 'Tidy your room right now or else there will be no pocket money for you this week!' In such a case, we can be confident that no-one would seriously think that the tort of intimidation has been committed. It is easy to see why. The mother would be perfectly entitled not just to withhold the child's spending money, but also to threaten to withhold it. As Lord Reid explained in *Rookes v Barnard*:

> [S]o long as the defendant only threatens to do what he has a legal right to do he is on safe ground … but I agree with Lord Herschell that there is a chasm between doing what you have a legal right to do and threatening to do what you have no legal right to do.[161]

From this we may infer that the tort of intimidation requires a threat to do something that one is not legally entitled to do. The reasoning would appear to be as follows. The very fact that what I threaten to do would not be something that I am legally entitled to do, necessarily colours the threat that I make and gives it the capacity to be treated as independently unlawful. Put perhaps more simply, the fact that I am prohibited by law from doing what I threaten to do causes my words to cross the line that separates lawful persuasion from unlawful coercion.[162]

Yet, this only takes us so far since the bare notion of 'threatening to do what you have no legal right to do' fails to illuminate sufficiently the range of possible threatened illegal acts that might count for these purposes. One might argue, for example, that threats to commit crimes, torts and breaches of contract should all qualify as unlawful threats on the straightforward footing that crimes, torts and breaches of contract are all things that we have no legal right to do.[163] However, Carty thinks – bearing in mind Lord Hoffmann's assertion in *OBG* that cases which formerly would have constituted three-party intimidation ought now to be seen as falling within the unlawful means tort – that only threats to commit civil wrongs will fit the bill. She thinks this way because she believes that in relation to instances of the unlawful means tort involving intimidation, 'threatened unlawful acts are [to be] equated to the unlawful acts themselves',[164] and that two-party cases should follow suit [and insist on civil wrongs] to ensure the rational development of the law.[165]

[161] *Rookes* (n 130) 1168. In similar vein, see *Crofter* (n 1) 467 (Lord Wright). For an important qualifier, see the law on lawful act duress in cases such as *CTN Cash & Carry v Gallagher* [1994] 4 All ER 714 (CA) and *Kent* (n 157) [230]; *Pakistan International Airline Corporation v Times Travel (UK) Ltd* [2021] UKSC 40.

[162] Note however that a mere threat to do something unlawful will not by itself suffice: the threat must succeed in being coercive: *Newsgroup Newspapers* (n 137) 204 (Stuart-Smith LJ).

[163] For example, in *Morgan v Fry* [1968] 2 QB 710 (CA), 724, Lord Denning MR expressed the view that threats of 'violence or a tort or a breach of contract' would all suffice.

[164] Carty (n 24) 120. She makes exactly the same claim in H Carty, 'The Economic Torts in the 21st Century' (2008) 124 *LQR* 641, 668.

[165] Carty (n 24) 113.

Because of her desire to equate the threat with the act threatened, Carty rules out the possibility that making a threat to commit a crime that has no tort law counterpart could count as an unlawful threat. And while it is true that there may only be a few such crimes, it is nonetheless important to recognise that insistence on equating the threat with the act threatened causes us to miss something crucial, namely, that unlawful threats have independent juridical significance. They have such significance because they interfere with the victim's decision-making freedom. That, in turn, feeds into the most crucial point of all, namely, that intimidation, properly understood, is not a tort specifically concerned with the protection of economic interests.

Before that point can be explored in more detail, however, it is important to demonstrate why Carty is mistaken in thinking that an unlawful threat must be equated with a particular civil wrong that has been threatened. After all, their Lordships did express considerable praise for what they regarded as the helpful analysis contained in her book.[166]

Three main grounds may be given for thinking that her treatment of this matter is flawed.[167] The first is simple enough to state. As noted already, their Lordships in *OBG* sought to show how the unlawful means tort had its origins in the seventeenth century case of *Garrett v Taylor*[168] (where the defendant had threatened would-be purchasers of quarried stone with 'mayhem' if they continued to buy from the claimant). Carty even applauds the fact that their Lordships 'followed a "back to basics" approach'[169] whereby *OBG* represented an attempt to align the unlawful means tort with its progenitor. But – and this is the crucial point – there is precisely nothing in *Garrett* (or any of the other ancient cases) that suggests that unlawful threats are to be equated with the acts actually threatened.

Secondly, the notion that the threat made ought to be equated with the act threatened is inconsistent with Lord Hodson's declaration in *Rookes* that, 'the vice of the respondents' action is the threat to break [a contract] and not the breach itself'.[170] So saying clearly afforded independent, juridical significance to the unlawful threat in that case.

Thirdly, Carty's suggested approach employs a legally ungrounded conception of unlawful threats. For her, only threats to do something that would or could be an actionable wrong against the person threatened will count in a three-party case.

[166] No fewer than three of their Lordships acknowledged the general helpfulness of Carty's analysis of the economic torts: see *OBG* (n 2) [65], [195] and [306] (Lord Hoffmann, Lord Nicholls and Baroness Hale, respectively). There is, therefore, a danger that without exposing the flaws in Carty's analysis on this matter, their Lordships might be taken implicitly to have signed up to it when, in reality, they were entirely silent on her examination of the relationship between the threats made and the acts threatened.

[167] For a fuller account than is offered here of why Carty's insistence on equating the threat with the act threatened is wrongheaded, see J Murphy, 'Understanding Intimidation' (2014) 77 *MLR* 33, 39–44.

[168] *Garrett v Taylor* (n 128).

[169] *Ibid.*

[170] *Rookes* (n 130) 1200–01.

She does not say this explicitly,[171] but it is something that can safely be inferred from the conjunction of two other claims that she does make. The first, already noted, is that there ought to be 'a rational development' of intimidation alongside the unlawful means tort (for which rational development she sees a common meaning of unlawfulness to be essential).[172] The second is her central claim that in cases of three-party intimidation, the threats in question must be 'equated to the unlawful acts'. From a conjunction of these two points it must follow that, in her view, whatever counts as unlawful means in the context of the *OBG* tort will also, of necessity, govern the threats that will count for the purposes of intimidation. But the view seems to rule out a very obvious case of intimidation that would not meet Carty's definition.

Imagine a scenario in which X threatens Y that he will physically harm Y's son, S, unless Y agrees to quit working for Z forthwith. In such a case, if the threat were to be equated with the act threatened, then the relevant act would be the battery of S rather than some or other tort committed directly against Y. As such, according to Lord Hoffmann's definition of unlawful means in *OBG*, there would be no action available to Z here *unless* the threat were treated as independently actionable by Y. Equating the threat made to Y with the commission of a battery against S is not something that would ordinarily confer a right of action upon Y,[173] and for this reason would leave both Y and Z with no remedy. But this must surely be wrong. It flies in the face of Lord Hodson's insistence that threats to break contracts must be seen as distinct from breach itself.[174] And it is also hard to reconcile with the fact that, in the parallel context of duress in contract law, it is now well established that threats to commit a tort against the employees of the claimant will suffice insofar as they coerce the will of the claimant.[175]

At bottom, Carty's narrow conception of unlawful threats causes us to lose sight of what is genuinely wrong with the making of unlawful threats: the coercion of the threatened person. And this is the key point. The examination of what unlawful threats entail has led us to uncover what seems to be the gist of two-party intimidation, namely, coercion of the victim. In order to achieve this, a sizeable array of threats – and not just threats to commit an actionable civil wrong against the claimant herself – will suffice. These include threats to commit civil wrongs against third parties, such as those with whom the

[171] Oddly, however, she does make this claim explicitly in relation to two-party intimidation (Carty (n 24) 121). That said, just a few paragraphs earlier, she expresses the view that 'the two-party tort of intimidation is in fact a "case apart"': *ibid*, 120.

[172] Carty (n 24) 115.

[173] One might seek to argue that it would still be a tort against Y if one knew that beating up Y's son would lead to Y quitting his job with Z in order to nurse his son. But there can be no guarantee that Y would act in this way. For example, his son might be an independent adult, or have health insurance that would cover the nursing costs, or Y may suffer from a disability that would prevent him from nursing his son. In short, there is no basis for thinking that the battery of Y's son must necessarily entail a tort against Y, as well.

[174] *Rookes* (n 130) 1200–01.

[175] *Gulf Azov Shipping Co Ltd v Idisi* [2001] 1 Lloyd's Rep 727 (CA).

threatened person enjoys a strong bond of affection, and possibly also those with whom the threatened person enjoys a valuable trading (or other economic) relationship.

I would also submit that threats to commit crimes of any complexion ought to suffice on the strength of Lord Devlin's having said as much in *Rookes*.[176] I recognise that this is not an uncontroversial matter, for it is perfectly true that in the wake of *Lonrho Ltd v Shell Petroleum Co Ltd*[177] there may be legitimate doubt about whether a threat to contravene a purely penal statute will suffice in this context. The current edition of *Clerk and Lindsell on Torts* certainly considers it to be an 'absurdity that they [ie, the defendants in that case] would be liable if they threatened [to breach the statute], but not liable if they deliberately inflicted the damage by the same illegal means'.[178] However, with respect, this is to miss the point. Thinking this way involves being seduced by the same illusory equation of the threat made and the act threatened that Carty insists upon. The fact that the breach of a purely penal statute may not ground a tort action is irrelevant to the question of whether an unlawful threat has coerced the person threatened into a certain course of conduct.

ii. The Crux of Actionability

It is entirely possible that some readers will find unattractive my suggestion that two-party intimidation attends primarily to coercion of the victim because placing coercion front and centre inevitably occludes any argument that this is best thought of as a tort concerned with the protection of economic interests. And yet the law's emphasis on coercion here should come as no surprise. The wrongfulness of coercion is firmly entrenched (via the duress idea) in both criminal law and contract law. In both contexts, it is the coercive effect of the threat that is key. In the criminal law, the wrongfulness of blackmail attaches to the coercive nature of the threat *even though* the threat made may have been to do something lawful.[179] Similarly, in contract law, cases of so called 'lawful act duress' are now also well established.[180] In both cases, the importance attributed to the coercion of the victim could not be clearer. There is no obvious reason, therefore, to resist the idea that tort law might similarly focus on the coerciveness of the threat; *especially where* (in contrast to these two examples) the threat in question relates to something one has no lawful right to do.[181]

[176] *Rookes* (n 130) 1206–07.

[177] *Lonrho v Shell* (n 1).

[178] Jones (n 136) 1767.

[179] *Cf Murray* (n 156) (a case of two-party intimidation, but involving a blackmail-like threat) where there was arguably a civil wrong threatened when the defendant said he would reveal to the claimant's wife and family the fact that the claimant had been using an internet dating agency.

[180] *Pakistan International Airline Corporation v Times Travel (UK) Ltd* [2021] UKSC 40 (SC); *Gallagher* (n 161); *Kent* (n 157).

[181] *In theory* it is conceivable that threats to do something lawful could suffice (though this runs counter to Lord Reid's definition of the threats required in *Rookes* (n 130) 1168). This is because tort

A wealth of authority would appear to confirm tort law's doing just this. In *Morgan v Fry*, Lord Denning stated bluntly that only 'the person damnified *by the compliance [with a threat]* can sue for intimidation'.[182] Equally, in *Newsgroup Newspapers Ltd v SOGAT '82* Stuart-Smith J opined:

> If a threat is little more than idle abuse and is not to be taken seriously, then it would not be sufficient to found an action for intimidation. Indeed, the tort is not complete unless the person threatened succumbs to the threat.[183]

What is clearly to the fore, in both these dicta, is the idea that coercion of the threatened person's will is vital to the commission of the tort.[184] Such thinking is also evident in the leading case of *Rookes* where Lord Devlin said: '*[t]he essence of the offence is coercion* … [and] the plaintiff who suffers by the aversion of the act threatened can legally claim that he is illegally injured'.[185] A little later in his speech, he added: '[a]ll that matters to the plaintiff is that, metaphorically speaking, a club has been used'.[186] No less explicitly, Lord Evershed also remarked that, 'the threat, properly understood … *had a real and substantial coercive force*' and '[a]s such … [the] threat itself constituted a cause of action'.[187]

A slightly more elaborate iteration of just such thinking was supplied, once again, by Lord Denning MR in *JT Stratford & Son v Lindley* when he said:

> it is essential to the cause of action that the person threatened should comply with the demand. If he has the courage to resist it … then the party threatened has no cause of action for intimidation … [for] they have suffered no damage by the threat … [and it] is *essential to the cause of action that the threat should be a coercive threat* … It must be intended to coerce a person into doing something that he is unwilling to do or not doing something that he wishes to do.[188]

What all of these cases consistently stress is that it is *coercion by way of an unlawful threat* that forms the gist of this tort. They make plain that the wrong inheres in the fact that the threatened person has been forced into a course of conduct that he or she would not otherwise have chosen to pursue. The interest at stake, in other words, is the claimant's decision-making freedom.[189]

law, at a certain level of abstraction, concerns itself with purposive activity (against which backdrop all the rights and duties recognised by tort law become intelligible): see EJ Weinrib, 'Correlativity, Personality, and the Emerging Consensus on Corrective Justice' (2001) 2 *Theoretical Inquiries in Law* 1, 13–20. From this it follows that, just because one may lawfully do X (even if so doing causes loss to another), does not necessarily entail that threatening to do X, simply in order to coerce another, must also fall within the purview of the protected pursuit of one's own projects.

[182] *Morgan* (n 163) 724 (emphasis added).

[183] *Newsgroup Newspapers* (n 137) 204.

[184] However, coercion is not the be all and end all. As noted earlier, for the coercion to count, it must have been brought about by an unlawful threat.

[185] *Rookes* (n 130) 1207 (emphasis added).

[186] *Ibid*, 1209.

[187] *Ibid*, 1189 (emphasis added).

[188] *Stratford* (n 159) 283 (emphasis added).

[189] In earlier work (Murphy (n 167)), I described the claimant's interest in terms of 'autonomy'. I have elected to eschew the use of that term here because its use becomes awkward in relation to corporate

Two other jurists to have noted the centrality of coercion to this tort are Jason Neyers[190] and Robert Stevens. According to the latter:

> [i]f D threatens to break X's legs unless he ceases to trade with C, D is [by getting X to act in this way] using X, or perhaps more accurately the right of X, for his own ends in order to cause loss to C.[191]

But note: it is only once X accedes to the threat made that D can be said to have abused the 'the right of X' to free agency: the right, in other words, to choose for himself the way he would like to act in a given set of circumstances.[192]

Much as it is tolerably easy to identify the claimant's decision-making freedom as the gist of this tort, there is a crucial supplementary point that must be made here. Unlike the kinds of threat that will ground an action for assault (a tort which is actionable *per se*), the threats which animate the tort of intimidation are not, by themselves, enough to ground a cause of action.[193] They must always be accompanied by – indeed, cause – a loss. But this, as we shall see in due course, is a mere condition of the claimant's ability to sue. For this reason, it is best to describe the *crux* of actionability in terms of the coercion, the loss of the freedom to decide matters for oneself.

In *Morgan v Fry* Lord Denning highlighted this by stressing that 'the person so threatened must comply with the demand rather than risk the threat being carried into execution.[194] And likewise, in *Godwin* – where a woman was kept as a 'household drudge', someone who was 'virtually a slave'[195] – Dillon LJ was content to allow her to sue on the basis of two-party intimidation noting 'intimidation … consisted of intentional unlawful coercion'.[196]

The fact that the woman was forced to work exhausting, excessive hours in this case is especially noteworthy for our purposes since, although the claimant suffered no economic or other material loss,[197] she very vividly suffered a gross violation of her decision-making freedom. Grasping this point serves to fortify the claim advanced in this chapter that two-party intimidation ought not to be viewed as a purely *economic* tort.

bodies that claim damages. This does not mean that it is *meaningless* to speak of company autonomy: see, eg, *Johnson v Gore Wood (No 1)* [2002] 2 AC 1 (HL), 36 (Lord Bingham). Rather, it is simply more convenient to refer to coercion of a victim than to set out a particular legal conception of autonomy.

[190] See his chapter on intimidation in Botterell (n 150) 920.

[191] Stevens (n 5) 190.

[192] For the most developed account of the centrality of free agency to the operation and understanding of tort law generally, see EJ Weinrib, *The Idea of Private Law* (Cambridge, Massachusetts, Harvard University Press, 1995) Ch 4.

[193] Assault involves threats which affect psychological integrity. It could well be argued that intimidatory threats do likewise (by causing C to suffer enduring anxiety about whether the threat-maker will actually go through with his or her threat). This raises interesting questions about just which forms of psychological harm should be compensable in tort law, and in what circumstances. But they are not questions relevant to this chapter.

[194] *Morgan v Fry* (n 163), 724 (emphasis added).

[195] *Godwin* (n 152) 65.

[196] *Ibid.*

[197] To her credit, Carty also acknowledges this point: see Carty (n 24) 116 and 121.

D. Merits and Potential

To a large extent the merits and future potential of two-party intimidation mirror those of lawful means conspiracy, sketched in the first part of this chapter. Also in keeping with lawful means conspiracy, two-party intimidation is rarely invoked as a freestanding tort. But this in no way undermines the fact that it played a critical role in enabling their Lordships in *Total Network* to revitalise the tort of unlawful means conspiracy. Key in this regard was the fact that it confirmed the existence of liability beyond the three-party framework to which the unlawful means tort and inducing breach of contract are necessarily confined. Equally, in much the same way that lawful means conspiracy can be used to make accountable in tort those whose conduct strays into the realm of utterly reprehensible wrongdoing, so too can two-party intimidation be put to such uses. Indeed, in the relatively recent *Kent* case, Leggatt LJ suggested that cases of blackmail would give rise to an action for intimidation.[198]

Of course, it could be said that there is nothing especially novel about countenancing an action for intimidation in cases of blackmail. It might be argued that in any such scenario one is merely allowing the action to redress the fact that D has extorted money (or its equivalent) from C. And that being the case – so the argument would go – the tort would simply be protecting the claimant's economic interests and thus operating just as one would expect of an economic tort. By way of reply, however, it might be said that such extortion – albeit involving a form of economic loss – does not involve economic loss of the kind that is classically associated with the economic torts. As may be recalled from chapter two, monists maintain only that the 'purpose of the economic torts is to protect a person in relation to his trade, business or livelihood',[199] and that their 'fundamental rationale … is to maintain the integrity of the competitive process'.[200]

Furthermore, there would appear to be no reason in principle why someone who has been intimidated should not be able to sue for, say, any mental distress caused by the relevant unlawful threat.[201] Consider, for example, the ancient case of *Gilbert v Stone*.[202] There, 12 armed men threatened to kill Stone unless he

[198] *Kent* (n 157) [230]. Interestingly, Leggatt LJ also expressed the view – contrary to what Lord Reid had said in *Rookes* – that there need not be a threat to do something unlawful. In this, he was seeking to align the tort with the nascent lawful act duress principle in contract law. But his saying this formed no part of the ratio of the case.

[199] S Deakin and Z Adams, *Markesinis and Deakin's Tort Law*, 8th edn (Oxford, Oxford University Press, 2019) 458.

[200] Deakin and Randall (n 97) 520.

[201] Blackmail does not necessarily involve the threat of doing something unlawful. But allowing any case in which a blackmailer threatened to do something lawful to fall within the compass of two-party intimidation would require a departure from Lord Reid's insistence in *Rookes* that the threat must be to do something that one has 'no legal right to do'. Accordingly, the better view is that, when it comes to grounding an action for intimidation, the only cases of blackmail that will suffice are those in which an unlawful threat has been made. *Cf* the obiter remarks of Leggatt LJ in the *Kent* case.

[202] *Gilbert* (n 135).

trespassed on Gilbert's land and stole Gilbert's horse. Stone complied and was later sued in trespass by Gilbert. The case actually concerned the question of whether Stone could raise a defence of duress. The court rejected the defendant's duress plea in relation to his trespassing upon the claimant's land, but it nonetheless accepted that, in respect of the bandits' forcing him to do this, 'the defendant hath remedy against those that compelled him'.[203] No indication is given in the report – which runs to just one paragraph – of what that remedy would have been for, but it is not difficult to imagine a similar sort of case in which D coerces C into doing something perilous, but not unlawful (so as to head off any possibility of the illegality defence), that would carry a risk of C suffering mental distress. In any such case, I think C should in principle be permitted to sue for intimidation. And any objection along the lines that intimidation would be adding nothing to the tort of assault here could be averted by imagining that the threat was to something other than infringe C's bodily integrity. D might, for example, threaten to set fire to C's house, or injure C's child.

And one final point, here: both of my examples involve just the kinds of especially egregious wrongdoing that I argue in this book is characteristic of a good deal of the modern usage of the general economic torts.

E. Other Reservations

I have already tackled several objections that might be raised in connection with my suggested understanding of the gist, and possible uses of two-party intimidation. But there are several others that must also be addressed before any firm conclusions concerning the extant, as well as potential, merits of this tort can firmly be drawn. Most of the remaining objections can be captured by one simple proposition, namely, that existing principles of contract law render this tort more or less redundant. But there is also one further objection which relates to my claim that there can be no instance of three-party intimidation (to be dealt with now under the rubric of the unlawful means tort) unless we first recognise the vitality of two-party intimidation. I address them each in turn.

i. Contract Law and Two-Party Intimidation

The first putative problem concerning the relationship between intimidation and contract law centres on the idea that contract law already deals adequately with the various situations that could be regarded as instances of two-party intimidation. Indeed, it is possible that it was just this overlap with contract law that Lord Hoffmann had in mind when he suggested that cases of two-party intimidation raise 'altogether different issues'. Nicholas McBride and Roderick

[203] *Ibid.*

Bagshaw certainly see this potential inter-relation with existing principles of contract law as '[o]ne reason why Lord Hoffmann did not simply confirm the existence of the [two-party] tort'.[204] More particularly, the thinking here is that, '[t]he claimant already has sufficient protection and remedies … [via] his contract rights – including the right to sue for anticipatory breach – when the threat to break the contract is made by the defendant'.[205] The most recent edition of *Clerk and Lindsell on Torts* also refers to this overlap with the doctrine of anticipatory breach of contract in assessing the modern day significance of two-party intimidation.[206]

In addition to the point concerning anticipatory breach, there is, in the minds of some, a further problematic overlap with the doctrines of duress and economic duress which are considered the more appropriate means of resolving a case that might otherwise be pursued on the basis of intimidation. As regards the overlap itself, it has certainly been said of the duress principle that 'neither a defence to a contractual claim nor a claim in tort can succeed unless it is shown that the will of the "victim" has been coerced'.[207] And, cognisant of this concurrence, McBride and Bagshaw worry that,

> it would be unsatisfactory if these doctrines [of duress and economic duress] said that the contract was enforceable, or the money could be retained, but tort law insisted that B should be compensated by A for the loss caused by the threat.[208]

There may well be cause for concern in what McBride and Bagshaw say; but it is important to get clear just what that concern is. Properly understood, the worry being expressed is that tort law might furnish a remedy where contract law would not. And that is a far cry from establishing the redundancy of two-party intimidation. Indeed, as we shall see presently, none of the areas of overlap just sketched, really serve to anchor the idea that this tort is surplus to requirements.[209]

a. Duress and Economic Duress

At least three major obstacles obstruct our acceptance of the suggestion that two-party intimidation is rendered redundant by virtue of the law of contract's capacity to deal adequately with coercive threats via the duress and economic duress doctrines.[210] The first is a fairly obvious one, though commentators seem

[204] McBride and Bagshaw (n 71) 654.

[205] Carty (n 24) 119. For a judicial hint of the possibility that anticipatory breach might enjoy a degree of overlap, see *Rookes* (n 130) 1207 (Lord Devlin).

[206] Jones (n 136) 1770–71.

[207] *Dawson* (n 141) [32] (Tomlinson LJ).

[208] McBride and Bagshaw (n 71) 654.

[209] The suggestion of redundancy is deducible from the regularity with which Lord Hoffmann stressed the claim that the economic torts could be rationalised into a simple, two-tort structure affording conceptual space to only the unlawful means tort and inducing breach of contract.

[210] For a philosophically oriented account of the distinction between coercive threats (which require primary attention to be afforded to the 'perspective of the dominant party') and duress (which is a

to have overlooked it. It is this: there is no *a priori* reason why there must be a contractual nexus between the person threatened and the person making the threat. Yet it is only in such circumstances that the duress and economic duress doctrines become salient. Coercive threats come in many different varieties and contexts. There is simply no reason why they may only take the form of either A coercing B into making an unwanted contract (duress), or A forcing B to accept an unfavourable variation of an existing contract (economic duress).

A second obstacle to accepting the proposition that the doctrine of economic duress caters perfectly well for threats made in a two-party setting can be illustrated by reference to *D & C Builders Ltd v Rees*.[211] This is because this case helps highlight the fact that the respective remedies in contract and tort can be very different (making the choice between an action in tort and one in contract a choice of real value).[212] The wife's threat to the builders in that case was, effectively, a threat to pay a sum considerably lower than the amount actually owed under the contract, or nothing at all. From the perspective of economic duress, the appropriate remedy was the setting aside of a putative accord and satisfaction. No such remedy would be available in tort law.

Furthermore, an unfavourable variation in the contract may result in a loss to C that goes beyond the original contractual price and the new (unfavourable) price. Tort law could well attend to this further loss as the following hypothetical illustrates. Suppose that A and B agree a contract for the sale of product X made by B, which is to be delivered to A some months later. Suppose also that a third business, C, unexpectedly goes into liquidation without being able to honour a huge debt owed to B such that the viability of B's own business now hangs in the balance. Next, imagine that taking advantage of B's precarious position, A declares, 'I know you are desperate just now, so you will have to accept half the agreed price in full settlement or else I'll pay you nothing at all'. Finally, assume that B accedes to this threat, and that, as things turn out, the reduced sum proves inadequate to keep B's business afloat (though payment of the full amount would have kept B above water). In consequence, B becomes bankrupt and suffers various knock-on losses in the form of several pre-arranged, extremely lucrative contracts falling through.[213]

In such circumstances, the economic duress principle, if invoked, would furnish B with a remedy equating to the difference between the original contract price and the price actually paid by A. It would not, however, make good the consequential losses associated with B's bankruptcy. Tort law, on the other hand, would

'victim-centred concept' concerned with whether the victim's conduct is excusable), see G Lamond, 'Coercion, Threats and the Puzzle of Blackmail' in AP Simester and ATH Smith (eds), *Harm and Culpability* (Oxford, Oxford University Press, 1996) 219–21.

[211] *D & C Builders Ltd v Rees* [1966] 2 QB 617 (CA).

[212] *Cf* J Goudkamp and D Nolan, *Winfield & Jolowicz on Tort*, 20th edn (London, Sweet & Maxwell, 2020) 554.

[213] Such cancellation is possible, by court order, under the Insolvency Act 1986, s 345.

provide a remedy that was attentive to this aspect of B's loss.[214] In other words, this hypothetical illustrates the way in which relying on the tort of two-party intimidation does not simply replicate the redress available under the auspices of economic duress. And since the two remedies may – as in this example – be very different indeed, it follows that it is inappropriate to conclude that two-party intimidation is redundant in this context.

A Canadian decision allows us to push the remedial distinction a little further. The case in point is *Gershman v Manitoba Vegetable Producers' Marketing Board*.[215] There, among other things, the defendant Marketing Board was held liable for causing the claimant to miss out on a very lucrative share option by virtue of its intimidatory conduct. Not only did the claimant sue successfully for the losses caused by the defendant's intimidation, he also received a sizeable sum by way of punitive damages.[216] Orthodox principles of contract law would never permit such a remedy.[217]

At bottom, what characterises these various situations is the presence of concurrent liability, the prospect of which was confirmed in *Kolmar Group AG v Traxpo Enterprises Pvt Ltd*.[218] There, the exploitative threat in question was considered capable of being viewed in terms of economic duress.[219] But even though he made this observation, Christopher Clarke J actually disposed of the case on the basis of two-party intimidation. After acknowledging the presence of economic duress, he said this:

> The tort of intimidation is established where (i) the defendant makes a demand backed by a coercive and unlawful threat; (ii) the plaintiff complies with that demand because of the coercive and unlawful threat; (iii) the defendant knows or should have known that compliance with its demand will cause loss and damage to the plaintiff and (iv) the defendant intends its demand to cause loss and damage to the plaintiff … Those requirements are, as it seems to me, satisfied … [and] [a]ccordingly, Kolmar is entitled to $1,405,566.61 as damages for intimidation.[220]

[214] The existing cases do not make clear which test for remoteness of damage applies in the context of intimidation. But this is immaterial here, since either the 'reasonably foreseeable type of harm' test (associated with *The Wagon Mound (No 1)* [1961] AC 388 (PC)) or that based on 'all direct consequences' (and associated with *Re Polemis* [1923] 3 KB 560 (CA)) would serve B equally well in this example. That said, it is submitted that the direct consequences test is the stronger candidate for use in cases involving intimidation, since this test is generally applied to torts based on intentional wrongdoing. Yet perhaps relevant, too, would be Lord Lindley's dictum in *Quinn* (n 39) 537 to the effect that the presence of intentional wrongdoing does away with question of remoteness of damage.

[215] *Gershman v Manitoba Vegetable Producers' Marketing Board* (1976) 65 DLR 181 (3d) 114.

[216] *Ibid*, [20].

[217] *Cassel & Co v Broome* [1972] AC 1027 (HL). Not only does contract law not currently countenance punitive damages, it also sets its face against the insertion into a contract of a penalty clause (which might be viewed as an attempt to obtain punitive damages 'by the back door'). As to why contract law does not permit punitive awards, see SA Smith, *Contract Theory* (Oxford, Oxford University Press, 2004) 417–20.

[218] *Kolmar Group* (n 153).

[219] 'I am quite satisfied from the evidence … that Kolmar agreed to amend the letters of credit … as a result of illegitimate pressure amounting to economic duress on the part of Traxpo': *ibid*, [93] (Clarke J).

[220] *Ibid*, [119]–[121]. It is submitted that the financial losses identified here were compensable merely because they were consequential upon the coercion of the claimant's will in just the same way that

A third basis on which to refute the argument that the economic duress doctrine functions as a genuine and complete alternative to two-party intimidation, and thus renders it redundant, inheres in the fact that the former only attends to threats which cause the claimant to accept an unfavourable variation in the contractual arrangements that *he himself* has with the defendant.[221] Thus, if A should say to B, 'I will not honour my side of our contract unless you make it clear to X that you are unprepared to engage in any future commercial dealings *with him*', the threat cannot possibly constitute economic duress because, although it forced B into an undesired variation in his extant contractual relations, it did not cause B to accept less advantageous terms *in his contract with A*.

b. Intimidation and Anticipatory Breach

As noted earlier, Carty has suggested that part of the reason for thinking that two-party intimidation is redundant is because a claimant already enjoys significant protection via her right to sue for anticipatory breach should the defendant threaten a breach of contract.[222] Such thinking, however, is equally vulnerable to the objection that there is no good reason to suppose that the person threatened will be in a contractual nexus with the threat-maker. Furthermore, even if such a contractual nexus does exist, the supposition that two-party intimidation is rendered redundant by the anticipatory breach doctrine is entirely misguided. The reason why probably requires some explanation.

Let us suppose for now that Carty is right in thinking that it could amount to anticipatory breach for A to threaten B that A will not honour his side of the bargain at the due date for performance, *unless* B does something stipulated by A. In any such scenario, there is no reason to think that the redress available in tort law would merely replicate any remedy available in contract.

But let us now question the supposition itself. For, the two options – the one contractual, the other tortious – could never in fact overlap. Where a threat amounting to an anticipatory breach is made, and the claimant seeks to accept that breach and sue for damages (situation 1), the claimant will not have acted in accordance with any threat in order to keep the contract alive. By contrast, for the tort action to be available (situation 2), the claimant must always accede to the threat and behave in a certain way stipulated by the defendant. He must be coerced into a course of conduct that he would not otherwise have chosen *in order*

damages are available for consequential economic loss in the tort of negligence where the defendant has caused the claimant property damage. The balance of authority does *not* require C to have suffered financial loss in order to be able to sue for intimidation. Indeed, as the *Godwin* case makes clear, the degradation associated with being treated as a slave will suffice. The better view, therefore, is that all that is required is some form of recognised damage that stems from C's coercion: see text associated with n 183, above.

[221] The term 'economic duress' is generally only applied to those cases where D has coerced C into an unfavourable variation of an existing contract: for examples, see E Peel, *Treitel: The Law of Contract*, 14th edn (London, Sweet and Maxwell, 2015) 500–503; J O'Sullivan, *O'Sullivan and Hilliard's Law of Contract*, 9th edn (Oxford, Oxford University Press, 2018) 265–74.

[222] Carty (n 24) 119.

to prevent the contract being broken. In situation 1, a breach (which is accepted) occurs; while in situation 2, no breach occurs. The bases for the two remedial options are mutually exclusive.

And there is a further difference, too, which also serves to highlight the way that tort and contract come apart in this setting. In the hypothetical just given, we simply assumed that A's threat was one of non-performance *unless B acted in a particular way*, and that this threat could amount to anticipatory breach. But any such assumption is misplaced. In a case of anticipatory breach, the 'threat' of non-performance will be of a categorically different kind to the sort of threat required by the tort of intimidation. In the latter context, the threat must be of the 'or else' variety. In a case of anticipatory breach, however, the kind of 'threat' involved is better described as a bare declaration by the defendant that she no longer intends to honour her side of an agreement: it involves a simple renunciation of contractual duty. And, as Devlin J explained in *Universal Cargo Carriers Corpn v Citati (No 1)*,[223] 'a renunciation can be made either by words or conduct, *provided it is clearly made*';[224] the test being 'whether the party repudiating has acted in such a way as to lead a reasonable person to the conclusion that he does not intend to fulfil his part of the contract'.[225] There is no contingency here (as there must always be in a case of intimidation). There is no 'or else' in play. The defendant's 'threat' to break the contract is not issued in terms that require the claimant to do anything at all. Yet, as Lord Denning explained, '[a] bare threat without a demand does not to my mind amount to the tort of intimidation'.[226]

The unavoidable conclusion, then, is that there exists no scope whatever for the anticipatory breach doctrine to eclipse the tort of two-party intimidation.

ii. Three-Party Intimidation Cases Depend on the Recognition of Two-Party Cases?

The idea that three-party intimidation cases – now subsumed, after *OBG*, within the unlawful means tort – require us to recognise the vitality of two-party intimidation might be challenged on the following basis. In a three-party case, it is perfectly possible that the defendant did not intend to harm the intermediary, whereas in a two-party intimidation case, an intention to harm the claimant would be necessary. Accordingly, it could be argued that a three-party case can, after all, be established in the absence of a two-party case.

Whatever its ostensible appeal, however, this argument may be dismissed. In a two-party case, what must be intended is that the person at whom the threat is directed should be coerced into doing a certain thing, quite regardless of whether

[223] *Universal Cargo Carriers Corpn v Citati (No 1)* [1957] 2 QB 401.
[224] *Ibid*, 436 (emphasis added).
[225] *Ibid.*
[226] *Stratford* (n 188) 283.

she suffers tangible harm. Tangible harm serves as a mere *condition of actionability*. But it does not constitute an element of the tort in the strict sense. It is just the same with the tort of deceit – which also protects decision-making freedom (as we shall see in chapter six). For this reason we may usefully invoke here Stephenson LJ's explanation (from that context) of the difference between an ingredient of the tort and a condition of actionability. He said: '[i]n deceit … the false representation … has to cause damage to be actionable, but no damage to the plaintiff is necessary for the tort to be committed'.[227] The same is true here: C must be coerced into acting in a particular way for the tort of intimidation to be committed; but he must also suffer measurable loss in order to be able to sue for damages.

F. Final Remarks

In the second main part of this chapter, I have tried to show that, according to the most defensible interpretation of the leading cases, two-party intimidation is a vital tort (in the strict sense), and that its gist is the wrongful coercion of the claimant's will, rather than injury to his or her economic interests. The *Godwin* and *Kolmar* cases certainly endorse this point; while my hypothetical – based on an adaptation of the facts of *Gilbert v Stone*, and in which the threatened person's mental health, rather than his economic interests, were put at risk – also supports this contention.

I also argued that, freed from a groundless pre-commitment to the idea that intimidation must be confined to the protection of economic interests, it can – in the same way as lawful means conspiracy – be used in connection with certain forms of especially reprehensible wrongdoing in relation to which it is not obvious that other torts may be applied. It is hard to imagine that anyone would consider a case like *Godwin* to be a regrettable development in the law merely because it departs from the 'tradition' of applying intimidation to cases in which the claimant suffers some form of trade or business loss. In just the same way that lawful means conspiracy was seen to be alive and well with a positive role to play going forwards, so might the same be said of two-party intimidation.

[227] *Diamond v The Bank of London and Montreal* [1979] QB 333 (CA), 349.

6

The Misrepresentation Torts

I. Introduction

There are three final torts relevant to this study that may conveniently be considered together, within a single chapter, given that they all involve misrepresentations that cause loss. As with the discussion of the general economic torts in the preceding three chapters, my principal concern here will be with the same questions that I addressed in relation to those other torts, namely, questions concerning the vitality of these torts, the range of interests they protect and their future prospects.

II. Passing Off

The vitality of passing off – a tort classically understood to involve a misrepresentation about the source of goods or services – is not in doubt. It is safe to say that, although it shares some common ground with the statutory rules concerning trade marks, it has in no way been eclipsed by them. However, for all that its existence is secure, there are nonetheless various important uncertainties that surround this action. For one thing, although it is regularly referred to as a tort of strict liability,[1] this depiction is far too simplistic. In truth, passing off has a less-than-straightforward liability basis which reflects the way it developed over the course of roughly the last century, which is not to say that this is when the tort first emerged. In fact, its precise origins remain obscure.[2] It certainly existed in the seventeenth century, from which period there is *some* evidence to suggest that it was, at that time, treated as a peculiar form of action, analogous to deceit, in which a defendant trader would use a distinctive mark in order to deceive a purchaser. The action, however, was not brought by the deceived consumer, but by the trader whose mark it was, *suing on his own behalf*.[3] By the nineteenth century, the need

[1] See, eg, P Cane, *The Anatomy of Tort Law* (Oxford, Hart Publishing, 1997) 45; H Carty, *An Analysis of the Economic Torts*, 2nd edn (Oxford, Oxford University Press, 2010) 226; C Wadlow, 'Passing Off at the Crossroads Again' (2011) 33 *European Intellectual Property Review* 447, 455.

[2] WL Morison, 'Unfair Competition and Passing-off – The Flexibility of a Formula' (1956) 2 *Sydney Law Review* 50, 53–54.

[3] In one case it was said: 'it was not the single act of making use of the mark that was sufficient to maintain the action, but doing it with a fraudulent design': *Blanchard v Hill* (1742) 2 Atk 484, 485 (Lord Hardwicke LC).

for any fraudulent intent on the part of the defendant had gone – at least in cases where an injunction was sought.[4] But even though the need to show fraud has disappeared, it cannot be said, today, that the relevance of intentional misrepresentations has disappeared with it.

Secondly, although *AG Spalding & Bros v AW Gamage Ltd*[5] is broadly regarded as having introduced a 'coherent theoretical basis of this tort',[6] centred around three key requirements – misrepresentation, goodwill and damage – it is observably the case that this so-called 'classical trinity'[7] of ingredients has been so stretched and distorted in some of the leading cases that a great deal of uncertainty now envelops the outer margins of the tort. Thirdly, it is also hard to discern a clear *raison d'être* for the tort. What began its existence as an action designed for the benefit of traders,[8] seems now to have metamorphosed – at least in the minds of some judges – into one that should be developed in line with a capacity to protect consumers, *even though* it is not the consumers themselves who are able to invoke the tort. A prime example of such thinking was provided by Lord Diplock when he said in one leading case that:

> Parliament … beginning in the 19th century has progressively intervened in the interests of consumers … [and where] [o]ver a period of years there can be discerned a steady trend in legislation which reflects the view of successive Parliaments as to what the public interest demands in a particular field of law, development of the common law in that part of the same field which has been left to it ought to proceed upon a parallel rather than a diverging course.[9]

The idea that the protection of consumers might nowadays be seen as forming *part of* the tort's rationale has also garnered support in *some* academic quarters.[10] But even so, there remains, as yet, no consensus amongst either judges or jurists about exactly what forms the primary function or purpose of this tort.

Fourthly, the question of whether the tort of passing off might be stretched to encompass the misappropriation of goodwill *in the absence of a misrepresentation* remains unsettled. This is because, to the extent that the question has been addressed in the case law, it has been dealt with inconclusively. The preponderance of the case law stands against such a development; yet, here and there, one finds dicta that support such an extension. At the same time, no satisfactory answer can be found in the relevant scholarship. Jurists who have voiced objections to such

[4] See, eg, *Millington v Fox* (1838) My & Cr 338, 3: 'it does not appear to me that there was any fraudulent intention [here] … That circumstance, however, does not deprive the Plaintiffs of their right to the exclusive use of those names'.

[5] *AG Spalding & Bros v AW Gamage Ltd* [1915] 32 RPC 273 (HL).

[6] H Carty, '*Spalding v Gamage* (1915)' in J Bellido (ed), *Landmark Cases in Intellectual Property* (Oxford, Hart Publishing, 2017) 181.

[7] See *Conzorsio del Prosciutto di Parma v Marks & Spencer Plc* [1991] RPC 351 (CA), 358 (Nourse LJ).

[8] See Morison (n 2) 53–54.

[9] *Erven Warnink BV v J Townend & Sons (Hull) Ltd* [1979] AC 731 (HL), 743 Note, also, the dictum of Fisher J in *Tots Toys Ltd v Mitchell* [1993] 1 NZLR 325, 341.

[10] See, eg, S Naresh, 'Passing-Off, Goodwill and False Advertising: New Wine in Old Bottles' [1986] *CLJ* 97, 120; Wadlow (n 1) 499; Carty (n 1) 267–68.

expansion in the scope of the tort have been either misdirected in what they say, or unconvincing in their opposition to it by virtue of their merely presupposing (but failing to substantiate) the necessary rigidity of the 'classical trinity'.[11]

Against this rather unsettled background, my aim in this part of the chapter is threefold. To begin with, I seek to demonstrate that passing off is, unlike all the other torts in this book, exclusively concerned with the protection of trade or business interests. Secondly, I aim to show that – for all that orthodoxy posits that this is a strict liability tort[12] – it is one that is nevertheless highly attentive to egregious wrongdoing. Thirdly, I endeavour to explain both the deficiencies in the arguments typically made against this tort being developed so as to tackle cases of misappropriation as well as the possible merits of taking such a step. As will be seen, although the scholarly objections so far voiced against such a development all founder, this does not mean that such a step should be taken without hesitation. I shall argue that, in theory, there could be development along these lines, but not without first resolving the awkward question of how (lawful) appropriation may satisfactorily be distinguished from (unlawful) *mis*appropriation. And although I express no firm view on that issue, I do commit to the contention that *any* future development of this tort should prescind from the public interest in consumers knowing the true provenance of goods and services.

Before dealing with these matters, however, it is important to make one final, prefatory point. This is that, in the course of my discussion, I shall eschew any analysis of two well-known, contentious issues surrounding this tort that do not impinge upon the major themes of this book. I shall avoid any engagement with the awkward question of whether passing off can and should protect what is sometimes called extra-territorial goodwill.[13] And, likewise, I shall leave to one side the tricky definitional matter of what counts as a misrepresentation in this context.[14]

A. Protected Interest

In *Erven Warnink BV v J Townend & Sons (Hull) Ltd*, Lord Diplock set out five 'characteristics' of passing off – namely:

[11] For Carty, the damage requirement would be undermined ('the aim is to submerge the concept of goodwill under the nebulous concept of misappropriation'): Carty (n 1) 277; for Wadlow, it is the centrality of the misrepresentation limb that would be tested ('liability for misappropriation … obviously extends well beyond cases of misrepresentation'): Wadlow (n 1) 450.

[12] According to Wadlow, the historically pertinent requirement of fraud is now an 'obsolete element': C Wadlow, *The Law of Passing-off: Unfair Competition by Misrepresentation*, 5th edn (London, Sweet & Maxwell, 2016) 18.

[13] See, eg, CW Ng, 'Goodwill Without Borders' (2018) 134 *LQR* 285 as well as the various sources cited therein.

[14] See, eg, A Walton, 'A Pervasive But Often Not Explicitly Characterised Aspect of Passing Off' (1987) 9 *European Intellectual Property Review* 159.

> (1) a misrepresentation (2) made by a trader in the course of trade; (3) to prospective customers of his … (4) which is calculated to injure the business or goodwill of another trader (in the sense that this is a reasonably foreseeable consequence) and (5) which causes actual damage to a business *or* goodwill of the trader.[15]

Lord Fraser set out an alternative five-part description;[16] but neither of these formulations has gained the same degree of traction as the so-called 'classical trinity'.

What all three depictions of this tort have in common is a firm commitment to the idea that passing off is centred upon the protection of a trader's commercial interest in goodwill. It is for this reason that the tort has a good claim to be regarded as a specifically *economic* tort even though, as we saw in chapter one, that phrase is sometimes used by authors only in conjunction with the torts considered in chapters three to five. The appellation is warranted by virtue of the fact that the tort is concerned *exclusively* with a trader's commercial interest in goodwill. But that said, it is apt to note that goodwill is no mere synonym for the claimant's trade or business interests.[17] Although described by Lord Macnaghten as the 'attractive force which brings in custom',[18] goodwill, by his own more detailed description, 'is composed of a variety of elements [that come in no fixed proportions such that] … [o]ne element may preponderate here, another one there'.[19] In fact, the cases reveal only two such elements: reputation and an established (or at least anticipated) customer connection.[20] As Lord Neuberger put it in *Starbucks (HK) Ltd v British Sky Broadcasting Group (No 2)*: 'mere reputation is not enough … [since in addition] [t]he claimant must show that it has a significant goodwill, in the form of customers'.[21]

Customer connection is, of course, to the fore in cases where sales have been diverted from claimant to defendant; and *Erven Warnink* was just such a case. There, the claimants had an established record of making a liqueur called 'Advocaat' before the defendants began marketing their rival product which, in terms of ingredients, was a very different drink indeed. The defendants nonetheless named it 'Keeling's Old English Advocaat' and, in so doing, captured a sizeable

[15] *Erven Warnink* (n 9) 742 (emphasis added).

[16] *Ibid*, 755–76: '[The claimant must show] (1) that his business consists of, or includes, selling in England a class of goods to which the particular trade name applies; (2) that the class of goods is clearly defined … (3) that because of the reputation of the goods, there is goodwill attached to the name; (4) that he … is the owner of goodwill … (5) that he has suffered, or is really likely to suffer, substantial damage to his property'.

[17] As noted in previous chapters, 'trade or business interests' is how the term 'economic interests' is typically understood in the context of the economic torts. *Cf* the meaning ascribed to the phrase in P Cane, *Tort Law and Economic Interests*, 2nd edn (Oxford, Oxford University Press, 1996) 1: 'an economic interest … is an interest for the invasion of which a finite sum of money can provide complete recompense'.

[18] *Inland Revenue Commissioners v Muller & Co's Margarine Ltd* [1901] AC 217 (HL), 224.

[19] *Ibid*, 244.

[20] See, eg, *Elida Gibbs Ltd v Colgate-Palmolive Ltd* [1983] FSR 95.

[21] *Starbucks (HK) Ltd v British Sky Broadcasting Group (No 2)* [2015] 1 WLR 2628 (SC), [52].

share of the English market for 'Advocaat' that had previously been held by the claimants. This amounted to tortious damage to the claimant's goodwill.

On other occasions – as Lord Macnaghten indicated – it will be the other component of goodwill (ie, reputation) that is front and centre. That the reputation of a trader (or the reputation of her product[22]) can contribute significantly to the attractive force that brings in custom is obvious enough.[23] But even so, reputation alone will not suffice. It cannot be treated as a synonym for goodwill. Lord Neuberger, as already noted, was crystal clear about this in *Starbucks*. And Oliver LJ, offering rather more by way of explanation, once expressed the point in these terms: 'reputation which may … exist without any supporting local business … does not by itself constitute a property which the law protects'.[24]

In drawing attention to the fact that reputation alone is not enough to constitute goodwill, I do not mean to suggest that tort law is not interested in the protection of reputation *per se*: it is, but only via the torts of defamation and injurious falsehood. Rather, my point in adverting to the distinction between goodwill and reputation is to show that, in the context of passing off, reputation does not enjoy freestanding significance. It is merely one of two critical elements – between which there is a symbiotic relationship – that comprise goodwill. Carty gets close to capturing this symbiotic relationship when she writes: 'the property right is in the customer connection emanating from the reputation of the plaintiff's products. In essence, therefore, the tort protects the trading activity that has created a reputation for the plaintiff's goods'.[25]

Although she fails to stress the point, Carty obviously recognises that not only can C's reputation generate an even greater customer connection, but also that an existing customer connection may serve to augment C's reputation. Satisfied customers are likely to return and contribute to the augmentation of C's reputation; while those who have not previously bought C's product may well be enticed to do so by virtue of C's established reputation.

Since goodwill is a composite of customer connection and reputation, it follows that an action for passing off is possible even if, on the facts of a given case, there is only damage to one of these (*so long as* both elements are present). In the same way that the proprietary interest in ownership[26] may be violated in more than one way – by, say, an infringement of the owner's right to exclusive possession,

[22] It does not matter that the reputation attaches not directly to a trader, but to their distinctive product. As was said in the 'Jif Lemon' case: '[w]hether the public is aware of the plaintiff's identity as the manufacturer or supplier of the goods or services is immaterial, as long as they are identified with a particular source which is in fact the plaintiff': *Reckitt & Colman Products Ltd v Borden Inc* [1990] 1 WLR 491 (HL), 499 (Lord Oliver).

[23] Lord Diplock captured well the relationship between the two phenomena when he said, 'it is the reputation that that type of product itself has gained in the market by reason of its recognisable and distinctive qualities that has generated the relevant goodwill': *Erven Warnink* (n 9) 747.

[24] *Anheuser-Busch Inc v Budejovicky Budvar NP* [1984] FSR 413 (CA), 470 (Oliver LJ).

[25] H Carty, 'Passing Off and the Concept of Goodwill' [1995] *Journal of Business Law* 139, 139.

[26] For a landmark elaboration of eleven distinct 'incidents of property', see AM Honoré, 'Ownership' in AG Guest (ed), *Oxford Essays in Jurisprudence* (Oxford, Oxford University Press, 1961) 107.

or perhaps her right to exclusive use – so too is it possible for goodwill to be infringed either by damage to C's reputation *or* by damage to her existing customer connection. This does not mean, however, that passing off is *not* confined to the protection of economic interests simply because an action may be brought where all that C can show is that D has damaged C's reputation. Because goodwill is a composite of reputation and customer connection it is perfectly legitimate to say that I have caused damage to another's goodwill whether I damage her reputation, her customer connection or both. It is no different than the veracity of saying I damage another's bicycle whether I damage the wheels, the frame or both. Furthermore, the notion that passing off protects only an economic interest can be shored up by reference to the fact that the only reputation that counts for this tort is the claimant's *trading reputation*. His or her reputation *qua* dignitary interest[27] is an immateriality.[28]

It is important to make this point because the so-called celebrity endorsement cases sometimes feature successful claimants whose reputation was adversely affected though no discernible loss of custom occurred. In *Irvine v Talksport Ltd*,[29] for example, an image of the claimant (a motor racing driver) was used without the claimant's authorisation in the defendant's promotional material in such a way as to suggest that the claimant had endorsed the defendant's radio station. He had done no such thing (although he had, through a promotions agency, endorsed other products in the past). Nor was the claimant a rival broadcaster who would lose listeners (and presumably advertising revenue) as a consequence of the defendant's entry into the market. Nonetheless, the claimant argued that his reputation had been misappropriated, and his claim in passing off succeeded. Laddie J specifically spelled out that 'it is not necessary to show that the claimant and the defendant share a common field of activity or that sales of products or services will be diminished either substantially or directly'.[30]

In the light of this decision, one might be forgiven for thinking that passing off may in practice be invoked on the basis of wrongs involving one's image rights. But it would be a mistake to think this way. For as the Court of Appeal made clear in *Fenty v Arcadia Group Brands Ltd (No 2)* – where an image of the pop star, Rihanna, was used on a t-shirt sold by Topshop – although '[t]here is in English law no "image right" or "character right" which allows a celebrity to control the use of his or her name or image [in general terms]',[31] a misappropriation of a particular posed image may be actionable harm insofar as it constitutes, 'a loss of control over her reputation in the fashion sphere'.[32] The damage, in other words, must be cashed out in terms of damage to her business interests. Where would her celebrity

[27] For an explanation of why reputation is ordinarily best seen as a dignitary interest, and how dignitary interests come apart from economic interests, see Cane (n 17) 4–5.
[28] *Bhayani v Taylor Bracewell LLP* [2017] ETMR 14, 28.
[29] *Irvine v Talksport Ltd* [2002] 1 WLR 2355.
[30] *Ibid*, 2368.
[31] *Fenty v Arcadia Group Brands Ltd (No 2)* [2015] 1 WLR 3291 (CA), [74] (Kitchin LJ).
[32] *Ibid*, [23].

endorsement business be if anyone who wanted to, could use any image at all of her, whenever they liked and without payment?

B. The Relevance of Reprehensible Conduct

The idea that reprehensible wrongdoing might be thought relevant to the tort of passing off seems, on the surface, hard to reconcile with the fact that, according to orthodoxy, it is a strict liability tort.[33] If, so the argument goes, a defendant can be held liable even though she acts innocently, then it is clearly a non-starter to argue that the reprehensibility of her conduct can be a relevant consideration. Things, however, are not quite so simple.

Even though, formally, one must go back to the days before the unification of the jurisdiction of the courts of equity and common law to identify fraud as a necessary ingredient of the common law action for passing off,[34] it is observably the case that, even today, the courts will afford significance to especially reprehensible wrongdoing. Thus, although the basic question in relation to the misrepresentation limb of the tort is whether, objectively, the defendant's marketing of a product was 'calculated to deceive',[35] the courts will not make its usual enquiry into whether a sizeable sector of the general public would, on the balance of probabilities, be misled into purchasing the defendant's product, where a deliberate attempt to deceive is present.[36] Rather, as Lord Scarman explained in *Cadbury Schweppes Pty Ltd v Pub Squash Co Pty Ltd*, '[w]here an intention to deceive is found, it is not difficult for the court to infer that the intention has been, or in all probability will be, effective'.[37] And likewise, in *Office Cleaning Services Ltd v Westminster Window and General Cleaners Ltd*, Lord Simonds stated: 'if the intention to deceive is found, it will readily be inferred that deception will result'.[38]

Perhaps even more forcefully, Earl Loreburn made no secret of the extent to which he was prepared to afford salience to the defendant's deliberate attempt to deceive in *Claudius Ash, Sons & Co Ltd v Invicta Manufacturing Company Ltd*.[39] On the facts of that case it was not proved that the defendants had acted dishonestly, yet his Lordship said the following:

[33] *Gillette UK Ltd v Edenwest Ltd* [1994] RPC 279, 291 (Blackburne J): 'I can see no good reason why, if damages are recoverable from the innocent infringer of a registered trademark, they should not equally be recoverable for innocent passing off'.

[34] It was not, however, required if what C sought was an injunction to restrain D from passing off his goods as those of C: see, eg, *Edelsten v Edelsten* (1863) 1 De G, J & S 185, 199 (Lord Westbury): 'this Court will act on the principle of protecting property alone, and it is not necessary for the injunction to prove fraud in the Defendant'.

[35] *Erven Warnink* (n 9) 742.

[36] *Neutrogena Corp v Golden Ltd* [1996] RPC 473 (CA).

[37] *Cadbury Schweppes Pty Ltd v Pub Squash Co Pty Ltd* [1981] 1 WLR 193 (PC), 203.

[38] *Office Cleaning Services Ltd v Westminster Window and General Cleaners Ltd* (1946) 63 RPC 39 (HL), 42–43 (Lord Simonds). In similar vein, see *British Sky Broadcasting Group Plc v Sky Home Services Ltd* [2007] FSR 14.

[39] *Claudius Ash, Sons & Co Ltd v Invicta Manufacturing Company Ltd* (1912) 29 RPC 465 (HL).

> It is said in this case that the Defendants intended to deceive – not that the goods were calculated even innocently to deceive – but that there was a fraudulent intention on the part of the Defendants. *That is a material fact* which would be weighed duly and to which no doubt great weight would be attached by any Court if it were established, because no Court would be astute when they discovered an intention to deceive, in coming to the conclusion that a dishonest defendant had been unsuccessful in his fraudulent design.[40]

Leaving to one side these cases of intentional deception, it is also notable that the courts have been determined to extend the reach of passing off to those whose especially sharp practices are difficult to reconcile with the three central requirements of passing off. *Glaxo Plc v Glaxowellcome Ltd*[41] provides a good example. In that case, the claimants were major pharmaceutical companies with worldwide reputations and very considerable goodwill in their respective names. A press release dated 23 January 1995 reported a take-over bid by the first claimant (Glaxo Plc) for the second claimant (Wellcome Plc). It announced that, if the bid succeeded, the first claimant would change its name to 'Glaxo-Wellcome Plc'. On 24 January 1995, the third defendant – a company registration agent – applied to register the first defendant (a shelf company) under the name of 'Glaxowellcome Limited'. The application was successful and the company was duly incorporated on 30 March 1995. The second and third defendants were both subscribers to that company.

The claimants sought a mandatory injunction to require the defendants either to sell the shelf company to them at the third defendant's standard rate of £1000, or change the first defendant's name to something that did not include either the words 'Glaxo' or 'Wellcome' (or any other related words with the capacity to confuse). For their part, the defendants demanded £100,000 for the company. In its assessment of the facts, the court found that the third defendant had acted dishonestly in two key ways. He had supplied a false address at the time of the application for registration of the shelf-company; and he had also tampered with the date on the statutory declaration in support of the registration so as to make it appear that the application had been prepared prior to the press release concerning the claimants' proposed merger.

Despite these findings, the third defendant maintained that he had acted with complete honesty and integrity throughout and that the registration of the shelf company had been planned in advance of the announcement of the proposed merger. He also stated that the choice of name was nothing more than an interesting combination of words, and that it had been made without either of the claimants in mind. Finally, he said that there was no intention that the first defendant would ever trade under its registered name, or seek to exploit the choice of name. In response to these contentions, in a judgment that ran to just three and a half pages, Lightman J was bluntly dismissive. 'All I need say in regard to these

[40] *Ibid*, 475 (emphasis added).
[41] *Glaxo Plc v Glaxowellcome Ltd* [1996] FSR 388.

suggestions', he said, 'is that there are limits to judicial credulity'.[42] Of the defendant's letter offering to sell the shelf company to the claimants, he added: 'it is not a bona fide effort to settle the dispute between the plaintiff and the defendant. It is a threat to damage the plaintiff unless the totally unwarranted sum demanded was paid'.[43] Then, just prior to granting an injunction 'specifically requiring [the three defendants] … to take all such steps as lie within their power to change or facilitate the change of name',[44] Lightman J stated forthrightly:

> The court will not countenance any such pre-emptive strike of registering companies with names where others have the goodwill in those names, and the registering party then demanding a price for changing the names. It is an abuse of the system of registration of companies' names.[45]

Similarly, in *Direct Line Group Ltd v Direct Line Estate Agency Ltd* – a case in which the defendants had a track record of incorporating companies with names which were the same as others' famous trade marks and then offering them for sale to the original proprietors for profit – Laddie J was insistent that 'this court will view with extreme displeasure any attempt by traders to embark upon a scam designed to make illegitimate use of other companies' trade marks'.[46] He duly issued the interlocutory relief sought in the case.

What seems to have been the main driver in these cases is the egregious conduct of the defendant rather than the fact that they fall neatly or obviously within the compass of passing off. In *Glaxo*, it is hard to see how the mere shelf company in that case – which never actually traded, and was never intended as a vehicle for trade – could be said to have satisfied the misrepresentation or damage elements of the tort. And the exact same problems beset the decision in *Direct Line* insofar as it concerned two of the three companies that had been incorporated in that case; for they too had never actually traded. Indeed, it is hard to disagree with Carty's assessment of all of the cases in this bracket when she writes:

> even where it is not clear that all elements of the tort have been proved … [and in particular] there would appear to be some difficulty in showing either a misrepresentation or harm to goodwill … the courts in these cases got round the problem by not alluding to it.[47]

In similar vein, albeit on the other side of the Atlantic, the Ontario Court of Appeal in *Orkin Exterminating Co Inc v Pestco Co* was also driven primarily by a desire to hold the defendant accountable for its egregious wrongdoing. For Morden JA, '[t]he spectre of Orkin having a monopoly in Ontario … [was] considerably less troubling than the deceptive use of its name and symbol by another'.[48] And without

[42] *Ibid*, 391.
[43] *Ibid*.
[44] *Ibid*, 392.
[45] *Ibid*, 391.
[46] *Direct Line Group Ltd v Direct Line Estate Agency Ltd* [1997] FSR 374.
[47] Carty (n 1) 227.
[48] *Orkin Exterminating Co Inc v Pestco Co* (1985) 19 DLR (4th) 90, [45].

so much as a nod to the fact that this tort is one of strict liability, he continued: 'I need not, and do not, say that the defendant's bad faith alone will confer a cause of action … but it surely must be a relevant factor to take into account'.[49]

By contrast, the courts are notably more reluctant to draw adverse inferences where the defendant is entirely innocent. In *Stringfellow v McCain Foods (GB) Ltd*, for example, the defendants were alleged to have committed the tort of passing off by virtue of their having given to their frozen chips the same name that the claimant had given to his nightclub. In declining the interlocutory relief sought, Slade LJ said:

> the court should not, in my opinion, readily infer the likelihood of resulting damage to the plaintiffs, as against an innocent defendant in a completely different line of business. In such a case the onus falling on plaintiffs to show that damage to their business reputation is in truth likely to ensue and to cause them more than a minimal loss is in my opinion a heavy one.[50]

In sum, it is clear that the courts, in developing this tort over the last century or so, have quite often been swayed by considerations of particularly reprehensible conduct on the part of the defendant. Carty quite rightly observes that 'in some of the more surprising decisions there is an underlying judicial disapproval of the defendant's activities'.[51] And Christopher Wadlow, too, points out that, 'far from unfolding in a consistent and purposeful manner passing off has largely developed through ad hoc decisions which were often motivated primarily by a desire not to let an unmeritorious defendant escape liability'.[52] In short, although liability for passing off is formally strict, a deliberate attempt to deceive customers still counts for a very great deal in this tort, as does the defendant's employment of especially sharp practices.

C. The Future

Despite the considerable potential for overlap between the protection offered by the tort of passing off and the Trade Marks Act 1994, the idea that the former is in danger of being eclipsed by the latter is completely without foundation. This is so for at least four reasons. First, at the point in time when D is alleged to have invaded C's right, C may not have registered her trade mark. Without such registration, there can be no action under the Act.[53] Secondly, C's trade mark may have been erroneously registered and may thus be declared invalid.[54] Thirdly, even where a trade mark has been correctly registered, the defendant may still be able to invoke one of the various defences contained within the 1994 Act. These defences

[49] *Ibid*, [48]. For further discussion of the case see Carty (n 25) 153–54.

[50] *Stringfellow v McCain Foods (GB) Ltd* [1984] RPC 501 (CA), 545–56. In similar vein (at 547), Stephenson LJ held that, '[w]hen the alleged "passer off" seeks and gets no benefit from using another trader's name … there must, in my judgment, be clear and cogent proof of actual or possible confusion or connection, and of actual damage or the real likelihood of damage'.

[51] Carty (n 1) 236–37.

[52] Wadlow (n 12) 20.

[53] Trade Marks Act 1994, s 2(2).

[54] *Ibid*, s 47.

have no purchase in relation to the common law tort.[55] Finally, the tort of passing off – which was famously described by Lord Diplock as our 'most protean'[56] tort – extends beyond the purview of the 1994 Act insofar as it also protects things that could not qualify as trade marks such as 'slogans or visual images, which radio, television or newspaper advertising campaigns can lead the market to associate with the plaintiff's product'.[57]

Although it is clear that passing off has a secure future, it is by no means easy to map with precision just what that future might look like. Both the compass and the trajectory of the tort have been uncertain for decades. Indeed, the image of passing off as a tort 'at the crossroads' is one that two leading scholars – writing well over a decade apart – have both seen fit to invoke.[58] The metaphor reflects well the fact that the future direction of this tort is yet to be settled by the courts. But even leaving to one side the fact that its future evolution defies prediction, it is far from easy to say whether all existing uses of this action will be regarded as legitimate in the years to come. Judicial doubts about certain uses have been expressed here and there, and these doubts are reflected in juristic writing about the 'proper' purview and purpose of this tort. Some scholars take a conservative (or traditional) approach, and stick firmly to the conviction that the parameters of passing off should be configured according to the classical trinity. There are others, however, who are more progressive, more expansionist, in their outlook. They are happy to applaud the fact that this tort has played a role in relation to some or all of the following: character merchandising,[59] dilution,[60] unfair competition,[61] and misappropriation.[62]

[55] Section 11 of the Trade Marks Act 1994 contains a fairly sizeable array of defences (such as the use by D of his own name (s 11(2)(a)), and use of a term which is necessary to convey what the product is designed to do (s 11(2)(d)).

[56] *Erven Warnink* (n 9) 740.

[57] *Cadbury* (n 37) 200 (Lord Scarman). For examples, see *United Biscuits Ltd v Asda Stores Ltd* [1997] RPC 513 (D's *Puffin* biscuit an imitation of C's famous *Penguin* biscuit: trade mark infringement claim failed, action based on passing off succeeded).

[58] See, eg, H Carty, 'Passing Off at the Crossroads' (1996) 18 *European Intellectual Property Review* 629; Carty (n 1) 269; Wadlow (n 1).

[59] See, eg, *Mirage Studios v Counter-Feat Clothing Co Ltd* [1991] FSR 145; SCG Burley, 'Passing Off and Character Merchandising: Should England Lean Towards Australia?' (1991) *European Intellectual Property Review* 227. *Cf* H Carty, 'Character Merchandising and the Limits of Passing Off' [1993] *Legal Studies* 289.

[60] The idea here is that whatever is distinctive about C's product is undermined by the introduction into the market of D's. For example, when it came to the damage element in *Taittinger SA v Allbev Ltd*, Peter Gibson LJ pointed to the 'erosion of the uniqueness that now attaches to the word "champagne"' while Mann LJ focused on the 'gradual debasement, dilution or erosion of what is distinctive': [1993] FSR 641, 669 and 674 respectively. In similar vein, see *British Telecommunications v One in a Million* [1998] 4 All ER 476 (CA), 497 (Mann LJ). But for doubt about such an extension, see *Harrods Ltd v Harrodian School* [1996] RPC 697 (CA), 715–16 (Millett LJ) and Wadlow (n 1) 454.

[61] See, eg, S Deakin and Z Adams, *Markesinis and Deakin's Tort Law*, 8th edn (Oxford, Oxford University Press, 2019) 693.

[62] See, eg, J Davis, 'Why the United Kingdom Should Have a Law against Misappropriation' [2010] *CLJ* 561. *Cf* M Spence, 'Passing Off and the Misappropriation of Valuable Intangibles' (1996) 112 *LQR* 472; Wadlow (n 1) 452–53.

Without wishing to endorse *tout court* any of these progressive uses of the tort, it is worth noting the weakness of the conservative approach which insists on a strict fidelity to the classical trinity – at least in the ways that the conservative approach has been advanced in the relevant literature. Carty, for example, maintains that the trinity should be adhered to faithfully because '[t]he certainty thereby provided is a fundamental factor in planning and pursuing commercial and competitive activity'.[63] But what grounds this contention? It is hard to accept that such certainty is as fundamental as she suggests given that commercial and competitive activity seems generally to have thrived *despite the fact* that passing off has for decades languished in what one commentator has called a 'state of confusion'.[64] Indeed, by Carty's own admission, the tort has been stuck at the crossroads for years, hence her repeated calls for clarification of the law.[65] If this be true, and if the tort has been functioning at least tolerably well for the last 20 or 30 years, it follows that it cannot be true that a rigid adherence to the trinity is anything like as fundamental as she claims.

Also against the conservative approach is Naresh's observation that, 'any evaluation that proceeds solely upon the basis that the departure from old established common law rules by itself renders the principle suspect would be misguided'.[66] This must be right. For, any putative argument that simply assumes the very thing that is in issue – namely, whether development of this tort absolutely *must* occur within the tramlines set by the classical trinity – is one that merely begs the question.[67]

On the other hand, the fact that there is no intrinsic merit in adhering strictly to the tort's three established ingredients does not mean that we must accept uncritically some of the developments that seem to have departed from them over the past 50 years. In the remainder of this section of the chapter, I do not propose to dwell at length on most of these. Partly, this is because they have received considerable academic attention already; but mainly it is because most of them do not impinge significantly on the major claims of this book. It suffices to say – though this is not a set of claims I defend in any detail – that those who are happy to stretch beyond the tort's recognised ingredients in order to bring character merchandising within the fold of passing off have had the better of that debate,[68] while those

[63] H Carty, 'Passing Off: Frameworks of Liability Debated' (2012) *Intellectual Property Quarterly* 106, 117.

[64] Spence (n 62) 472.

[65] Carty (n 1) 270, Carty (n 58) 114.

[66] Naresh (n 10) 119.

[67] Another way of putting it is to say that the argument is circular. It is reducible to the proposition that liability beyond the confines of the classical trinity is not possible because liability beyond the confines of the classical trinity is not possible.

[68] For details of the stretching involved, and a rebuttal of the one-time objection that the claimant and defendant in such cases may not share a 'common field of activity', see Carty (n 1) 234–35. See also, C Ng, 'The Law of Passing Off – Goodwill Beyond Goods' (2016) 47 *International Review of Intellectual Property and Competition Law* 817, 830–31 and J Phillips and A Coleman, 'Passing Off and the "Common Field of Activity"' (1985) 101 *LQR* 142.

who prefer to see passing off as a tort of unfair competition,[69] or one that protects against dilution,[70] have come off second best in those disputes.

The two unresolved matters concerning the future of this tort that do require closer consideration are as follows: first, whether the public interest in knowing the genuine provenance of goods should, as some seem to think, provide all or part of this tort's *raison d'être*; and, secondly, whether passing off ought to be developed so as to become more responsive to instances of misappropriation of goodwill in circumstances where there was no accompanying misrepresentation. Each is considered in turn.

i. The Relevance of Public Interest?

In *British Telecommunications Plc v One in a Million Ltd*, Aldous LJ displayed a marked preparedness to justify the tort of passing off on the basis that it serves to protect the public interest in knowing the true provenance of goods. He did so by quoting with approval something that had originally been said by Lord Diplock in the *Erven Warnink* case. It was the part of his dictum, quoted earlier,[71] in which his Lordship suggested that the common law of passing off ought to be developed in line with the consumer welfarism that underpinned various related statutory interventions.[72] Even more clearly, Fisher J said in *Tots Toys v Mitchell* that, 'there is a legitimate private interest in protecting business goodwill … [But] [e]ven more importantly, there is a strong public interest in preserving the means of identifying the source of the products'.[73]

A number of scholars agree. Naresh, for instance, contends that '[t]he objective of protecting consumers against misrepresentations is of course, a laudable one'.[74] And Wadlow makes substantively the same point,[75] while Carty is only a little more circumspect in saying that 'the public interest is an important but indirect justification for the tort'.[76]

I take a different view. I do so because I fail to see how the existence of a common law right of action might properly be thought to hinge upon the question of whether its exigibility will promote the (non-actionable) interests of

[69] See, eg, Davis (n 62) 561.

[70] To my mind, the single most compelling argument against the protection of dilution is that there is nothing belonging to C (including a right) that is adversely impacted. What, in other words, has C got to complain about? For a summary of the other major arguments both for and against the protection against dilution (together with resounding support for the second of these two positions), see Wadlow (n 1) 454 and H Carty, 'Dilution and Passing Off: Cause for Concern' (1996) 112 *LQR* 632.

[71] See text associated with (n 9), above.

[72] *British Telecommunications* (n 60) 486.

[73] *Tots Toys v Mitchell* [1993] 1 NZLR 325, 341.

[74] Naresh (n 10) 120.

[75] In his view, 'passing off not only protects the private interests of individual claimants … it is fully justified by the public interest': Wadlow (n 1) 449.

[76] Carty (n 1) 266–67.

third parties.[77] Common law torts (unlike those created by statute) ought not to be crafted by judges with a view to having them serve nakedly instrumentalist goals;[78] and claimants in such cases are not public champions. Rather, they have standing to sue on their own behalf, either in connection with rights that are personal to them that have been wrongfully invaded, *or* (less often[79]) in connection with certain losses that have been wrongfully caused by the defendant.[80]

Even if this were not the case, it is questionable whether the public interest will always be enhanced (on balance) by a tort that serves to curb the incidence with which copycat products appear on the market. Competition in the form of similar goods being available will both augment consumer choice and exert a downward pressure on prices. This is basic micro-economics. Accordingly, although judges have sometimes treated consumer interests as part of the rationale for this tort, it is by no means certain that the existence of passing off (conceived as a tort based on the protection of consumer interests) is more conducive to the promotion of such interests than its absence.[81]

ii. Protection against Misappropriation in the Absence of Misrepresentation

The question of whether passing off should become more attentive to the simple misappropriation of goodwill is a much trickier matter. The most rigorous and expansive existing examination of this issue can be found in an article by Michael Spence, the stated aim of which was 'to demonstrate how difficult it is to mount an argument of principle for the development of a broadly framed tort of misappropriation of valuable intangibles'.[82] In it, he describes what he considers to be three general hurdles that face anyone intent on creating such a tort. And, on top of this, he outlines the shortcomings of four possible bases that might be suggested for any such development. In my view, his arguments about the general hurdles are misconceived, while his rejection of the four putative justifications is inconclusive.

The three general obstacles he describes are as follows. First, he asserts that it can be very difficult – perhaps even impossible – to identify the creator of an

[77] For compelling accounts of why the courts shy away from nakedly policy-driven decision-making, see R Stevens, *Torts and Rights* (Oxford, Oxford University Press, 2007) 312–14; A Beever, *Rediscovering the Law of Negligence* (Oxford, Hart Publishing, 2007) 3–8.

[78] It is true that in adjudicating cases according to specific *legal norms*, a judge's decision may ultimately be justified by instrumentalist concerns *because the legal norms are themselves justified by policy considerations*: see J Gardner, *Torts* and *Other Wrongs* (Oxford, Oxford University Press, 2019) 116. But this does not license overt judicial recourse to just any policy in adjudicating tort cases.

[79] I sketch all the major exceptions to the rule that torts involve rights infringements in J Murphy, 'The Heterogeneity of Tort Law' (2019) 39 *OJLS* 455, 462–68.

[80] For a first-rate defence of this position, see JCP Goldberg and BC Zipursky, *Recognizing Wrongs* (Cambridge, Massachusetts, Harvard University Press, 2020) Ch 3.

[81] For fine-grained, economic analysis of this point, see J Murphy, '*Erven Warnink v Townend* (1979)' in J Gardner *et al* (eds), *Landmark Cases in Consumer Law* (Oxford, Hart Publishing, 2022).

[82] Spence (n 62) 473.

intangible asset, making it unclear in whom the rights of a creator should reside. For this reason, he continues, it is difficult to justify a tort of passing off that responds to acts of misappropriation. He gives the example of a case centred on the bushman character, Mick Dundee, from the film *Crocodile Dundee*. He quite rightly identifies the character as having possessed great product endorsement value, but goes on to ask who created that value: 'was it the makers of the film, those who had contributed to the development of the bushman tradition or the public at large? And in what proportion?'.[83] With no clear answer to these questions, he concludes, it is hard to say in whom any right to sue for passing off should reside.

His second supposed obstacle is a related one: it stems from the difficulty in claiming that a corporate entity is the creator of an intangible asset. He puts it this way:

> [i]f many valuable intangibles which a corporation seeks to protect are in fact 'created' by employees or groups of employees, and if it is difficult to speak of the corporation as itself 'creating' the relevant intangible in such circumstances, serious problems arise for the justification and application of a tort of misappropriation.[84]

Thirdly, he suggests that there is also a problem in the shape of the fact that the creation of a tort of misappropriation would be contrary to the public interest insofar as 'the development of culture and maintenance of economic competition depend upon our ability to imitate one another'.[85]

In my view, all of these objections founder. The first two fail because they focus upon those who *create* the intangible asset. Such a focus is of course apt in connection with *intellectual property* where someone's creative effort is always in play: someone must have written the book that is now protected by copyright; someone must have invented the device that is now protected by a patent; someone must have designed the mark or get-up that is protected by a registered trade mark. But in passing off things are different. It is a tort concerned with the protection of the claimant's goodwill; and while goodwill and intellectual property are both forms of *intangible* property, they are by no means synonymous with one another. Goodwill, *choses in action*, domain names and trade secrets are all forms of intangible property, but not one of them warrants the label intellectual property. None of them arises from a creative enterprise in the same way as inventions, authored works or fancy packaging. Moreover, there is no reason to think that tort law is only concerned with rights in or over property the claimant has created. Tort law recognises the rights I possess in relation to the house that I bought but did not build, just as it recognises my rights in relation to a great many chattels that I also purchased but did not make.

On top of this – perhaps even more importantly – misappropriation is by no means an alien concept within tort law when it comes to the protection of

[83] *Ibid*, 480.
[84] *Ibid*, 481.
[85] *Ibid*, 482.

property. Rather, as Peter Cane notes in relation to property-based wrongs generally, '[a]ppropriation … is tort law's main concern'.[86] And in support of that claim he sketches, at considerable length, many different instances in which tort provides such protection.[87] What he does not mention, however, is the historical fact – helpfully unearthed by Wadlow – that 'from its very earliest beginnings passing off has always been as much concerned with misappropriation, as with misrepresentation'.[88] Accordingly, Cane's contention that only land and chattels may be appropriated,[89] is a questionable one (and one we shall return to).

Spence's third general hurdle can be rebuffed much more straightforwardly. It is reducible to the idea that a tort's validity can be determined by reference to its communitarian credentials. But as we have already seen, there is little that can be said in favour of public interest-based rationales for the tort of passing off (or, indeed, any tort). The value to the general public of A's capacity to sue B for a given tort is immaterial when it comes to justifying the existence of a right of action that A holds against B. When the common law grants A the right to sue B in tort, it does so because in some way or other B has wronged A; and not because B has wronged society as a whole.

Having dismissed as misdirected these three general hurdles in the way of passing off becoming a tort concerned with misappropriation *regardless* of whether D misrepresented anything, what can be said of Spence's objections to the four putative justifications that have been put forward for its fulfilling this role? The answer is that, quite apart from individual shortcomings,[90] they are necessarily inconclusive. To explain: even if Spence is right to find fault in the four justifications that have been offered in favour of making passing off a tort of misappropriation, this does not preclude the possibility of a fifth, successful justification. Expressed in shorthand: just because rule of law *x* cannot be justified by reference to putative reasons *a–d*, does not mean that rule of law *x* can never be justified because, however flawed the justificatory credentials of factors *a–d* may be, there logically remains the possibility of a different justification – factor *e*.

Given that none of Spence's objections are compelling, can there be raised any other, more conclusive reasons for rejecting the extension of passing off to cases of misappropriation? I don't think that there can. True: Jacob LJ's memorable words in *L'Oreal v Bellure* might be regarded as the source of a plausible objection. He said:

[86] Cane (n 17) 25.
[87] *Ibid*, 25–48.
[88] Wadlow (n 1) 449.
[89] See below, text associated with (n 99).
[90] For example, the fact that he doubts that a misappropriation role for passing off can plausibly be anchored to a concern to protect a creator from the harm caused by imitations (see Spence (n 62) 483–86), reveals once again his misplaced fixation with creator's rights.

> I am not sure where I first saw the word [misappropriation] used in this context, though I believe it to have come from the United States. I wish to state that I think it very unhelpful. We are all against misappropriation, just as we are all in favour of mother and apple pie.[91]

Yet this is mere rhetoric. Neither in this passage, nor in his judgment generally, was there the faintest engagement with the American case law. And yet one can hardly expect one's dismissal of a body of case law as 'unhelpful' to be seen as convincing when one fails to give it serious consideration. Furthermore, Wadlow is no more persuasive when he contends that judges should not extend the tort of passing off to cases of misappropriation *without misrepresentation* for the simple reason that this would involve them in the laying down of rules of unfair competition (which, in his view, is a matter properly for the legislature).[92] It is true that developing the tort in this way would indeed impact competitive freedom. But it would only do this by way of side-effect.[93] The principal concern would be with the protection of property. More fully: however broad or narrow one's preferred conception of misappropriation may be, the term has an inescapable proprietary dimension to it. And it is this inescapable proprietary aspect that forces us to accept that actions based on misappropriation are fundamentally about the protection of C's property rights and *not* chiefly about fair competition. What may be legally done in the name of competition is affected, but only indirectly.

Carty is a third jurist who has expressed hostility to the idea that passing off should be seen as an action for misappropriation. In her case, the objection is that, if the courts were to treat misappropriation as the key issue, then '[t]he rationale [for the tort must be seen as] the protection of already successful traders'.[94] But as we have noted, this conclusion is unwarranted since a tort of misappropriation is more naturally interpreted as being first and foremost about the protection of a claimant's property rights; and in this there is nothing remotely untoward. Indeed, to the contrary, tort law's protection of property rights is an entirely quotidian phenomenon,[95] while tort law's promotion or protection of fair competition is not. The former interpretation seems altogether more appealing since it explains why the claimant has standing to sue. Adopting Carty's interpretation renders it a mystery why any given individual should be entitled to sue.

[91] *L'Oreal v Bellure* [2008] RPC 8 (CA), [160].

[92] See, eg, Wadlow (n 1) 453: 'the misappropriation doctrine erects barriers to entry and imposes additional costs on new market entrants, who must go through the motions of re-inventing the wheel not only once, but time and time again'.

[93] Catherine Ng thinks likewise. She claims that, in so far as passing off protects against unfair competition, the fact that it does this is not 'sustainable as a rationale for the law' but a mere 'incidental and occasional' occurrence: see C Ng, 'A Common Law of Passing-Off: English and Scottish Perspectives' (2009) 13 *Edinburgh Law Review* 134, 139.

[94] Carty (n 1) 266. Her saying this was anchored to the fact that Sir Michael Kerr LJ once said (obiter) that the key issue in a particular case was 'whether this was a misappropriation': see *Harrods* (n 60) 722.

[95] As one leading scholar notes, there are 'at least four different types of disputes about property with which the law of tort deals: title disputes, user disputes, interference with use (or "amenity damage") disputes, and physical damage disputes. These types of dispute correspond to different incidents of the right of property': see Cane (n 17) 104.

At this point it is probably worth summarising why, despite the widespread hostility to this development, I do not consider it *necessarily* to be off limits to extend passing off to cases where D misappropriates C's goodwill (without D making the kind of misrepresentation that is ordinarily associated with this tort). To begin with, objections rooted in the sanctity of the classical trinity are circular. Secondly, arguments – such as those advanced by Spence – which centre on the difficulties associated with identifying the creator of the goodwill are misguided, since they are germane only to invasions of *intellectual property* rights (and goodwill is not intellectual property). Thirdly, the failure of the four putative justifications that have so far been offered in no way precludes the possibility of a more compelling justification being found. Fourthly, arguments grounded in considerations of aggregate public interest can be dismissed as blind to the juridical norm that torts classically are centred upon various forms of *injuria* suffered by the claimant. Finally, the objection that a tort attentive to misappropriation must be regarded as beyond the bounds of legitimate judicial law making because it would render passing off a tort of unfair competition (an inescapably political matter) must also be put to one side since a tort that responds to misappropriations is best seen as one that protects a claimant's proprietary rights rather than one concerned with fair competition or securing the position occupied by already successful traders.

With all these flawed objections laid bare, is there anything, then, that can be said in favour of passing off becoming a tort that responds to misappropriations in cases in which D has not made a misrepresentation? One possible argument stems from something said by Lady Hale in *OBG Ltd v Allan*, namely, that 'once the law recognises something as property, the law should extend a proprietary remedy to protect it'.[96] In similar – though more expansive – vein, Green and Randall have argued that:

> to provide protection for property rights in tangible assets but not for the same rights in intangible assets is to discriminate between situations which, though physically dissimilar, are legally similar ... and is not consistent with a coherent legal response to interference with property rights.[97]

But these remarks are not quite conclusive. For one thing, the majority of their Lordships in *OBG* were adamant that the tort of conversion could only be invoked to protect tangible assets on the basis that *only tangible assets* are capable of being possessed. On the strength of their Lordships having expressed this view, it could be argued that talk of misappropriating goodwill is meaningless given that goodwill is an intangible asset. Wadlow certainly thinks that what was said in *OBG* precludes passing off from becoming a tort of misappropriation.[98] Cane, writing before *OBG* was decided, adopted a similar view. For him, the idea that goodwill and other forms of intangible property can be misappropriated is an impossibility given that 'misappropriation is a wrong that can only be committed in

[96] *OBG Ltd v Allan* [2008] 1 AC 1 (HL), [311].
[97] S Green and J Randall, *The Tort of Conversion* (Oxford, Hart Publishing, 2009) 131.
[98] Wadlow (n 1) 450–52.

relation to land and chattels'.[99] And although Green and Randall have argued forcefully that it is in fact possible (for the purposes of conversion) to possess and therefore convert certain forms of intangible property, it seems unlikely that even they would consider goodwill to be one such form of intangible property.[100]

On the other hand, maybe all of these commentators are missing something. As regards Cane, it is, as intimated already, questionable whether he is right to suggest that it is only possible to misappropriate land or chattels. And as for Wadlow, he seems to overlook an important difference between conversion and passing off with the result that his willingness to be led (analogically) by what was said in *OBG*, may be a tad too hasty. The problems that beset the various contentions made by these authors are dealt with in turn.

Cane invokes a common parlance conception of misappropriation in what he says. It is one that clashes with an alternative meaning of misappropriation already at work in the law. Under the law of theft, the concepts of appropriation and deprivation are necessarily separate ones; for an appropriation that is unaccompanied by an intention permanently to deprive is not theft.[101] In other words, appropriation is subtly, but importantly different, from X simply taking something away from Y. The fact that, under the relevant legislation, acts of appropriation come apart from acts effecting dispossession was made clear in *R v Morris* where Lord Roskill defined appropriation as 'an act by way of adverse interference with *or* usurpation of those rights [of the owner]'.[102] On this approach, a misappropriation can occur where there is mere interference with '*any of the rights* of the owner'.[103] If this understanding of misappropriation were to be applied to the tort of passing off, it would be enough to show that D marketed a product designed to imitate one made by C and that his doing so led to a diversion of sales away from C. So doing, to use Honoré's well-known phrase, would constitute a usurpation of the 'right to the income of the thing'.[104] There would, in other words, be misappropriation of a proprietary right without any dispossession of a tangible asset in such a case.

[99] Cane (n 17) 26.

[100] Their argument is fairly complex, but the essential claim is that, in order to establish possession 'there must be at least one manual element and at least one cognitive element present': Green and Randall (n 97) 110. The cognitive element would be unproblematic since claimants in passing off cases undoubtedly intend to exclude others. But they would not, it seems, be able to demonstrate the manual control upon which these authors would also insist. The concept of manual control requires that the asset in question display both of two key characteristics, namely, excludability and exhaustibility: Green and Randall (n 97) 111.

[101] Theft Act 1968, s 1.

[102] *R v Morris* [1984] AC 320 (HL), 332 (emphasis added). He went on to stipulate that, for the purposes of the Theft Act 1968, such acts of appropriation must be without the owner's consent. This aspect of his definition *for the purposes of s 3* was later rejected in a subsequent House of Lords decision. But the idea that an appropriation involves an act which adversely interferes with, or constitutes a usurpation of, the owner's rights was adopted without qualification: see *DPP v Gomez* [1993] AC 442 (HL), 460 (Lord Keith).

[103] *Ibid* (emphasis added).

[104] This right, for Honoré, was one of 11 so-called 'incidents of ownership': see Honoré (n 26) 113. *Cf* the view that this right to the income of a thing is merely one *aspect* of a unitary concept of property (anchored to the concept of a right to exclusive use), see JE Penner, 'The Bundle of Rights Picture of Property' (1996) 43 *UCLA Law Review* 711, 765.

Furthermore, even if we leave the meaning of appropriation found in English criminal law to one side, it is still possible to identify other common law jurisdictions in which the idea of appropriating intangibles has been recognised by the civil law. In Australia, for example, there has been judicial acceptance of the idea that passing off may comprise a 'wrongful appropriation of business reputation'.[105] Equally, in the United States of America, there has been formal recognition of a tort of appropriation of likeness since as early as 1905 when the Georgia Supreme Court – in a case in essence identical to *Fenty* – accepted the common law right of an individual to control the commercial use of his picture.[106] (The tort's recognition now finds expression in section 652C of the *Restatement (Second) of Torts*.[107])

In Canada, too, there has been acceptance that an action in tort will lie for the misappropriation of a claimant's personality where his or her image is used without permission, as a marketing device.[108] In none of these instances has there been any objection raised to the idea that an intangible asset might be misappropriated. Seen against this backdrop, it is perhaps unsurprising that there has been some judicial receptiveness in this country to the idea that '[t]he traditional form of passing off … is no longer definitive of the ambit of the cause of action'.[109] The trinity may be classical, but it seems not to be sacred.

As to Wadlow's view that *OBG* provides clear guidance on the direction that passing off should take, it is worth remembering that although *dispossession* is central to the workings of conversion, this is not true of passing off.[110] The requirement of dispossession in the tort of conversion makes it perfectly proper to conclude that goodwill cannot be converted. So long as the claimant retains some customer connection, it is hard to think of her as having been dispossessed – in the sense of completely deprived – of her goodwill. But in passing off there is no requirement that the defendant should dispossess the claimant of her property. It is enough that the defendant infringes rights associated with that property. Injury to goodwill (not dispossession) is the gist of the tort.

In fact, I think the single biggest difficulty in developing the tort along the lines discussed in the preceding paragraphs would be the awkward matter of deciding at which point mere appropriation gives way to *mis*appropriation.[111] Jacob J rightly pointed out in *Hodgkinson Corby Ltd v Wards Mobility Services Ltd (No 1)* that:

[105] *Henderson v Radio Corp Pty* [1969] RPC 218 (H Ct NSW), 236 (Evatt CJ).

[106] *Pavesch v New England Life Insurance Co*, 122 Ga 190, 50 SE 61 (1905).

[107] The section bears the title, 'Appropriation of Name or Likeness' and it imposes liability on anyone 'who appropriates to his own use or benefit the name or likeness of another'. (I am indebted to John Goldberg for drawing this to my attention.).

[108] *Athans v Canadian Adventure Camps Ltd* (1977) 80 DLR (3d) 583. For discussion, see BM Hylton and P Goldson, 'The New Tort of Appropriation of Personality: Protecting Bob Marley's Face' [1996] *CLJ* 56, 61.

[109] *Arsenal Football Club Plc v Reed (No 2)* [2003] RPC 39, [70].

[110] So, eg, there was no conversion in *Fouldes v Willoughby* (1841) 8 M & W 540 where D removed C's horses from a ferry and deposited them on the shore but never sought to deprive C of them.

[111] Although, in addition to the arguments considered here, Hazel Carty purports to identify a series of further objections against passing off becoming a tort attentive to misappropriation, it is clear that these are misdirected. Thus, while 11 pages of her book are ostensibly devoted to this question (Carty (n 1) 271–81), it is clear that her real gripe is with dilution – of which she speaks repeatedly – being the

> [t]here is no tort of copying. There is no tort of taking a man's market or customers. Neither the market nor the customers are the Plaintiff's to own. There is no tort of making use of another's goodwill as such. There is no tort of competition.[112]

With this dictum in mind, it is clear that the key question we face concerns the basis – perhaps bases – on which any given appropriation may appropriately be characterised as wrongful, as a *mis*appropriation. Arguably, a naked attempt to free-ride on the back of the claimant's goodwill will suffice. Indeed, had this approach been taken in the well-known 'Spanish Champagne' case,[113] the decision might well have been less controversial than it ultimately proved to be. The various claimants in that case – all of whom produced wine in the Champagne district of France and sold it in the UK – applied for an injunction to restrain the defendant from passing off a sparkling wine made in Spain and marketed in the UK as 'Spanish Champagne'. The defendant argued, not implausibly, that it had not misrepresented anything since its addition of the word 'Spanish' to the name of its own wine precluded its being mistaken for Champagne produced in France. Only by recourse to the observation that there exist 'persons whose life or education has not taught them much about the nature and production of wine … [and] who are likely to be misled by the description "Spanish Champagne"'[114] was the judge in that case able to identify a misrepresentation.

Instead of relying on the putative gullibility of an uneducated sector of society, it might have made for a more edifying dictum had Danckwerts J placed greater emphasis on the fact that there had been 'a blatant attempt to secure to the sale of the defendant company's wine the advantage of the goodwill connected with the word "champagne" and the business of the plaintiffs'.[115] Equally, the judge could conceivably have given more weight to the fact that the defendant had marketed the exact same wine in Spain under the name 'Perelada', where it already had an established customer base. It had only labelled it 'Spanish Champagne' for the purposes of the UK market where it hoped to free-ride on the reputation attached to the wine of the claimants. In short, the case was clearly one in which there was an attempt to misappropriate the claimant's goodwill and the defendant had undoubtedly resorted to deeply reprehensible tactics in order to do this.

D. Final Remarks

There is no doubt that passing off has historically been, and continues to be, overwhelmingly concerned with the protection of the claimant's goodwill. For the most

basis of a claim. A more open admission of this can be found in an article written some years later in which she said: 'in this context these terms – dilution/misappropriation – amount to the same thing': Carty (n 63) 119.

112 *Hodgkinson Corby Ltd v Wards Mobility Services Ltd (No 1)* [1995] FSR 169, 174.

113 *J Bollinger SA v Costa Brava Wine Co Ltd (No 4)* [1961] 1 WLR 277.

114 *Ibid*, 291.

115 *Ibid*.

part, the courts have sought strenuously to deal with each novel challenge for this tort – whether it be a case of character merchandising, extraterritorial goodwill, inverse passing off or whatever – by reference to the classical trinity of goodwill, misrepresentation and damage. To the extent that they have done this successfully, the tort rightly deserves to be regarded as one specifically concerned with the protection of an economic interest. But it must be acknowledged that in some cases the concept of goodwill has been stretched almost beyond recognition. For example, the courts' attempts to bring within the fold of goodwill the interests of certain professional governing bodies or charities that do not aim to generate profits[116] might reasonably be described as strained. The same can be said of the pre-launch advertising cases (which establish that one may have goodwill even before one has commenced trading).[117]

As regards the significance of especially reprehensible conduct, this may still count for a great deal in passing off even though, formally, the tort is one of strict liability. The case law amply reveals that the courts will treat instances of 'innocent passing off' in an appreciably more lenient way than cases in which the defendant has intentionally set out to deceive consumers.[118] That the courts have done this serves to buttress one of the key claims of this book, namely, that, within the sphere of the so-called economic torts, egregious wrongdoing often accounts for novel developments.

Finally, it has also been seen that although the recognition of actions for passing off in the absence of a misrepresentation will strike some as heretical – as a development that would drive a coach and four through the classical trinity – it *might* nonetheless be a welcome one. But whether it be a welcome development or not, it is not yet safe to say that passing off has formally broken free from the requirement of a misrepresentation. The strongest indications to date that such a development might occur can be traced to the decisions in *Glaxo* and *Direct Line* considered earlier. Yet the courts in those cases did not overtly say that there was no longer a need to show a misrepresentation by the defendant: they avoided the problem by simply steering clear of addressing it head on. They are therefore inconclusive authorities. All that can be said with confidence, here, is that if the courts were prepared to entertain a case in which there has been no clear misrepresentation, they would thereby create a means by which a case like *Erven Warnink* could more straightforwardly be decided. As things stand, though, it is

[116] See, eg, *The Law Society of England and Wales v Society of Lawyers* [1996] FSR 739; *The British Diabetic Association v The Diabetic Society* [1995] 4 All E.R. 812. For discussion see Ng (n 68) 831.

[117] See, eg, *WH Allen & Co v Brown Watson Ltd* [1965] RPC 191; *BBC v Talbot Motor Co Ltd* [1981] FSR 228. For criticism, based on the idea that goodwill equates to 'the tendency to return to an old and familiar place', see Wadlow (n 1) 44. Also, contrast *Cruttwell v Lye* (1810) 17 Ves Jr 335, 346 (Lord Eldon): 'good-will … is nothing more than the probability, that the old customers will resort to the old place'; *Muller* (n 18), 224 (Lord Macnaghten): '[Goodwill] is the one thing which distinguishes an old-established business from a new business at its first start'.

[118] The *Office Cleaning Services* case (n 38), appears to reverse the burden of proof in relation to the misrepresentation limb of the tort. The fact that deception will 'readily be inferred' in such cases places the onus on D to show that there was no deception.

hard – when sticking rigidly to the classical trinity – to square the outcome in that case with Lord Diplock's admission that, as a matter of fact, 'it could not be shown that any purchaser of "Keeling's Old English Advocaat" supposed or would be likely to suppose it to be goods supplied by Warnink or to be Dutch advocaat of any make'.[119]

Furthermore, I think the fear of allowing claims based on misappropriation *in the absence of a misrepresentation* must be seen in perspective. For one thing, any claimant who over-zealously invoked the tort of passing off to defend their monopoly against just the faintest suggestion of an imitation of their product could well see their action struck out before it actually troubled a competitor. Furthermore, the fact that the Supreme Court has in recent years extended the tort of malicious prosecution to cases involving civil actions might well have a deterrent effect upon those who are unscrupulous in their desire to see off unwelcome competition.[120] In deciding whether to allow such claims for malicious prosecution, it is conceivable that the courts would be guided by the way the legislature has tackled the problem of groundless threats to litigate for breach of intellectual property rights via the Intellectual Property (Unjustified Threats) Act 2017.[121]

III. Injurious Falsehood

A. Vitality

Injurious falsehood cases are fairly few and far between. To some extent, the tort's limited popularity is explicable by reference to the fact that it overlaps with three other torts that are better known and which, for various reasons, are typically preferred. They are the torts of causing loss by unlawful means, passing off and defamation. On top of this, claimants will sometimes have the option of invoking one of two statutory actions (considered below) which also circumscribe the need to rely on injurious falsehood. But even so, the common law tort remains vital in the strict sense of that word.[122] It has a pedigree stretching back nearly 450 years,[123] and, to date, there has been no suggestion from the courts that it is an otiose cause of action. That said: there are several jurists who now consider injurious falsehood to be a redundant cause of action, despite the fairly steady trickle

[119] *Erven Warnink* (n 9) 739.
[120] See *Willers v Joyce* [2018] AC 779 (SC).
[121] The Act introduced amendments to this in each of the Registered Designs Act 1949, the Patents Act 1977, the Copyright, Designs and Patents Act 1988 and the Trade Marks Act 1994. For details of the way these statutes make accountable for unjustified threats of suit the owners of such intellectual property rights, see L Bentley *et al*, *Intellectual Property Law*, 5th edn (Oxford, Oxford University Press, 2018) 1302–1305.
[122] See J Murphy, 'The Vitality of Injurious Falsehood' (2021) 137 *LQR* (2021) 137 *LQR* 657.
[123] The earliest reported case – one involving slander of title – was *Bliss v Stafford* [1573] 74 ER 82.

of reported cases each year. The plausibility of their claims cannot be dismissed summarily, and they are therefore considered at length in subsection D, below. For now, however, it is enough to note that the courts continue to treat this tort as one that is alive and well.

B. Protected Interests

The name injurious falsehood reveals nothing about the interests protected by this tort. But then nor (very accurately) do any of the other names by which it has been known at various points in its history. Although the original actions on the case – variously labelled 'slander of title', 'disparagement of title', 'slander of goods', 'disparagement of goods' and 'trade libel'[124] – all seem to provide clues as to its remit, none of these names (which have all lapsed into desuetude) capture very accurately the full scope of the modern tort. Indeed, in the present era, the only serious rival to the label 'injurious falsehood' is 'malicious falsehood'. But it is not the label used here. For one thing, malice is a doubtful ingredient, having become an element of the tort by mistake.[125] And in any event, the meaning of 'malice' in this tort is out of line with the way that word is used elsewhere in tort law.[126] True: the name 'injurious falsehood' is also a little misleading since the tort's gist is not *injuria* (as that name suggests) but *damnum* (in the shape of special damage). But it is a good deal less misleading than those names which suggest that slander, or that title of some sort, must be in issue; and it at least has in its favour the fact that it was the name first given to the modern version of the tort by John Salmond around the turn of the twentieth century.[127]

Despite the confusion that surrounds the nomenclature, it is generally accepted that this tort is concerned solely with economic losses. According to Prosser, it 'consists of the publication, or communication to a third person, of false statements concerning the plaintiff, his property, or his business, which cause him pecuniary loss'.[128] In similar vein, Carty maintains that 'it must be economic harm that is caused'.[129] Conspicuously, however, neither author provides an authority for what they say. By contrast, the current edition of *Clerk and Lindsell on Torts* does purport to anchor essentially the same claim to a particular authority. It states: 'in *Royal Baking Powder Co v Wright, Crossley & Co* [130] the essentials of the action were defined as: false words which are maliciously published and which

[124] For details of the various rather dated cases in which these (and closely related) labels have been used, see FH Newark, 'Malice in Actions on the Case for Words' (1944) 60 *LQR* 366.

[125] See Murphy (n 122) 659–60.

[126] See J Murphy, 'Malice as an Ingredient of Tort Liability' [2019] *CLJ* 355.

[127] J Salmond, *The Law of Torts: A Treatise on the English Law of Liability for Civil Wrongs*, 1st edn (London, Stevens & Haynes, 1907) 417.

[128] WL Prosser, 'Injurious Falsehood: The Basis of Liability' (1959) 59 *Columbia Law Review* 425, 425.

[129] Carty (n 1) 203.

[130] *Royal Baking Powder Co v Wright, Crossley & Co* (1901) 18 RPC 95 (HL).

are calculated to cause (and do cause) the claimant *pecuniary loss*'.[131] But this is not quite right. The precise words used in that case were that:

> [t]o support such an action it is necessary for the [claimant] to prove (1) that the statements complained of were untrue; (2) that they were made maliciously – that is, without just cause or excuse; (3) that the [claimant] had suffered thereby.[132]

From this we may properly conclude that it is the general concept of 'special damage' rather than the narrow one of 'pecuniary loss' that, on House of Lords authority, forms the gist of injurious falsehood. Of course, the obvious rejoinder here is that there is no difference between special damage and pecuniary loss. It is a rejoinder that those making it might seek to fortify by reference to the fact that section 3 the Defamation Act 1952 clearly identifies pecuniary interests as being protected by this tort. There can be no doubt that the Act does in fact do this;[133] but conceding this point does not require us to accept that the tort is limited to the protection of such interests. Just because the statute confines itself to cases of pecuniary loss provides no licence for supposing that, as a matter of common law, the terms 'pecuniary loss' and 'special damage' must be treated as synonyms. Indeed, as a matter of established common law, all that special damage entails is 'actual'[134] – ie, measurable or material – damage. In certain slander cases, for example, it has been held to encompass a loss of voluntary hospitality shown to one by friends;[135] and it probably also stretches to cover the loss associated with separation from a spouse.[136]

Of course, it is true that, in practice, it will normally be pecuniary loss that prompts the claimant to bring an action for injurious falsehood. So much is obvious from the fact that, ordinarily, D's untruthful and disparaging remarks about C (or her goods or business) will, in the natural run of things, lead to C losing custom. But the relevant case law would seem to suggest that *other forms of loss* may also suffice to ground an action. In *Ratcliffe v Evans*, for example, Bowen LJ said that special damage should be understood in terms of any 'particular damage (beyond the general damage), which results from the particular circumstances of the case' and that, here, particular damage simply 'denotes the actual and temporal

[131] M Jones (ed), *Clerk and Lindsell on Torts*, 23rd edn (London, Sweet & Maxwell, 2020) 1704 (emphasis added).

[132] *Royal Baking Powder* (n 130) 99 (Lord Davey).

[133] This provision, specifically dealing with injurious falsehood, relieves C from the requirement of proving that the words complained of were calculated to cause C pecuniary damage if they were (i) in writing (or other permanent form) or (ii) uttered in respect of any office, profession, calling trade or business.

[134] This was the term preferred by Bowen LJ in *Ratcliffe v Evans* [1892] 2 QB 525 (CA), 527: 'an action will lie for written or oral falsehoods, not actionable per se … where they do produce, actual damage'.

[135] *Davies v Solomon* (1871–2) LR 7 QB 112, 114 (Blackburn J): 'the loss of the hospitality of friends is sufficient special damage to sustain an action like the present'.

[136] *Lynch v Knight* (1861) 9 HL Cas 577 (HL), 595 (Lord Brougham): 'the late Lord Chancellor, I know, entertained a strong opinion … that the consequential damage arising to the wife in such a case afforded her a good ground of action … I am strongly inclined to think that the view taken by my late noble friend was correct'.

loss which has, in fact, occurred'.[137] Even more clearly, in *Chamberlain v Boyd*, Coleridge CJ specifically referred to harm other than that which is of the pecuniary variety. He said that words 'can become actionable only when they have been followed by pecuniary *or temporal damage*'.[138] His only caveat in relation to the recoverability of those other forms of 'temporal damage' was that they not be 'unsubstantial and shadowy'.[139] In yet another case, Lord Robertson similarly omitted any reference to the need to show pecuniary loss. Couching what he understood to be the gist of the tort in negative (yet conspicuously non-specific) terms, he said: '[u]nless the plaintiff has in fact suffered loss which can be and is specified, he has no cause of action'.[140] All that is required on this formulation is that the claimant be able to point to loss of one form or another that can be specified.

Though these various dicta do not themselves provide examples of the other kinds of loss that might also be covered by the tort of injurious falsehood, they nonetheless indicate that their existence cannot be ruled out. One must also add to them the fact that the Supreme Court has recently indicated that personal injury and damage to chattels are both in principle recoverable under the banner of injurious falsehood. In *Secretary of State for Health v Servier Laboratories Ltd*,[141] two important hypotheticals were considered. The first involved D falsely informing a doctor that it was an unconscious patient's left leg that was due to be amputated rather than (as was in fact the case) the right leg. The second involved D telling the security services at an airport that baggage belonging to C had been left unattended for hours such that it was removed and destroyed, when in fact it had only been left unattended for a moment. According to Lord Hamblen, 'in both these examples, the claimant is likely to have a claim for malicious faslehood'.[142]

But what other forms of loss, beyond these clear-cut examples, might be recoverable under the auspices of this tort? The question of whether recovery for injured feelings is possible arose in *Fielding v Variety Inc*, where the defendant described the claimants' theatrical show, *Charlie Girl*, as being a 'terrible flop'. Recognising that special damage forms the gist of this tort, Lord Denning opined that claimants 'can only recover damages for their probable money loss, and not for their injured feelings'.[143] But in *Joyce v Sengupta* a differently constituted Court of Appeal questioned whether this was right. Addressing his mind to a hypothetical case in which

[137] *Ratcliffe* (n 134), 528.

[138] *Chamberlain v Boyd* (1883) 11 QBD 407 (CA), 412 (emphasis added). Bowen LJ gave an example of a temporal loss that would not be financial in its nature. He said: '[p]ossibly the membership of a club may be a matter of temporal advantage, and the deprivation of it may be an injury or damage of which the law will take cognisance': *ibid*, 415.

[139] *Ibid*, 412.

[140] *Royal Baking Powder* (n 130) 103.

[141] *Secretary of State for Health v Servier Laboratories Ltd* [2021] UKSC 24 (SC).

[142] *Ibid*, [85].

[143] *Fielding v Variety Inc* [1967] 2 QB 841 (CA), 850.

D has maliciously spread a rumour that C's business is in such financial difficulty that the appointment of a receiver is imminent, Sir Donald Nicholls V-C regarded injury to feelings as compensable, albeit under the banner of aggravated damages. He said:

> because of the effect the rumours are having on his business … [C] is worried beyond measure about his livelihood and his family's future. He suffers acute anxiety and distress. Can it be right that the law is unable to give him any recompense for this suffering against the person whose malice caused it? Although injury to feelings alone will not found a cause of action in malicious falsehood, ought not the law to take such injury into account when it is connected with financial damage inflicted by the falsehood?[144]

In *Khodaparast v Shad*,[145] taking a lead from what had been said in *Joyce*, the Court of Appeal went one step further and awarded aggravated damages for the claimant's injured feelings after she had been falsely portrayed by the defendant as having appeared in a pornographic magazine advertising telephone sex services. Those damages were described in exactly the same way that Sir Donald Nicholls' had portrayed them in his judgment in *Joyce*: as a parasitic award made on the back of a claim for special damage. As Stuart-Smith LJ put it:

> *once the plaintiff is entitled to sue for malicious falsehood*, whether on proof of special damage [or] by reason of section 3 of the Act of 1952, I can see no reason why, in an appropriate case, he or she should not recover aggravated damages for injury to feelings.[146]

The fact that the Court of Appeal in *Khodaparast* was persuaded by what had been said in *Joyce*, and the fact that it did not seek to contradict anything in the earlier case, may be significant. This is because, in *Joyce*, the Vice-Chancellor did not stop at saying that injured feelings may be compensated by way of aggravated damages. He also expressly countenanced the idea that such loss – or at least the distress that accompanies such injured feelings – might constitute special damage in its own right. He said: '[i]f distress can inflame the damages recoverable for pecuniary loss, the difference between awarding aggravated damages for that reason and awarding damages for distress *as a separate head is a difference in words only*'.[147] That particular part of his dictum was explicitly invoked and considered in *Khodaparast*,[148] and nothing was said in the later case to oppose or undermine it. It is therefore

[144] *Joyce v Sengupta* [1993] 1 WLR 337 (CA), 348.
[145] *Khodaparast v Shad* [2000] 1 WLR 618 (CA).
[146] *Ibid*, [42] (emphasis added). The inserted word 'or' appears in the headnote, but seems erroneously to have been omitted from the judgment itself. Whether aggravated damages are best seen as being awarded in respect of hurt feelings is questionable. The leading case, *Rookes v Barnard* [1964] AC 1129 (HL), would seem to anchor them to C's dignitary interest, which need not require consciousness of the insult, and hence hurt feelings, as anyone familiar with the story of *The Emperor's New Clothes* should recognise: see further, J Murphy, 'The Nature and Domain of Aggravated Damages' [2010] *CLJ* 353, 362–65.
[147] *Joyce* (n 144) 348–49 (emphasis added).
[148] *Khodaparast* (n 145) [37] (Stuart-Smith LJ).

an open question whether a claimant may bring a claim for injurious falsehood, arguing that his or her special damage took the form of distress (or injury to feelings[149]). The Vice-Chancellor's hypothetical in *Joyce* certainly provides a plausible enough example of how someone might suffer severe distress, as do the facts of *Khodaparast*. In fact, it is easy to imagine that, had the claimant in *Khodaparast* not lost her job as a teacher at an Iranian religious school, she would still have suffered very considerable distress at the thought that others in her community believed what had been said of her. McBride and Bagshaw recognise this point, yet they stop short of endorsing the idea that an injurious falsehood claim may be based on something other than the suffering of economic loss.

They are hesitant on two main grounds. First, because of the decision in *Quinton v Peirce*[150] and secondly because of a problem that they label the '*Wainwright objection*'. According to McBride and Bagshaw, Eady J in *Quinton* had insisted that 'damages could only be awarded in malicious falsehood if the defendant's falsehood resulted in the claimant suffering "actual financial loss"'.[151] This is true *of the case itself* but it is perhaps misleading as a guide to injurious falsehood more generally. The case concerned a Conservative councillor who claimed that by virtue of what had been said about him he lost his seat on the district council and, by extension, an allowance of nearly £3000 per annum that would have been available to him as a councillor. Eady J was quite specific in saying that were it not for section 3 of the Defamation Act 1952 – which relieves a claimant of the need to prove pecuniary loss where the relevant falsehood was in writing or uttered in respect of any trade, office or business – 'it would have been necessary to prove actual financial loss'.[152] But his dictum was not, I think, intended to be read as a general statement about an essential ingredient of the tort. It was merely an explanation of the effect of section 3 (which nowhere states that the tort is confined to the protection of purely pecuniary interests). Had it been a statement about the tort generally, and not one concerning the particular case before him, the learned judge would surely have said 'it *is necessary* to prove' rather than 'it *would have been* necessary to prove'. In short, *Quinton* – which is only a first instance decision – does nothing categorically to rule out damages for pure distress in injurious falsehood.

McBride and Bagshaw's '*Wainwright* objection' stems, predictably enough, from something said by Lord Hoffmann in a case bearing that name. It was this:

> In institutions and workplaces all over the country, people constantly do and say things with the intention of causing distress and humiliation to others. This shows lack of

[149] I include here the possibility that 'injury to feelings' might constitute the requisite special damage since it was hurt feelings (rather than distress) that were regarded by Stuart-Smith LJ as being the aggravating factor in *Khodaparast*. Furthermore, I am not alone in thinking that hurt feelings might suffice to ground a claim for injurious falsehood: see Cane (n 17) 100.

[150] *Quinton v Peirce* [2009] FSR 17.

[151] NJ McBride and R Bagshaw, *Tort Law*, 6th edn (London, Pearson, 2018) 672.

[152] *Quinton* (n 150) [47].

> consideration and appalling manners but I am not sure that the right way to deal with it is always by litigation.[153]

Here, again, though, their hesitancy seems misplaced. This is because what Lord Hoffmann said seems applicable only in a two-party case: where D fails to give proper consideration to C or treats C with dreadful manners. It surely cannot be a matter of bad manners, for example, for D to say something scurrilous about C *to a third party*. And yet it is according to just such a three-party structure that the tort of injurious falsehood operates. If this be right, then the *Wainwright* objection would seem to have no purchase in the injurious falsehood setting. More fully: for the purposes of injurious falsehood, it is not what D says to C that is in issue, but rather *the effect of* what D says to a third party, T, *about C*. Of course, if what D says to T is the kind of thing that will cause harm to C's reputation, then defamation may be the appropriate cause of action. But if all that C suffers is pure distress – perhaps because, as per Nicholl's V-C's hypothetical, D has simply spread a rumour that C is going out of business and C's fears that his existing customers will now go elsewhere to buy their goods – it is far from clear that C should have no remedy based on injurious falsehood.[154]

As with all the other torts in this book, it is arguably the case that injurious falsehood has considerably more remedial potential than is typically ascribed to it. It is not, at least on the authorities as they stand, *necessary* that it be confined to the protection of economic interests. It can provide redress for injured feelings via an award of aggravated damages. But in addition – on the strength of what has been said by the Court of Appeal – it seems possible that it might also be invoked by claimants who suffer distress or injured feelings in the absence of any pecuniary loss. This, however, is where I think the line must be drawn in relation to non-tangible loss. True: there exist dicta in two further cases which suggest that the tort might cover 'interests of personality' and 'reputation of property'. But these, in my view, are best seen as misguided claims.

It was in the context of a case concerning malicious prosecution that the former suggestion was made. In his attempt to unearth the nature and scope of the tort, Lord Steyn opined: '[t]he tort of malicious prosecution … must be seen in the context of overlapping torts, such as defamation and malicious falsehood, which serve to protect interests of personality'.[155] The second claim can be traced to a case decided just over a decade later. In it, Sedley LJ seemed equally keen to bracket injurious falsehood and defamation together. Offering a rather different conception of the interest protected, he said: 'both [torts] concern the protection of reputation, albeit one protects the reputation of persons and the other

[153] *Wainwright v Home Office* [2004] 2 AC 406 (HL), [46].

[154] It could be argued that, although Lord Hoffmann confined what he had to say to a two-party setting, he was generally opposed to the idea that mere distress could constitute a recognised form of damage in tort law. But against that, it is important to note that he expressly prefaced what he said in the text with a statement to the effect that he was reserving his opinion on the matter: *ibid*.

[155] *Gregory v Portsmouth City Council* [2000] 1 AC 419 (HL), 426.

the reputation of property, typically in the form of the goodwill of a business'.[156] Notably, neither of these assertions was rigorously defended; and both of them were uttered *obiter*. Accordingly, it is hard to afford any great weight to them. Furthermore, their implausibility is augmented once it is recognised (as I explain in subsection D) that – despite both judges seeking to emphasise a supposed link between injurious falsehood and defamation – there exist very good reasons for regarding them as two very different torts.

C. The Need for Malice

For the purposes of injurious falsehood, bare lies are not enough to ground an action.[157] It has long been established that, in addition to being untrue, the statement in question 'must [also] be malicious'.[158] In this context, however, 'malice' must not simply be taken to bear its everyday meaning of spite, or ill-will. Rather, drawing on what Lord Herschell said in *White v Mellin*,[159] malice may be of two broad types: either 'motive malice' or 'deceit malice'.[160] In order to constitute the former, 'the object of the publication must be to injure another person', whereas for the latter it is enough that the defendant 'published it with a knowledge of its falsity'.[161]

Of these two broad varieties, only 'motive malice' equates broadly with the meaning attributed to malice in common parlance. Although the courts have adverted to such malice in a variety of ways – like, for instance, emphasising the fact that D was actuated by 'mala fides',[162] or that D acted with a 'dishonest motive',[163] or one that was 'improper'[164] – there is still a common thread. It inheres in the fact that all such cases involve the deliberate infliction of loss. As Collins MR put it, using language substantially identical to that of Lord Herschell: the thing

[156] *Ajinomoto Sweeteners Europe SAS v Asda Stores Ltd* [2011] QB 497 (CA), [28].

[157] *Spain v Christie, Manson & Woods Ltd* [1986] 1 WLR 1120 (CA), 1129 (Sir Nicholas Brown V-C): '[i]f every man can protect the false use of his name or reputation by having a basic right so to do, why is it that the courts have developed the very limited class of cases in which an action for passing off or malicious falsehood can be brought?'. In other words, if making a false claim is, by itself, enough to create tortious liability, what purpose is served by the other elements in both the present tort and that of passing off?

[158] *Steward v Young* (1870) LR 5 CP 122, 126 (Byles J).

[159] *White v Mellin* [1895] AC 154 (HL).

[160] These terms are borrowed from Carty (n 1) 212.

[161] *White* (n 159) 160.

[162] *Halsey v Brotherhood* (1881) 19 Ch D 386 (CA), 388 (Lord Coleridge LCJ): 'there must be some evidence … that the statement was not only untrue, but was made male fide for the purpose of injuring the plaintiff'.

[163] *Greers Ltd v Pearman & Carder Ltd* (1922) 39 RPC 406 (CA), 417 (Scrutton LJ): 'maliciously … in the sense of being made with some indirect or dishonest motive'.

[164] *Balden v Shorter* [1933] Ch 427, 430 (Maugham J): 'malice in the law of slander of title and other forms of injurious falsehood means some dishonest or otherwise improper motive'.

complained of 'must be done with the direct object of injuring that other person's business'.[165] By contrast, cases of 'deceit malice' are markedly different.

At the heart of a 'deceit malice' case is the defendant's knowledge of, or recklessness as to, the falsity of the statement in question. In *Joyce v Sengupta*, it was held that an action for malicious falsehood lay against the author of an article that was published in a national newspaper alleging that the claimant had stolen private correspondence from a member of the royal family. Sir Donald Nicholls V-C highlighted the defendant's 'reckless indifference to the truth or falsity of the allegations' and held that malice could 'be inferred from the grossness and falsity of the assertions and the cavalier way they were published'.[166] A similar, but importantly different, formulation was employed in *Kaye v Robertson*. There, Glidewell LJ held that

> [m]alice will be inferred if it be proved that the words were calculated to produce damage[[167]] *and* that the defendant knew when he published the words that they were false or was reckless as to whether they were false or not.[168]

The difference between the two dicta inheres in Glidewell LJ's insisting that, in addition to the defendant's recklessness, the statement in question must have been calculated to do harm.[169] Of the two approaches, it is submitted that Glidewell LJ's is to be preferred. This is not merely because it chimes with Atkin LJ's having laid down the requirement that the words used must be calculated to cause harm in the earlier case of *Shapiro v La Morta*,[170] but also because this requirement helps restrict the tort's incursion into the freedom of speech afforded to all citizens.[171]

Crucially, even though the malice requirement in this tort may be satisfied without showing spite or ill-will, it remains arguable that injurious falsehood has developed into an action that is attentive to especially reprehensible wrongdoing.[172] Cases involving 'motive malice' – animated as they are by the notion of *male fides* – are self-evidently capable of being viewed in this way. But even cases of 'deceit malice' involve obviously deplorable conduct. Deliberate lying that causes

[165] *Dunlop v Maison Talbot* (1904) TLR 579 (CA), 581. But note *Wilts United Dairies v Robinson* [1957] RPC 220, 237 (Stable J): 'if you publish a defamatory statement about a man's goods which is injurious to him, honestly believing that it is true, your object being your own advantage and no detriment to him, you obviously are not liable'.

[166] *Joyce* (n 144) 345.

[167] The expression 'calculated to produce damage' merely means objectively likely to cause damage. As Mahon J put it in *Customglass Boats Ltd v Salthouse Boats Ltd* [1976] RPC 589, 603: '[t]he word "calculated" in this context is equivalent to "likely"'.

[168] *Kaye v Robertson* [1991] FSR 62 (CA), 67 (emphasis added).

[169] As to the requisite likelihood of harm, it has been held that a test of harm that is 'more likely than not' should be applied: see *Tesla Motors Ltd v BBC* [2011] EWHC 2760, [7].

[170] *Shapiro v La Morta* (1923) 40 TLR 201 (CA), 203: 'I shall assume that a statement made by a man who knows that it is likely to injure and knows that it is false is made maliciously and I shall make the same assumption if he knows that it is likely to injure and … makes it recklessly, not caring whether it is true or false'.

[171] For the salience of free speech in this setting, see subsection D below, and Carty (n 1) 294–96.

[172] It will be recalled from chapter one that some (but not all) of the torts considered in this book have always targeted especially egregious wrongdoing. Injurious falsehood, for the reasons given in this section, is one of them. Deceit, as we shall see in the next section, is another such tort.

harm – though not the source of tortious liability *tout court* – is clearly capable of being seen in such terms. For, as Stable J put it in one case, '[i]f a man says something that he knows to be untrue, it is malicious ipso facto, because he has said something that is false and something that he knows to be false'.[173] And in any case of deceit malice in which D has 'merely' been subjectively reckless[174] as to the truth of the statement in question, it is still possible to think in terms of D's deplorable conduct. In *R v G* – albeit that that was a criminal law case – Lord Bingham supplied a helpful explanation of why subjective (as opposed to objective) recklessness deserves to be seen as particularly reprehensible. He said:

> The most obviously culpable state of mind is no doubt an intention … but knowing disregard of an appreciated and unacceptable risk … would be readily accepted as culpable also. It is clearly blameworthy to take an obvious and significant risk of causing injury to another. But it is not clearly blameworthy to do something involving a risk of injury to another if … one genuinely does not perceive the risk.[175]

It is clear, then, that even its most attenuated form, and even though spite or ill-will need not be shown, the malice requirement in injurious falsehood serves to ensnare only those who bear especial moral culpability. As one Australian court put it, malice 'conveys the imputation that his conduct is open to moral reprobation'.[176] Furthermore, it is important to note that a tort enlivened by recklessness cannot be seen as somehow a halfway house between negligence on the one hand, and a tort in which intention is required, on the other. This is because the tort of negligence, properly understood, requires no mental element at all. It is enlivened purely by a failure to meet a certain, legally-prescribed standard of conduct. Torts such as injurious falsehood in which recklessness can attract liability are much closer in kind to those that require intention;[177] and they must certainly be distinguished from negligence. Whereas the latter is characterised by not taking reasonable care, recklessness is characterised by simply *not caring*.[178]

D. Future Prospects

As noted earlier, the tort of injurious falsehood overlaps to some extent with five other actions. Three of these comprise the common law torts of defamation, passing off and causing loss by unlawful means. The other two are statutory

[173] *Wilts* (n 165) 235.

[174] Lord Ellenborough made clear in *Pitt v Donovan* (1813) 1 M & S 639 that objective recklessness will not suffice. He said: '[t]he question then distinctly and substantively is, whether in the communication which he [the defendant] made, he acted bona fide … they are no slander of the title, if he believed them': *ibid*, 647.

[175] *R v G* [2004] 1 AC 1034 (HL), [32].

[176] *Clarke v Meigher* (1917) 17 SR (NSW) 617, 621–22.

[177] In *OBG* (n 96), two of their Lordships were prepared to treat cases in which D turned a blind eye as meeting the requirement of intention: see *ibid*, [40] and [70] (Lord Hoffmann); [192] (Lord Nicholls).

[178] See further, P Cane, '*Mens Rea* in Tort Law' (2000) 20 *OJLS* 533, 537.

actions: the first being an action for misuse of another's trade mark in the course of comparative advertising;[179] the second, statutory recourse for what are generally called threats actions (ie, actions based on an ungrounded threat made by D that he will sue C for infringement of some or other intellectual property right held by D). Against this backdrop, the question that naturally arises is whether alone or in combination, these various other possible actions have effectively eclipsed the tort of injurious falsehood. Is what was always a tort of limited practical importance now, in other words, best seen as one that is more or less redundant?

If the answer to this question is 'No', then a further question – equally concerned with the future of this tort – is whether, in theory, injurious falsehood has greater remedial potential than has hitherto generally been acknowledged. Each of these questions will be considered in turn.

i. Impending Redundancy?

Ever since it became possible under modern trade mark legislation[180] to use another's trade mark in comparative advertising, there have been numerous cases in which it has been alleged that one trader has overstepped the bounds of what is permissible. Very loosely, what is permitted in this context is the making of factually correct claims about a rival's product; but claims that are disparaging and untrue are not allowed since they tend to cause loss of custom with no justification. In any such circumstances, the claimant will have a choice between an action for trade mark infringement,[181] and one for injurious falsehood. In acknowledging the possibility of an action on either basis, Jacob J was adamant in *Cable & Wireless Plc v British Telecommunications Plc* that the former would always be preferable. He said:

> Cable and Wireless were suing for infringement of their trade marks … They were also suing for malicious falsehood. I could not see what the latter cause of action could possibly add to trade mark infringement. It merely adds the burden (and costs) of proof of malice.[182]

Though Jacob J was in no doubt that injurious falsehood should be seen as redundant *in this context*, what he said provides no licence for regarding the common law tort as having been completely – or even significantly – eclipsed by virtue of the statutory action. For one thing, the statute only applies to those cases in

[179] This is a form of advertising 'where trader A uses trader B's trade mark to refer to qualities or characteristics of trader B's goods or services in comparison with those supplied by trader A': D Bainbridge, *Intellectual Property*, 10th edn (Harlow, Pearson, 2018) 631.

[180] Originally the Trade Marks Act 1994, s 10(6); but now the Business Protection from Misleading Marketing Regulations 2008, Reg 4. Such advertising is permitted so long as it is not misleading and so long as it does not denigrate the advertiser's competitor.

[181] Trade Marks Act 1994, ss 10(4)(e) and 14(1).

[182] *Cable & Wireless Plc v British Telecommunications Plc* [1998] FSR 383, 385.

which the defendant has engaged in comparative advertising. It has no impact at all in cases where the claimant's title is attacked, or those – including leading cases like *Ratcliffe*, *Kaye* and *Cruddas v Calvert*[183] – in which the defendant is merely a publisher rather than a trade rival. Furthermore, even where the claimant *is* a trade rival – though this, apparently, will commonly not be the case[184] – the action for injurious falsehood will still be attractive where the validity of the trade mark is in doubt,[185] or where it is plainly invalid. Accordingly, even if the statutory action will typically be preferred in cases involving comparative advertising, its availability will constitute only a limited inroad into the established domain of injurious falsehood.

A similar conclusion can be reached in connection with the fact that defamation sometimes overlaps with injurious falsehood. True: where the two torts intersect, an action based on defamation will probably appear preferable. After all, a claimant relying on injurious falsehood must prove considerably more than one who relies on defamation. He must prove that the statement complained of was untrue[186] (whereas in defamation – so long as the statement is defamatory – it falls to the defendant to establish truth as a defence); and he must also always establish malice,[187] unlike the claimant relying on defamation (who will only need to prove malice to defeat a privilege invoked by the defendant). On the other hand, it is important to appreciate that defamation law only overlaps with the tort of injurious falsehood to a limited degree and that, as a matter of history, they were always distinct. Thus, as one commentator notes, '[f]rom the beginning … the [injurious falsehood] action appears to have been recognized as only loosely allied to defamation, and to be rather an action on the case for the special damage resulting from the defendant's interference'.[188] More concrete evidence of the limited common ground between the two torts inheres in the fact that disparaging statements made about a person's business or goods – while enough to ground liability for injurious falsehood – will count for nothing from the perspective of defamation if they do not also affect the claimant's *personal* reputation. In order to see this distinction at work, one need look no further than the leading case of *Ratcliffe*[189] where the defendant's false assertion that the claimant had ceased trading was in no way defamatory: it did not impinge at all upon the personal reputation of the claimant.

To the fact that injurious falsehood is capable of being invoked in cases beyond those involving personal disparagement can be added a further significant distinction. It is as follows: while the claimant in a case of injurious falsehood must show

[183] *Cruddas v Calvert* [2015] EMLR 16 (CA).

[184] According to Wadlow's comprehensive trawl of the authorities, '[t]he whole body of decided cases on injurious falsehood … is not large, and a large proportion of those are on facts of no direct relevance to competitive situations': Wadlow (n 12) 381.

[185] See, eg, *Compaq Computer Corp v Dell Computer Corp Ltd* [1992] FSR 93.

[186] *Royal Baking Powder* (n 130) 99 (Lord Davey).

[187] *Cruddas* (n 183) [2] (Jackson LJ).

[188] Prosser (n 128) 425.

[189] *Ratcliffe* (n 134).

special damage, this is still a lower damage threshold than obtains within the law of defamation. By virtue of legislation passed in 2013, it must now be shown in a defamation case that the 'offending' publication would cause (or be likely to cause) 'serious harm' to the reputation of the claimant.[190] By contrast, special damage (for the purposes of injurious falsehood) need not be particularly severe. It need only be damage of the right type.

It follows from all of the foregoing that injurious falsehood is of considerably wider scope than defamation in terms of its remedial capacity. It operates according to a wider range of recognised harms and it has a lower threshold of actionability. As such, it cannot plausibly be said that defamation law substantially eclipses what remains of injurious falsehood after the impact of the trade mark legislation has already been taken into account. And nor does the tort of passing off.

Although, again, some overlap is in evidence, the tort of passing off intrudes only minimally into the terrain covered by injurious falsehood. This point may be illustrated by reference to *Rima Electric Ltd v Rolls Razor Ltd*.[191] In that case, the defendants falsely represented that they – unlike other retailers who stocked the claimant's hairdryers – could sell them at no more than cost price, plus a small handling charge. So saying clearly annoyed other stockists, and for this reason they complained to the claimants about the defendants' false claims. The claimants investigated the matter and discovered that the defendants were in fact selling different hairdryers. There was a prospect that the claimants, as well as the stockists who had complained to them, would lose custom going forwards. With this worry in mind, the claimants sought an injunction to restrain the defendants from continuing to make this false claim. It was sought on two alternative bases: that is, the statement was either an injurious falsehood or it amounted to passing off. The court, however, was clear that no relief could be granted on the basis of passing off as there was a critical absence of confusion about the source of the goods. As Wilberforce J put it, 'it does not seem to me that the evidence, such as it is, at this stage, is enough to establish a case of passing-off' since '[t]here is no actual evidence of confusion; there is no case of an order having been placed for a Magicair [hairdryer] and a Covergirl having been supplied [instead]'.[192] On the other hand, he was equally clear that an injunction *could be granted* on the basis of injurious falsehood. The defendants' false claim was:

> likely to cause a severe dislocation in their [ie, the claimants'] trade, because, it causes other dealers in Magicairs to complain that they are not able to obtain goods at the same price and causes them, consequently, to discontinue … [dealing with] the plaintiff company.[193]

[190] Defamation Act 2013, s 1(1).
[191] *Rima Electric Ltd v Rolls Razor Ltd* [1965] RPC 4.
[192] *Ibid*, 6.
[193] *Ibid*, 7.

So, even though a loss of custom may be key in both injurious falsehood and passing off cases, one cannot conclude on the basis of this observation that the latter is a redundant cause of action. That there need not be any overlap between the two torts seems obvious, in fact, so long as one accepts that, as a general matter, in passing off, defendants make false claims about the *source of goods that they themselves supply* whereas in injurious falsehood the statement will typically be about the *quality of goods supplied by the claimant.*[194]

A fourth incursion into the domain of injurious falsehood exists in the form of various statutory actions that may be brought under the Intellectual Property (Unjustified Threats) Act 2017 against those who threaten to sue on the basis of an alleged infringement of various kinds of intellectual property right.[195] It is true that such 'threats actions' constitute an inroad of sorts into injurious falsehood, but again it is important to get a sense of perspective. First, although it may well amount to injurious falsehood to claim untruthfully that X is infringing your patent or trade mark, it by no means follows that most (or even many) injurious falsehood claims are of this kind. Secondly, although statutory threats actions are available in connection with most types of intellectual property right, there is no such action created in relation to allegations concerning alleged breaches of copyright. For a combination of these reasons, it would be wrong to see the actions under the legislation of 2017 as doing much to render redundant the common law tort.

By far the most significant challenge to the survival of injurious falsehood comes from its overlap with the tort of causing loss by unlawful means. In *Gatley on Libel and Slander*, it is suggested that 'every statement about a trader which amounts to malicious falsehood and causes damage should amount to causing loss by unlawful means'.[196] Were this true, then the redundancy of injurious falsehood as a free-standing tort would be assured. But it is by no means clear that it is true. In order to see why not, we must first try to understand the thinking behind the claim inserted into a footnote in *Gatley*, since unfortunately, *Gatley* itself fails to provide any proper explanation of what is understood to ground the contention made there. Happily, a similar claim has been made by Robert Stevens who does helpfully explain how he arrives at the conclusion that there is little future need for injurious falsehood. He begins his explanation by reference to *National Phonograph Co Ltd v Edison-Bell Consolidated Phonograph Co Ltd.*[197]

[194] The reference may, however, be an indirect one: *Riding v Smith* (1876) 1 Ex D 91. In this case the statement referred not to the claimant himself, but to his wife. The defendant's claim was that she was an adulterer. So saying caused the claimant (because of his obvious association with her) a significant loss of custom. He could sue for this loss.

[195] Intellectual Property (Unjustified Threats) Act 2017, ss 1–6. The rights in question are, patents, trade marks, registered designs and design rights.

[196] A Mullis *et al* (eds), *Gatley on Libel and Slander*, 12th edn (London, Sweet and Maxwell, 2013) para 21.4 (fn 30).

[197] *National Phonograph Co Ltd v Edison-Bell Consolidated Phonograph Co Ltd* [1908] 1 Ch 335 (CA).

The significance of that case inheres in the fact that, in *OBG*, it was highlighted by Lord Hoffmann as one of the exceptional cases in which an action for the unlawful means tort would lie *even though* the unlawful means complained of would not themselves be actionable by the third party against whom they were directed. *National Phonograph* involved a defendant (who was a retailer on a suspended dealers list) fraudulently inducing a third party to sell it phonographs that had been made by the claimants and which had been bought wholesale by that third party. The wholesale purchase had occurred on the condition that the third party would not later sell those phonographs to companies or persons on the suspended retailers list. Yet by virtue of the fraud, the third party was duped into making such a sale to the defendant. As things turned out, the third party did not itself suffer any loss as a result of this sale. It was therefore unable to bring an action in deceit against the defendant.

The question arising from this case, and the one upon which Lord Hoffmann reflected in *OBG*, was whether the non-actionability of the fraud by the third party in *National Phonograph* would serve to obstruct an action by the claimants based on the unlawful means tort. The question was a significant one because, elsewhere in his speech, Lord Hoffmann was keen to clarify that 'unlawful means' should be equated with actionable wrongs committed against a third party (through whom the defendant struck at the claimant).[198] Without resiling from his general position, Lord Hoffmann did however confirm that an exception would exist if 'the only reason why [the means in question] … are not actionable is because the third party has suffered no loss'.[199] Having explained this exception, he was then able to confirm that there had been sufficient unlawful means in the *National Phonograph* case, because the defendant's fraud 'would have been actionable if the third party had suffered any loss'.[200]

Now, according to Stevens, the treatment of the *National Phonograph* case in *OBG* 'illustrates that lies are wrongful per se';[201] and so, he continues, '[o]nce lies are accepted as sufficient to constitute unlawful means, the scope for an independent tort of malicious falsehood is much reduced'.[202] Such thinking is presumably what undergirds the more forceful claim in *Gatley* that anyone with a viable claim for injurious falsehood might now pursue an action based on the *OBG* tort instead. But it is demonstrably the case that Stevens makes too much of the vindication in *OBG* of the decision in *National Phonograph*. This is because at no point did Lord Hoffmann consider *mere lies* to be enough to constitute unlawful means. What he actually said was this:

> [where] the defendant intentionally caused loss to the plaintiff by *fraudulently inducing* a third party to act to the plaintiff's detriment. The *fraud was unlawful means* because

198 *OBG* (n 96) [49].
199 *Ibid.*
200 *Ibid.*
201 Stevens (n 77) 189. For a similar claim, see T Weir, *Economic Torts* (Oxford, Clarendon Press, 1997) 16.
202 Stevens (n 77) 189.

> it would have been actionable if the third party had suffered any loss, even though in the event it was the plaintiff who suffered. In this respect, procuring the actions of a third party *by fraud* (dolus) is obviously very similar to procuring them by intimidation (metus).[203]

What this passage highlights is that Lord Hoffmann very specifically spoke of *fraud*. And there is a critical difference between mere lies and fraud as was recognised as long ago as 1789 in the foundational deceit case of *Pasley v Freeman* in which Buller J said: 'an action cannot be supported for telling a bare naked lie'.[204] Fraud, in contrast to a bare untruth, requires that, in addition a to the defendant uttering a falsehood, the person to whom the false statement was made must have been induced to act in reliance on what they were told. In *National Phonograph*, the intermediary clearly was induced to act in a particular way. As Alverstone LCJ noted, 'the defendants, *by fraud*, induced the [intermediary] … to sell instruments to them'.[205] And in similar terms, in the same case, Buckley LJ observed that, 'the defendants, *by deceit*, induced the [intermediary] … to sell to the defendants contrary to the duty … contractually owed to the plaintiffs'.[206] Accordingly, *pace* Stevens, it is wrong to suggest that bare lies are wrongful *per se* and that they are enough to constitute unlawful means.

On the other hand, noting this does nothing to preclude the possibility that the *OBG* tort has now effectively superseded injurious falsehood. This is because, in just the same way that there can be no fraud without an act of reliance on the part of the intermediary, nor can there be an actionable injurious falsehood in the absence of such reliance. There must always be special damage *caused by the reaction of third parties to the falsehood they are told*. It follows that, if the enduring vitality of injurious falsehood can be shown, it must be shown by reference to some important way in which it comes apart from the unlawful means tort. This, I think, has been identified by Carty who points to the fact (not mentioned by Stevens or *Gatley*) that, for the purposes of the unlawful means tort, the defendant must have intended the harm caused.

Thus, although Carty – like Stevens and *Gatley* – notes the possible overlap between the two torts,[207] she is astute to point out that the overlap is not complete. As she puts it, 'though the tort [of injurious falsehood] has obvious affinities with the unlawful means tort, its roots lie in liability for falsehoods uttered at peril, rather than intentional harm through unlawful means'.[208] Accordingly, she continues, in a case like *Wilts* – where the defendant's intention was to harm the very persons at whom the falsehood was directed rather than the claimant – there could be no liability on the basis of the unlawful means tort,

[203] *OBG* (n 96) [49] (emphases added).
[204] *Pasley v Freeman* (1789) 3 Term Rep 51, 56.
[205] *National Phonograph* (n 197) 357 (emphasis added).
[206] *Ibid*, 358 (emphasis added).
[207] Carty (n 1) 221.
[208] *Ibid*, 221–22.

even though a claim for injurious falsehood could succeed since 'the defendant uses lies, inherently likely to cause harm'.[209] Her claim here seems to be perfectly true; particularly when one recalls that a defendant's recklessness in the tort of injurious falsehood need only pertain to the veracity of what is said. Put otherwise, the malice required for the tort of injurious falsehood cannot be equated with the intention element in the unlawful means tort. In *Kaye*, it will be recalled, Glidewell LJ was clear that '[m]alice will be inferred if it be proved that the words were calculated to produce damage *and* that the defendant … was *reckless as to whether they were false or not*'.[210] Thus, although recklessness may also suffice to ground liability based on the unlawful means tort, in that second setting the recklessness must pertain to the loss caused as opposed to the truth of a particular statement.[211]

The distinction becomes even clearer if one thinks through the following hypothetical. Suppose D, purely as a joke, makes a false claim about trader C in something like the same way the defendant said what he did in *Wilkinson v Downton*.[212] In such circumstances – which a Canadian case reveals to be far from fanciful[213] – it is possible that the harmful consequences of D's intended joke could form the basis of an action for injurious falsehood. But it could never ground one framed in terms of the unlawful means tort. For the purposes of the latter, D would lack the requisite intention to cause harm to C. D's words, after all, were *ex hypothesi* spoken only in jest.

An even more significant gap between the two torts will exist where the publisher of a newspaper is sued for injurious falsehood in circumstances where it bore no ill-will towards the claimant. Imagine, for example, the publication of a disparaging story about a particular individual, where the publisher of the newspaper was subjectively reckless as to the truth of that story. In such a case, the publication might be regarded as simply 'good copy'; and certainly not as an instrument of harm. The publisher could be said to be reckless as to the truth of story, and yet her conduct would fall beyond the compass of the unlawful means tort. As Lord Hoffmann emphatically stated in *OBG*, 'one is not liable for loss which is neither a desired end nor a means of attaining it but merely a foreseeable consequence of one's actions'.[214] The publisher's indifference to the claimant's foreseeable loss would rule out liability on this footing.

[209] *Ibid*, 222.

[210] *Kaye* (n 168) 67 (emphasis added).

[211] In *OBG* (n 96) [62], Lord Hoffmann was clear that intention should be gauged according to a test based on ends, means and consequences, and 'one is not liable for loss which is neither a desired end nor a means of attaining it but merely a foreseeable consequence of one's actions'.

[212] *Wilkinson v Downton* [1897] 2 QB 57.

[213] In *Manitoba Free Press Co v Nagy* (1907) 39 SCR 340 the defendants were held liable for causing the loss of a house sale by informing a potential purchaser that it was haunted by ghosts. It was never clearly established whether the defendants meant this sincerely.

[214] *OBG* (n 96) [62].

Overall, it is undeniable that the various actions discussed in the preceding paragraphs have made some incursions into the territory covered by what was always only a 'minor' tort.[215] But at the same time it seems equally clear that it has not yet been rendered redundant. Whether it stands ready to be revitalised – as has occurred in Australia[216] – is the matter that must next be discussed.

ii. Expansion of the Tort

The main limitation on the availability of injurious falsehood is the requirement that the claimant prove malice. So long as this endures, there is little prospect of this tort's use becoming commonplace. Establishing 'motive malice' is notoriously difficult, not least because – as with the tort of simple conspiracy – no action will lie if the defendant can show that his preponderant objective was to further his own interests.[217] Where an alternative action exists, it is easy to see why a claimant would prefer to opt for that.

So far as 'deceit malice' is concerned, however, it is possible to perceive a way in which, if not the popularity, then at least the scope, of this tort might be extended. It would involve abandoning the putative requirement that the statement in question should have referred – directly or indirectly – to the claimant, her goods or her business. Though such a need is routinely mentioned by jurists[218] in line with what was said in *White v Mellin*,[219] there can be found, here and there in the case law, indications that an action for injurious falsehood may be pursued despite the absence of any such reference to the claimant. Take, for example, *Danish Mercantile Co Ltd v Beaumont*.[220] In that case, the defendant (falsely claiming to be the director of a certain company) claimed in letters sent to potential buyers of sugar harvesting machinery that his company were the 'only authorised importers or manufacturers of … [that] equipment'. This was flatly untrue. Indeed, the company in whose name he sent the letters had not even been incorporated at that time. In reality, it was the claimant who held sole distribution rights in Great Britain and Ireland. Although the claimant was never actually named by the defendant in what he said, Roxburgh J was adamant that:

> the statements made in the two letters which I have read were the plainest possible trade libel upon the first Plaintiff … It seems to me that an action of this kind will lie for damage wilfully and intentionally done without just occasion or excuse, and in my judgment that is precisely applicable to the state of affairs as it existed at the date of the

[215] Stevens (n 77) 190.

[216] See A Gemmell, 'Injurious Falsehood Emerges from the Wings' (2008) 46 *Law Society Journal* 69.

[217] See *Dunlop* (n 165) 581 (Collins MR): 'it was not malice if the object of the writer was to push his own business, though at the same time it might incidentally injure another person's business'.

[218] See, eg, Wadlow (n 12) 363; Mullis *et al* (n 196) para 21.4.

[219] *White* (n 159) 165 (Lord Watson).

[220] *Danish Mercantile Co Ltd v Beaumont* (1950) 67 RPC 111.

> issue of this writ and there is not the least doubt that it was calculated to damage the first Plaintiff.[221]

Carty refers to this case as one involving 'inverse malicious falsehood'.[222] Writing just over a decade ago, she considered this a possible growth area for injurious falsehood. With the advantage of hindsight, however, we can now say with some confidence that the seeds of possibility sown in *Danish Mercantile* – a mere first instance decision – appear to have landed on barren soil.[223]

In addition, a second case that Carty cites as being broadly supportive of such a development is, properly understood, not one of 'inverse malicious falsehood' at all. That second case was *Marathon Mutual Ltd v Waters*.[224] In it, there were two claimants whose businesses were so closely interlinked that any harmful falsehood spoken of the first claimant would foreseeably also cause loss to the second. In the course of his judgment, Judge Moloney QC refused to strike out a claim by the second claimant (whose name was never mentioned). Yet a close reading of the case reveals that the mutual fund that was falsely claimed by the defendant to be beset by serious financial difficulties was just as much 'part of its own business'[225] as it was the first claimant's. Accordingly, the falsehood was in fact one that could be regarded as referring to both claimants simultaneously. It was just that in the case of the second claimant, the reference was indirect. Armed with this interpretation of the facts, it becomes clear why, elsewhere in his judgment, Judge Moloney expressly endorsed the orthodox view that direct or indirect references are needed. He said this:

> the law must require that there be some reference, direct or indirect, in the words complained of to the claimant or to his business, property or other economic interests, though it is not necessary to go further and establish identification of the claimant in the minds of the publishees.[226]

In addition to the fact that there is precious little case law that genuinely supports the idea that 'inverse malicious falsehood' might be actionable, there is, rather conspicuously, a further factor that speaks against the abandonment of the requirement that the statement in question must refer to the claimant or her business. It takes the form of a concern on the part of the courts to strike an appropriate balance between tortious liability based on falsehoods and the right of free speech. As is well known, this concern has been evident for some time in the law relating

[221] *Ibid*, 112.

[222] Carty (n 1) 212. The idea at work is that in saying a certain thing, A, about entity X, it must also follow that another thing, B, is true about entity Y.

[223] The only other clear-cut case on offer hails from New Zealand rather than England and Wales: *Customglass Boats* (n 167).

[224] *Marathon Mutual Ltd v Waters* [2010] EMLR 63.

[225] *Ibid*, 72.

[226] *Ibid*, 71.

to defamation[227] and the law on misuse of private information.[228] But its relevance to injurious falsehood has also been judicially acknowledged. In the *Marathon Mutual* case, the judge expressly noted that there was:

> [a] need to ensure that the restrictions imposed on [the defendants'] freedom of expression by the law of malicious falsehood are duly prescribed by law and not disproportionate to the purposes towards which the restrictions are directed.[229]

Taking this into account alongside the paucity of case law supportive of 'inverse malicious falsehood', Carty's suggestion that it is 'not inconceivable that claimants might persuade the courts to apply the tort generally even though there is no reference to the claimant himself',[230] appears to be mistaken. What seems altogether more likely is that the tort will continue to be one of limited practical significance. On the other hand, it does not follow that those who are harmed by false claims that do not refer to them will be left without a remedy in all cases. This is because some cases of what would amount to 'inverse malicious falsehood' might instead be presented as cases of inverse passing off. Think again about the *Danish Mercantile* case. The defendant's representation in that case was admittedly, on one view, essentially a claim about title – namely, that of being the sole distributor in Great Britain and Ireland of a certain product. But on another view, it could easily be considered a misrepresentation that something which *in truth* had been sold by the claimant (ie, all the sugar beet harvesters that had already been sold by it in this country) had instead been sold by Beaumont. So saying might create the impression that the defendant was the seller of well-respected goods and thereby divert custom from the claimants to themselves, in just the same way as occurred in the actual inverse passing off case of *Bristol Conservatories Ltd v Conservatories Custom Built Ltd*.[231]

E. Final Remarks

Although in practical terms a marginal tort, injurious falsehood remains vital in the strict sense. This is because, although there have been numerous legislative and common law incursions into its traditional domain, they have by no means managed to eclipse it. At the same time, however, the courts' general concern not to develop torts that undermine freedom of speech, the need to prove malice and the requirement that the defendant's falsehood should refer to the claimant (or

[227] See, eg, *Jameel (Yousef) v Dow Jones & Co Inc* [2005] QB 946 (CA); *Jameel (Mohammed) v Wall Street Journal* [2007] 1 AC 359 (HL).

[228] See, eg, *McKennitt v Ash* [2008] QB 73 (CA); *PJS v News Group Newspapers Ltd* [2016] AC 1081 (SC).

[229] *Marathon Mutual* (n 224) 71.

[230] Carty (n 1) 287.

[231] *Bristol Conservatories Ltd v Conservatories Custom Built Ltd* [1989] RPC 455 (CA).

her business) serve, in combination, to render it unlikely that injurious falsehood will expand in any significant way in the foreseeable future. Even the prospect, once floated by Cane,[232] of its being a source of exemplary damages seems faint at best.[233]

Like the other torts considered in this book, injurious falsehood is one that can be used to obtain damages for something other than harmed economic interests. True: according to the strict letter of the available authorities, awards in respect of injured feelings are presently only available as 'aggravated damages'. But various compelling obiter dicta also support the argument that distress and injured feelings might be considered forms of special damage and thus be directly (as opposed to parasitically) recoverable. Equally, in keeping with the other torts considered in the preceding chapters, injurious falsehood – in its modern incarnation, anyway – is also one that conspicuously links actionability to especially reprehensible wrongdoing. This is true regardless of whether the claimant relies on 'motive malice' or 'deceit malice'. In either case, deeply immoral wrongdoing is to the fore. This is obvious in cases of 'motive malice' since malice here equates broadly to the wilful infliction of harm. In cases of deceit malice, by contrast, the moral culpability of the defendant is not so obvious. Indeed, the fact that this form of malice may be inferred from mere reckless falsehoods might be thought to render it a stretch to describe the wrongdoing as especially reprehensible. But on close analysis, such doubts dissolve. True: in *Ajinomoto*, the Court of Appeal held that defamation law's single meaning rule[234] does not apply to injurious falsehood,[235] perhaps leading one to think that that case effectively undermines the claim that this tort targets especially reprehensible wrongdoing (given that a defendant could be held liable on the strength of a secondary meaning that he never intended). But *Cruddas* negates any such thinking. In that case, Jackson LJ qualified what was said in *Ajinomoto* in these terms:

> Since the test for malice is subjective, knowledge of falsity must be assessed by reference to the meaning which the defendant intends to convey. In my view, if (a) an article has one correct meaning which is true but is susceptible to a second incorrect interpretation by some cynical readers which is untrue, (b) the author intends the article to convey its correct meaning but foresees that some cynical readers will place upon it the

[232] Cane (n 17) 100.

[233] Presumably, Cane's thinking here was along these lines. Following *Cassell v Broome* [1972] AC 1027 (HL), it should in theory be possible to obtain exemplary damages where A makes a malicious, false claim about B with a view to capturing some of the latter's customers thinking he will make more out of his tort than he would lose by paying compensatory damages to B. But the theory breaks down because if B loses customers X, Y and Z to A, then A's gain and B's loss will be identical. There will be no excess gain, and therefore no basis for exemplary damages.

[234] This is the rule that even ambiguous statements should be treated as having only one meaning, namely, 'the natural and ordinary meaning of the words': *Slim v Daily Telegraph Ltd* [1968] 2 QB 157 (CA), 176 (Diplock LJ).

[235] *Ajinomoto* (n 156) [35] (Sedley LJ).

incorrect interpretation, then that does not constitute malice for the purpose of malicious falsehood.[236]

In the wake of *Cruddas*, in other words, it is not enough merely to show that a defendant recognised the possibility that some, rather uncharitable, readers would be impressed with a false image. Rather, he must be reckless as to the prospect that a number of *reasonable readers* would form this view. Accordingly, the prospect of being held liable for some barely culpable conduct disappears. A defendant in such double-meaning cases will only be held liable where he has adopted an obviously cavalier attitude to the truth of what he said.[237]

IV. Deceit

The third and final misrepresentation tort is deceit. From the perspective of tort theory, it raises a number of difficult and interesting questions – such as why detrimental reliance is required, why it operates according to a remoteness rule based on losses that flow directly from the wrong (rather than the more common one based on reasonably foreseeable types of harm),[238] and why pleas of contributory negligence are unavailable to defendants in such cases. None of these questions, however, is relevant for present purposes.[239] Nor need we dwell on whether this tort is alive and well. Its vitality is not in doubt, and nor has it ever been in doubt ever since the landmark decision in *Pasley v Freeman*.[240] Equally, although suggestions have periodically been made along the lines that deceit might occasionally be available in the odd three-party scenario,[241] these proposals have been conclusively quashed by the courts (adding considerably to a claim advanced fully in chapter seven, that there is no structural uniformity to be found among the economic torts).

In fact, bearing in mind the principal theses advanced in this book, there are only two issues that need be addressed here. The first is whether it is appropriate

[236] *Cruddas* (n 183) [111].

[237] But note there is still no recklessness as to harm required!

[238] See, eg, *Doyle v Olby (Ironmongers) Ltd* [1969] 2 QB 158 (CA), 167 (Denning MR): 'it does not lie in the mouth of the fraudulent person to say that they [ie, the losses suffered] could not reasonably have been foreseen'.

[239] For discussion of these matters, see J Murphy, 'Misleading Appearances in the Tort of Deceit' [2016] *CLJ* 301.

[240] *Pasley* (n 204).

[241] Three possible candidates for such expansion can be identified. First, where D lies to a third party, T, who, in reliance on what she has been told, acts to the detriment of C. This is a non-starter. It will certainly constitute an instance of the unlawful means tort, but it will not give rise to liability for deceit: see text associated with nn 197 to 200. Secondly, where an agent is bribed by D into acting to the detriment of the principal, the better view is that this, too, does not amount to deceit: see, *Petrotrade Inc v Smith* [2000] 1 Lloyd's Rep 486, 490 (Steel J): 'the claim based on bribery is not a species of deceit but a special form of fraud where there is no representation made to the principal of the agent let alone reliance'. Thirdly, and analogously, where D persuades a trustee to act in breach of trust, this is best viewed as a form of accessory liability – namely, knowing assistance in breach of trust: see *Royal Brunei Airlines Sdn Bhd v Tan* [1995] 2 AC 378 (PC), 384 (Lord Nicholls).

to regard deceit as 'economic tort' in the sense that it protects *only* economic interests.[242] The second is the extent to which it is aptly considered a tort in which especially egregious wrongdoing is afforded salience.

A. Protected Interests

Although in practical terms deceit is usually engaged by claimants who have been duped into making unfavourable commercial arrangements or bargains,[243] this is not ineluctably so. True: the classic cases of *Pasley*,[244] *Derry v Peek*,[245] *Doyle v Olby (Ironmongers) Ltd*[246] and *East v Maurer*[247] are all ones that fall within this bracket, but when Viscount Maugham set out the ingredients of this tort in *Bradford Third Equitable Building Society v Borders*, he made no mention of the need to show economic loss. Rather, in very general terms, he said:

> First, there must be a representation of fact made by words, or, it may be, by conduct … Secondly, the representation must be made with a knowledge that it is false … Thirdly, it must be made with the intention that it should be acted upon by the plaintiff, or by a class of persons which will include the plaintiff, in the manner which resulted in damage to him … Fourthly, it must be proved that the plaintiff has acted upon the false statement *and has sustained damage* by so doing.[248]

There was no specific stipulation here that *economic loss* be shown, although the occasional judge and some scholars seem to think that it must.[249] Nor was there any suggestion that such loss comprises the gist of the tort. Accordingly, the various cases in which other types of loss have been held to be actionable under the auspices of deceit should be seen as completely unobjectionable; and there

[242] The idea that these are the economic interests to which the economic torts attend belongs to Simon Deakin and John Randall: see S Deakin and J Randall, 'Rethinking the Economic Torts' (2009) 72 *MLR* 519, 523.

[243] Indeed, the origins of the tort have a markedly close association with early 'contract law' – if it be fair to characterise the early rules on false warranties in that way – see D Ibbetson, *A Historical Introduction to the Law of Obligations* (Oxford, Oxford University Press, 1999) 84–85.

[244] *Pasley* (n 204).

[245] *Derry v Peek* (1889) 14 App Cas 337 (HL).

[246] *Doyle* (n 238).

[247] *East v Maurer* [1991] 1 WLR 461 (CA).

[248] *Bradford Third Equitable Building Society v Borders* [1941] 2 All ER 205 (HL), 211 (emphasis added).

[249] In *Dura Pharmaceuticals, Inc v Broudo* 544 US 336, 343 (2005), the court stated that 'the common law has long insisted that a plaintiff … [must show] that he suffered actual economic loss'. Dobbs takes the view that it is 'a stand-alone economic or commercial tort that causes financial harm without causing physical harm either to person or to property': DB Dobbs, *The Law of Torts* (St Paul, Minnesota, West Academic, 2000) 1344. Also, some leading textbooks on torts treat deceit as an economic tort. Witting, for example, discusses deceit in a chapter allotted to '[t]orts based on false statements protective of financial interests' (C Witting, *Street on Torts* (Oxford, Oxford University Press, 2018) 335), while McBride and Bagshaw place their discussion of deceit in a chapter that bears the heading 'The Economic Torts' (McBride and Bagshaw (n 151) Ch 20).

are several of these. For example, the claimants in both *Langrdige v Levy*[250] and *Burrows v Rhodes*[251] were able to claim successfully in respect of personal injuries that they suffered. These decisions are not anomalies. Rather, they contribute significantly towards the broad coherence of tort law[252] in that they align the tort of deceit with negligence law under which it is firmly established that a claimant's reliance upon a careless statement that leads to physical injury is actionable.[253] The law in relation to civil liability for false statements would be odd indeed if it allowed recovery for, say, a broken leg attributable to a negligent misstatement, but ruled out recovery for the self-same injury caused by an intentionally or recklessly uttered falsehood. Furthermore, one might even consider the tort to be one of perversely narrow scope if it did not protect such interests given that bodily integrity is generally considered more worthy of protection than purely economic interests.

Physical inconvenience, too, has been held to be recoverable in deceit. In the novel case of *Mafo v Adams*,[254] the claimant was duped into quitting his protected tenancy. He spent some time staying with a friend after he discovered that he had been tricked into thinking that he had acquired the lease to alternative premises by the defendant's ex-wife. Finding in the claimant's favour, Sachs LJ said:

> The plaintiff apparently still has not got a tenancy with an equally sure protection, and for that he is entitled to compensation. In addition, he is entitled upon accepted principles to compensation for the *physical inconvenience* suffered when put in the position to which I have already adverted.[255]

Even mental distress, should not be ruled out. Although no such harm was alleged in *Doyle v Olby*, Winn LJ nonetheless said that, in addition to relatively easily measured pecuniary losses: 'one considers other consequences … [such as] *strain, anxiety and unhappiness* … [since] in some cases such considerations might well be appropriate'.[256] And in *Shelley v Paddock*,[257] the Court of Appeal affirmed a first instance decision of Bristow J that included in the damages awarded to the claimant a sum reflecting the distress she suffered when she was swindled in connection with the purchase of a house in Spain.[258]

[250] *Langrdige v Levy* (1837) 2 M&W 519. The injury suffered was a shotgun wound.

[251] *Burrows v Rhodes* [1899] 1 QB 816. The injuries suffered were sustained in battle conditions after C had been duped into joining an illegal fighting force in South Africa.

[252] Tort law is only, however, broadly coherent. There are significant aspects of the law that for one reason or another may be regarded as outliers from the perspective of coherence: see, J Murphy, 'Contemporary Tort Theory and Tort Law's Evolution' (2019) 32 *Canadian Journal of Law and Jurisprudence* 413.

[253] See, eg, *Perrett v Collins* [1998] 2 Lloyd's Rep 255 (CA). The case concerned the negligent certification of a light aircraft as airworthy.

[254] *Mafo v Adams* [1970] 1 QB 548 (CA). See also *Saunders v Edwards* [1987] 1 WLR 1116 (CA).

[255] *Mafo v Adams, ibid*, 554 (emphasis added).

[256] *Doyle v Olby* (n 238) 170 (emphasis added).

[257] *Shelley v Paddock* [1980] QB 348 (CA).

[258] In similar vein, see *Burki v Seventy Thirty* [2018] EWHC 2151 and *Kinch v Rosling* [2009] EWHC 286 (QB).

Taken together, these various illustrations of non-economic losses that have been recognised by the courts put beyond doubt the fact that, in common with all the other torts considered in this book bar passing off, there is no especial reason to consider deceit an action that is confined purely to the protection of economic interests. The better view is that it is concerned with the protection of the claimant's right to decision-making autonomy. On this view, it is a rights-based tort and not, as some scholars argue, one that is loss-based and in which measurable damage forms the gist.[259] But before substantiating this particular rights-based understanding of deceit, it is important that I deal with three other such accounts which I think must be rejected.

The first rival account belongs to Stevens. In his view, the gist of this tort is 'our right not to be lied to'.[260] He does not contend that bare lies are enough to ground an action, but instead adds the caveat that a claimant must *also show* actionable loss. In saying this, however, he makes clear that he does not regard proof of recognised loss to be a required ingredient of the tort: it is considered a mere condition of actionability made necessary by the fact that '[i]t would, of course, be unacceptable for the law to make actionable all of the minor deceptions that we practise upon one another'.[261] Presumably, Stevens' thinking here is that the need to show tangible loss serves to stave off a floodgates problem. It may well have some such effect. Yet Stevens' analysis is contradicted by existing case law. In the well-known case of *Wilkinson v Downton*, the defendant had untruthfully told the claimant that her husband had suffered a very severe injury in an accident. In other words, she had been lied to. As a consequence of this 'joke', the claimant suffered a serious physical reaction: a measurable loss! Yet Wright J refused to allow a claim in deceit for the illness suffered.[262] If Stevens were right in saying that deceit is animated by a combination of the infringement of a right not to be lied to and consequential loss, then the refusal of a remedy for the claimant in *Wilkinson v Downton* appears mysterious. But even leaving this aspect of his argument to one side, we have already observed that in *Pasley v Freeman* the court made plain the difference between fraud on the one hand and a 'bare naked lie on the other'.[263]

A second rights-based understanding of the gist of deceit has been put forward by Neyers. He rejects the idea that the tort is anchored to a right not to be lied to. He contends, instead, that 'the secret to the tort of deceit … is that the tort does not protect just one right but rather it protects all of our rights (to things, to money, to

[259] Carty (n 1) 188 erroneously attributes this understanding to Lord Blackburn's opinion in *Smith v Chadwick* (1884) 9 App Cas 187. However, his Lordship never in fact said this. The closest he came to such a statement was when he said (*ibid*, 195): '[w]hatever difficulties there may be as to defining what is fraud and deceit, I think no one will venture to dispute that the plaintiff cannot recover unless he proves damage'.

[260] Stevens (n 77) 8.

[261] *Ibid*, 89.

[262] *Wilkinson v Downton* (n 212) 58.

[263] See above, text associated with n 204.

contracts, to our bodies) from non-consensual dispossession'.[264] And it is not just his rejection of the centrality of a right not to be lied to that places clear blue water between his and Stevens' understandings, since he is also unpersuaded by Stevens' adherence to the idea that loss is a mere condition of actionability. In Neyers' view, this understanding is 'incoherent since the justification for the liability (actual reliance) is being arbitrarily cut off by the unrelated requirement that the claimant suffer consequential loss in order to delimit liability'.[265] But for someone who seems committed to the idea that explanatory theories should fit the law as laid down in the cases,[266] Neyers would appear to be riding roughshod over Stephenson LJ's dictum in *Diamond v The Bank of London and Montreal* along the lines that: '[i]n deceit ... the false representation ... has to cause damage to be actionable, but no damage to the plaintiff is necessary for the tort to be committed'.[267]

And there are other problems, too. Recall his central claim that the tort of deceit 'does not protect just one right but rather it protects all of our rights (to things, to money, to contracts, to our bodies) from non-consensual dispossession'. Despite ostensible appeal, this claim too runs aground when the nature of the rights to which he adverts are considered closely. The idea that we have a right to money, for example, seems highly implausible. Indeed, Neyers is elsewhere on record as being someone who signs up to the generally held view that there is no such right.[268] And correctly so, for it is trite to say that tort law does not recognise a right to money or to financial wellbeing.

Equally, although his inclusion of a right 'to our bodies' is doubtless a nod to *Langridge v Levy*, look again at his contention. It is not that deceit protects this right *per se*, it is that deceit protects this right against non-consensual dispossession. The problem here, of course, is that our right to bodily integrity is an inalienable right. If I punch you on the nose, I certainly infringe your right to bodily integrity. But it is not a right of which you are thereby dispossessed. It is just as much a tort if I punch you on the nose a second time. And contractual rights, too – unless they are treated as a species of quasi-property (which treatment itself is problematic, as we saw in chapter three) – are only exigible against those privy to the contract. So, in sum, Neyers has a great deal of work to do if he is to persuade us that deceit – in the absence of any cases saying this – protects the array of rights that he identifies, *in the way that he suggests*.

A third, rights-based understanding of the modern tort has been supplied by Goldberg, Sebok and Zipursky. In contrast to Stevens – who, as we have seen, takes the gist of the tort to be a right not to be lied to, despite such a right being denied

[264] J Neyers, 'Form and Substance in the Tort of Deceit' in A Robertson and J Goudkamp (eds), *Form and Substance in the Law of Obligations* (Oxford, Hart Publishing, 2019) 325.

[265] *Ibid*, 316.

[266] *Ibid*, 322: '[i]t seems clear ... that the conventional English conception of damage in the tort of deceit is an inadequate interpretation of the tort as we find it'.

[267] *Diamond v The Bank of London and Montreal* [1979] QB 333 (CA), 349.

[268] See J Neyers, 'The Economic Torts as Corrective Justice' (2009) 17 *Torts Law Journal* 1, 26.

in *Derry*[269] – these authors suggest, somewhat periphrastically, that the right in play is the rather hazy right to decision-making autonomy that they describe thus:

> [T]he core of the legal wrong that has historically been labelled 'fraud' or 'deceit' is the wrong of interfering with a particular interest of the victim, namely her interest in making certain kinds of choices in certain settings free from certain forms of misinformation.[270]

This, too – despite getting a good deal closer to the true gist of this tort than do either Stevens or Neyers (given that it is an understanding that is contradicted by neither existing law nor legal history) – clearly fails to pin down with adequate clarity the decision-making right in issue. The phrases 'certain kinds of choices', 'certain settings' and 'certain forms of misinformation' do little to clarify matters. They simply cause us to wonder: What kinds of choices? Which settings? What kinds of misinformation? But Goldberg *et al* are, I think, heading in the right direction. Their description merely needs some refinement.

For one thing, as a matter of English law, we can dispense with the qualifier 'certain forms of misinformation' since the types of misinformation which count for the purposes of deceit are tolerably well settled. We can simply replace the last six words in the above claim with the phrase 'free from the kinds of misrepresentation laid down in *Derry v Peek*'.[271] Equally, it is unclear how much weight we must attribute to the authors' suggestion that deceit is only available in 'certain settings'. For one thing, in the course of their rather lengthy article, they only actually refer to the qualifier, 'certain settings', twice; and on neither occasion do they offer any positive elaboration of what those settings might be. Instead, they put forward only the negative claim that there is no *a priori* reason why deceit should be confined to what the authors call the 'exchange setting'.[272] So can we improve upon this? Perhaps we can: by revisiting the well-known case of *East v Maurer*.[273]

In that case, the defendant owned two hairdressing salons and offered to sell one to the claimants promising not to continue working in the second if the claimants bought it. This assurance was very important to the claimants, since they feared that the clientele at the salon they proposed to buy would simply defect (out of customer loyalty) to the defendant's second salon after the sale of the first one. The defendant, contrary to his assurance, did continue working in the second salon. The claimants' fears were realised. The claimants then successfully sued for deceit, and among the losses recovered was a sum reflecting the opportunity

[269] *Derry* (n 245) 350, Lord Bramwell said: 'to say that there is "a right to have true statements only made", I cannot agree, and I think it would be much to be regretted if there was any such right'.

[270] JCP Goldberg, AJ Sebok and BC Zipursky, 'The Place of Reliance in Fraud' (2006) 48 *Arizona Law Review* 1001, 1011.

[271] In *Derry* (n 245) 374, Lord Herschell laid down the test: see text associated with n 277 below.

[272] Writing about exchange settings, the authors assert: 'it is not obvious to us that this sort of case exhausts the domain of fraud': Goldberg, Sebok and Zipursky (n 270) 1011.

[273] *East v Maurer* (n 247).

cost associated with buying the defendant's first salon instead of another salon in another location which would have yielded greater income. In other words, since the damages covered 'the kind of profit which the second plaintiff might have made if the representation which induced her to buy the [first salon] … had not been made',[274] it was effectively established that a claimant in deceit may sue for the opportunity cost attributable to a defendant's false statement.

On the logic of this case, then, it would seem that, quite regardless of the setting in which the deceitful statement is made, any fraudulently induced course of action that results in a measurable opportunity cost has the potential to support an action for deceit. If this be right, then the second of the qualifiers in the Goldberg *et al* statement also becomes otiose. We can disregard as ungrounded the claim that deceit is available only in 'certain settings'. There remains, then, only one outstanding ambiguity in their depiction of the gist of deceit: the reference to 'certain types of choices'.

Yet even here it is possible to be more precise. We have already identified the fact that deceit requires a claimant to show measurable loss so we can safely replace the vague reference to 'certain types of choices' with the proposition that, so far as the claimant's decision-making is concerned, the tort requires the claimant to have 'made a choice in reliance on the defendant's untruthful statement that results in some recognised form of harm for the claimant'. This suggestion is borne out by the case law. In *Wilkinson v Downton*, when Wright J treated as recoverable the cost of transporting friends to the place where the victim had been told that her husband lay injured, he said the following:

> As to this 1s 10½d, expended in railway fares on the faith of the defendant's statement, I think the case is clearly within the decision in *Pasley v Freeman*. The statement was a misrepresentation intended to be acted on to the damage of the plaintiff.[275]

Notice the complete absence of any insistence that the election to send friends to the site of the supposed accident must fall within some or other category of protected choices. No more was required by Wright J than that the representation should have been 'acted on'. Thus, if all that need be shown is that the claimant has in some way detrimentally 'acted on' the defendant's false claim, it is difficult to see what might anchor the contention that deceit is enlivened only where the claimant has made 'certain types of choices'.

In summary, the gist of deceit can be identified with the claimant's decision-making autonomy; and this, in turn, can be said to have been sufficiently interfered with where the choice into which the claimant is drawn by the defendant's falsehood results in a recognised form of harm. Although Goldberg, Sebok and Zipursky's original formulation must be dismissed as too vague a description of what lies at the heart of this tort, we can at least distil from it

[274] *Ibid*, 467.
[275] *Wilkinson v Downton* (n 212) 58.

the following, more precise one: 'The gist of deceit is an interference with the victim's decision-making autonomy that occurs by virtue of one of the established types of misinformation (laid down in *Derry v Peek*) and which results in a recognized form of harm'. Accordingly, like all but one of the other torts considered in this book, the tort of deceit is seriously mischaracterised when it is portrayed as being attentive only to economic losses. At its heart is C's decision-making autonomy; and it is the fact that C has been duped into making decisions that result in self-inflicted harm *of various different types* that grounds a successful action.[276]

B. Egregious Wrongdoing

Although several of the torts considered in previous chapters have only recently exhibited a clear concern to attend to egregious behaviour, deceit has always done this. The requirement that the defendant must have acted in an especially reprehensible fashion was made clear in the landmark case of *Derry v Peek*. There, on the basis of certain claims made in a company prospectus about its trams running on steam power (rather than being horse-drawn) in the future, the claimant invested in that company. However, before being allowed to implement the use of steam power, it was necessary to obtain Board of Trade approval, and this the defendants had failed to do. They did, however, at the time of publication of the prospectus, believe that such authorisation would be forthcoming. As it turned out, no such consent was ever given, the company was wound up and the claimant sued for deceit. Lord Herschell laid down the firmly entrenched test for the tort. He said this:

> in order to sustain an action of deceit, there must be proof of fraud, and nothing short of that will suffice. Secondly, fraud is proved when it is shewn that a false representation

[276] Neyers (n 264) 322–25 argues vigorously against my conception of the gist of deceit. He has three principal objections. The first (at 322) is that 'as a general matter, autonomy as a right appears to be too wide a concept to explain the law'. This criticism misses the mark because I very carefully limit the right in question to the right to choose one's future projects. I make no claim about autonomy in general. His second criticism (at 323) rests on the decision in a Canadian case, in which the plaintiff was deceived into having unprotected sex which led to his becoming a father: *PP v DD*, 2016 ONSC 258, 129 OR (3d) 175 (affirmed *PP v DD*, 2017 ONCA 180). Quite apart from the fact that a Canadian case cannot *per se* unsettle the law in England and Wales, it is also telling that Neyers admits that when the Ontario Court of Appeal dismissed the claim for damages for being denied the right to choose when to become a father, it emphasised *not* the fact that decision-making autonomy was not the gist of deceit, but rather the fact that involuntary parenthood had never previously been recognised as actionable damage. Neyers' third criticism (at 324) is that 'a right to decision-making autonomy does not meaningfully link with the requirement of damage (understood as some form of loss)'. This is perhaps true, but in order for the criticism to bite, it must be shown *first* either that I say that it does possess such a link *or* that such elegance in the law is a firm and accepted requirement rather than just a theoretical aspiration on Neyers' part. He does neither of these things.

> has been made (1) knowingly, or (2) without belief in its truth, or (3) recklessly, careless whether it be true or false.[277]

What is not always appreciated is that his Lordship did not quite stop there. Indeed, in the very next sentence he added these words:

> [a]lthough I have treated the second and third as distinct cases, I think the third is but an instance of the second, for one who makes a statement under such circumstances can have no real belief in the truth of what he states.[278]

The point of citing this addendum, although it is infrequently quoted, is to help draw attention to what was a central issue in the case, namely, the question of whether there could be liability for negligently uttered falsehoods. For Lord Herschell, it was important to point out that liability in deceit would only attach to those who deliberately lie to others or those who engage in conduct that is a very close approximation to deliberate lying. This, in other words, was the point of his stressing that a man who recklessly says something that is untrue 'can have no real belief in the truth of what he states'.

The notion that deceit is a tort that attends to misstatements that are deeply morally culpable comes through loud and clear in the case. Lord Bramwell colourfully signed up to the definition of fraud propounded by Lord Herschell when he declared that 'a man who makes a statement without care and regard for its truth or falsity commits a fraud. He is a rogue'.[279] Lord Bramwell was also attentive to the moral gulf between deceit and mere negligence, stressing the difference between 'unreasonableness of belief as evidence of dishonesty, and unreasonableness of belief as of itself a ground of action'.[280] Lord Herschell (again) made a more or less identical remark;[281] while Lord Fitzgerald, too, was keen to stress that '[i]t is essential to the action that moral fraud should be established'.[282]

Perhaps the clearest statement of all in the case that something particularly culpable is required in order to impose liability for deceit belongs to Lord Herschell. He was quite emphatic in saying:

> A man who forms his belief carelessly, or is unreasonably credulous, may be blameworthy when he makes a representation on which another is to act, but he is not, in my opinion, fraudulent in the sense in which that word was used in all the cases from *Pasley v Freeman* down to that with which I am now dealing.[283]

277 *Derry* (n 245) 374.
278 *Ibid*, 374.
279 *Ibid*, 349.
280 *Ibid*, 352.
281 *Ibid*, 361: 'To make a statement careless whether it be true or false, and therefore without any real belief in its truth, appears to me to be an essentially different thing from making, through want of care, a false statement, which is nevertheless honestly believed to be true'.
282 *Ibid*, 356.
283 *Ibid*, 369.

Since this momentous decision was handed down, various commentators have unreservedly laid stress upon the required moral turpitude of the defendant in deceit cases. Carty traces the requirement back as far as *Pasley*.[284] Fleming, too, understood liability in this tort to be calibrated to the degree of fault on the defendant's part. Writing about the situation in which there existed a reasonable expectation that a misrepresentation directed to X would also be forwarded to Y, he described the courts' refusal to impose liability for deceit in such cases as 'a reminder of the law's pervasive concern lest liability for misrepresentation entail an excessive burden out of all proportion to the fault'.[285] Finally, in much the same way that I do here, Stoljar interprets *Derry* as displaying a 'strong insistence on the seller's moral fraud' in those cases where X is induced to buy something from Y.[286]

Precisely the same emphasis on particularly reprehensible conduct has, in fact, been consistently enunciated by the courts. Setting the tone right from the start, Buller J said in *Pasley* that, 'if a man will wickedly assert that which he knows to be false, and thereby draws his neighbour into a heavy loss … [then] I say *ausis talibus istis non jura subserviunt*'.[287] And although Kenyon CJ, in that self-same case, did not invoke the language of 'wickedness', he was equally keen to stress the fact that 'the defendant's conduct was highly immoral'.[288] *Derry*, as already noted, marked a distinct refusal on the part of the House of Lords to dilute the requirement that there be a marked moral wrong; and just four years after it was decided, Lord Esher MR expressed firmly the view that, 'a charge of fraud is such a terrible thing to bring against a man that it cannot be maintained in any court unless it is shown that he had a wicked mind'.[289]

C. Final Remarks

In common with its sister misrepresentation torts of passing off and malicious falsehood, deceit is yet another action that – despite the way it is often portrayed – does a good deal more than protect against the wrongful infliction of trade or business losses. The fact that, on good authority, it is capable of providing a remedy in respect of such things as physical injury and mental distress lends weight to one of the principal theses of this book, namely, that the label, 'the economic torts', is apt to mislead, that it is a misnomer. The gist of deceit is not damage, but the decision-making autonomy of the claimant.

[284] On her reading, '[w]hat was emphasized [in *Pasley*] was the dishonesty element': Carty (n 1) 182.

[285] JG Fleming, *The Law of Torts*, 9th edn (Sydney, Law Book Company, 1998) 710.

[286] SJ Stoljar, *Mistake and Misrepresentation: A Study in Contractual Principles* (London, Sweet and Maxwell, 1968) 142 (fn 91).

[287] *Pasley* (n 204) 61.

[288] *Ibid*, 65.

[289] *Le Lievre v Gould* [1893] 1 QB 491 (CA), 498.

Whether for good or ill, the formulation of the relevant rules governing this tort took place at a time when the courts were very much in the thrall of the *caveat emptor* principle.[290] Accordingly, the bar was set high for claimants who, using the law of tort, wanted amends for (or to escape the clutches of) imprudent bargains into which they had been led by a seller's false claims. This high threshold of actionability comes through most strongly in the courts' repeated insistence that there be a marked moral stain on the defendant's conduct, that the falsehood be uttered deliberately or recklessly.

V. Conclusion

Although passing off and deceit are unquestionably of more practical significance than injurious falsehood, it remains true to say – despite the doubts expressed by some jurists – that all three actions remain vital in the strict sense of that word. But they are also vital in the other accepted sense: that is, they each provide distinctive avenues of relief, recourse not replicated (or, at least, not guaranteed to be replicated) by other civil actions. Passing off, most strikingly, will avail claimants who have failed entirely to register their trade mark, or who have not validly registered one, or who have succeeded in registering their mark, but may be faced with a statutory defence if they seek to rely on an action under the trade mark legislation. Similarly, for all that injurious falsehood shares some common ground with a range of other civil law actions, it nonetheless enjoys a discrete sphere of operation, and cannot safely be declared redundant.

Deceit, too, has a well-established and distinctive role within the law of torts. The rules governing such liability are so well established and provoke such little controversy that it seems unlikely that the tort will evolve very much in at least the foreseeable future. By contrast, we cannot be so certain about the future compass of both passing off and injurious falsehood. The former has considerable capacity to expand its protective borders in various ways, though it seems for the present to be dogged by inertia, stuck fast at the crossroads (as others have put it). Similarly, although in principle injurious falsehood could be developed by abandoning the need to show malice (which only ever became an ingredient of the tort by mistake[291]), or relaxing the putative requirement that the 'offending' statement must refer to the claimant, neither of these developments looks likely at the time of writing.

[290] See, eg, WH Hamilton 'The Ancient Doctrine Caveat Emptor' (1931) 40 *Yale Law Journal* 1133, 1186: 'Not until the nineteenth century, did judges discover that caveat emptor sharpened wits, taught self-reliance, made a man – an economic man – out of the buyer, and served well its two masters, business and justice'; Stoljar (n 286) 142 (fn 91): '[*Derry*] … in actual result, if not in its reasoning, displays a pronounced bias in favour of caveat emptor'.

[291] For an account of this historical oddity see Murphy (n 122).

From a theoretical perspective, all three of the torts considered in this chapter are especially noteworthy. It is sometimes said that there is something exceptional – perhaps even anomalous – about the three-party structure some of the general economic torts considered in the preceding chapters. The fact that passing off and injurious falsehood also operate according to this three-party structure tends to weaken the force of such claims. At the same time, the ineluctable two-party nature of deceit combines with what remains of the independent tort of intimidation and some cases of conspiracy to confound any possible suggestion that, the elusive golden thread that unites the economic torts can be found in their tripartite structure. Finally, the notions of intention and recklessness at work in both deceit and injurious falsehood contrast markedly with the mental elements one finds in the torts considered in chapters three, four and five raising questions about the work done by intentionality in the so-called economic torts. These are all matters I explore in depth in the next chapter.

7

Connections and Distinctions

I. Monism Revisited

In chapter two, we considered several monistic accounts of the economic torts – accounts, that is, that attempt to identify some sort of golden thread that unites the various actions dealt with in this book. We saw, first, that for some commentators, these torts are all about, *and only about*, the protection of economic interests. Thus, we noted (for example) Simon Deakin's belief that, for the purposes of these torts, 'unless a direct interference with trade, business or employment is made out, a vital element of the wrong is missing'.[1] Secondly, we alighted upon Allan Beever's rival view – which could scarcely be more different – along the lines that:

> The wrongdoing with which they [ie, the economic torts] are concerned is coercion of the plaintiff by the defendant through another: indirect control. The coercion is not a violation of the plaintiff's property or contractual rights. It is a violation of the plaintiff's innate right.[2]

In other words, whereas Deakin thinks that *direct* invasions of *economic interests* provide the elusive link, Beever thinks that *indirect* violations of an abstract, innate human right are key.

Third, we also noted in chapter two several other prominent monistic accounts of the economic torts, and in particular those proffered by Hazel Carty and Jason Neyers. We observed that while the accounts advanced by Carty and Neyers share *some* common ground with those of Deakin and Beever respectively, they also diverge in various significant ways from what these authors argue. In relation to all four of these monistic accounts, significant shortcomings were identified in the shape of major inconsistencies with the law as it presents itself. The conclusion reached in chapter two, therefore, was that none of these scholars has succeeded in providing a very satisfactory account of the economic torts, and still less one that identifies a unifying feature.

Against this backdrop, the following four chapters were designed to provide a fresh start, unblinkered by assumptions that are frequently made about the *raisons d'être* of the torts in view.[3] In the course of those chapters, a variety of quite different

[1] S Deakin and J Randall, 'Rethinking the Economic Torts' (2009) 72 *MLR* 519, 533.

[2] A Beever, *A Theory of Tort Liability* (Oxford, Hart Publishing, 2016) 124.

[3] For the avoidance of doubt, talk here of the 'proper *raisons d'être*' is to be understood in descriptive rather than prescriptive terms. In other words, the phrase refers to rationales that demonstrably

rationales (or prime concerns) applicable to the various torts was unearthed.[4] The closest we come to a characteristic that is shared by all the torts considered in this book is the fact that *in the modern era* they are all particularly attentive to especially reprehensible wrongdoing.[5] Notably, it is a feature of the economic torts that has been picked out by one of our most senior judges. In *Revenue and Customs Commissioners v Total Network SL*, speaking generally about the various actions with which we are concerned, Lord Scott said:

> It is not all conduct foreseeably likely to cause, and that does cause, economic harm to another that is tortious. Nor should it be. The circumstances must be such as to make the conduct sufficiently reprehensible to justify imposing on those who have brought about the harm liability in damages for having done so.[6]

But much as this is true, especially reprehensible conduct cannot, for at least two reasons, be taken to constitute the elusive golden thread that unifies and gives specific identity to the economic torts. To begin with, if egregious wrongdoing were to be treated as the organising feature of a group of torts, then that group ought also to include the actions that exist for abuse of process, malicious prosecution and misfeasance in a public office. Since no-one would regard these as being members of the economic torts family,[7] it follows that especially reprehensible wrongdoing is not capable of constituting the key feature that identifies and unites the torts with which this book is concerned. Secondly, the attentiveness of some of these torts to especially egregious wrongdoing is more a characteristic of modern developments than a trait that they have borne ever since their inception. The reader is reminded here, in particular, of the twenty-first century uses of unlawful means conspiracy, and the stretching of passing off to cases in which D resorts to especially underhand methods even though the outcome in these cases is not always easy to reconcile with the original judicial conception of goodwill.

It is against the background of the failure of existing monists' accounts, as well as the inability of an alternative monistic explanation (based on egregious wrongdoing) to identify a compelling unifying feature, that this chapter seeks to explain why, as Lord Neuberger has acknowledged, 'it is a mistake to group these "torts" together'.[8] The extent to which this would indeed be a mistake will be demonstrated

underscore the various cases as we find them, rather than an idealised view of the purposes to which the torts in question should be put.

[4] The exception was inducing breach of contract where a clear rationale remains elusive.

[5] We noted in passing that this feature has always been possessed by deceit and injurious falsehood; and we noted, too, that the presence of such wrongdoing can make a material difference to the way a court will approach a case of passing off, even though strictly speaking this is a strict liability tort.

[6] *Revenue and Customs Commissioners v Total Network SL* [2008] 1 AC 1174 (HL), [56].

[7] It was said in *Northern Territory v Mengel* [1995] HCA 65, [60] (Mason CJ, Dawson, Toohey, Gaudron, and McHugh JJ) that misfeasance in a public office could be seen as a 'counterpart to' the general economic torts in that, it too, requires the intentional infliction of loss. But it was never regarded as being an economic tort.

[8] *Total Network* (n 6) [224]. It was an *acknowledgement* (rather than an assertion) on Lord Neuberger's part because the quoted words actually belong to Robert Stevens: see R Stevens, *Torts and Rights* (Oxford, Oxford University Press, 2007) 297.

by making good on one of the central claims in this book: the contention that there is a great deal more that divides than there is that unites these torts.

Three main types of difference will be addressed. In section II, the focus is upon juridical distinctions (with particular attention devoted to two prominent features, namely 'required mental elements' and 'unlawful means'). In section III, attention shifts to the important structural differences that exist; while in section IV the focus is upon the significant functional variations among these torts. In section V, I draw things together with a series of conclusions about the overwhelming – perhaps inevitable – *disunity* we encounter in this setting.

II. Juridical Links and Distinctions

Within the economic torts, two juridical features stand out: first, the fact that they are overwhelmingly 'intentional wrongs' (in the strict sense[9]), and secondly, the fact that they frequently require some sort of 'unlawful means'. The first of these features is more pervasive than the latter, though, in its own right, the need for unlawful means comprises an essential ingredient in nearly half of the torts in view.[10] In this section of the chapter, my aim is to demonstrate that, although these two characteristics seem ostensibly to forge an important juridical link between the various torts in which they comprise elements of liability, they in fact constitute the source of very significant divergence. I address first the intentionality component, highlighting the differences between the various mental elements that are required. I then turn to the rival meanings that are ascribed to the term 'unlawful means' in the torts of causing loss by unlawful means, and unlawful means conspiracy.

A. Mental Elements

With the exception of passing off – which, formally, constitutes an example of strict liability within tort law – all of the torts considered in this book contain a mental element that must be satisfied in order for liability to be imposed. It is not possible, however, simply to say that they are all torts of *intention*, and still less that it is intentionality that forms the elusive golden thread that unites them.

[9] Although the trespass torts are frequently referred to as 'intentional torts', this is, in one sense, a misleading label. They are torts that require deliberate conduct (ie, that D volitionally do the act in question); but they do not require 'intention' in the sense that a particular outcome is desired. So, for example, if D deliberately mows grass that he mistakenly believes to be his own, but which in fact belongs to C, he commits the tort of trespass to land: *Basely v Clarkson* (1682) 3 Lev 37. It is only where D intends a particular outcome that a tort can be described in terms of D intentionally *wronging* C.

[10] It is obvious that unlawful means are required in the torts of causing loss by unlawful means and unlawful means conspiracy; but the same is true, also, of intimidation since liability for this tort requires that an unlawful threat be made. See further subsection B, below.

Any attempt to recast them as 'the intentional torts' would be to take a view of them that is both under- and over-inclusive. It would be too narrow a label for them insofar as making intention the organising concept would result in the torts of injurious falsehood and lawful means conspiracy (both of which are enlivened by malice rather than intention[11]) being excluded from the analysis.

At the same time, reconceptualising the economic torts as 'the intentional torts' would also be too broad an approach because there are a number of other well-known torts that could be brought within this category. Battery, assault and false imprisonment are probably the most obvious examples of tort actions that no-one would ever seek to bracket with the torts with which this book is concerned. But they are by no means the only ones. Intentionality in one form or another also plays a critical role in various abuse of power torts,[12] as well as in the recently revitalised rule in *Wilkinson v Downton*.[13] The most we can say, then, is that the group of torts familiarly referred to as the economic torts typically contain a *mens rea* element,[14] but this, by itself, is a relatively vacuous and unilluminating observation. For example, such vague language would tend to mask the fact that, in the tort of inducing breach of contract there is no need to show intention *per se*, since recklessness (in the form of turning a blind eye) will also suffice.[15]

As we shall see in the remainder of this section, when the spotlight is cast upon the *mens rea* or fault elements one finds at work in this setting, it transpires that there is a good deal more that divides than unites the relevant actions.

Intention features as an ingredient of liability in no fewer than five of the torts in view: the unlawful means tort, inducing breach of contract, two-party intimidation, unlawful means conspiracy and deceit.[16] However, the fact that it may be regarded as an ingredient of liability in each of these torts does not warrant its being regarded as a *common element* because intention, as we shall see, is a protean concept, the meaning and object of which varies from one action to the next. Counterintuitively, then, the fact that intention (or, more accurately, some notion of intentionality) plays a central role in the ascription of liability in the majority of

[11] Lawful means conspiracy is animated by a conception of malice that equates to an improper purpose. The self-same conception of malice also *sometimes* operates in the tort of injurious falsehood though, for that tort liability can also be imposed on the basis of 'deceit malice' (namely, saying something in the belief that one's statement may be false).

[12] For the intentionality – or, more accurately, malice – requirements of the torts of abuse of process, misfeasance in a public office and malicious prosecution, see J Murphy, 'Malice as an Ingredient of Tort Liability' [2019] *CLJ* 355, 358–62.

[13] *Wilkinson v Downton* [1897] 2 QB 57 (rescued from desuetude in *O v Rhodes* [2016] AC 219 (SC)).

[14] Although, strictly, this term belongs in the sphere of the criminal law, I take my lead from Peter Cane in using it as a term of convenience to encompass the various mental states in play in the torts considered here: see P Cane, '*Mens Rea* in Tort Law' (2000) 20 *OJLS* 533.

[15] 'If the defendant deliberately turned a blind eye and proceeded regardless he may be treated as having intended the consequence he brought about': *OBG Ltd v Allan* [2008] 1 AC 1 (HL), [172] (Lord Nicholls). As such, *mens rea* would not mean the same thing in all of these torts.

[16] Intention is not the only mental element in deceit. But where intention is present, it unquestionably operates as an element of the tort.

the economic torts, is more an indicium of difference than of commonality. This contention requires some elaboration.

i. Intentionality in the General Economic Torts

In *OBG Ltd v Allan*, Lord Hoffmann, who delivered the leading speech, made clear the need for intention in both inducing breach of contract and the unlawful means tort. He said: 'In the *Lumley v Gye* tort, there must be an intention to procure a breach of contract. In the unlawful means tort, there must be an intention to cause loss'.[17] One might think that his saying this in a single sentence was indicative of considerable common ground between the two actions. This, however, would be a mistake (and one that even a senior judge made in that very same case[18]). For, although his Lordship took the view that the *meaning* of intention was identical in both actions – that is, a person intends a particular occurrence if it is either a desired end in itself, or simply a means to an end[19] – he was equally adamant that the intended outcomes were very different indeed. Whereas harm to the claimant must be intended in the unlawful means tort, no such outcome must be intended in order to justify an action based on inducing breach of contract. Indeed, in explaining in more detail the intention element in the latter, Lord Hoffmann assiduously steered clear of any mention of the need for intended harm. All that is required, he made clear, is the following:

> you must know that you are inducing a breach of contract. It is not enough to know that you are procuring an act which, as a matter of law or construction of the contract, is a breach. You must actually realise that it will have this effect. Nor does it matter that you ought reasonably to have done so.[20]

The fact that the emphasis was placed upon there being an intended breach of contract rather than intended harm was doubly significant. For one thing, it provided the basis for overruling the disagreeable decision in *Millar v Bassey*.[21] But, more importantly for present purposes, it also enabled Lord Hoffmann to highlight an important distinction between inducing breach of contract and the unlawful means tort. He put it this way: '[t]he ends which must have been intended [in the two actions] are different … one may intend to procure a breach

[17] *OBG* (n 15) [62].

[18] In *OBG*, despite her expressing agreement with the 'conclusions and reasoning' of Lord Hoffmann, her Ladyship nonetheless said at one point in her speech that, '[t]he underlying rationale of both the *Lumley v Gye* … and the unlawful means torts is the same: the defendant is deliberately striking at his target through a third party': *OBG* (n 15) [302] and [306].

[19] *OBG* (n 15) [43], [62].

[20] *Ibid*, [39].

[21] *Millar v Bassey* [1994] EMLR 44 (CA). Shirley Bassey had broken her contract with a recording company; and a foreseeable consequence of this was that the recording company would, in turn, break its contracts with the musicians who had been engaged to play on the record. Critically, Bassey had never intended that the breaches of contract between the record company and the musicians should occur.

of contract without intending to cause loss'.[22] Elsewhere in his speech he illustrated the significance of this difference by reference to *South Wales Miners' Federation v Glamorgan Coal Co Ltd*,[23] a case in which a miners' union had called a strike (and thereby induced breaches of the miners' contracts of employment). The union argued that the inevitable restriction in coal production to which this strike would lead would cause there to be an increase in the price of coal; and thus, in Lord Hoffmann's words, 'far from wishing to cause the mine owners loss, they intended to make both owners and miners better off'.[24] But this did not matter. The owners did in fact sustain loss, and they were able to sue in respect of it.

The significance of this difference between the two torts has been noted by others. Thus, while Deakin and Randall believe that a test of 'harm ... aimed or targeted at the claimant would be preferable'[25] in cases of inducing breach of contract, they freely acknowledge that no such test presently exists in the law. And it is easy to see, also, why Davies should argue that because '*Lumley* does not require the defendant to intend to harm the claimant ... [this] is an important difference from the unlawful means tort'.[26]

The tort of intimidation also requires intentional wrongdoing. Stuart Smith J was adamant about this (in relation to both forms of the tort) when he stated in *Newsgroup Newspapers Ltd v SOGAT '82* that, '[t]he tort is one of intention and the plaintiff, whether it be B or C, must be a person whom A intended to injure'.[27] Of course, as we saw in chapter four, by virtue of the decision in *OBG*, only the two-party version of this tort now remains vital as an independent tort. Their Lordships in *OBG* made clear that any case of three-party intimidation should now be regarded as being but a classic example of the unlawful means tort. It follows from this, however, that the meaning and the object of intention in two-party intimidation cases must be the same as the meaning and the object of intention in the unlawful means tort.

My reasoning here runs thus. Since Stuart Smith J's dictum suggests that, historically, the meaning of intention was the same for both the two- and three-party cases of intimidation, it follows that, because three-party intimidation cases are simply examples of the unlawful means tort, there is now a common meaning of intention within two-party intimidation and the unlawful means tort. This must be so, for when the three-party version of intimidation was relabelled in *OBG*, it was not at the same time tweaked in terms of its key elements. The intention requirement – which was shared with case of two-party intimidation – was left untouched.

[22] *OBG* (n 15) [62].
[23] *South Wales Miners' Federation v Glamorgan Coal Co Ltd* [1905] AC 239 (HL).
[24] *OBG* (n 15) [8].
[25] Deakin and Randall (n 1) 552.
[26] PS Davies, *Accessory Liability* (Oxford, Hart Publishing, 2015) 158.
[27] *Newsgroup Newspapers Ltd v SOGAT '82* [1987] ICR 181 (CA), 204.

What, then, of the final general economic tort in which intention must be shown, namely, unlawful means conspiracy? In this connection there is certainly *a different* notion of intention in play. This was made abundantly clear in the leading case of *Total Network*. What also seems clear from that case is the fact that intention bears *a narrower* meaning in relation to unlawful means conspiracy than it does in connection with the unlawful means tort.[28] Lord Walker, who delivered the leading speech, was adamant that, in terms of intention, there exists a significant difference between unlawful means conspiracy and the tort of causing loss by unlawful means. He said: 'what sets conspiracy apart from other torts … [is] the intense focus, in the tort of conspiracy, on intention'.[29] Signalling that this 'intense focus' could be achieved via a test of 'targeted harm' (rather than the ends/means test promulgated by Lord Hoffmann in *OBG*), Lord Mance said this:

> Lord Hoffmann's criticism of the Court of Appeal's reasoning in *OBG* was that it first expanded the concept of 'unlawful means', and then sought to counteract the width of the concept 'by insisting upon a highly specific intention, which "targets" the plaintiff'; this, he considered, 'places too much of a strain on the concept of intention' … That problem does not to my mind arise with anything like the same force in the present context.[30]

Lord Hope, too, considered salient the fact that the 'criminal offence was directed at the commissioners'[31] in that case. True: their Lordships were not absolutely crystal clear in laying down a test of 'targeted harm', but the message that a narrower conception of intention is at work in unlawful means conspiracy comes through loud and clear.[32] For this reason, although the Court of Appeal has since stated that the same meaning of intention should be applied in both the tort of causing loss by unlawful means and unlawful means conspiracy,[33] it is hard to regard this statement as being anything other than at variance with what Lords Mance, Hope and Walker had to say on the matter.

By contrast, the other conspiracy tort – ie, lawful means conspiracy – does not operate according to any of the conceptions of intention considered thus far. Instead, as I explained at some length in chapter five, it works according to a requirement of predominant bad motive (or illegitimate purpose). It was for this reason that Lord Hoffmann referred to it in *OBG* as 'malicious *Quinn v Leathem*

[28] For discussion of which of these constructions of intention is the more appealing in normative terms, see H Carty, 'The Modern Functions of the Economic Torts: Reviewing the English, Canadian, Australian and New Zealand Positions' [2015] *CLJ* 261, 282–83.

[29] *Total Network* (n 6) [78].

[30] *Ibid*, [42].

[31] *Total Network* (n 6) [124].

[32] For the view that the difference that exists is 'slight', see PS Davies and P Sales, 'Intentional Harm, Accessories and Conspiracies' (2018) 134 *LQR* 69, 72.

[33] *Berryland Books Ltd v BK Books Ltd* [2010] EWCA Civ 1440 (CA), [48] (Etherton LJ). See also *Meretz Investments NV v ACP Ltd* [2008] Ch 244 (CA), [90] (Arden LJ); *Digicel (St Lucia) Ltd v Cable & Wireless Plc* [2010] EWHC 774, Annex I, [83] (Morgan J).

conspiracy'.[34] That this version of conspiracy employs a different intentionality requirement than its sister tort – one that draws attention to the fact that the defendant has engaged in some form of especially reprehensible conduct – was emphasised by Lord Walker in *Total Network*. He alighted upon the 'clear distinction between the requirement of predominant purpose under one variety of the tort of conspiracy and the *lower requirement of intentional injury* needed for the other variety'.[35]

What the foregoing paragraphs demonstrate is this: although it is easy to describe loosely the general economic torts as being torts of intention, careful scrutiny of the cases reveals considerable variation in the mental element required from one action to the next.[36] What is no less noteworthy is the fact that the differences between the various intentionality components employed in the economic torts become even more numerous once those that operate within the misrepresentation torts are taken into account.

ii. Mental Elements in the Misrepresentation Torts

As was observed in chapter six, there is no specific mental state required in order for there to be liability for passing off. It is a tort which, according to orthodoxy, is one of strict liability.[37] True – as was also noted in chapter six – a defendant's intention *may* be highly relevant to the question of whether there has been customer deception.[38] But the critical point is that no court has ever yet said that intention, or any cognate concept, is an *essential ingredient* of the tort. To this extent, the difference between passing off and all the other torts considered in this book could scarcely be more apparent. The other two misrepresentation

[34] *OBG* (n 15) [20]. There is a need to exercise care when speaking of malice in this context. For, although it is *always* true to say, that '[i]n tort law, bad motives are referred to as "malice"' [Cane (n 14) 539], it is not possible to say that malice in tort law *must* always be understood in terms of bad motives. Recall, for example, the second meaning attributed to malice in the tort of injurious falsehood.

[35] *Total Network* (n 6) [82] (emphasis added).

[36] It is precisely because the law is clear that those who would prefer different *mens rea* tests are forced to concede that what they want is something different from the orthodox one. For example, although Beever would prefer that throughout the economic torts intention be equated with purpose (that purpose being control of C), he is forced to concede that '[t]his understanding of intention is sure to attract criticism': Beever (n 2) 132. Equally, the argument advanced by Deakin and Randall (n 1) 541 that we should favour a test of targeting (instead of intention) is accompanied by the concession that this does not reflect the law: 'the general requirement for liability in tort for interfering with trade or business, including in the conspiracy torts' they suggest, 'should be restated in terms of the defendant "aiming at" or "targeting" his conduct at the claimant … [even though] [t]argeting or aiming is not quite the same as either intending to harm, or even being reckless'.

[37] *Gillette UK Ltd v Edenwest Ltd* [1994] RPC 279.

[38] See, eg, *Cadbury Schweppes Pty Ltd v Pub Squash Co Pty Ltd* [1981] RPC 429 (PC), 490 (Lord Scarman), '[w]here an intention to deceive is found, it is not difficult for the court to infer that the intention has been, or in all probability will be, effective'; *Office Cleaning Services Ltd v Westminster Window and General Cleaners Ltd* (1946) 63 RPC 39 (HL), 42–43 (HL) (Lord Simonds): 'if the intention to deceive is found, it will readily be inferred that deception will result'.

torts do, however, have *mens rea* requirements, and it is with these that the remainder of this section is concerned.

In deceit, there is ostensibly a return to familiar ground, for it is well established in this tort that the claimant must show (among other things) that the defendant's false statement was intended to induce an act of reliance on the part of the representee. As Viscount Maugham put it in the House of Lords in *Bradford Third Equitable Benefit Building Society v Borders*, '[the statement] must be made with the intention that it should be acted upon by the plaintiff, or by a class of persons which will include the plaintiff, in the manner which resulted in damage to him'.[39]

To the extent that the intention must have been to cause the representee to act in a particular way, it might be thought that a link could be made between the intentionality element in deceit and the one (considered earlier) in inducing breach of contract. At the same time, however, the fact that harm to C must have been the intended result of the act prompted by what was said by D might be thought to constitute a link between the intention component in deceit and the one at work in the unlawful means tort. On closer inspection, however, neither of these apparent links turns out to be very strong.

Whereas both deceit and inducing breach of contract require the defendant to have intentionally procured a certain type of conduct on the part of the person with whom the defendant communicates, the act procured in deceit must always be harmful. We already observed that this is not so in the case of inducing breach of contract. Thus, we can say this: in deceit, D must intentionally procure harmful conduct; but D need not intend to procure harmful conduct for the purposes of inducing breach of contract.

Equally, although both deceit and the unlawful means tort require, in some sense, an intention to cause harm to C, it is nonetheless the case that within the unlawful means tort, the intention must pertain to *the loss actually suffered*. Lord Hoffmann, employing his ends/means test of intention in *OBG*, was careful to state that, 'one is not liable for loss which is neither a desired end nor a means of attaining it but merely a foreseeable consequence of one's actions'.[40] It follows from this that the harm in respect of which one may be held liable must have been specifically intended by D (even if it was only intended as a means to an end). Lord Nicholls could not have been clearer when he said: '[t]he defendant must have intended to inflict the harm of which complaint is made'.[41] In the tort of deceit, however, things are very different. D need not have intended the specific harm complained of. It is enough that he has, in a very general sense, intended that the claimant should suffer harm. That no greater specificity than this is required is reflected in the fact that liability for deceit may be imposed in respect of *all directly caused harm*[42] and not just (as per the unlawful means tort) harm that was specifically intended.

[39] *Bradford Third Equitable Benefit Building Society v Borders* [1941] 2 All ER 205 (HL), 211.
[40] *OBG* (n 15) [62].
[41] *Ibid*, [141].
[42] *Doyle v Olby (Ironmongers) Ltd* [1969] 2 QB 158 (CA).

Finally, as the alternative name for injurious falsehood – ie, malicious falsehood – clearly suggests, it is malice rather than intention that comprises the intentionality component in the tort. As was noted in chapter six, this may take two forms: 'motive malice' and 'deceit malice'. Motive malice replicates the *mens rea* component in lawful means conspiracy, but deceit malice does not, despite the name, translate into the intention requirement found in the tort of deceit. This is because the intentionality in any such case pertains *only* to the truth of the injurious statement made. What is important, in other words, is that the defendant intended to tell a lie, and not that he intended also that his telling a lie should result in harm to the claimant (as is the case in deceit). Thus, in one case decided by the Supreme Court of Canada (where the law is more or less identical to the law in this country),[43] the defendants printed an untruthful story, with not the slightest suggestion that they believed it to be true, about a particular house being haunted by ghosts. It ran thus:

> There is a ghost in the north end of the city that is causing a lot of trouble to the inhabitants. His chief haunt is in a vacant house [that of the claimant] on St John Avenue, near to Main. He appears late at night and performs strange antics, so that timid people give the place a wide berth. A number of men have lately made a stand against ghosts in general, and at night they rendezvous in the basement and close around the haunted house to await his ghostship, but so far he still remains at large.[44]

It is fairly clear from the excerpt reproduced here that the story had been printed as a joke and that the defendants had not intended to cause loss to the claimant (whose action in injurious falsehood was based upon the fact that the planned sale of the house fell through). This, however, made no difference to the outcome of the case. The defendants were liable for the loss of the sale. The case, therefore, illustrates the significant difference between intending to cause harm via an untruthful statement, and simply intending to say something that is untrue. To put it another way: it is hard to see how one might plausibly infer an intention to cause harm (if inference rather than proof be permissible) from what was obviously considered a harmless joke about 'strange antics' on the part of a ghost that was referred to humorously as 'his ghostship'.

iii. Concluding Remarks on Intentionality

Although we have noted that some form of *mens rea* is required in the majority of the economic torts, we have also seen that there is great variability in the object of the intention. It varies from the defendant intending to bring about a breach of contract, to loss in general (in deceit), to some more specific loss (in the unlawful means tort). We also noted that a very specific form of intention – namely, targeted harm – is required in unlawful means conspiracy. What we did

[43] *Manitoba Free Press Co v Nagy* (1907) 39 SCR 340.

[44] The press report is reproduced in the decision: see *ibid*, 351.

not observe earlier, but may usefully mention now, is the fact that in some of these torts, subjective recklessness in the form of turning a blind eye will be equated with intention.[45] This stands in stark contrast to the torts of injurious falsehood and deceit where recklessness – as an alternative trigger for liability – bears its more usual *objective* meaning, and can clearly be distinguished from intention.

What all this confirms is that there is anything but commonality between the economic torts when it comes to the question of the mental element that must be shown in each case. At their least demanding, in terms of moral culpability, recklessness (as a concept distinct from intention) will suffice. But at their most demanding, nothing short of malice (*qua* ill-will or bad motive) will do. Intention ordinarily falls somewhere between these two extremes since it is entirely possible to intend to do a thing as a matter of deliberation without, at the same time, *emotionally* wanting to do that thing. Anyone who has acted under duress would readily attest to this point. Add to this the fact that observably different notions of intended harm can be distilled from the cases of unlawful means conspiracy and the tort of causing loss by unlawful means and what becomes apparent is that there is next to no unity between these torts when the various intentionality components are scrutinised.

Indeed, the only real commonality in this context is that each of these actions requires at least some clear measure of moral culpability. This may explain why the economic torts so readily permit the recovery of pure economic loss when the law of negligence – in which there is no mental element to satisfy – does not: the presence of such moral culpability is what justifies liability being stretched to what is generally regarded as a lowly-ranking protected interest.[46] But this, it must be appreciated, is scarcely a profound link because it is negative rather than positive in nature: it links the economic torts merely by reference to what they are not – ie, negligence. If, with the focus on intentionality, one looks for a positive link between the various torts, one searches in vain. In this regard my claim that there is more that divides than unites these torts is, I would submit, irresistible.

B. Unlawful Means

As indicated at the beginning of this section, it is in the torts of unlawful means conspiracy, causing loss by unlawful means and two-party intimidation, that one encounters the requirement that the defendant must have used unlawful means in causing harm to the claimant in order to be held liable. That this is an essential ingredient in the first two of these torts is obvious from their names. But it is

[45] *OBG* (n 15) [172] (Lord Nicholls).

[46] See, eg, NJ McBride, *The Humanity of Private Law* (Oxford, Hart Publishing, 2019) 124; Davies and Sales (n 32) 83; J Goudkamp and D Nolan, *Winfield and Jolowicz on Tort*, 20th edn (London, Sweet and Maxwell, 2020) 106.

true, too, that it operates as a liability component in intimidation, albeit that the way in which it does this requires some explanation.

In the tort of intimidation, there can be no liability if there has been no threat. Yet, for these purposes, only certain kinds of threat will do. If the threat made by the defendant was a legitimate one, then no tort will have been committed. As noted already in chapter five, Lord Reid said in *Rookes v Barnard*:

> [S]o long as the defendant only threatens to do what he has a legal right to do he is on safe ground … but I agree with Lord Herschell that there is a chasm between doing what you have a legal right to do and threatening to do what you have no legal right to do.[47]

This dictum makes plain the fact that, in order for there to be liability for intimidation, there must have been a threat to do something that one is not legally entitled to do. And as I explained at length when dealing with intimidation, the reason for this is easily grasped: if what I threaten to do would be an unlawful act, this inevitably colours the threat that I make and thereby enables that threat to be regarded as unlawful means. Put another way, the very fact that I am prohibited by law from doing what I threaten to do causes what I say to cross the line that divides lawful persuasion (on the one hand) from unlawful coercion (on the other).[48]

It is true that what I say here constitutes a greatly simplified account of what amounts to an unlawful threat. There is, I readily concede, a great deal of disagreement among commentators about whether the threat to commit just *any* unlawful act (as opposed to certain limited types of unlawful act – like breaches of contract) will suffice.[49] However, engagement in this debate is not necessary here; for there is at least universal acceptance that *whichever kinds of threat* do in fact trigger liability, there is no denying that threats of the requisite type will themselves constitute unlawful means.

Having thus established that unlawful means are required in all three of these torts, the pressing question for present purposes is whether the meaning of 'unlawful means' is consistent among them. The simple answer is that it is not. The most pronounced difference exists between the tort of causing loss by unlawful means, where only actionable civil wrongs (or potentially actionable civil wrongs) will do,[50] and unlawful means conspiracy, where common law crimes not actionable as

[47] *Rookes v Barnard* [1964] AC 1129 (HL), 1168. In similar vein, see *Crofter Hand Woven Harris Tweed Co Ltd v Veitch* [1942] AC 435 (HL), 467 (Lord Wright).

[48] Note, however, the threat must succeed in being coercive and that an ineffectual threat to do something unlawful will not by itself suffice: *Newsgroup Newspapers* (n 27) 204 (Stuart-Smith LJ).

[49] For lengthy engagement in this debate, and for the argument that the threat to commit crimes as a well as civil wrongs are actionable, see J Murphy, 'Understanding Intimidation' (2014) 77 *MLR* 33, 38–44.

[50] *OBG* (n 15) [45] (Lord Hoffmann). Lord Walker, Baroness Hale and Lord Brown agreed: *ibid*, [270], [302] and [320] respectively. Lord Nicholls dissented on the point saying, '[i]t would be very odd if … the law were to afford the claimant a remedy where the defendant committed or threatened to commit a tort or breach of contract against the third party but not if he committed or threatened to commit a crime against him': *ibid*, [152]. For an expression of sympathy with Lord Nicholls' view, see Davies and Sales (n 32) 72.

torts,[51] and acts amounting to a contempt of court – such as breach of a freezing order – will also count.[52]

There is even, in some circumstances, an appreciable difference between the two torts where purely civil law wrongs are alleged to constitute the unlawful means. This is because, in relation to the tort of causing loss by unlawful means, the defendant's act must, according to Lord Hoffmann, be 'intended to cause loss to the claimant by interfering with the freedom of a third party in a way which is unlawful as against that third party *and which is intended to cause loss to the claimant*'.[53] This, he went on, 'does not … include acts which may be unlawful against a third party but *which do not affect his freedom to deal with the claimant*'.[54] And however odd or unprincipled it may seem, this dealing requirement has since been firmly baked into the tort of causing loss by unlawful means by the Supreme Court in a case in which its status was directly challenged.[55] There is, however, no equivalent qualification in the tort of unlawful means conspiracy that the unlawful means must restrict the freedom of a third party (against whom they are directed) to deal with the claimant.

In *Douglas v Hello! Ltd*, the claimant magazine, *OK!*, had contracted for the exclusive right to publish photographs of the celebrity wedding of Michael Douglas and Catherine Zeta Jones. The defendant had obtained and published photographs that had been taken by a member of the paparazzi who had surreptitiously gained entry to the wedding, posing as a waiter or guest. On the facts, Lord Hoffmann held that no action could be brought against *Hello!* on the basis of causing loss by unlawful means because, although the defendant had certainly broken a duty of confidentiality owed to the Douglases, it was not the case that *Hello!*:

> did anything to interfere with the liberty of the Douglases to deal with *OK!* or perform their obligations under their contract. All they did was to make *OK!*'s contractual rights less profitable than they otherwise would have been.[56]

If we suppose, however, that *Hello!* had made a prior arrangement with the paparazzo to obtain the photographs – that they had conspired, in other words, to use unlawful means – then there might well have been liability based on the conspiracy tort, even though the change of facts would have made no difference at all to the action based on causing loss by unlawful means. The fact that, in this second set of circumstances, the breach of the duty of confidentiality could be attributed to a combination of actors would in no way impact the fact that the Douglases' freedom to deal with *OK!* was unaffected.

[51] *Total Network* (n 6) [94] (Lord Walker): 'criminal conduct engaged in by conspirators as a means of inflicting harm on the claimant is actionable as the tort of conspiracy, whether or not that conduct, on the part of a single individual, would be actionable as some other tort'. Lords Scott, Mance and Neuberger agreed: *ibid*, [47], [56] and [217] respectively.

[52] *JSC BTA Bank v Khrapunov* [2018] UKSC 19 (SC), [16] (joint speech of Lords Sumption and Lloyd-Jones, delivered on behalf of the entire Supreme Court).

[53] *OBG* (n 15) [51] (emphasis added).

[54] *Ibid*, [51] (emphasis added).

[55] *Secretary of State for Health v Servier Laboratories Ltd* [2021] UKSC 24.

[56] *OBG* (n 15) [129].

Whether or not the prospect of a different outcome, depending on which of the two torts is invoked, is to be regretted,[57] is a normative matter on which I need not dwell (though it is notable that, in *Total Network*, Lord Neuberger thought the difference a defensible one,[58] as did Lord Walker[59]). My aim in this chapter is – no more and no less – to show that, as the law presently stands, there is a significant difference between the concept of 'unlawful means' in the two torts. It is a difference that has been openly acknowledged at the highest judicial level, with Lord Walker commenting in *Total Network* that, 'as the economic torts have developed, "unlawful means" has a wider meaning in the tort of conspiracy than it has in the intentional harm tort'.[60] It is also one with a considerable historical pedigree,[61] and one that serves to substantiate the primary argument of this chapter.

It is hard to regard what counts as unlawful means in the context of the tort of intimidation as anything other than a civil wrong. This is not, *pace* Carty, because a defendant's threats 'are [to be] equated to the unlawful acts themselves',[62] but because the threats are intrinsically a recognised form of civil wrong. A point made in chapter five that warrants repetition here is that, the principal reason why threats cannot simply be equated with the acts threatened is because this would be inconsistent with Lord Hodson's declaration in *Rookes* that, 'the vice of the respondents' action *is the threat to break and not the breach itself*.'[63] In saying this, his Lordship clearly afforded independent, normative significance to unlawful threats. It is one thing to insist that an unlawful threat be parasitic or contingent upon an unlawful act, but it is altogether another to equate the former with the latter.

[57] Carty certainly considers it lamentable that a different result would be reached, depending on which tort was invoked: see H Carty, 'The Tort of Conspiracy as a Can of Worms' in SGA Pitel *et al* (eds), *Tort Law: Challenging Orthodoxy* (Oxford, Hart Publishing, 2013) 391, 407. For a more relaxed view, see P Edmundson, 'Conspiracy by Unlawful Means: Keeping the Tort Untangled' (2008) 16 *Torts Law Journal* 189, 206: 'now is the time for the tort to undertake a period of case-by-case development without necessarily looking for a clear and comprehensive test for what amounts to unlawful means'.

[58] For example, Lord Neuberger thought that allowing crimes to count as unlawful means in the conspiracy tort (even though they would not count as such in the tort of causing loss by unlawful means) was justifiable. He said: 'I would find it far less offensive to hold that unlawfulness can extend to a "mere" crime in unlawful means conspiracy, when it cannot do so in causing loss by unlawful means, than to hold that a "mere" crime cannot in any circumstances constitute unlawfulness in unlawful means conspiracy, when there is a tort of conspiracy to injure by means which are neither tortious nor criminal': *Total Network* (n 6) [224].

[59] *Ibid*, [104]. Elsewhere in his speech his Lordship was keen to stress that the notion that 'unlawful means' should mean the same in both unlawful means conspiracy and causing loss by unlawful means rested on nothing more than an assumption: *ibid*, [89].

[60] *Ibid*, [100].

[61] See M Lobban, 'Intentional and Economic Torts' in W Cornish *et al* (eds), *The Oxford History of the Laws of England: Volume XII – Private Law* (Oxford, Oxford University Press, 2010) 1065 *et seq*.

[62] H Carty, *An Analysis of the Economic Torts*, 2nd edn (Oxford, Oxford University Press, 2010) 120. In case it be thought that this is simply an infelicitous expression on her part, it is noteworthy that she makes exactly the same claim in H Carty, 'The Economic Torts in the 21st Century' (2008) 124 *LQR* 641, 668.

[63] *Rookes* (n 47) 1200–1201 (emphasis added).

Now, one vitally important consequence of attaching independent, normative significance to unlawful threats is that these then assume the mantle of the wrong for which a remedy is sought in any case of two-party intimidation. And it is just this wrong that creates the conceptual space for the idea – endorsed in *OBG* – that a case of three-party intimidation is a mere example or subspecies of the general tort of causing loss by unlawful means. Put another way: it is precisely because the threat is itself an actionable wrong that a third-party claimant seeking to invoke the unlawful means tort on the back of a threat made against an intermediary is able to do so. The unlawful threat constitutes the requisite unlawful means.

It cannot, however, be concluded from what has been said in the preceding paragraphs that the unlawful means tort and two-party intimidation employ *precisely the same* conception of unlawful means. It is certainly true that both torts require a civil wrong in order for the test of unlawful means to be met, but the civil wrongs that constitute unlawful means in relation to the unlawful means tort are not confined to unlawful threats. Thus, had there been, in *Douglas v Hello!*, a breach of confidence that *did affect the Douglases' freedom* to deal with *OK!* magazine, it seems likely that Lord Hoffmann would have reached a different conclusion about whether that tort was made out.

For the purposes of two-party intimidation, there is (just as with unlawful means conspiracy) no additional requirement that the threat should affect the liberty of the person at whom it is directed to deal commercially with a third party.

There are, then, three torts in which unlawful means comprise an essential ingredient of liability. But in each one an observably different meaning is attached to that term. In intimidation only unlawful threats count. In the tort of causing loss by unlawful means all actionable civil wrongs count provided they are liberty restricting. And in unlawful means conspiracy a host of legal wrongs – including civil wrongs of any stripe, common law crimes and acts that amount to a contempt of court – will meet the test.

C. Conclusion on Juridical Links and Distinctions

Two prominent, recurring aspects of the torts in view are the presence of an intentionality component and a requirement that there be use made by D of 'unlawful means'. But neither can be regarded as the source of juridical unity between the various actions. Indeed, it is a grave mistake to assume that they fulfil anything like this role. As Lords Sumption and Lloyd-Jones remarked in their joint speech in *JSC BTA Bank v Khrapunov*: '[s]ome of the elements of the torts, notably intention and unlawful means are common to more than one of them. But it is dangerous to assume that they have the same content in each context'.[64]

[64] *Khrapunov* (n 52) [6]. This exact point was reiterated with approval in *Racing Partnership Ltd v Sports Information Services Ltd* [2020] EWCA Civ 1300 (CA), [142] (Arnold LJ).

The trap of chasing simplicity (or at least uniformity of meaning) is one into which Carty seems to have fallen. In one article, she begins her analysis of what is meant by 'unlawful means' by sketching what she dubs the 'abstentionist policy' in *Allen v Flood*[65] and *OBG*. According to this supposed policy, a restrictive meaning is to be given to 'unlawful means' in order to limit the courts' powers of intervention in economic torts cases. The thinking runs thus: the fewer things that count as unlawful means, the narrower the scope of tortious liability. Having signalled her approval of this policy, Carty proceeds to criticise the expansive conception of unlawful means enunciated in *Total Network*. Her complaint is that the meaning attributed to 'unlawful means' in that case is 'at odds with the abstentionist agenda set by both *Allen* and *OBG*'.[66] But quite why this might constitute a valid criticism is unclear. After all, Carty openly admits that the courts, throughout the history of the economic torts, have vacillated between the so-called abstentionist policy and its rival, the 'interventionist policy'.[67] Both approaches, therefore, can be defended by reference to previous authority; and any preference for one policy over the other is inescapably a mere expression of her personal preference, and not one rooted in incontrovertible juridical orthodoxy.[68]

Furthermore, her dogged commitment to what was said in *Allen* might also be challenged on the footing that it is blind to the way the common law evolves.[69] Not infrequently in tort law, certain rules, concepts and doctrines undergo expansion in the usual process of incremental judicial exegesis of those rules, concepts and doctrines. The end result is the rather untidy common law of torts; but this untidiness is scarcely a revelation to anyone who knows this branch of the law well. And nowhere is the untidiness of tort law any more apparent than in relation to the various different meanings that have been given by the courts to the terms 'intention' and 'unlawful means'.

III. Structural Links and Distinctions

According to Tony Weir, 'while you can take direct action against a person's body or property, to ruin a person financially the action you take *must be indirect*, through another person, the source of his earnings or profits'.[70] If this were

[65] *Allen v Flood* [1898] AC 1 (HL).
[66] Carty (n 57) 405.
[67] *Ibid*, 393–99.
[68] Engagement with the politics associated with the economic torts is unnecessary for the purposes of this chapter; but it forms a central part of the discussion in the next one.
[69] See further chapter nine.
[70] T Weir, *A Casebook on Tort*, 10th edn (London, Sweet & Maxwell, 2000) 573 (emphasis added). This claim represents a hardening of his view over time given that, in an earlier text, he wrote less dogmatically that, 'one can bloody one's neighbour's nose unaided, but to ruin him *usually requires assistance*': see T Weir, 'Chaos or Cosmos: *Rookes*, *Stratford* and the Economic Torts' [1964] *CLJ* 225, 227 (emphasis added).

right, *and* if it were true that the economic torts genuinely are a set of actions confined to the protection of economic interests, it would necessarily follow that they would all conform to a three-party structure. But, in fact, neither of these claims is true. A person could easily be defrauded out of their life savings *directly*. There is therefore no *a priori* reason why all the torts considered in this book *must conform* to a three-party structure, even if, *arguendo*, we accept that their purpose is confined to the protection of economic interests.

An alternative reason for thinking that the economic torts must always function according to a three-party structure has been advanced by Allan Beever. Although he rightly rejects the idea that their common *raison d'être* is the protection of economic interests, he nonetheless holds firmly the conviction that, 'the so-called economic torts deal with cases in which one person attempts to control another *via the medium of a third party*'.[71] But this contention, too, is demonstrably without firm foundations. For, even if these torts were about the illegitimate, indirect control of others, as Beever suggests, just a moment's reflection would reveal that in *any case of conspiracy* the control is being exerted, by definition, by more than 'one person'. And although Beever gives the relevant part of his book – Part III – the title 'Indirect Control',[72] it is plain that not all of the economic torts conform to a three-party structure. Deceit, as noted already, is a prime example.

Now one possible response here would be that the term 'economic torts' is, properly, to be reserved for just the general economic torts. And, as we saw in chapter one, some authors adopt exactly this conception of the economic torts. This would exclude deceit from the list of actions that require an explanation. Remarkably, though, Beever does not accept this narrow conception: he specifically states that the economic torts are 'a set [of actions] that includes the torts of deceit, malicious falsehood [which, curiously, he re-names 'injurious falsehood' in chapter 11 of his book] and passing off'.[73] There is, then, no escaping the fact that deceit confounds his claim that the economic torts are ineluctably three-party torts.[74] And nor is it alone in doing so.

By definition, the very same point can be made by reference to cases of two-party intimidation. This is because, although there was some uncertainty concerning the future of this tort in the immediate wake of *OBG*, that uncertainty was laid to rest by the decision of the House of Lords in *Total Network* (where their Lordships relied heavily on two-party intimidation when it came to rescuing (or resurrecting) the tort of unlawful means conspiracy). And the significance of *Total Network* in relation to the structure of the economic torts did not stop there, for it was also expressly recognised that, on the facts of that case, the tort of unlawful

[71] Beever (n 2) 154 (emphasis added).

[72] *Ibid*, 99.

[73] *Ibid*, 100.

[74] The only possible salvation would require him to deny deceit is an economic tort as some jurists do. But even that manoeuvre is of limited use since (as discussed below) the conspiracy torts – universally considered to be economic torts – also often operate according to a two-party structure.

means conspiracy had been committed within a two-party framework. As Lord Hope put it: 'in this case there was no third party'.[75] The point was echoed in the speech of Lord Mance. He said:

> I accept that conspiracy can be categorised as a three- rather than two-party tort, in that liability depends on at least two persons joining together to injure another … Nevertheless, there is in my view a distinction between the infliction of harm through the intermediary of a third party (as in the case of the tort of causing harm by unlawful means under consideration in *OBG Ltd v Allan*) and the present situation where two wrongdoers join and act together to inflict injury directly upon another person or body.[76]

There is nothing here, of course, to say that liability for unlawful means conspiracy must always conform to a two-party structure. There may very well be cases in which D_1 and D_2 conspire to strike at C via a third party. As much is recognised in the current edition of *Clerk and Lindsell on Torts* where it states:

> a combination to cause loss to a claimant by threatening to break a contract with a third party *in order to persuade* that third party to cease dealing with the claimant can be treated as a conspiracy to commit the tort of intimidation.[77]

Any such case could therefore aptly be described as a three-party case of unlawful means conspiracy; and it is right to recognise the capacity of this tort to take either a two-party or three-party form.[78]

We saw at some length, in chapter three, that there are some commentators who insist that inducing breach of contract involves secondary or accessory liability and that it is not a tort proper. I acknowledged that there are arguments both ways, but ultimately defended the view that it is better seen as a freestanding tort (albeit a highly unusual one). What I did not do in that earlier chapter, however, is afford any great attention to the claim advanced by some that unlawful means conspiracy is best seen as a form of secondary liability. Nor do I do any more here than note that this conception has backers who are in no short supply of gravitas.[79] But insofar as this study has afforded primacy throughout to cases decided by our senior courts that are both crystal clear and authoritative in what they say, I feel justified in dismissing relatively swiftly this contention. Lord Walker emphatically quashed

[75] *Total Network* (n 6) [43].

[76] *Ibid*, [126]. As yet more evidence of Beever's wayward view of these torts, note that he claims, in spite of Lord Mance's very clear dictum, that 'causing loss by unlawful means and conspiracy are the same action, separated only by their unnecessary and invalid control mechanisms': Beever (n 2) 139.

[77] M Jones (ed), *Clerk and Lindsell on Torts*, 23rd edn (London, Sweet and Maxwell, 2020) 1800.

[78] *Fatimi Pty Ltd v Bryant* (2004) 59 NSWLR 678 was a two-party case in which the defendant sold off land at an undervalue to a fellow conspirator in order to prevent the claimant recovering a debt. The classic case of *Crofter v Veitch* (n 47) involved the infliction of harm via an intermediary: mill owners combined with trade union officials to persuade the third party (dockers) not to handle the claimant's yarn.

[79] See, eg, P Sales, 'The Tort of Conspiracy and Civil Secondary Liability' [1990] *CLJ* 491; PS Davies and P Sales, 'Intentional Harm, Accessories and Conspiracies' (2018) 134 *LQR* 69.

such an understanding of unlawful means conspiracy when he said in the *Total Network* case:

> any suggestion that the unlawful means conspiracy is a form of secondary liability, and must therefore have an actionable wrong as an essential ingredient, seems to me to be a circular argument which assumes what it sets out to prove.[80]

In the light of the foregoing paragraphs, it is clear that, in structural terms, the economic torts divide three ways. Inducing breach of contract, the unlawful means tort, passing off and injurious falsehood all follow what some consider to be a paradigmatic three-party structure.[81] The two conspiracy torts may take either a two- or three-party form; while deceit and intimidation (which now only exists in a two-party form) invariably conform to a purely bilateral structure. There is, in other words, just the same kind of disunity in relation to the structure of the economic torts as we observed in relation to their intentionality and unlawful means components. In the next section we shall see the pattern repeated when the spotlight switches to the various interests that these torts protect.

IV. Functional Links and Distinctions

In chapters three to six, I alighted upon various different *raisons d'être* for the torts considered in this book. We noted that only one of them – the tort of passing off – could accurately be described as being concerned purely with the protection of trade or business interests. In respect of most of the others, I highlighted various other forms of non-trade-related loss that the courts have treated (or at least recognised) as compensable. These included mental distress, anxiety and other such forms of emotional harm. Furthermore, careful analysis of *exactly* what was said in certain landmark decisions revealed that no objection rooted in the relevant authorities could be mounted against their being invoked in respect of yet other types of loss, such as loss of (or damage to) property.[82] The conclusion, to which this, I think, impels us, is that they cannot plausibly be portrayed as a close-knit

[80] *Total Network* (n 6) [104].

[81] Carty, for example, thinks that they should conform to this structure. She suggests that, 'after *OBG* it could be argued that the economic torts remained limited to their paradigm intermediary-use setting … [And] [t]his analysis would seem to be shaped by the fact that rivalrous intentional economic harm is unlikely to fit within the normal direct setting of tort law': Carty (n 57) 396. Her argument, however, is unpersuasive. She effectively claims that the economic torts should take a three-party form because that is the form that best lends itself to the protection of economic interests. But this, of course, presumes the very thing that must first to be shown, namely, that these torts genuinely are designed to protect economic interests.

[82] It is arguable that this was all but recognised in *Gilbert v Stone* (1641) Aleyn 35 – a case in which various persons intimidated the defendant into stealing the claimant's horse. On the facts, the claimant sued the defendant, but given that the court specifically recognised the intimidation of the defendant (saying (*ibid*): 'the defendant hath remedy against those that compelled him'), it is not much of a stretch to think of the claimant's loss as having been caused in a classic three-party intimidation scenario. And this, of course, would now be treated as an instance of the unlawful means tort.

family of civil wrongs, linked by a common, central concern to provide a remedy for harm caused to trade or business interests. And yet some commentators stick doggedly to this line.

Carty recognises the various departures from the protection of economic interests to which I have just adverted. But her treatment of these departures creates the impression that they constitute judicial aberrations or missteps. In the final chapter of her book, she remains insistent that the economic torts 'are all weapons in the policy to prevent "excessive" competition or economic endeavour. They are all about protecting your competitive edge – whether against lies, confusion or attacks on your commercial partners'.[83] She ends, in other words, just where she starts with the claim that 'these torts [should be seen] as protecting against the infliction of economic harm, against the background of competition'.[84]

Admittedly, her view plays out well in relation to some of the seminal cases. The momentous case of *Mogul Steamship Co Ltd v McGregor Gow & Co*[85] clearly centred on rival traders. And the early cases concerning disputes between trade unions and employers can also be portrayed in terms of litigants who were in economic competition with one another so long as one thinks of workers and employers as being economic competitors trading labour and wages respectively. Certainly, Cane takes this view. He writes:

> industrial action designed to improve wages and conditions is a form of competitive activity in the sense that the aim of the action is to achieve a redistribution of wealth from the employer to the employees, just as traders seek to divert wealth from their competitors to themselves.[86]

One momentous way in which the depiction of these torts as being means to control excessive competitive behaviour between economic rivals breaks down, is in relation to such central cases as *Allen* and *Rookes*. For both of these may aptly be regarded as labour v labour cases. In the former, the claimants were workers suing a union official. In the latter, another worker was suing former co-workers. Trade unions and co-workers are not an employee's trade rivals. Equally, it is easy to think of ways in which persons other than the claimant's trade rivals may either persuade a third party to break their contract with the claimant, or intimidate that third party into doing the same and thus trigger liability for inducing breach of contract[87] and causing loss by unlawful means,[88] respectively. Also, in much the

[83] Carty, *An Analysis* (n 62) 311.

[84] *Ibid*, 4.

[85] *Mogul Steamship Co Ltd v McGregor Gow & Co* [1892] AC 25 (HL).

[86] P Cane, *Tort Law and Economic Interests*, 2nd edn (Oxford, Oxford University Press, 1996) 472, fn 72.

[87] See, eg, *Stott v Gamble* [1916] 2 KB 504 (CA). The defendant licensing authority revoked the right to show a certain film at a theatre at which the claimant had obtained a contract to show a particular film for a fee. Although on the facts the defendant had a valid defence (public justification), the case illustrates the fact that licensing justices *could have been* liable for inducing a breach of contract without being rival film distributors.

[88] In *Garret v Taylor* (1620) Cro Jac 567, there is no suggestion that the defendant who threatened the claimant's would-be customers with mayhem was a trade rival. It is, however, hard to be sure given the brevity of the report.

same way, it is clear that conspirators need not be trade rivals of the claimant. The leading case of *Total Network* provides ample evidence in this regard (since the Inland Revenue is not a trader of any description). And there are also very clear dicta to this effect in relation to lawful means conspiracy.[89]

If we turn our attention to the misrepresentation torts, it is true to say that many of the leading cases do indeed fit the excessive economic behaviour paradigm. And yet a core claim of this book is that this characterisation of the actions in view must be rejected, that they are better regarded as having only a loose affiliation with one another. How then can such a claim be maintained? The answer is that, even within the setting of the misrepresentation torts, it is clear that economic interests of business competitors are not the be all and end all. In some key cases, the facts plainly obstruct their being seen in such terms. In others, the courts have clearly emphasised an altogether different rationale than the protection of trade and business interests.

Take, first, the foundational deceit case of *Derry v Peek*,[90] in which the claimant was deceived into *investing in* the defendants' company. By no stretch of the imagination can an investor in the defendants' business be regarded as a business rival. Indeed, 'business rival' seems a most inappropriate label to attach to any victim of deceit. The duped individual typically thinks that she is dealing with (rather than competing against) the defendant. Similarly, although many of the early cases of injurious falsehood undoubtedly involved commercial rivals – eg, defendants asserting a better title than the claimant to certain property – the landmark case of *Ratcliffe v Evans*[91] amply demonstrates that a newspaper proprietor can be held liable for this tort *even though* on no plausible grounds could he be regarded as the claimant's trade competitor.

The short point is that Carty and other monists adopt a demonstrably myopic view of the scope of the economic torts. A clear majority of the actions considered in this book have been used to do more than 'get the appropriate balance between policing competition and not unduly stifling it'.[92] And what is particularly telling, here, is the fact that this has been done in leading rather than minor, dubious or anomalous cases. If, however, it be thought that my claims so far about (1) these torts being able to protect a wide range of interests and (2) their being underpinned by non-economic rationales are rather light on authority, it is perhaps worth setting out in a bit more detail various further arguments and evidence that can be marshalled in support of these contentions.

[89] In *Gulf Oil (Great Britain) Ltd v Page* [1987] 2 Ch 327, 332–33, Parker LJ noted that defendants had 'no immediate interest of their own to protect against Gulf and no interest of their own to further as against Gulf' and yet there was 'a strong inference that the purpose of the [defamatory] display was simply to inflict upon Gulf the maximum possible damage … [and thus] a strong prima facie case in conspiracy to injure'.

[90] *Derry v Peek* (1889) 14 App Cas 337 (HL).

[91] *Ratcliffe v Evans* [1892] 2 QB 525 (CA).

[92] Carty, *An Analysis* (n 62) 311.

A. Torts Protecting a Range of Interests

In chapter three, I constructed an argument as to why – against the background of the ambivalence on the question in *OBG* – we should consider inducing breach of contract a freestanding tort. With this matter out of the way, I went on to consider the range of interests it protects. It was argued that, although it is inescapably an action tied to the interests generated by a contract, there is no reason to think that these must be commercial in nature. The simple fact is this: not all contracts have a commercial core. Contracts for the provision of medical or physiotherapy services could well result in damages in respect of setbacks to the claimant's health caused by a breach that has been induced. And where the contract in question is for the provision of entertainment or enjoyment, damages in respect of disappointment would be perfectly feasible.

In the tort of injurious falsehood, as noted in chapter six, the courts have not just allowed recovery in respect of consequential mental distress[93] and injured feelings.[94] They have also signalled a willingness to allow claims in respect of such losses to count as special damage in their own right.[95] Equally, within the tort of deceit, the courts have treated as compensable various non-economic losses including physical injury,[96] mental distress[97] and inconvenience.[98]

Besides these torts, in which there has been *express judicial recognition* of non-economic losses that are recoverable, there are also implicit suggestions in the case law to similar effect in relation to both unlawful means conspiracy and the tort of causing loss by unlawful means. In respect of the former, without specifying just what kinds of loss he had in mind, Lord Walker said in *Total Network* that 'the claimant need not be a trader who is injured in his trade'.[99] In relation to the latter, recognition must be unearthed in stages.

The first point to note is Lord Evershed's acknowledgement in *Rookes* that a claimant, A,

> might well, as a consequence of B's intimidation, suffer in many ways including health, and, if he did … his cause of action against B … would not be confined, by reference to the damage suffered, to interference with his business.[100]

The next point is that *Rookes* was reconceptualised in *OBG* as a case of causing loss by unlawful means. It follows from this that it would be fair to apply Lord Evershed's dictum to a case with suitable facts and allow recovery in respect

[93] *Joyce v Sengupta* [1993] 1 WLR 337 (CA).
[94] *Khodaparast v Shad* [2000] 1 WLR 618 (CA).
[95] There has even been some acknowledgement in the Supreme Court that an action based on injurious falsehood could well be brought in respect of physical injury where D untruthfully informs a surgeon that it is a patient's left leg that has been listed for amputation, when in fact it is her right leg: *Servier* (n 55) [85] (Lord Hamblen).
[96] *Langridge v Levy* (1837) 2 M&W 519.
[97] *Shelley v Paddock* [1980] QB 348 (CA).
[98] *Mafo v Adams* [1970] 1 QB 548 (CA).
[99] *Total Network* (n 6) [100].
[100] *Rookes* (n 47) 1194.

of injury to health on the basis of the unlawful means tort. To give one example, D may intimidate C's personal physiotherapist into treating C (against his better judgement) in such a way that C suffered some sort of physical setback. In any such case, it could not be complained that the facts fell foul of the so-called 'dealing requirement' we considered earlier; and the Supreme Court has recently left open the possibility of invoking the unlawful means tort in connection with non-economic losses.[101]

In respect of lawful means conspiracy, things are only slightly less clear. For one thing, in *Crofter Hand Woven Harris Tweed Co Ltd v Veitch*, Viscount Simon said in observably non-specific terms that 'the gist of the action is that damage was inflicted by defendants who combined together for the purpose of inflicting it'.[102] In addition, in *Gulf Oil (Great Britain) Ltd v Page*,[103] the Court of Appeal did not rule out the prospect of this tort being used to protect one's reputational interest in circumstances where the law of defamation would not be available.[104] So, although it cannot be said with a high degree of certainty that lawful means conspiracy can be used in conjunction with non-economic losses,[105] nor can this prospect be ruled out.

B. Torts with a Clear Alternative Rationale

As was seen in chapter five, in the tort of intimidation, the courts have repeatedly stressed the need for coercion. This, it may fairly be said, is what forms the gist of the tort.[106] In the *Newsgroup Newspapers* case Stuart-Smith J made clear that the tort is not complete unless the person who was the victim of the threat succumbs to the threat.[107] But firm insistence on coercion's centrality can be found in *Rookes* where Lord Devlin said that, '[t]he essence of the offence is coercion',[108] while Lord Evershed insisted that a threat which 'had a real and substantial coercive force … constituted a cause of action'.[109]

What these, and other dicta on the matter,[110] consistently urge is that it is the infringement of free agency by way of an unlawful threat that animates this tort.

[101] *Sevier* (n 55) [85] (Lord Hamblen).
[102] *Crofter v Veitch* (n 47) 444.
[103] *Gulf Oil* (n 89).
[104] The idea that lawful means conspiracy can be used to this end was, however, curtailed in the later case of *Lonrho Plc v Fayed (No 5)* [1994] 1 All ER 188 (CA). It was held that *damages* could not be awarded for injury to reputation (though so saying did nothing to rule out the prospect of injunctive relief, which is what had been sought in *Page*).
[105] For doubts about, but no outright rejection of, the prospect, see NJ McBride and R Bagshaw, *Tort Law*, 6th edn (London, Pearson, 2018) 671–72.
[106] For a fuller account of this argument, see Murphy (n 49).
[107] *Newsgroup Newspapers* (n 27) 204. My stressing the centrality of coercion is no way a denial of the need to show consequential harm. It is just that the suffering of measurable harm is best seen as a condition of actionability.
[108] *Rookes* (n 47) 1207. And notice the attention here to *injuria* rather than *damnum*.
[109] *Ibid*, 1189.
[110] See, eg, *Stratford & Son v Lindley* [1965] AC 269 (HL), 283 (Lord Denning MR).

The focus is squarely upon the fact that the claimant has been forced into a course of conduct that he would not himself choose to pursue. As I have argued at length elsewhere, the self-same interest animates the tort of deceit.[111] For in that setting, too, the claimant's complaint centres on the fact that she was caused by the defendant to make a decision that she otherwise would not choose to make. Stephen Smith is another jurist to have noted the connection (albeit that, for him, the concern is with how this link plays out in the contract arena). He writes,

> a court may deny a plaintiff's request to enforce a contractual right that was obtained by a fraudulent … misrepresentation on the same basis it may deny such a request when the contractual right was obtained by the plaintiff's wrongful threat.[112]

C. Conclusion on Functional Distinctions

It is incontrovertibly true that the economic torts cannot be unified according to an unswerving and shared focus on the protection of economic interests. A much more defensible view – and the one advanced here – is that properly unpicked, the leading cases often point to various non-economic interests that can perfectly well be protected by these torts. And in respect of some torts, a clear rationale that has nothing to do with economic welfare, and everything to do with decision-making autonomy, has repeatedly been advanced by the courts.

V. Overall Conclusion

In scholarly treatments of the so-called economic torts, the premise of Lord Wedderburn's famous comment that they 'have lacked their Atkin'[113] seems seldom to have been questioned.[114] Indeed, it seems broadly to be assumed by a sizeable number of commentators that these torts are (or ought to be) capable of being rationalised according to some or other commonality. There are even some judges who think this way, who believe, in other words, that there should be juridical consistency between the various actions. For example, in one case decided at the beginning of the twenty-first century, Laddie J remarked:

> There is much to commend the suggestion that the principles which apply to economic torts should be consistent with each other. After all, these are creations of the common law and it is difficult to see why, for example, an unlawful act which is sufficient to ground a cause of action for unlawful interference with trade should not also be sufficient to ground an action for unlawful means conspiracy and conversely why an unlawful act, if any, which is insufficient to support one should not also be insufficient

[111] J Murphy, 'Misleading Appearances in the Tort of Deceit' [2016] *CLJ* 301.
[112] SA Smith, *Contract Theory* (Oxford, Oxford University, Press, 2004) 367.
[113] KW Wedderburn, 'Rocking the Torts' (1983) 46 *MLR* 224, 229.
[114] One notable exception, already mentioned, is Stevens (n 8) 297.

> to support the other. If different types of unlawfulness will support different common law causes of action it would give rise to a degree of obscurity in the law which serves no useful purpose.[115]

Yet, as we have seen, this particular line of argument was openly rejected in *Total Network*. No-one put it more vividly that Lord Neuberger when he observed that, the economic torts 'present problems even if they are considered individually (and yet more problems arise if they are treated as a genus)'.[116] It is true that in *OBG* Lord Hoffmann made a valiant effort to rationalise the economic torts by proposing that we 'return to the two torts identified by Lord Watson in *Allen v Flood*'.[117] Yet the resuscitation in *Total Network* of unlawful means conspiracy, two-party intimidation and lawful means conspiracy almost immediately put an end to that ambition.

In my view, the Law Lords were on very solid ground in doing this in *Total Network*, since Lord Hoffmann seems to have read into Lord Watson's speech in *Allen v Flood*, rather more than Lord Watson actually intended should be read into it. The precise words used by the latter were as follows: '[t]here are, in my opinion, two grounds only upon which a person who procures the act of another can be made legally responsible for its consequences'.[118] This statement, *pace* Lord Hoffmann, cannot be equated with the view that *all* of the so-called economic torts can either be repackaged as cases of inducing breach of contract, or causing loss by unlawful means. The barrier to such an interpretation is the carefully inserted qualifier that what was being said was intended to be applied only where 'a person procures the act of another'. In other words, Lord Watson was only addressing those torts where A in some way or other causes B to act to the detriment of C. There is nothing in this qualifier that could possibly impact deceit or two-party intimidation. And nor need it *necessarily* impact either of the conspiracy torts; for as we have seen, both versions of conspiracy may be committed directly – that is, without the involvement of an intermediary. Furthermore, in *Allen* itself, Lord Macnaghten was perfectly aware of the fundamental difference between cases involving the unlawful means tort and cases involving conspiracy. He said:

> in my opinion the decision of this case can have no bearing on any case which involves the element of oppressive combination. The vice of that form of terrorism commonly known by the name of 'boycotting', and other forms of oppressive combination, seems to me to depend on considerations which are, I think, in the present case conspicuously absent.[119]

Rather than there being simplicity and elegance in relation to the so-called economic torts, what we find is a group of eight distinct torts that are characterised, in various ways, by a number of factors that speak more to their mutual independence than their unity. They diverge significantly in juridical terms, in structural terms and in functional terms. They will, I think, be awaiting their Atkin indefinitely.

[115] *Michaels v Taylor Woodrow Developments Ltd* [2001] 2 WLR 224, [22].
[116] *Total Network* (n 6) [216].
[117] *OBG* (n 15) [33].
[118] *Allen* (n 65) 96.
[119] *Ibid*, 153.

8

Genesis and Evolution

I. Introduction

This chapter seeks to demonstrate that – although they are supposed by many to have a common *raison d'être*, a shared purpose – the various economic torts have nonetheless emerged and developed in a fairly ad hoc and un-coordinated way. It will contest the core claim of Hazel Carty – probably the leading commentator in the field – that the key to understanding the development, and key juridical features, of these torts can be gleaned from an appreciation of the influence exerted by two competing policies. According to her, 'the real development of *all these torts* took place in the late nineteenth century' and '[t]o understand this development it is important to underline [that] the choices made by the judges in this era … were the result of two antithetical policies', namely 'abstentionism' and 'interventionism'.[1] In using these terms, what she means is (respectively) the absence and presence of a general judicial willingness to set limits on what can be done to advance one's own economic interests at the expense of those of one's competitors.

I reject the simple, binary nature of this analysis. I disagree in particular with the contention that the 'real development' of the actions in view took place when she says it did, that is, in the late nineteenth century. For, although this period was unquestionably significant, the claim that Carty makes is not in fact true of 'all these torts'. Moreover, I would also argue that gaining a full understanding of the development of the economic torts requires that an altogether more complex story be told of their emergence and subsequent development by several generations of judges. And I think that this more complex – more complete – story serves to reinforce the central claim of the previous chapter, namely, that there is more that divides than unites the torts considered in this book.

The alternative account, presented in this chapter, identifies a sizeable range of factors that have all left their imprint on the content and contours of the actions in view. By acknowledging this diverse range of influences, my aim is twofold: first, to render intelligible the various peculiarities – often glibly described as anomalies – that characterise some of these torts; and secondly, to explain the various twists and turns that they have taken in the course of their development.

[1] H Carty, *An Analysis of the Economic Torts*, 2nd edn (Oxford, Oxford University Press, 2010) 5 (emphasis added).

The analysis proceeds as follows. In section II, attention is devoted to the significance of the dates at which certain landmark cases were decided. For as we shall see, so doing helps ground the claim that those cases can best be understood as reflective of a (then) prevailing ideology or public sentiment. Recognising the significance of timing also helps to explain why various apparent *volte faces* might have occurred in the course of the development of these torts: as one particular dominant ideology or public sentiment gave way to another, so too did the law keep step.[2] Thus, although Carty is quite right to identify the tussle between capital and labour at the turn of the twentieth century as an important factor behind the creation and early development of *some* of the general economic torts,[3] the struggle between employers and unions offers no explanation of the various novel uses to which they have since been put in the twenty-first century. That the influence of industrial relations should have waned is, of course, unsurprising given that the problems posed by closed shops, secondary pickets and winters of discontent are pretty much things of the past.[4] If, however, we regard recent developments in the law as being products of a distinct modern era, with its own concerns and pervasive ideology, they appear much less aberrant and incoherent than when measured against the much-too-simplistic yardstick of the regulation of competitive behaviour by trade rivals.[5]

For the purposes of this section, three time-related influences stand out for comment. First, the fact that many of the foundational principles of the general economic torts were forged on the anvil of late nineteenth century industrial disputes which posed a series of rather novel challenges for the courts. The second spirit-of-the-age influence was the marked judicial distrust of juries that existed (again) in the latter part of the nineteenth century. The third was the indirect effect of legislation introduced during the twentieth century which, on the one hand, created certain immunities for trade unions and, on the other, gave legal effect to a growing popular concern for consumer welfarism.

In section III, attention shifts to the effect that political considerations have played in the development of these torts. The phrase 'political considerations' is used here as an umbrella term encompassing three different, though related, factors. The first of them is a discernible judicial commitment to the liberty of the individual in the late nineteenth and early twentieth centuries. It is sometimes referred to as individualism. And although it had nothing specifically to do with

[2] For a fairly sophisticated argument along broadly similar lines, see J Stapleton, *Three Essays on Torts* (Oxford, Oxford University Press, 2021) 4–10.

[3] HW Arthurs, 'Tort Liability for Strikes in Canada: Some Problems of Judicial Workmanship' (1960) 38 *Canadian Bar Review* 346, 362.

[4] They were, of course, still around in the 1960s when *Rookes v Barnard* [1964] AC 1129 (HL) was decided, giving the stamp of approval to a tort of intimidation, hence Carty's observation that, 'in the 1960s and 1970s the further growth and development of these torts sprang from judicial alarm at the disruption caused by trade union activity (and indeed by unofficial action)': Carty (n 1) 11.

[5] In any event, as noted in chapters one and seven, some of the milestone cases involved litigation between labour and labour: *Rookes*, *ibid*, and *Allen v Flood* [1898] AC 1 (HL) are obvious examples!

the economic torts, it assuredly impacted their development. The second political consideration is a more or less enduring judicial preference for free and competitive markets. This policy – dubbed abstentionism by Carty – was closely bound up with the economic torts as they were initially conceived. But it was not a policy whose influence was confined to these torts. It also affected other areas of private law, such as the law of contract.[6] The last political influence was an early *judicial hostility* towards trade unions (which should not be confused with a fear of the public disorder that such unions could cause). As we shall see, there was a fairly widespread distrust of unionism among judges at the end of the nineteenth century. But in the case of a handful of *key* judges – by which I mean judges who decided landmark cases – there was raw contempt, rooted in personal political convictions that were, at best, thinly concealed.

In sections IV and V the spotlight turns to two further factors – exclusively twentieth and twenty-first century phenomena – that have also helped shape the torts with which we are concerned. They are, respectively, the unusually high degree of influence that has been enjoyed in this setting by the work of a select number of prominent scholars, and the salience ascribed to certain types of litigants in various milestone cases. In relation to this second matter, as we shall see, the courts in recent years have made an obvious effort to extend the use of the economic torts beyond the classic framework of trade competition in order to bring within the maw of the law various forms of egregious conduct that might otherwise escape legal sanction.

Section VI concludes with a contention, namely that, given tort law's role as the common law's Swiss army knife,[7] it is neither, surprising nor especially alarming, that the torts considered in this book have developed in an observably unsystematic fashion.

II. *Zeitgeist*

There is nothing very novel in the observation that developments in tort law are often intimately bound up with what, at the relevant time, were the prevailing social conditions and ideology. For example, as Mitchell has carefully demonstrated, the mood music supplied by two world wars exerted an appreciable influence over the way in which pockets of tort law developed during the relevant periods of time.[8]

[6] See, eg, PS Atiyah, *The Rise and Fall of Freedom of Contract* (Oxford, Oxford University Press, 1979) 464: 'The classical model of contract law … left each party to a contract to rely on his own judgment … Neither party owed duties to the other to volunteer information, or even to undeceive him when he plainly laboured under some misapprehension. Further, there was no presumption that the terms of the contract bore any particular relationship to the price agreed upon.'

[7] This metaphor is taken from A Beever, *Rediscovering the Law of Negligence* (Oxford, Hart Publishing, 2007) 197.

[8] For details, see P Mitchell, *A History of Tort Law 1900–1950* (Cambridge, Cambridge University Press, 2014) Ch 2.

Thus, the fairly unsympathetic approach that was taken towards a Scottish fishwife who attempted to sue in negligence for the effects of nervous shock was, according to one distinguished Law Lord, based on 'a robust wartime view of the ability of the ordinary person to suffer horror and bereavement without ill effect'.[9] The judiciary made no secret of the fact that it felt obliged to develop the law in line with the extant material conditions of life. And a particularly pertinent acknowledgement that the courts will mould and apply the law to fit prevailing conditions can be found in the speech of Lord Herschell in *Allen v Flood*. He said: '[i]t is the function of the Courts to apply established legal principles to the changing circumstances and conditions of human life'.[10] Similarly, Letwin – in an article concerned with the law's treatment of those exploiting (or seeking to exploit) monopoly power – observes that, 'the common law at any given time reflects the economic theories and policies then favored by the community, and may change as radically as those theories and policies'.[11]

For present purposes, one of the most influential factors in relation to the genesis and early development of the economic torts was the rise of trade unionism during the latter part of the nineteenth century. Indeed, it is no exaggeration to say that the emergence of civil liability for conspiracy represents, in significant measure, the civil law's attempt to 'tame the beast'. It is certainly widely recognised that, around this time, the law on conspiracy 'became entangled with the wider debate on the emerging trade unions and labour competition'.[12] The full details of this story – most comprehensively dealt with in an exemplary work of legal history by Michael Klarman[13] – cannot be recounted here. But a fair summary of what happened was supplied by Lord Walker in *Revenue and Customs Commissioners v Total Network SL* when he highlighted the fact that there was:

> at the end of the 19th century … [a] largely unarticulated … [but nonetheless] deep suspicion which the governing class had, in Georgian and Victorian England, of collective action in the political and economic spheres, as potential threats to the constitution and the framework of society'.[14]

His Lordship was clear, too, that the judiciary formed part of this 'governing class';[15] and the significance of the particular political sympathies of some key judges during this period is a matter to which I shall return in more detail below.

[9] *White v Chief Constable of South Yorkshire* [1999] 2 AC 455 (HL), 501 (Lord Hoffmann).

[10] *Allen* (n 5) 127–28.

[11] WL Letwin, 'The English Common Law Concerning Monopolies' (1954) 21 *University of Chicago Law Review* 355, 355.

[12] H Carty, 'The Modern Functions of the Economic Torts: Reviewing the English, Canadian, Australian and New Zealand Positions' [2015] *CLJ* 261, 266.

[13] MJ Klarman, 'The Judges Versus the Unions: The Development of British Labour Law, 1867–1913' (1989) 75 *Virginia Law Review* 1487.

[14] *Revenue and Customs Commissioners v Total Network SL* [2008] 1 AC 1174 (HL) [78]. This understanding of the origins of tort liability for conspiracy was endorsed in the joint speech of Lords Sumption and Lloyd-Jones in *JSC BTA Bank v Khrapunov* [2018] UKSC 19 (SC) [7].

[15] *Total Network*, *ibid*, [78].

However, it is apt to mark here the general attitude in society towards trade unions at this time. Of especial note is the fact that the 'Sheffield Outrages' of the 1860s – a series of violent acts, including two murders, perpetrated against non-union labour – generated a good deal of anti-union sentiment among the general public. Indeed, in the wake of these 'outrages', a Royal Commission was established to investigate union practices; and as Cornish and Clark note, on the heels of what happened in Sheffield, '[e]ven the moderate *Daily News* could insist "the unions must be stamped out as a public nuisance"'.[16] So widespread was the condemnation of what happened in Sheffield, that even some people who were generally sympathetic to the trade union movement, admitted that they were appalled at the assaults and the destruction of property that took place. For instance, one member of that Commission – the Oxford jurist, Frederic Harrison (who was a regular contributor to the trade unionist publication, *The Beehive*, and a firm supporter of the trade union movement) – thought that, if such acts of violence became commonplace, they would 'undoubtedly demand the unqualified extirpation of unionism'.[17]

Happily, there was no repeat of the Sheffield Outrages either in Sheffield or anywhere else. But high profile union protests about members' vulnerability to criminal prosecution[18] on what were thought to be inadequate grounds, did persist well into the next decade. Thus, quite regardless of the particular *political* beliefs of the judges at this time, there was certainly a fear on their part about the threat to public order posed by trade unions. It was a fear that lingered into the early years of the twentieth century, in part fuelled by reports (in the largely pro-capital press) of threats of 'organised terrorism'.[19] Also, as one anonymously written article in the *Solicitors' Journal* in 1905 records, the more lenient treatment shown by the courts to combinations in the form of cartels was thought justifiable on the basis that '[w]orkmen's disputes lead more readily than the rivalry of traders to violence and personal oppression'.[20]

If we add to the mix the fact that the Conspiracy and Protection of Property Act 1875 significantly curtailed the prospect of criminal sanctions being imposed upon workers taking industrial action, it is easy to see why the courts felt obliged to act. They did so, as Bob Simpson explains, by creating novel forms of liability in tort. In his words:

> When the trade union legislation … placed important limits on the criminal sanctions which could be imposed on those organising or taking part in strikes or other forms of industrial action, some of the judiciary responded positively to employers' recourse to

[16] WR Cornish and G de N Clark, *Law and Society in England 1750–1950* (London, Sweet and Maxwell, 1989) 315.

[17] *Eleventh and Final Report of the Royal Commission on Trade Unions* (1869) 40.

[18] There were, in particular, two offences under the Combinations of Workmen Act 1925 for which a criminal sanction might be imposed: they were molestation and obstruction. For application of these offences to seemingly innocuous trade union picketing, see *R v Druitt* (1867) 16 LTR 855.

[19] *The Times*, 20 December 1903 (editorial concerning the *Taff Vale* case (discussed below)).

[20] (1905) 49 *Solicitors' Journal* 455, 455.

> civil proceedings as a reaction to actual or threatened strikes .... *Quinn v Leathem* and other decisions at the beginning of the twentieth century showed that the judiciary were reluctant to tolerate [certain] labour practices.[21]

A second factor that contributed to the shaping of the economic torts in the latter part of the nineteenth century was the judicial distrust of juries. During this period, the judges' taking the first tentative steps towards a duty of care idea that, in time, would become the cornerstone of the modern tort of negligence, was in significant measure attributable to their desire to arrogate to themselves (under the rubric of duty) matters that had previously been left to the discretion of juries to whom it fell to determine whether the defendant had failed to meet the standard of conduct demanded by the law. More specifically, the courts transformed into a doctrinal (and therefore, legal) question, something that had previously been considered a question of fact. This meant that they could, at an anterior stage, exert greater control over the outcome of cases that would probably otherwise have attracted claimant-friendly treatment at the hands of jurors.

As is well known, this desire for greater judicial control was particularly prominent in cases in which judges did not trust juries not to exhibit a strong predisposition towards injured claimants who were seeking to sue a corporate defendant.[22] This distrust of juries was openly admitted by Lord Bramwell in one case of malicious prosecution – a tort in which the requirement of an absence of reasonable and probable cause was likewise transformed into a question of law. In *Abrath v North Eastern Railway Co*, he said: 'everyone ... knows that the only reason why a railway company is selected for an action of this sort is that a jury would be more likely to give a verdict against a company than against an individual'.[23]

More pertinently for present purposes, this self-same distrust of juries is also apparent in the context of the economic torts. In *Lumley v Gye*, very clear salience was afforded to malice on the part of the defendant.[24] Its centrality to liability for inducing breach of contract was subsequently confirmed by the majority of the Court of Appeal in *Bowen v Hall*. Longmore LJ was very clear in this respect. He said:

> if a man endeavours to persuade another to break his contract and succeeds in his endeavour, yet if he does this without what the law calls 'malice,' the damage which results, however great, is not in itself a cause of action.[25]

[21] B Simpson, 'Trade Disputes Legislation and the Economic Torts' in TT Arvind and J Steele (eds), *Tort Law and the Legislature* (Oxford, Hart Publishing, 2012) 127–28.

[22] For a particularly good account, see DJ Ibbetson, 'The Tort of Negligence in the Common Law in the Nineteenth and Twentieth Centuries' in EJH Schrage (ed), *Negligence: The Comparative Legal History of the Law of Torts* (Berlin, Duncker & Humblot, 2001).

[23] *Abrath v North Eastern Railway Co* (1886) 11 App Cas 247 (HL), 252.

[24] *Lumley v Gye* (1853) 2 El & Bl 216, 224, 233 and 238 (Crompton, Erle and Wightman JJ, respectively).

[25] *Bowen v Hall* (1881) 6 QBD 333 (CA), 343. In similar vein, Brett LJ stated, '[m]erely to persuade a person to break his contract, may not be wrongful in law or fact ... But if the persuasion be used for the

Coleridge LJ, however, dissented; and his reason for so doing stemmed in part from his having very clear doubts about the ability of juries to deal with such issues. He said, 'I think the inquiries to which this view of the law would lead are dangerous and inexpedient inquiries for courts of justice; judges are not very fit for them, and *juries are very unfit*'.[26]

It was ultimately Coleridge LJ's view that prevailed. Thus, roughly two decades after *Bowen* had been decided, Lord Macnaghten made clear in *Quinn v Leathem* that malice was no longer an essential component in the tort of inducing breach of contract.[27] This juridical transformation appears firmly to have been linked to a worry about juries handling questions of malice. True: Lord Macnaghten did not overtly echo in *Quinn v Leathem* the fear that had been expressed by Coleridge LJ; but that he did in fact share that fear is beyond doubt. Just a few years earlier, in *Allen v Flood*, he had made plain what he thought about the fitness of juries to deal with questions of malice. In addressing the question of whether liability ought ever to be tethered to a defendant's malicious acts, he expressed concern about, not the possibility, but what he saw as the '*probability* of injustice being done by juries in a class of cases in which there would be ample room for speculation and *wide scope for prejudice*'.[28] Lord Herschell was of a similar view. He could not have been more alarmist when he said:

> I can imagine no greater danger to the community than that a jury should be at liberty to impose the penalty of paying damages for acts which are otherwise lawful, because they choose, without any legal definition of the term, to say that they are malicious. … The result would be to put all our actions at the mercy of a particular tribunal whose view of their propriety might differ from our own.[29]

And so it was that one of the most important decisions in the field of the economic torts was to an appreciable extent influenced by a judicial perception of there being a danger of biased decision-making by juries. This hostility towards malice-based liability carried with it a rejection of the prima facie tort doctrine[30] which figured prominently in the development of the economic torts on the other side of the Atlantic.[31] But it was a rejection of the prima facie tort doctrine that cannot solely be attributed to a perception that that principle was *juridically* unsound.

indirect purpose of injuring the plaintiff, or of benefiting the defendant at the expense of the plaintiff, it is a malicious act which is in law and in fact a wrong': *ibid*, 338.

[26] *Ibid*, 344 (emphasis added).

[27] *Quinn v Leathem* [1901] AC 495 (HL), 510.

[28] *Allen* (n 5) 153 (emphasis added).

[29] *Ibid*, 118.

[30] Under this doctrine, the intentional infliction of harm by an act that is ordinarily lawful will be treated as a tort if it is motivated by malice. For discussion of it (and criticism on pragmatic grounds), see T Weir, *Economic Torts* (Oxford, Clarendon Press, 1997) 73.

[31] See *Tuttle v Buck* 119 NW 946 (Minn 1909). (A wealthy banker set up a barber's shop in the vicinity of one owned by the claimant, and he did so purely to undercut the latter's prices and thereby drive him out of business.)

The time at which particular actions crystalised has also been significant in the context of the misrepresentation economic torts. Passing off, in particular, can be seen to have been influenced by prevailing ideologies, both at its inception and, subsequently, in the course of its development. In *Erven Warnink BV v J Townend & Sons (Hull) Ltd*, in the course of discussing the misrepresentation limb of the tort, Lord Diplock specifically noted the fact that the common law, at the time the action first got going, was very much a reflection of the then ascendant credo of *caveat emptor*. And he also suggested that, just as successive governments had introduced consumer welfarist legislation in line with public sentiment, the courts should follow suit in their development of the common law. As may be recalled from chapter six, he said this:

> The market in which the action for passing off originated was no place for the mealy mouthed; advertisements are not on affidavit; exaggerated claims by a trader about the quality of his wares … [were] permitted by the common law as venial 'puffing'… Parliament, however, beginning in the 19th century has progressively intervened in the interests of consumers to impose on traders a higher standard of commercial candour than the legal maxim *caveat emptor* calls for … [and] the increasing recognition by Parliament of the need for more rigorous standards of commercial honesty is a factor which should not be overlooked by a judge … [Thus] [w]here over a period of years there can be discerned a steady trend in legislation which reflects the view of successive Parliaments as to what the public interest demands in a particular field of law, development of the common law in that part of the same field which has been left to it ought to proceed upon a parallel rather than a diverging course.[32]

Over time, the courts became markedly less tolerant of misleading descriptions of products, and in this way the tort of passing off acquired an increased capacity to reduce the scope for consumer confusion.[33]

That *Zeitgeist* should have played such an important role in relation to the introduction of the economic torts would not have struck Dicey as odd or alarming. He, after all, in his *Lectures on the Relation between Law and Public Opinion in England During the Nineteenth Century* remarked as long ago as 1905 that, '[n]owhere have changes in popular convictions or wishes found anything like such rapid and immediate expression in alterations of the law as they have in Great Britain during the nineteenth century, and more especially during the last half thereof'.[34] I imagine also that Dicey would have been equally unsurprised to see further such changes in popular convictions exert a comparable effect on the twentieth century development of those torts.

[32] *Erven Warnink BV v J Townend & Sons (Hull) Ltd* [1979] AC 731 (HL), 742.

[33] Curiously, Lord Diplock's words had more of an effect on other elements of the tort of passing off than the one that lay at the heart of the *Erven Warnink* case. For details, see J Murphy, '*Erven Warnink v Townend* (1979)' in J Gardner *et al* (eds), *Landmark Cases in Consumer Law* (Oxford, Hart Publishing, 2022).

[34] AV Dicey, *Lectures on the Relation between Law and Public Opinion in England During the Nineteenth Century* (London, Macmillan, 1905) 8.

III. Politics

A. The Commitment to Individualism

It is all too easy to treat the Victorian judges' commitment to individualism and the hostility shown by some of them towards trade unions as mere opposite sides of the same coin. But I nonetheless think that to do so is a mistake. The Bench during this era accepted that the Trade Union Act 1871 had abolished the prospect of trade unionists being held criminally liable for conspiracies in restraint of trade. And it was accepted, too, that this Act eliminated the possibility that trade union agreements could be struck down as void or voidable on the basis of their unlawfulness.[35] The courts even acknowledged without criticism the extension of trade unions' criminal law immunity under the Conspiracy and Protection of Property Act 1875. But certain judges took a markedly different view when it came to union activities that interfered with individual liberty. Thus, as Klarman notes, although the courts recognised that it was lawful to join a union and make union agreements, they nonetheless held it to be:

> impermissible to: (1) compel unwilling members of a union to abide by such an agreement; (2) coerce an employer into conceding the union's demands by threatening a (perfectly lawful) strike; (3) persuade, even peacefully, non-union labor to stay away from a struck shop; or (4) pressure workers to join a union.[36]

At work here was a concern to protect individualism rather than a desire per se to suppress unions. It was a concern that went beyond the parameters of the economic torts. For example, it was manifest, too, in the way the law of negligence first began to take shape during the nineteenth century. As Ibbetson observes:

> [t]he acute individualism which had characterised Victorian England … [made] it obvious that an individual who caused harm to another while pursuing his own economic self-interest should be liable only if it could be shown that he had not taken reasonable care.[37]

But perhaps predictably, this concern for individualism was especially pronounced in the context of the formulation of the early iterations of the general economic torts.

The tone was set in 1967 in *R v Druitt* – a case decided before the introduction of either of the two Acts mentioned above. It was a case concerning peaceful picketing, an activity that could lead to a conviction for the crime of obstruction. In that case, Baron Bramwell held that, 'the liberty of a man's mind and will, to say how he should bestow himself and his means, his talents, and his industry,

[35] Trade Union Act 1871, ss 2–3.
[36] Klarman (n 13) 1561.
[37] Ibbetson (n 22) 259.

is as much a subject of the law's protection as is that of his body'.[38] Likewise, Sir William Erle, in his extra-judicial capacity as chairman of the 1867–1869 Royal Commission on Trade Unions, wrote:

> [e]very person has a right under the law, as between him and his fellow subjects, to full freedom in disposing of his own labour or his own capital according to his own will. It follows that every other person … is prohibited from any obstruction to the fullest exercise of this right which can be made compatible with the exercise of similar rights by others.[39]

Klarman doubtless goes too far in stating that 'most of the major judicial decisions in British trade union law from the early 1890s until the First World War can be understood as an effort to return to the mid-Victorian regime of unfettered individualism', for other considerations were also treated as salient. But even so, the courts' desire to protect and promote individualism certainly played its part in the landmark decision in *Quinn* which, it is submitted, is far too simply described when it is portrayed as being merely an example of the court following an interventionist agenda. In it, Lord Brampton not only cited with approval the words of both Baron Bramwell and Sir William Erle just quoted,[40] he also added that

> [t]he Legislature in conferring upon trades unions such privileges as are contained in the Trade Union Acts … has not conferred upon any association or any member of it a licence to obstruct or interfere with the freedom of any other person in carrying on his business or bestowing his labour in the way he thinks fit.[41]

In saying this, Lord Brampton was not single-mindedly seeking to regulate competitive dealings as per the policy of interventionism. Rather, his overwhelming concern was to defend individual liberties.

B. Faith in Competitive Markets

Alongside the commitment to individualism among English judges in the latter part of the nineteenth century, there was also widespread judicial support for free, competitive markets. Like their belief in individualism, the judges' acceptance of the virtues of free-competition – something that persists even today[42] – deserves to be seen separately from the trenchant hostility that at least some of them had towards trade unions. The reason for my saying this is that competition between economic actors need not – and typically does not – involve trade unions: it is an

[38] *R v Druitt* (n 18) 858.
[39] *Eleventh and Final Report of the Royal Commission on Trade Unions* (n 17) 77.
[40] *Quinn* (n 27) 525.
[41] *Ibid*, 526.
[42] See, eg, *Total Network* (n 14) [142], where Lord Nicholls remarked: '[c]ompetition between businesses regularly involves each business taking steps to promote itself at the expense of the other … Far from prohibiting such conduct, the common law seeks to encourage and protect it'.

altogether more widespread phenomenon which plays out, ordinarily, in relation to rival traders.

That the judiciary did generally favour competitive markets at the time that the economic torts were first being crafted seems clear enough. Based on the evidence he managed to unearth, one distinguished legal historian concludes that, the Victorian judges were 'influenced by philosophical radicalism and political economy, inclining them to believe in market competition and the natural selection of the economically fit'.[43] But even before the Victorian era – as far back as the middle ages, in fact – the English courts had vigorously favoured competitive markets.[44] By the nineteenth century, there was so much judicial support for competitive practices that, according to Letwin, it was fair to say that, '[t]he common law put a higher value on the freedom of entrepreneurs to use any means short of violence to outstrip competitors than on the right of the public to enjoy the advantages of competition'.[45]

This general approach certainly had its impact on some of the foundational cases within in the economic torts setting, including some in which there was no trade union presence. In *Mogul Steamship Co Ltd v McGregor Gow & Co*, for example, Bowen LJ began by setting out a list of prohibited acts (such as threatening violence against a rival's customers or inducing them to breach their contracts with the claimant). He then proceeded to condone what the defendants had done in that particular case on the basis that they were mere acts of aggressive (but not excessive or illegitimate) competition. In his words:

> They [the defendants] have done nothing more against the plaintiffs than pursue to the bitter end a war of competition waged in the interest of their own trade. To the argument that a competition so pursued ceases to have a just cause or excuse when there is ill-will or a personal intention to harm, it is sufficient to reply (as I have already pointed out) that there was here no personal intention to do any other or greater harm to the plaintiffs than such as was necessarily involved in the desire to attract [a greater market share].[46]

In *Allen*, Lord James was conspicuously, positively in favour of moulding the law along pro-competition lines. In the context of his consideration of whether it should be regarded as tortious to induce one person not to contract with another, he objected:

> Every competitor for a contract who alleged that he was the best person to fulfil it would be liable to an action. Take the case of an architect who seeks to be employed

[43] J Getzler, 'The Fate of the Civil Jury in Late Victorian England: Malicious Prosecution as a Test Case' in K O'Donovan and GR Rubin (eds), *Human Rights and Legal History: Essays in Honour of Brian Simpson* (Oxford, Oxford University Press, 2000) 207.

[44] FD James, 'Historical Development of the Law of Business Competition' (1926) 35 *Yale Law Journal* 905.

[45] W Letwin, 'The English Common Law Concerning Monopolies' (1954) 21 *University of Chicago Law Review* 355, 379.

[46] *Mogul Steamship Co Ltd v McGregor Gow & Co* (1889) 23 QBD 598 (CA), 614 (affirmed [1892] AC 25).

> to the exclusion of his rivals. He says: 'My plans are the best, and following them will produce the best house at the least cost. Therefore employ me and not A or B'. If he be so employed the architect would, according to the dicta in *Bowen v Hall*, be liable to an action at the suit of his rivals. For he has induced a person not to enter into a contract with a third person, and his object clearly was to benefit himself at the expense of such third person.[47]

Insofar as the courts were prepared in key cases to allow the perceived desirability of free competition to decide who should be the winners and losers, it is arguably – but only arguably – appropriate to describe the courts as pursuing an abstentionist agenda.[48] However, as should be clear by now, these were not the only relevant cases, and abstentionism was by no means the only (or even dominant) factor that helped mould the economic torts as a whole into the form in which we find them today. Carty therefore overstates things when she suggests that '[t]he development of the economic torts has been guided expressly by the issue of free competition and the need to map out the limits of permissible behaviour in the marketplace'.[49] There is a good deal more to the story than a desire to foster free competition.[50] Indeed, as we shall see in the next section, the political commitments of some of the key judicial architects of these torts had a much more profound influence over the shape that they took.

C. Judicial Hostility Towards Trade Unions

Perhaps the best-known puzzle in the present setting is how to reconcile the decisions in *Quinn v Leathem* and *Allen v Flood*. The Royal Commission on Trade Disputes and Trade Combinations, for example, made the point that the decision in *Quinn* (in the wake of what had been said in *Allen* about malice being insufficient to transform an ordinarily lawful act into one that was tortious), was 'bound to produce contradiction and uncertainty'.[51] For Carty, the only distinction to be

[47] *Allen* (n 5) 179. Lord Shand, too, was openly supportive of competition. He asked, 'what would be the thought of the application of the word "malicious" to the conduct of a tradesman who induces the customer of another tradesman to cease making purchases from one with whom he had long dealt, and instead to deal with him, a rival in trade': *ibid*, 164.

[48] For doubts about whether the courts ever can or do pursue particular agendas, see the discussion in chapter nine.

[49] Carty (n 1) 2.

[50] And in any case, some judges who might fairly be described as abstentionists, were not obviously in favour of competition. It is just that they saw rule-making in this sphere as a task that was not suitable for judges. For example, in the context of injurious falsehood, Lord Herschell opined that, the courts should not be used as 'a machinery for advertising rival productions by obtaining a judicial determination which of the two was the better': *White v Mellin* [1895] AC 154 (HL) 16. In similar vein, see *Janson v Driefontein Consolidated Mines Ltd* [1902] AC 484 (HL), 500 (Lord Davey); *OBG Ltd v Allan* [2008] 1 AC 1 (HL), [56] (Lord Hoffmann).

[51] *Royal Commission on Trade Disputes and Trade Combinations*, 1903–6, Report, Cmnd 2825 (London, HMSO, 1906) 84 (Sir George Lushington).

drawn between the two cases is that there was a combination in *Quinn*,[52] but no such combination in *Allen*.[53] She then registers her doubts about how suitable a distinction that is.[54]

For Beever, the conflict is illusory, nothing more than a figment of modern jurists' imagination.[55] In his view, the best interpretation of the majority view in *Allen* is that they considered the defendant to have behaved responsibly (rather than coercively), and for that reason concluded that tortious liability ought not to be imposed. He thinks that, by contrast, in *Quinn*, the defendants 'were trying to control the way in which he [the claimant] ran his business'[56] and on that basis could be considered tortfeasors.

The truth is that there are dicta that support both interpretations of these cases.[57] To my mind, an equally – perhaps more – important contradiction in the law reveals itself when the decisions in *Quinn* and *Mogul Shipping* are contrasted. This is because, in both cases, the claimant's loss arose by virtue of the ostensibly lawful means employed: a combination. In *Quinn*, those combining were trade unionists, in *Mogul*, they were traders forming a cartel. The most plausible distinction between these two cases has been said to reside in the fact that some of the judges who decided them had a particular, personal dislike, not so much of combinations per se, but of trade unions in particular. Lobban, for example, writes: 'judges were generally more hostile to trade unions than political opinion was'; and yet '[a]t the same time, the judiciary was much less hostile to businessmen or property owners using their economic power or assets in an aggressive way'.[58] It is certainly the case that *some judges* during the latter part of the nineteenth century, though still generally hostile to those who acted in restraint of trade, showed a measure of tolerance towards *certain* agreements made between traders not to compete against one another. For example, in *Jones v North*,[59]

[52] Carty (n 12) 266: 'Though the facts were essentially the same as *Allen*, the *Quinn* court used the additional allegation of conspiracy to create a new version of the conspiracy tort'. A similar conclusion as to the key difference is reached by Cornish and Clark (n 16) 330.

[53] Under the relevant union rules, Allen had complete discretion to deal with the problem that had arisen by himself.

[54] Carty (n 1) 11, fn 75. One judge who favoured it in *Quinn* was Lord Lindley. In his view, it was a salient difference, because while '[a] man may resist without much difficulty the wrongful act of an individual … it is a very different thing … when one man has to defend himself against many combined': *Quinn* (n 27) 511.

[55] A Beever, *A Theory of Tort Liability* (Oxford, Hart Publishing, 2016) 125: 'The abstentionist/interventionist divide is a creature of modern legal analysis'.

[56] *Ibid*, 128.

[57] Lord Watson's speech in *Allen* is unquestionably, as Carty stresses, abstentionist in tone. But Lord Shand was in the majority in both cases; and in *Allen* he certainly treated as significant the fact that the defendant was acting from the best of motives: see *Allen* (n 5) 164: 'the defendant was bent, and bent exclusively, on the object of furthering the interests of those he represented … and not a desire, to use the words of the learned judge, "to do mischief to the plaintiffs"'.

[58] M Lobban, 'Intentional and Economic Torts' in W Cornish *et al* (eds), *The Oxford History of the Laws of England – Vol XII: 1820–1914* (Oxford, Oxford University Press, 2010) 1049–50.

[59] *Jones v North* (1874–75) LR 19 Eq 426.

four quarry owners agreed between themselves that three of them would sell stone to the fourth, and that the fourth one alone would deal with stone sales made to the Birmingham Corporation. It was held on demurrer that this agreement, to buy and sell coal *inter se*, was not void on the basis of its being in restraint of trade. The Vice Chancellor expressly ruled out that suggestion. He treated the agreement as one that should be seen in terms of the freedom of the three traders to make what they considered to be acceptable bargains for the sale of their own stone with a fourth such trader.[60]

Similarly, in the *Mogul Shipping* case, Lord Halsbury was unwilling to treat the combination of traders who sought to exclude the claimants from the Chinese tea trade as being in restraint of trade. Instead, like Bowen LJ in the court below,[61] he emphasised the competitive nature of the defendant traders' behaviour: that is, the fact that they were offering financial advantages to those who dealt with the cartel's members. In short, he treated the defendants' reducing their prices as a legitimate exercise of their right to trade, and not as an illegitimate interference with the trading rights of others. He began with the observation that, 'in pursuance of the conspiracy people were "bribed" … to agree to forbear and to forbear from shipping cargoes by the steamers of the plaintiffs'.[62] He then went on: '[i]f the word "bribed" is satisfied by their offering lower freights and larger discounts, then that is proved; but then the word "bribed" is robbed of any legal significance'.[63]

By contrast, where it was a trade union that was in the frame for tortious liability, a markedly different approach was sometimes taken.[64] According to Cornish and Clark:

> whatever might be thought of the differentiation of joint from individual action, it remained an utter puzzlement to many that 'malicious' secondary pressure when practised by a union became for a business cartel the pursuit of legitimate self-interest. Never was the law more nakedly the partisan of masters against men.[65]

For Lobban, it was clear that, 'the outcome of cases depended on whether the judges approved or disapproved of the economic activity in question'.[66] This led

[60] *Ibid*, 430.

[61] 'The truth is', Bowen LJ said, 'that the combination of capital for the purposes of trade and competition is a very different thing from such a combination … as falls under the head of an indictable conspiracy': *Mogul* (n 46) 609.

[62] *Mogul Steamship Co Ltd v McGregor, Gow & Co* [1892] AC 25 (HL), 40.

[63] *Ibid*.

[64] But not always! On the other hand, the revelation by a judge of his hostility towards a trade union was not always needed on the facts of a case. As Wedderburn noted, 'the exceptional "non-interventionist" decisions of judge-made law have tended to occur when the interests of a union coincide, rather than conflict, with the predominant interests of employers and the State': KW Wedderburn, *The Worker and the Law*, 3rd edn (London, Penguin, 1986) 94.

[65] Cornish and Clark (n 16) 330. See also, in similar vein, M Macnair, 'Free Association versus Juridification' (2011) 39 *Critique* 53, 76: the courts were simply 'finding a stick to beat unions and strikers'.

[66] Lobban (n 58) 1033.

to 'rules that were inconsistent with those governing functionally similar areas of the law'.[67]

Of course, it is important not to overstate things here, and present an image of a judiciary that was united across all of its ranks in a deep-seated loathing of trade unions together with an equal and opposite respect for commercial entities. In *Hilton v Eckersley*, for example, Crompton J saw no problem in treating members of a cartel as indictable conspirators.[68] And whilst he was Attorney-General in 1873, Lord James – a member of the panel that decided *Allen* – had been supportive of reforms that would protect trade unions. But even so, it is fair to observe that *some* of the main architects of the economic torts (and the satellite rules concerning trade unions) allowed a raw, personal, anti-union sentiment to insinuate its way into their judgments in a number of the landmark cases. And it is equally to be noted that, although other members of the Bench in the years that followed did not overtly display the same *virulent hostility* towards trade unions, a conspicuous *distrust* of them is nonetheless evident in their judgments and extra-judicial writings.

Four judicial figures stand out as being worthy of comment. Two are representative of the early years; two are drawn from the more recent past. They are identified not because they were much more hostile to unions than all other judges; but because their hostility was expressed in key cases. Thus, although Lord Hoffmann has pointed out in relation to Lord Esher MR's judgment in *Temperton v Russell (No 1)*[69] that, '[o]ne cannot read the description of the union's actions by the Master of the Rolls [in that case] without seeing disapproval dripping from every sentence',[70] it is important to appreciate that Lord Esher was much less influential in the development of these torts.

i. Halsbury

It would be hard to deny the influence that Lord Halsbury had in shaping the general economic torts. He was a member of the appellate panel that decided all three of the foundational cases: *Mogul*, *Allen* and *Quinn*. His decisions in those cases tend to confirm the claim in this chapter that it is too simplistic to label some judges 'interventionists' and others, 'abstentionists'. He was in the majority in *Mogul*, the minority in *Allen* and the majority in *Quinn*. In other words, he was unprepared to use the common law to regulate the competition between traders

[67] Klarman (n 13) 1488. Somewhat charitably, he associates this attitude with 'judges' unconscious class prejudices' (*ibid*, 1574), but as we shall see below, in some cases there was nothing unconscious about the approach taken by several other judges.

[68] *Hilton v Eckersley* (1855) 6 El & Bl 47, 53: 'I think that combinations like that disclosed in the pleadings in this case were illegal and indictable at common law, as tending directly to impede and interfere with the free course of trade and manufacture'.

[69] *Temperton v Russell (No 1)* [1893] 1 QB 715 (CA).

[70] L Hoffmann, 'The Rise and Fall of the Economic Torts' in S Degeling *et al* (eds), *Torts in Commercial Law* (Pyrmont, NSW, Thomson Reuters, 2009) 109.

in *Mogul* (even though there was a combination in that case in the shape of a cartel); yet he was only too keen for tortious liability to be imposed in *Allen* and *Quinn* (where unions featured prominently). Indeed, as is well known, as Lord Chancellor, he took the remarkable step in *Allen* of summoning eight High Court judges to advise the House of Lords. The step was an extraordinary one not merely because there was little justification for requesting such advice after the introduction of Lords of Appeal in Ordinary in 1877, but also, more importantly, because he selected them without consulting any of the other Law Lords who heard the case.[71] It was, in the words of Lord Hoffmann, a blatant attempt 'to pack the court and to intimidate the Law Lords by invoking the ancient practice of summoning the judges to advise them'.[72] His thinking was that, 'having appointed many of these judges for their political views … he could rely on them in his hour of need'.[73] But he was wrong. For, despite his attempt to engineer matters, the majority held that no tort had been committed in *Allen*. Undaunted, just a few years later, in *Quinn*, he left nothing to chance.[74] He carefully selected the panel of Law Lords who would sit with him to hear that case. And when it came to formulating his judgment, he made no attempt to conceal his hostility towards the unions.

In his speech, he was almost contemptuous of the decision that had been reached in *Allen*. Completely undeterred by the fact that it was hard to reconcile the decisions in *Allen* and *Quinn*, he opined that a problem only arises if one 'assumes that the law is necessarily a logical code' yet 'every lawyer must acknowledge that the law is not always logical at all'.[75] He saw the restraint of union power via the decision in *Quinn* as necessary on the basis that, if he were to hold otherwise, 'it could hardly be said that our jurisprudence was that of a civilized community'.[76] And when, some years later, Parliament went some way to undoing the effect of *Quinn* via the immunities conferred on trade unions in the Trade Disputes Act 1906, Lord Halsbury said (of the relevant section, as the Act was passing through Parliament): 'I venture to say that so disgraceful a section has never appeared in an English Statute before … Was there ever such a thing heard of in a civilised country?'.[77] Then, just a few paragraphs later, he added: 'anything more tyrannical I can hardly conceive'.[78]

[71] See RFV Heuston, *Lives of the Lord Chancellors 1885–1940* (Oxford, Clarendon Press, 1964) 118–122.

[72] Hoffmann (n 70) 110.

[73] R Stevens, *Law and Politics: The House of Lords as a Judicial Body, 1800–1976* (London, Weidenfeld & Nicholson, 1979) 93.

[74] As the *Oxford Dictionary of National Biography* records, he engaged in 'manipulation of the panel in order to exclude Lords Davey and James [who were sympathetic towards the trade unions] from hearing the appeal': www.oxforddnb.com/view/10.1093/ref:odnb/9780198614128.001.0001/odnb-9780198614128-e-33395?rskey=hnoqt5&result=2.

[75] *Quinn* (n 27) 506.

[76] *Ibid*, 506.

[77] HL Deb 4 December 1906, vol 166, col 705.

[78] HL Deb 4 December 1906, vol 166, col 707.

That he should have held such a trenchant view is anything but surprising. After all, he had (in a former life) assisted his father as the Editor of *The Standard* in which, as the *Oxford Dictionary of National Biography* puts it, 'the tory cause was uncompromisingly advanced'.[79] But that he should have allowed this to infect his role as a Law Lord is harder to comprehend, and even more difficult to justify.

ii. Farwell

Although not a case that directly left its mark on the *ingredients* of any of the general economic torts, the decision in *Taff Vale Railway Co v Amalgamated Society of Railway Servants*[80] provided a very strong and influential indication of what those torts existed for; and in significant measure, it paved the way for the momentous decision in *Quinn* which was handed down just two weeks later. The Law Lords in *Taff Vale* held, ultimately, that a trade union could be sued in its own name even though a trade union is neither an individual nor a corporate body. In so holding, their Lordships (in a series of very short speeches) reinstated the decision that had been reached at first instance by Farwell J, who himself had been appointed to the Bench by Lord Halsbury. And it is in this first instance judgment that we find his barely concealed suspicions about trade unions. In reaching the conclusion that unions could be sued in their own name – a matter on which the various Trade Union Acts of the 1870s were entirely silent – Farwell J expressed the fear that:

> they would [otherwise] be at liberty … to disseminate libels … or to hire men to reproduce the rattening methods that disgraced Sheffield thirty or forty years ago, and their victims would have nothing to look to for damages but the pockets of the individuals, usually men of small means, who acted as their agents.[81]

Quite why he thought unions would suddenly do such things when they had not done so for getting on for half a century was not explained. But he did not stop at a mention of what had happened in Sheffield. He said that before he refused to hold unions liable in their own name, '[i]t would require very clear and express words of enactment to induce me to hold that the Legislature had in fact legalised the existence of such irresponsible bodies with such wide capacity for evil'.[82]

His view of trade unions did not soften as the years passed. Even after he had been elevated to the Court of Appeal, he was, in *Conway v Wade*,[83] excoriating in his analysis of the Trade Disputes Act 1906 (a statute that had afforded trade unions tortious immunity for certain acts done in furtherance of a trade dispute[84]).

[79] See www.oxforddnb.com/view/10.1093/ref:odnb/9780198614128.001.0001/odnb-9780198614128-e-33395?rskey=hnoqt5&result=2.
[80] *Taff Vale Railway Co v Amalgamated Society of Railway Servants* [1901] AC 426.
[81] *Ibid*, 430.
[82] *Ibid*, 431.
[83] *Conway v Wade* [1908] 2 KB 844 (CA).
[84] Trade Disputes Act 1906, s 3.

He said of the relevant provision that it was in 'entire contradiction of those doctrines of personal freedom and equality before the law which have hitherto been its main aim and object'[85] and that its purpose was to 'destroy liberty'.[86] His personal politics could hardly have influenced his decision-making more openly; and thanks in significant measure to his judgment in the *Taff Vale* case, the notion that the economic torts are intimately bound up with the struggle between capital and labour was able to take root. This in turn fuelled the idea – that I have strenuously sought to counter in this book – that these torts are confined to the protection of trade and business interests.

iii. Denning

Lord Halsbury and Farwell LJ were by no means the only judges from the late nineteenth and early twentieth century who were conspicuously anti-union in their decision-making. For example, Lord Brampton, like Lord Esher whom we have already considered, said of the defendant trade union in *Quinn* that it was 'a powerful and dangerous engine … employed by the defendants for the perpetration of organized and ruinous oppression'.[87] And Brett LJ, too, would have extended the tort in *Lumley* to cases in which people were induced not to enter contracts in the first place.[88] Yet, the degree of influence that these judges exerted over the shape (and the understanding among jurists) of the economic torts during their early years was of an appreciably lower order. For a politically-driven influence that rivals that of Lord Halsbury and Farwell LJ, the clock must be rolled forwards to the 1960s; for it was in this decade that Lord Denning began what Carty calls 'a vigorous campaign … to expand economic tort coverage in the face of the increasing muscle of trade unions'.[89]

This supposed 'Denning agenda' was slightly better concealed than had been the hostility towards unions of Lord Halsbury, Lord Brampton and Farwell LJ. But only slightly; for it was still fairly easy to unearth where certain types of union activity were in the spotlight. As Bogg puts it: 'Lord Denning was notoriously hostile to secondary industrial action, and this policy commitment infused the discharge of his judicial responsibilities in applying and developing the law'.[90] This is unquestionably correct.

[85] *Conway* (n 83) 855.
[86] *Ibid*, 856.
[87] *Quinn* (n 27) 531.
[88] *Temperton v Russell* [1893] 1 QB 715 (CA), 728. Lord Hoffmann has since written of this case that '*Temperton v Russell* in 1893 was the critical case in which Lord Esher MR [as Brett LJ became] enthusiastically embraced *Lumley v Gye* as a weapon against the unions': Hoffmann (n 70) 109.
[89] H Carty, 'The Tort of Conspiracy as a Can of Worms' in SGA Pitel *et al* (eds), *Tort Law: Challenging Orthodoxy* (Oxford, Hart Publishing, 2013) 395.
[90] A Bogg, 'Common Law and Statute in the Law of Employment' (2016) 69 *Current Legal Problems* 67, 87, fn 80.

To begin with, Lord Denning held secondary action to be unlawful in *Associated Newspapers Group Ltd v Wade*.[91] And then later – after the obscurely worded immunity in section 17 of the Employment Act 1980 had been enacted – he took advantage of the opaque language in that provision in *Hadmor Productions v Hamilton*[92] to hold that secondary action remained unlawful: it was not, *on his reading of the Act*, within the immunity created by Parliament. Denning's impact on the law went further, though. For, as Carty rightly notes, even in the 1960s, he was active in giving a very wide meaning to the phrase 'unlawful means' so as to bring within the maw of tort law a wide range of other union activities. Take, for example, his decision in *Torquay Hotel Co Ltd v Cousins*, a case in which he set about minting a hybrid tort – one that mixed elements of inducing breach of contract with elements of the tort of causing loss by unlawful means.[93] (The putative tort created was that of interfering with contract by unlawful means.) In that case, he declared in relation to the unlawful means element that: 'if one person deliberately interferes with the trade or business of another, and does so … *by an act which he is not at liberty to commit*, then he is acting unlawfully'.[94] In other words, he was prepared to countenance acts that went beyond 'merely' recognised crimes or torts. Also, just a year earlier, using an equally expansive phrase, he had stated that the requirement of unlawful means would be satisfied if the defendant had acted with 'no sufficient justification'.[95] Naturally, his giving a very broad meaning to unlawful means in these cases – one that would, for example, include aiding and abetting the breach of an injunction[96] – meant that there was more for which trade unions could potentially be held liable in tort.

Though in everyday speech, as well as in labour law circles,[97] it seems apt to speak of 'a right to strike', no such right could be squared with what Lord Denning said in another case, namely, that:

> when Parliament granted immunities to the leaders of trade unions, it did not give them any *rights*. It did not give them a *right* to break the law or to do wrong by inducing people to break contracts. It only gave them immunity if they did.[98]

The italicised words appear in the original text, and lend ample support to Davies and Freedland's summary of this dictum as follows: 'the contrast between rights

[91] *Associated Newspapers Group Ltd v Wade* [1979] 1 WLR 697 (CA), 713: 'when strikers choose to picket, not their employers' premises, but the premises of innocent third persons not party to the dispute – it is unlawful'.

[92] *Hadmor Productions v Hamilton* [1981] 3 WLR 139 (CA), 151. He began by observing, '[i]t is the most tortuous section I have ever come across', yet despite the confusion concluded, 'I think I can discern the general legislative purpose of section 17. It is to retain the statutory immunity for primary action, but to remove the immunity for secondary action'.

[93] The existence of this tort was, of course, rejected in *OBG* (n 50).

[94] *Torquay Hotel Co Ltd v Cousins* [1969] 2 Ch 106 (CA) 139 (emphasis added).

[95] *Daily Mirror Newspapers Ltd v Gardner* [1968] 2 QB 762 (CA), 781.

[96] *Acrow (Automation) Ltd v Rex Chainbelt Inc* [1971] 1 WLR 1676 (CA).

[97] See, eg, P Davies and M Freedland, 'Labour Law' in JL Jowell and JPWB McAuslan (eds), *Lord Denning: The Judge and the Law* (London, Sweet and Maxwell, 1984) 377–411.

[98] *Express Newspapers v McShane* [1979] ICR 210 (CA), 218.

and immunities is stressed and trade unionists become "law-breakers" upon whom special protections are conferred by Parliament'.[99] To put it another way, there is nothing here that is perceived as being done in the exercise of a right. Rather, trade unions were seen by him as bodies that, prima facie, act unlawfully when they engage in industrial action.

iv. Hoffmann

It is very easy to cite the landmark case of *Rookes v Barnard*[100] as an example of the courts' hostility towards trade unions. It is true, after all, that their Lordships formally minted the tort of intimidation in that case and that, in so doing, they identified a gap in the cloak of immunity created by the Trade Disputes Act 1906 behind which unions had been able to shelter for over half a century. And it is true, also, that, around the time of that decision, the country was witnessing 'a new period of economic disruption caused by mounting union power' in which *Rookes* 'marked the beginning of a new period of judicial activism … which extended economic tort liability beyond the hitherto recognised limits'.[101] But it does not follow from this that the decision in *Rookes* – in which Lord Denning played no part, at any level – was driven by anti-union convictions on the part of their Lordships. Indeed, the closest we get to any such sentiment is in the speech of Lord Evershed who, conscious of the prevailing conditions in society, opined: 'it seems to me that in the year 1963 it is not possible or sensible to deny such a wrong [as intimidation]'.[102] Yet he made clear later in his speech that his reasons for believing that a tort of intimidation should be recognised were not political. He said: 'I hope and believe that the trade unions in our country are sufficiently responsible and influential to see that acts done by their members in the course of trade disputes are not wholly irresponsible'.[103] In other words, his willingness to acknowledge the existence of the tort was based squarely on jurisprudential grounds.

Against this backdrop, it is not immediately obvious why Lord Hoffmann, writing extra-judicially about the rise and fall of the economic torts, should preface his discussion of *Rookes* with the observation that 'in the 1960s … excessive use of trade union power, often by small factions within the unions, had alienated the judges'.[104] But the reason is not long in coming, for he soon afterwards applauds the formal creation of a tort of intimidation in these terms: 'this new tort *had the advantage* of not being protected by the 1906 Act'.[105] And lest there be any

[99] Davies and Freedland (n 97) 393.
[100] *Rookes* (n 4).
[101] Simpson (n 21) 106.
[102] *Rookes* (n 4) 1182.
[103] *Ibid*, 1196.
[104] Hoffmann (n 70) 112. Simpson (n 21) 106 gives a fairer description when he writes: 'the House of Lords' decision [in *Rookes*] marked the beginning of a new period of judicial activism … which extended economic tort liability beyond the hitherto recognised limits'.
[105] Hoffmann (n 70) 112 (emphasis added).

lingering doubt about why he saw this development in the common law as being a meritorious one, he was quick to add the following:

> During the 1970s the union leaders exercised power free from any restraint, whether external or even internal within their unions. This experiment in total *laissez faire* was based on the social theories of Professor Otto Kahn-Freund, a refugee from the Nazis, who was very influential with the Labour government of the day and believed strongly that the law should play no part in industrial relations. I remember him at Oxford, a most learned, gentle and charming man who did more damage to the United Kingdom than any German since Hitler.[106]

Of course, the fact that Lord Hoffmann made these comments in an extra-judicial capacity negates any suggestion that they *directly* influenced the shape of relevant tort doctrine. But what his words arguably do contribute towards, is the perpetuation of the notion that the economic torts are ultimately about the control of excessive conduct in the commercial setting. Moreover, it is a conception of the purpose for which they exist that is readily reinforced by his insistence in *OBG* that 'the essence of the [unlawful means] tort [is] … a wrongful interference with the actions of a third party *in which the claimant has an economic interest*'.[107] So, rather than expanding the scope or practical utility of the economic torts, in the way that the decisions in *Quinn*, *Taff Vale* and (for a time, anyway) *Torquay Hotel* did, he can, I think, fairly be identified as saying things that serve to stifle their future development.[108] He might even be accused of trying to kill them off, mindful of the fact that they are seldom used in industrial relations cases any more. He did, after all, admit that:

> [t]he message intended to be conveyed by *OBG* was that in regulating industrial relations, the economic torts have run their course and nothing needs to be done about them. In regulating competition, the common law should be modest in its ambitions and confine itself to preventing the crude and obvious forms of unfair competition, which seldom in practice occur. It is significant that, apart from the flurry of trade union cases in the 1960s and 1970s, cases on causing loss by unlawful means have come at the rate of about one a century.[109]

It cannot be denied that the days of closed shops and secondary picketing are behind us. But it does not follow from this, as Lord Hoffmann would seemingly wish, that 'cases on the economic torts will become rare curiosities, of little practical consequence'.[110] In recent years there have been several milestone cases which

[106] *Ibid*, 112.

[107] *OBG* (n 50) [47] (emphasis added). This requirement – or, more precisely the requirement that the unlawful means should impact the third party's freedom to deal with C – was recently confirmed as an ingredient of the tort, and proved decisive in holding that the defendant was not liable in *Secretary of State for Health v Servier Laboratories Ltd* [2021] UKSC 24 (SC).

[108] It is certainly true that the Supreme Court has recently been minded to treat Lord Hoffmann's dealing requirement as a desirable 'control mechanism': *Servier*, *ibid*, [92] (Lord Hamblen).

[109] Hoffmann (n 70) 114.

[110] *Ibid*, 116.

found their way to the highest court in the land, in all of which there was not even a whiff of the historically commonplace tussle between capital and organised labour. Rather, the torts in view were invoked in connection with (1) an attempt to cheat the Inland Revenue by way of a carousel fraud,[111] (2) an attempt, contrary to an order of the court, to put beyond the reach of the English legal system the proceeds of embezzlement,[112] and (3) an attempt to use deceit against an intermediary in order gain a monopoly and impose monopoly pricing.[113] None of these seems a particularly edifying pursuit. Indeed, they all appear to be just the sort of thing – ie, egregious conduct causing harm to others – about which tort law ought rightly to have something to say.

Against this backcloth, characterisations of these torts such as the one supplied by Lord Hoffmann run the risk of creating the image that the economic torts have purely a small (and dwindling) role to play in the sphere of economic competition, whether that be competition between business rivals or competition between employers and employees. Naturally, the magnitude of the risk that such a limited agenda could conceivably be set for the economic torts via the medium of extra-judicial writing (or other academic commentary) depends on how much influence such literature typically exerts in the cases that actually come before the courts. But as we shall see in the next section, the degree of influence that such writing has had is by no means inconsiderable.

IV. The Influence of Juristic Literature[114]

In *Common Law and Modern Society*, published in 2015, Lady Arden spent an entire chapter discussing the economic torts. She gave it the title 'Economic Torts in the Twenty-first Century', and in it, she could not have disagreed more with Lord Hoffmann about the future vitality of these actions. In line with my own perceptions about this area of law, she declared in the very first sentence that: 'as recent case law suggests … it is a field ripe for development, and indeed it is in the course of development'.[115] Then, within the space of just a couple of lines, she openly acknowledged the fact that the evolution of these torts owes much to

[111] *Total Network* (n 14).

[112] *Khrapunov* (n 14).

[113] *Servier* (n 107). True: the action in this case failed. But it was nonetheless recognised (obiter) by their Lordships that on slightly different facts (ie, facts in which C could, unlike in *Servier*, satisfy the dealing requirement), it would be possible for C to sue D on the basis of the unlawful means tort: *ibid*, [86] (Lord Hamblen). The particular example in connection with which this was said involved a hoaxer (rather than a business rival trade union) deceiving the operators of Heathrow into believing that a bomb had been planted so as to prompt the closure of the airport and thus cause loss to British Airways which uses Heathrow as its hub.

[114] For present purposes, I treat extra-juridical writing as part of the body of juristic literature in view.

[115] M Arden, *Common Law and Modern Society: Keeping Pace with Change* (Oxford, Oxford University Press, 2015) 64.

academic scholarship. She wrote: 'I would like to begin by paying tribute to the work of scholars in this field … [since] [d]evelopment of the law in this area is undoubtedly assisted by their work'.[116]

This is, at first sight, a somewhat surprising way for a judge to begin an essay about a particular area of law. After all, as Duxbury notes in his study of the influence that scholarly writing has had over judicial decision-making, there has been a clear convention in the courts of England and Wales that living jurists should not be cited by judges.[117] In *Donoghue v Stevenson*, Lord Buckmaster put it this way: 'the work of living authors, however deservedly eminent, cannot be used as authority'.[118] In saying this, his Lordship was largely echoing the view expressed by Kekewich J about 50 years earlier that, 'it is much to be regretted, and it is a regret which I believe every Judge on the bench shares, that text-books are more and more quoted [by barristers] in Court'.[119] And the tendency appears to be an enduring one, for, as Duxbury further explains, '[e]ven though the English courts are nowadays generally more inclined to cite academic commentary, such practice is by no means routine'.[120]

The willingness of the courts to be guided by academic commentary when it comes to the economic torts stands in stark contrast to this tradition, just as Lady Arden suggests in her book. Take, for example, the fact that it was Sir John Salmond who first proposed the existence of a tort of intimidation. This suggestion was readily accepted by their Lordships in *Rookes* where, as noted previously, that tort was first formally introduced. Lord Devlin was perfectly open in saying: 'in my opinion there is a tort of intimidation of the nature described in Chapter 18 of *Salmond on the Law of Torts*'.[121] Likewise, Lord Evershed remarked that although counsel for the defendants had argued forcefully that it 'was in truth invented by Sir John Salmond', he was nonetheless of the view that, by 1963 it was 'too late to deny the reception of the tort of intimidation into the company of English wrongs'.[122] It is hard to imagine an academic lawyer having so profound an influence in any other department of tort law, for *Rookes* was unquestionably a milestone. As Lord Hoffmann later acknowledged, '*Rookes v Barnard* … ushered in an era of extensive judicial development of economic tort activity'.[123] And even though Lord Hoffmann was rather sceptical in *OBG* about the merits of two-party

[116] *Ibid*, 64.
[117] N Duxbury, *Jurists and Judges: An Essay on Influence* (Oxford, Hart Publishing, 2000) 62–77.
[118] *Donoghue v Stevenson* [1932] AC 562 (HL), 567. There appears, historically, to have been less resistance to the judicial citation of academic work *after the author's death*: see Duxbury, *ibid*, 78–84.
[119] *Union Bank v Munster* (1887) 37 Ch D 51, 54.
[120] Duxbury (n 117) 61.
[121] *Rookes* (n 4) 1205.
[122] *Ibid*, 1185.
[123] Hoffmann (n 70) 128. Essentially the same point is made in S Deakin and J Randall, 'Rethinking the Economic Torts' (2009) 72 *MLR* 519, 524–25: *Rookes* was, they contend, 'the catalyst for a series of judicial innovations which, from the mid-1960s to the mid-1980s, seemed to throw the economic torts … into chaos'.

intimidation[124] – a version that Salmond had specifically spelled out in his textbook – the decisions in *Godwin v Uzoigwe*,[125] and *Newsgroup Newspapers Ltd v SOGAT '82*,[126] still stand as concrete examples of that tort's acceptance by the courts.

Carty, the modern doyen of the economic torts, has been influential too in this sphere. Lord Hoffmann's lengthy attempt to bring clarity to what had become a very muddled area of law in *OBG* concluded with this frank admission:

> In arriving at these statements of general principle, I have derived great assistance from many who have written on the subject in addition to those whom I have specifically cited and in particular, if what I have said does anything to clarify what has been described as an extremely obscure branch of the law, much is owing to Hazel Carty's book *An Analysis of the Economic Torts* (2001).[127]

Equally, Lady Hale – who was also a member of the panel in that case – said: 'I too have found the discussion by my former colleague, Hazel Carty ... most helpful'.[128] But Carty was not the only academic whose work proved influential in *OBG*. Roderick Bagshaw's treatment of the pivotal concept of 'unlawful means' was also expressly adopted by Lord Hoffmann.[129] Between them, then, Carty and Bagshaw can be seen to have contributed significantly to the unlawful means tort's being afforded a much more restricted role for the twenty-first century than Lord Nicholls, by contrast, would have given it.[130]

The decision in *Total Network* was regarded in some quarters[131] as something of a *volte face* in the wake of *OBG*. The fact that the House of Lords adopted a different meaning of 'unlawful means' for the purposes of conspiracy liability than it had been given in the tort of causing loss by unlawful means was at the very least eyebrow raising. And so, too, was the basis on which this step was taken.

Conscious of the clash, Lord Neuberger, justified the attribution of a different meaning to a shared phrase by reference to a pair of academic sources. He said:

> the notion of a single consistent approach as to what constitutes unlawfulness in relation to all the economic torts can said to be inconsistent with what *Clerk & Lindsell on*

[124] *OBG* (n 50) [61].
[125] *Godwin v Uzoigwe* [1993] *Fam Law* 65 (CA).
[126] *Newsgroup Newspapers Ltd v SOGAT '82* [1987] ICR 181 (CA).
[127] *OBG* (n 50) [65].
[128] *Ibid*, [306].
[129] *Ibid*, [59].
[130] In general terms, Carty's analysis of the economic torts advocates an abstentionist role. This approach shares with Bagshaw (see R Bagshaw, 'Can the Economic Torts be Unified?' (1998) 18 *OJLS* 729, 732), a preference for 'unlawful means' to be interpreted narrowly. Lord Nicholls, by contrast, would have given the phrase a wide meaning – one that included criminal as well as civil wrongs – and would thus have granted the unlawful means tort a wider sphere of operation.
[131] See, eg, H Carty, 'The Economic Torts in the 21st Century' (2008) 124 *LQR* 641, 642 ('the *Total* decision has arguably undermined the prospect for clarity that *OBG* represented, and thrown the economic torts back into the mess in which they were before *OBG*'); Deakin and Randall (n 123) 519 ('Lord Hoffmann's leading judgment is not easily reconcilable with ... the approach taken in a subsequent House of Lords decision, *Total Network*').

> *Torts*, 19th ed refer to, at para 25-001, as the 'ramshackle' nature of the economic torts and with the statement in Stevens on *Torts and Rights* (2007) 297 that the economic torts 'have no inherent unity' and that it is 'a mistake to group these "torts" together'.[132]

Once again, the influence of these writers can properly be regarded as having been momentous. For, in taking a lead from 'mere jurists' who expressed the view that the economic torts lacked unity, the court was able to breathe new life into a cause of action that Lord Hoffmann had hoped to side-line by advocating, in this field, a simple, *two-tort* approach as per the judgment of Lord Watson in *Allen v Flood*.[133] At the same time, their Lordships acknowledged two further dimensions to this disunity: they accepted the continued vitality of two-party intimidation and lawful means conspiracy,[134] and they stated forthrightly, *pace* Lord Hoffmann, that the economic torts might sometimes operate according to a two-party structure,[135] the case before them being a prime example. So at stroke, taking a lead from the work of jurists, their Lordships resuscitated three torts that Lord Hoffmann would have been happy to expunge from the tort law canon, while the supposedly paradigmatic three-party structure of the economic torts was shown not to be a defining characteristic of all the torts in this field.[136]

What the preceding paragraphs reveal is that, in developing the economic torts, the courts have been unusually attentive to, and openly influenced by, academic discussion of the various actions with which this book is concerned. In most cases, it is no exaggeration to say that that influence has had a very important, and clearly measurable, impact on this particular constellation of torts.

V. Especially Reprehensible Defendants

It might be thought that the question of who exactly the defendants are in a particular tort case should be an irrelevance. In the context of civil law litigation, the job of the judge – one would think – is to apply, even-handedly and dispassionately, the rules of law as they have been laid down in the past. It should make no difference, one might say, that a particular defendant has (or could easily obtain) liability insurance.[137] Indeed, Viscount Simonds once opined that, 'in determining

[132] *Total Network* (n 14) [224].
[133] *OBG* (n 50) [33].
[134] For details, see chapter five.
[135] Carty notes this effect of *Total Network*, but erroneously portrays the decision as one that took the economic torts 'beyond the *Quinn* framework into the uncharted (and radical) concept of two-party economic torts': Carty (n 1) 15. It is wrong to say this, however, because deceit has only ever been a two-party tort, and the two-party intimidation case of *Godwin* (n 125) also predates the decision in *Total Network*.
[136] Carty (n 89) 393: 'intermediary-use liability is the paradigm setting for the economic torts'.
[137] See J Stapleton, 'Tort, Insurance and Ideology' (1995) 58 *MLR* 820, 823–24.

the rights *inter se* of A and B the fact that one or other of them is insured is to be disregarded'.[138] And yet, this is not what happens in the modern law of negligence. Several studies make clear that judges in the present era adopt a very different approach. In line with some of what might be described as Lord Denning's more 'maverick' judgments,[139] there are numerous clear examples of the courts these days paying particular attention to the insured (or insurable) status of the defendant.[140] And it is not just the liability rules in negligence that have been affected in this way. In a leading case concerning vicarious liability, it was made clear by the Supreme Court that, '[t]here is no difficulty in identifying a number of policy reasons that usually make it fair, just and reasonable to impose vicarious liability on the employer' including the fact that '[t]he employer ... can be expected to have insured against that liability'.[141]

Being attentive to the particular attributes of the defendant has also been a driver of development within the economic torts. As already noted, it has counted for a great deal in a number of landmark cases that the defendant was a trade union. But the presence of other types of defendant has also proved to be a material consideration in developing the law. Where justice has (in the eyes of the court) demanded that a particular outcome be reached, the courts have been willing to stretch or adapt existing doctrines so as to impose liability.[142]

Unlike in the trade union cases considered in an earlier section of this chapter, the courts have not always been entirely candid about doing this. But there are certainly hints here and there which I think license a certain amount of reading between the lines. For example, although none of the judges in *Lumley v Gye* put it in quite such overt terms, Lord Hoffmann is almost certainly right to think that the 'sudden emergence of ... inducing breach of contract ... in the last quarter of the nineteenth century, was the result of ... the ungentlemanly behaviour of a London opera impresario'.[143] The judges in *Lumley* were appreciably more reserved in what they said. But that broad notions of justice and particularly reprehensible behaviour were seen as important to the outcome comes through clearly enough in the judgment of Crompton J. He said:

> the servant or contractor may be utterly unable to pay anything like the amount of the damages sustained entirely from the wrongful act of the defendant: and it would

[138] *Lister v Romford Ice and Cold Storage Co Ltd* [1957] AC 555 (HL), 576–77.
[139] *Nettleship v Weston* [1971] 2 QB 691 (CA), 699: '[m]orally the learner driver is not at fault; but legally she is liable ... because she is insured'; *Morris v Ford Motor Co Ltd* [1973] QB 792 (CA), 798: '[t]he courts ... would not find negligence so readily ... except on the footing that the damages are to be borne, not by the man himself, but by an insurance company'.
[140] For details, see J Morgan, 'Tort, Insurance and Incoherence' (2004) 67 *MLR* 384; R Lewis, 'Insurance and the Tort System' [2005] *Legal Studies* 85, 101–103.
[141] *Catholic Child Welfare Society and Others v Various Claimants* [2013] 2 AC 1 (SC), [35] (Lord Phillips).
[142] See further, chapters four and nine.
[143] Hoffmann (n 70) 105.

> seem unjust, and contrary to the general principles of law, if such wrongdoer were not responsible for the damage caused by his wrongful and malicious acts.[144]

With such considerations to the fore, Crompton J was perfectly content to extend the extant, narrow rule of law concerning the tortious enticement of a servant (which status, strictly speaking, Wagner did not possess). He said:

> I think that we are justified in applying the principle of the action for enticing away servants to a case where the defendant *maliciously procures* a party, who is under a valid contract to give her exclusive personal services to the plaintiff for a specified period, to refuse to give such services.[145]

Erle J said something very similar.[146] So it seems a fair characterisation of the decision in *Lumley* that it was an exercise in judicial legislation prompted by conduct on the part of the defendant that was regarded as especially reprehensible. As we saw in chapter three, the arguments about whether the rule introduced in that case should or should not be regarded as a thoroughbred tort are fairly evenly balanced. And yet the court in that case, even in the absence of a cast iron authority to follow, was clearly determined to concoct some sort of action that would allow justice to be done. The decision was, as Waddams puts it,

> the only way to prevent Gye from profiting from his own wrongdoing … [and] [t]he whole gist and tenor of the judgments … is that Gye was seeking to reap where he had not sown and that he ought not to profit at Lumley's expense.[147]

The self-same phenomenon of gap filling in order to do justice – whether by stretching, adding to, or simply reinterpreting existing doctrine – can be seen in other leading cases on the economic torts. In fact, they provide a first-class example of tort fulfilling the role of the common law's Swiss army knife:[148] the legal category that can be called upon to supply imaginative solutions to novel, often unforeseen, problems. Yet Carty objects to the fact that claimants in this field sometimes – but especially in the twenty-first century – have sought 'to broaden the remit of these torts so that they are no longer simply "stretching" existing liability but are gap-filling, creating new civil liability where … civil liability might be problematic or lacking'.[149] Her objection is largely based on what she takes to be the original conception of their purpose. In the context of her discussing the first manifestations in English law of these torts, she writes: they 'simply stretched existing civil liability … [and][w]hat they did not do was fill gaps in the common law by making tortious behaviour that did not already involve a civil wrong'.[150]

[144] *Lumley* (n 24).
[145] *Ibid*, 231 (emphasis added).
[146] *Ibid*, 234.
[147] S Waddams, 'Johanna Wagner and the Rival Opera Houses' (2001) 117 *LQR* 431, 449–50.
[148] The metaphor is taken from A Beever, *Rediscovering the Law of Negligence* (Oxford, Hart Publishing, 2007) 197.
[149] Carty (n 12) 264.
[150] *Ibid*, 263.

I offer a full response to these statements in chapter nine. But I nonetheless take the opportunity to note here a fundamental problem with Carty's objection. It is that she simply presumes the very thing that needs to be shown: that is, that the economic torts should not be used in novel circumstances. Showing that a tort originally did *x* or *y*, is, by itself, not a cast iron objection to its now being used to do *z*. The logical conclusion to which such argumentation propels us is that the law of torts is in a more or less ossified state, incapable of developing in anything like a dynamic way. That, however, is clearly not the lesson that history teaches us. Think, for example, of the breakthrough decision in *Hedley Byrne & Co Ltd v Heller & Partners Ltd*[151] in relation to the recovery of pure economic loss caused by a negligent misstatement. And think, too, of the milestone decision in *Willers v Joyce*,[152] in which a tort that had originally been confined to those who maliciously initiate criminal proceedings was extended to the malicious pursuit of civil actions. With those widely-welcomed examples of torts being stretched into new territory in mind, can one really consider it objectionable that, for example, the tort of intimidation was afforded entirely novel usage so as to provide a remedy for the woman who had been treated as a slave in *Godwin*? Should it have been considered fatal to her claim that she could not frame her complaint in terms of economic loss?

It certainly seems that neither the House of Lords nor the Supreme Court has accepted Carty's restricted conception of the proper scope and purpose of the economic torts. The fact that these torts were originally used to resolve disputes between commercial competitors was seen as no obstacle to their being used to impose liability in the *Total Network* and *Khrapunov* cases.[153] In the first of these, it will be recalled, fraudsters committed the common law crime of cheating the Revenue. They were most certainly *not* commercial competitors of the Revenue; but as Lord Mance said in that case, '[l]ike others of your Lordships, I think that there would be an evident lacuna if the law did not respond to this situation by recognising a civil liability'.[154] Similarly, Lord Hope noted that: '[t]he conspirators cannot, on the commissioners' primary contention, be sued as joint tortfeasors because there was no independent tort actionable by the commissioners. This is a gap which needs to be filled'.[155]

Lord Scott, as observed in chapter four, presented things slightly differently. He justified the novel use of the tort of unlawful means conspiracy in that case according to the lessons he learnt in his youth, as a law student. He referred to the fact that the action on the case had always been regarded as flexible enough to respond incrementally to losses inflicted by those whose conduct could be regarded as '*sufficiently reprehensible* to require the conclusion that they ought to be held

[151] *Hedley Byrne & Co Ltd v Heller & Partners Ltd* [1964] AC 465.
[152] *Willers v Joyce* [2018] AC 779.
[153] See n 14.
[154] *Total Network* (n 14) [120].
[155] *Ibid*, [44].

responsible for the harm'.[156] Yet, for all that his Lordship endeavoured to present the case as a classic example of incremental decision-making, it is questionable whether *Total Network* ought to be viewed in this way. After all, their Lordships were not simply employing a broader notion of unlawful means than had been employed in *OBG*, and re-opening questions that had seemingly been closed in the latter case. They were also making plain (contrary to orthodox understandings) the existence of certain two-party economic torts.[157]

As we also noted in chapter four, the Supreme Court in *Khrapunov* went even further. It recognised the possibility of liability for unlawful means conspiracy where a former bank chairman diverted huge sums of money from the bank's coffers to his own, and was assisted by his son-in-law in moving some of those assets to a safe place in breach of a worldwide freezing order. Just as in *Total Network*, the tort was used in a setting other than one involving commercial rivals. And in order to make sure that this particularly contemptible wrongdoing did not slip through the net, the court stretched the meaning of 'unlawful means' to include a contempt of court.

In combination, the two cases not only gave a new lease of life to unlawful means conspiracy, but also considerably expanded its field of operation. It therefore seems wrongheaded to consider the tort, as Carty does, 'an unimportant "legal backwater", adding little to economic tort liability'.[158] And it is noteworthy, too, that its revitalisation was not driven by concerns to capture the *Zeitgeist*, to hold trade unions in check or to promote a free-market economy. Rather, it was plainly the desire to bring within the clutches of tort law defendants whose conduct could fairly be described as especially reprehensible.

Egregious wrongdoing also helps to explain important developments that have occurred in the misrepresentation torts. In *Royal Baking Powder Co v Wright, Crossley and Co*,[159] Lord Davey clarified the classic ingredients of the tort of injurious falsehood. In setting these out, he insisted that,

> [t]o support such an action it is necessary … that the Plaintiffs have suffered special damage … [for] damage is the gist of the action, and therefore, according to the old rules of pleading, it must be specially alleged and proved.[160]

But in *Kaye v Robertson*,[161] a significantly different approach was taken as we saw in chapter six. It will be recalled that in that case a popular actor, Gordon Kaye, had been injured in a freak accident during a storm. A journalist and photographer from a tabloid newspaper, the *Sunday Sport*, obtained graphic photographs plus an 'interview' with a very disorientated Mr Kaye who was, according to doctors, in no fit state to be interviewed. The journalist and photographer managed to do what they did by gaining unauthorised access to his room. And they did this despite

[156] *Ibid*, [56] (emphasis added).
[157] For details, see chapter four.
[158] Carty (n 131) 267.
[159] *Royal Baking Powder Co v Wright, Crossley and Co* (1901) 18 RPC 95 (HL).
[160] *Ibid*, 99.
[161] *Kaye v Robertson* [1991] FSR 62 (CA).

there being a notice on his door instructing others to keep out. In order to prevent publication of this 'scoop', Mr Kaye sought an injunction on the basis of several possible torts, one of which was injurious falsehood. In relation to the injurious falsehood claim, Glidewell LJ (with whom Bingham and Leggatt LJJ agreed), said this:

> As to damage … [i]t needs little imagination to appreciate that whichever journal secured the first interview with Mr Kaye would be willing to pay the most. Mr Kaye thus has a potentially valuable right to sell the story of his accident and his recovery when he is fit enough to tell it.[162]

Notably, in so saying, Glidewell LJ dispensed with the requirement spelled out in *Royal Baking Powder* that a claimant must prove damage already suffered. As the excerpt from his judgment reveals, he thought it was enough that Mr Kaye should have lost a potential future sale of his story. There was no indication that this was what Mr Kaye actually intended to do. He had suffered brain damage and was still a long way from being his usual self by the time of the trial. Commenting on the fact that he had been forced to sue via his next friend, Glidewell LJ remarked: 'Mr Kaye is at present incapable of managing his own affairs'.[163] Since he was incapable of managing his own affairs, it follows that it was a matter of pure speculation whether Mr Kaye would at some stage seek to sell the story of his accident to the Press. Accordingly, the injunction in that case can be seen to have been granted on the basis of *a possible loss* and not (as orthodoxy then had it) on the basis of a proven (if hard to calculate) loss.[164]

The reason underpinning the court's willingness to extend the existing law in this way is thinly veiled. Glidewell LJ obviously took a dim view of the *Sunday Sport* in general terms. He said: '[a] copy of a recent edition of *Sunday Sport* which was put in evidence before us shows that many of the advertisements contained in it are for various forms of pornographic material. This indicates the readership it seeks to attract'.[165] More pertinently, the court's obvious desire to see justice done in relation to a newspaper that had invaded Mr Kaye's privacy when 'it was quite apparent to the reporter and photographer from *Sunday Sport* that Mr Kaye was in no condition to give any informed consent to their interviewing or photographing him'[166] comes through very clearly. As Bingham LJ put it, invoking a general notion of fair-mindedness (but no firm authority):

> Any reasonable and fair-minded person hearing the facts which Glidewell LJ has recited would in my judgment conclude that these defendants had wronged the plaintiff. I am therefore pleased to be persuaded that the plaintiff is able to establish, with sufficient

[162] *Ibid*, 68.
[163] *Ibid*, 63.
[164] *Ratcliffe v Evans* [1892] 2 QB 524 (CA) 532–33 (Bowen LJ): 'As much certainty and particularity must be insisted on, both in pleading and proof of damage, as is reasonable, having regard to the circumstances and to the nature of the acts themselves by which the damage is done. To insist upon less would be to relax old and intelligible principles'.
[165] *Kaye* (n 161) 63.
[166] *Ibid*, 68 (Glidewell LJ).

> strength to justify an interlocutory order, a cause of action against the defendants in malicious falsehood.[167]

The urge to fill a gap in the law – one that would have existed had there not been a preparedness to treat Mr Kaye's *loss of a chance* to sell his story as special damage – is obvious, here. The learned Lord Justice admitted to being propelled towards the conclusion he reached on the strength of the facts alone. A similar desire to make this particular defendant accountable by filling the apparent gap in the law is also evident in what Glidewell LJ had to say. Right from the very start of his judgment he bemoaned the fact that 'in English law there is no right to privacy', and that 'accordingly there is no right of action for breach of a person's privacy'.[168] His stretching the concept of special damage to embrace the loss in this case – the loss of a kind that, by his own admission, came to his mind with a 'little imagination'[169] – was clearly his Lordship's way of filling that gap and of holding the *Sunday Sport* liable in tort for the underhand methods it had employed to fill its apparently not-so-newsworthy pages.

The tort of passing off has also been developed at times in ways that have facilitated the imposition of liability on particularly reprehensible defendants. As was seen in chapter six, there are several types of case in which the courts have been prepared to hold tortiously accountable certain types of defendant who would not neatly or obviously fall within the traditional compass of the tort. We noted there, for example, *Direct Line Group Ltd v Direct Line Estate Agency Ltd*:[170] a case in which the defendants had a track record of (1) incorporating companies with names which were the same as other companies' famous trade marks and then (2) offering those companies for sale to the original proprietors at exorbitant prices. As may be recalled, Laddie J stated forthrightly that, 'this court will view with extreme displeasure any attempt by traders to embark upon a scam designed to make illegitimate use of other companies' trade marks'.[171] And we noted, too, that the courts were prepared to grant a remedy even where the company making the copycat product had never actually done any trading, making it a sizeable stretch to say that it had cashed in on the claimant's goodwill.

It was also observed in that chapter that, despite passing off's being, technically, a strict liability tort, the courts will happily attach significance to the fact that a given defendant has quite deliberately tried to deceive those who would usually be customers of the claimant by relaxing the rules on proof of damage. Thus, in *Office Cleaning Services Ltd v Westminster Window and General Cleaners Ltd*, Lord Simonds said that, 'if the intention to deceive is found, it will readily be inferred

[167] *Ibid*, 70.

[168] *Ibid*, 66. He went on, laying emphasis upon the particular circumstances, to say in the very next sentence: 'The facts of the present case are a graphic illustration of the desirability of Parliament considering whether and in what circumstances statutory provision can be made to protect the privacy of individuals'.

[169] *Ibid*, 68.

[170] *Direct Line Group Ltd v Direct Line Estate Agency Ltd* [1997] FSR 374.

[171] *Ibid*, 376.

that deception will result'.[172] The willingness to modify the tort – at least in terms of what must be proven – was openly driven by a desire to bring within the reach of tort law those whose conduct is particularly reprehensible.

Taken as a whole, what the cases considered in this section of the chapter illustrate is that egregious wrongdoing has counted for a very great deal when it comes to the way that both the general and the misrepresentation economic torts have developed over the past century or so. The courts have, at times, grasped with both hands the idea that existing tort rules and doctrines are flexible; that they can be stretched, modified or simply added to in order to plug gaps in the law through which particularly reprehensible conduct might otherwise slip.

VI. Conclusion

In addition to the juridical and structural disjunctions between the economic torts that were highlighted in the previous chapter, this chapter has sought to show that many different influences affected the introduction and subsequent development of the actions in view. The ad hoc ways that this range of influences affected the various torts only adds to the impression that they are more readily seen in terms of their heterogeneity than their unity. The trajectory of their development has not been governed solely by ebbs and flows in the rival policies of abstentionism and interventionism as Carty would have us believe. The story is an altogether more complex one than that. More specifically, the influence of each of the different factors has varied over time, and varied also as between the different torts. Thus, although there is more than a grain of truth in the claim made by Lobban that, 'the outcome of cases depended on whether the judges approved or disapproved of the economic activity in question',[173] that is only a fraction of the story.

In similar vein, it is far too limited a description of recent developments in the general economic torts to state that they have 'experienced something of a resurgence, finding a new role in resolving the boundaries of commercial ethics, of what can and cannot be done to further one's own economic interests at the expense of competitors'.[174] For in none of the three most recent Supreme Court

[172] *Office Cleaning Services Ltd v Westminster Window and General Cleaners Ltd* (1946) 63 RPC 39 (HL), 42–43. In similar vein, see *British Sky Broadcasting Group Plc v Sky Home Services Ltd* [2007] FSR 14.

[173] Lobban (n 58) 1033.

[174] J O'Sullivan, 'Intentional Economic Torts, Commercial Transactions and Professional Liability' (2008) 24 *Professional Negligence* 164, 165. For a broadly similar account, arguing that industrial action dictated the early evolution of the economic torts, while rivalry between businesses has done more to dictate their modern development, see Deakin and Randall (n 123) 524 ('the priorities of industrial action law came to overshadow the evolution of the economic torts') and 531 ('as modern competition law began to develop, the role of the economic torts in market regulation became an adjunct one to that of statute'). In fairness to all these authors, though, they were writing before *Khrapunov* (n 14) was decided.

cases – ie, *Total Network*, *Khrapunov* and *Secretary of State for Health v Servier Laboratories Ltd*[175] – were the respective defendants and claimants commercial rivals.

As was seen, the particular era and ideological climate in which certain cases fell to be decided could count for a great deal. Negative influences – such as public sentiment following the Sheffield outrages – played a part. But so too, sometimes, did more positive developments. The common law tort of passing off, for example, was avowedly[176] developed in the *Erven Warnink* case to achieve alignment with various consumer welfarist statutes that had been introduced. But that said, and by way of obvious contrast, the economic torts have sometimes been developed as a reaction *against* statutory interventions. The introduction of statutory immunities for certain trade union activities, for instance, prompted a number of important developments in the field of economic tort liability.[177]

Perhaps most startling of all is the role that the political predilections of certain key judges has played in shaping these torts. Overt expressions of faith in free markets and the ideology of individualism can be found in the case law, as can a marked (and arguably class-based[178]) distrust of organised labour. In recent times, the most striking departures from orthodoxy have generally been characterised by a clear determination to ensure that especially egregious wrongdoing should fall within the reach of the economic torts. And finally, more obviously than in any other area of tort law, the courts have been guided in this sphere – in even some of the landmark cases – by what jurists have said about the various actions with which this book is concerned.

The result of all these influences is a bunch of torts that is often described as chaotic.[179] I reject that pejorative description and prefer to describe these torts, more charitably, as an excellent microcosm of the heterogeneity and questionable coherence of tort law in general.[180] The early House of Lords cases certainly reflect the fact that, 'typically Lords of Appeal of this era … [were] chosen primarily for their political achievements rather than for their professional successes'.[181] But the

[175] *Servier* (n 107).

[176] I say 'avowedly' because it is not entirely clear, under economic analysis, whether this has been achieved since, very crudely, although a wide-ranging tort of passing off cuts back the chance of consumer deception, it also stifles competition. For much more detail on the economic analysis of passing off, see Murphy (n 33).

[177] Pertinently, if not perfectly accurately, it has been argued that, '[T]he evolution [of the economic torts] has been a strange and even rather artificial one, directed above all by plaintiffs' attempts to circumvent the immunities': see Deakin and Randall (n 123) 531. See also, Simpson (n 21) *passim*.

[178] For a sustained defence of this view, see Klarman (n 13) 1575–91.

[179] See chapter one.

[180] On tort law's heterogeneity, see J Murphy, 'The Heterogeneity of Tort Law' (2019) 39 *Oxford Journal of Legal Studies* 455; and on tort law's incoherent development, see J Murphy, 'Contemporary Tort Theory and Tort Law's Evolution' (2019) 32 *Canadian Journal of Law and Jurisprudence* 413.

[181] N Duxbury, 'Lord Wright and Innovative Traditionalism' (2009) 59 *University of Toronto Law Journal* 265, 275.

justice-driven, interstitial law-making that characterises the more recent cases aptly reflects the point made by Toulson LJ in *Meretz Investments NV v ACP Ltd* that, 'the common law in this area is designed only to enforce basic standards of civilised behaviour'.[182] And the desire to do justice, to make accountable in tort law those who engage in especially reprehensible conduct, has certainly triumphed over any concerns for juridical tidiness.

[182] *Meretz Investments NV v ACP Ltd* [2007] EWCA Civ 1303 (CA) [174].

9

Future Province of the Economic Torts

I. Introduction

In chapters three to six, I endeavoured to unearth both the existing and the potential province of each of the eight torts considered in this book. In order to do this, I focused upon exactly what the relevant cases say (if anything) about the limits of their uses. To some extent, these chapters were also intended to serve as a corrective to the various monistic claims about the economic torts that have been made by a number of prominent commentators. For, it is only once we free ourselves from the tramlines set by these unduly narrow depictions of the purpose and purview of these torts that we stand any chance of evincing the truth concerning their probable and possible future uses.

It is, for example, clear that we will be misled regarding the uses to which the economic torts may be put if we accept uncritically Carty's proclamation that, 'in the general economic torts the defendant seeks to attack the claimant, whereas in the misrepresentation economic torts the defendant seeks to make a gain that properly belongs to the claimant'.[1] And we will be misled because her division between the two sets of torts is inaccurate. Take, for instance, the decision in *Lumley v Gye*[2] – the foundational case in the general economic tort of inducing breach of contract. This clearly fits the function that Carty ascribes to the misrepresentation torts given the fact that Gye was attempting to obtain money from opera-goers who would, in the absence of any attempt to attract Wagner to his own opera house, have been paying money to his rival, Lumley, to hear her sing at his premises. At the same time, many cases of injurious falsehood (a misrepresentation tort) involve defendants who are not the claimant's trade rivals (as they would have to be to meet Carty's description). *Ratcliffe v Evans*[3] is a good example. There, the defendant was a newspaper editor, and by no stretch of the imagination someone who could be described as the claimant's competitor. And the same is true of a typical deceit case in which C is duped into thinking that she is doing business *with* (rather than competing against) D. In neither of these types of case is there any issue of C suing in respect of misdirected gains.

[1] H Carty, *An Analysis of the Economic Torts*, 2nd edn (Oxford, Oxford University Press, 2010) 3.
[2] *Lumley v Gye* (1853) 2 El & Bl 216.
[3] *Ratcliffe v Evans* [1892] 2 QB 525 (CA).

What these last two examples also highlight is the fact that it is plainly too simplistic to claim, as Carty does, that '[t]he development of these torts [ie, injurious falsehood and deceit] has been dictated by the caution of the common law in allowing competitors to control commercial misrepresentations'.[4] And, in any case, deceit is clearly not a tort confined to the commercial setting: modern internet and telephone scams affect plenty of people besides those who work in the world of commerce.[5]

Another general claim that must be resisted if the true (potential) role of these torts is to be appreciated is the one advanced forcefully by Deakin, namely, that the economic torts are (or should be) confined to the protection of interests in 'trade, business and employment'.[6] This particular combination of words can be traced to section 3 of the Trade Disputes Act 1906.[7] But the idea that a statutory defence should define the parameters of the various economic torts – including intimidation, to which tort that Act never applied – seems clearly misguided. No-one, for example, would think that because a defence may be invoked by those who publish peer reviewed claims in scientific or academic journals[8] that the law of defamation is (or should be) confined to statements about scientific or academic matters. Nor, likewise, are the various kinds of interference protected by the law of private nuisance limited to those in respect of which the defence of abatement may be claimed.

To some extent, when commentators speak about the 'chaos of these torts',[9] they do so because the torts in question resist confinement within the artificial parameters that they (and not the courts) have constructed. And it is just the same when it comes to claims about the redundancy or terminal decline of some of these actions. It is true that many of the early cases involving the general economic torts centred on disputes between labour and capital. And it is true, too, that the regulation of such matters is now overwhelmingly governed by statute. But several milestone cases cannot be fitted within this paradigm: some – such as *Allen v Flood*[10] and *Rookes v Barnard*[11] – effectively involved litigation between labour and labour,[12] while others involved disputes between one business and another.[13]

[4] Carty (n 1) 7.

[5] And for an older case involving a non-commercial victim, see, eg, *Langridge v Levy* (1837) 2 M & W 519.

[6] See, eg, S Deakin and J Randall, 'Rethinking the Economic Torts' (2009) 72 *MLR* 519, 533.

[7] Similar, but not exactly the same words – ie, 'trade, business or livelihood' – were used in *Keeble v Hickeringill* (1706) 11 East 574. But as noted in chapter four, *Keeble* was a nuisance case and not one that set the parameters of the economic torts.

[8] Defamation Act 2013, s 6.

[9] Carty (n 1) 10. See also Deakin and Randall (n 6) 525; JA Weir, 'Chaos or Cosmos: *Rookes, Stratford,* and the Economic Torts' [1964] *CLJ* 225, 226.

[10] *Allen v Flood* [1898] AC 1 (HL).

[11] *Rookes v Barnard* [1964] AC 1129 (HL).

[12] See, eg, *Huntley v Thornton* [1957] 1 WLR 321.

[13] See, eg, *Mogul Steamship Co Ltd v McGregor, Gow & Co* [1892] AC 25; *Lonrho Plc v Fayed (No 1)* [1992] 1 AC 448 (HL).

Accordingly, it is myopic to announce or predict the demise of these torts for the reason given by Lord Hoffmann (extra-judicially), namely, that:

> [as a] result of Mrs Thatcher's legislation … in the area of industrial relations, there is no longer any interest in the common law economic torts … Parliament has taken over the task of delimiting what industrial action should be lawful or unlawful, without regard to contractual relationships.[14]

In truth, *most* of the economic torts – and not just the general ones that are historically bound up with litigation arising out of industrial relations – are very much alive and well. It is a matter of record that there is a fairly steady flow of reported cases involving claims based on the unlawful means tort, inducing breach of contract, passing off and deceit. Even unlawful means conspiracy[15] – a tort that need not be relied upon in many cases because of the overlap it enjoys with the established rules on joint tortfeasance – is invoked with (all such things considered) surprising frequency.[16]

The remaining economic torts, it is true, seldom arise in practice. But this does not mean that they can be dismissed as being either redundant or in terminal decline. The crime of treason cannot be described as redundant simply by virtue of the paucity of cases involving this offence. Rarity and redundancy are very different beasts. Thus, the rarity with which any given tort is invoked is not an indicium of decline or demise. And nor can it be assumed that there is a positive correlation between the importance of a wrong and the frequency with which it is committed. Taking that approach would lead to an obviously erroneous view of the relative significance of murder on the one hand, and minor traffic offences, on the other. Put tersely: it is clearly wrong to consider moribund, or to marginalise, certain torts simply because, in practice, they are relatively infrequently invoked.

Most of my defence of the vitality and future potential of the eight torts considered in this book has already been supplied. In chapters three to six, I explained how – especially in recent years – most of the economic torts have been put to a range of uses that have nothing to do with the regulation of wrongs committed by one trade

[14] L Hoffmann, 'The Rise and Fall of the Economic Torts' in S Degeling *et al* (eds), *Torts in Commercial Law* (Pyrmont, NSW, Thomson Reuters, 2009) 113.

[15] According to a *Westlaw* search conducted at the end of April 2021, there had been over the previous 12 months, no fewer than 22 cases in which the prospect of liability for unlawful means conspiracy was considered.

[16] As Lord Hoffmann observed: 'if one of the conspirators has committed a tort, the others would be liable as accessories to that tort without there being a separate tort of conspiracy … [so] [i]t comes into play [only] when people conspire to do something which causes loss by means which are unlawful, but not otherwise tortious on the part of any of the conspirators': Hoffmann (n 14) 115. *Cf* PS Davies and P Sales, 'Intentional Harm, Accessories and Conspiracies' (2018) 134 *LQR* 69, 73-74. These authors point out a reason why the inventive use of unlawful means conspiracy may even flourish. It runs as follows. If C can identify that D had a co-conspirator (even one who performed no act herself), C will be able to rely on D's common law crimes as unlawful means in a way that would not be open to C if he were to seek to rely on the unlawful means tort.

rival against another. I argued also that, properly understood, the key authorities seldom (if ever) conclusively limit the role of these torts to the fulfilment of such a function. But two further things remain to be done in this chapter.

In section II, I defend *as a general matter* the capacity of torts (including the ones in view) to be put to novel purposes. True, I have already defended certain particular instances of individual torts being used as gap-fillers. Recall, for example, my discussion of various possible inventive uses of unlawful means conspiracy, injurious falsehood and passing off. What I have not so far supplied, however, is (1) a *general warrant* for *all* the torts in this book to be so used, or (2) an account of the limits of such an enterprise.

In section III, conscious of the prescriptive dimension to some of the arguments marshalled in section II, I offer a defence of why an element of normativity is acceptable within a study that purports to offer an interpretive account of the *true* purview of the economic torts. At the heart of this defence is the claim that no interpretation of what the law will allow in relation to foreseeable (but yet-to-be-litigated) circumstances can ever be without a prescriptive dimension. What matters, I shall argue, is that this prescriptive dimension be kept within precedent-respecting bounds, that it be (in other words) inoffensive from the perspective of retroactive law-making. To this end, my analysis of these yet-to-be litigated matters may be said to be offered from the standpoint of a 'precedent-respecting progressive'. In dealing with these issues, I distance myself from both those I describe as 'precedent-respecting conservatives' and those I label 'precedent-ignoring mavericks'. Section IV offers a brief conclusion.

II. The Future of the Economic Torts

Arguably, the most certain claim that can be made about the overhaul of the general economic torts undertaken in *OBG Ltd v Allan*[17] is that it raised almost as many questions as it answered. Among the most pressing of these were the following: (1) Do these torts have any role to play in two-party settings? (2) Is unlawful means conspiracy now redundant (mindful of *both* the extant rules on joint tortfeasance, *and* Lord Hoffmann's insistence that, in future, there should be a simple, two-tort structure in this arena)? (3) Is lawful means conspiracy best seen as an historical anomaly, as an action that can safely be regarded as having died a long overdue death?

While the decision in *Revenue and Customs Commissioners v Total Network SL*[18] answered some of these questions, it also raised others of its own. Little wonder, then, that Carty should have suggested in the wake of *Total Network* that 'the ripples of uncertainty that flow from the revitalised tort of conspiracy will

[17] *OBG Ltd v Allan* [2008] 1 AC 1 (HL).
[18] *Revenue and Customs Commissioners v Total Network SL* [2008] 1 AC 1174 (HL).

ultimately call into question the future function of the unlawful means tort'.[19] Others, too, were prompted to contemplate the less-than-certain future of these torts in several other jurisdictions.[20] In the remainder of this section I join the fold by considering two matters: first, the merits, in general terms, of using these torts as gap-fillers; and, secondly, the related issue of the extent to which, in addressing perceived lacunae in the law, these torts may legitimately come apart from their original juridical and purposive moorings in an effort to keep pace with societal values and expectations.

A. The Legitimacy of Judicial Gap-Filling

The *idea* that judges may act as interstitial law-makers can be traced to Justice Holmes' dissent in *Southern Pacific Co v Jensen* in 1917.[21] But the first sustained *defence* of the practice – along the lines that the judge legitimately 'fills the open space in the law'[22] so long as she 'keep[s] within those interstitial limits which … other judges through the centuries of the common law have set to judge made innovation' – was not advanced until a few years later. That defence was proffered by another influential American judge-cum-jurist.[23] Since then, a very sizeable body of literature associated with judicial law-making has emerged. But of particular note is the especially pertinent claim of Lord Mance (in the *Total Network* case) that their Lordships were fully justified in using the tort of unlawful means conspiracy to plug a gap in the law. As noted in a previous chapter, his justification placed considerable weight on the fact that 'there would be an evident lacuna if the law did not respond to this situation by recognising a civil liability'.[24]

His saying this, however, cannot *per se* be read as licensing a similar gap-filling use of the other economic torts. And nor was it a claim about the use of unlawful means conspiracy with which all of the other judges on the panel agreed. Indeed, Lords Hope and Neuberger expressly registered their disagreement with Lord Hope on this front. But having said that, it is important to note the basis of their disagreement. They did not stand in opposition to judicial, interstitial law-making as a general matter. They simply thought it wrong for judges to fill in *gaps in legislation* (as opposed to gaps in the common law). Lord Neuberger opined that it was,

[19] H Carty, 'The Modern Functions of the Economic Torts: Reviewing the English, Canadian, Australian, and New Zealand Positions' [2015] *CLJ* 261, 265.

[20] See, eg, JW Neyers, 'Causing Loss by Unlawful Means: Should the High Court of Australia follow *OBG Ltd v Allan*?' in Degeling *et al* (n 14); Davies and Sales (n 16) 72; P Edmundson, 'Conspiracy by Unlawful Means: Keeping the Tort Untangled' (2008) 16 *Torts Law Journal* 189.

[21] *Southern Pacific Co v Jensen* 244 US 205 (1917), 221. See also, *Hardie Finance Corp Pty Ltd v Ahern (No 3)* [2010] WASC 403, [709].

[22] BN Cardozo, *The Nature of the Judicial Process* (New Haven, Yale University Press, 1921) 113.

[23] *Ibid*, 103.

[24] *Total Network* (n 18) [120].

'unconvincing and unattractive that the common law should be invoked to "fill in the gaps" in a taxing statute'.[25] And in similar vein, Lord Hope said:

> the regime for the administration and collection of VAT which is set out in the 1994 Act is indeed comprehensive and does not admit the use by the commissioners of [common law] means for collecting VAT which are not provided for by the statute.[26]

We may therefore safely put to one side their remarks. Not only were they *not* aimed at the practice of interstitial law-making *in general*, they were also based on the false belief that the Value Added Tax Act 1994 constituted an exhaustive regime for the recovery of VAT. The erroneous nature of this belief was exposed by Lord Walker in his leading speech when he pointed out that the commissioners have ancillary powers to those contained in the statute of 1994 under which they are specifically permitted to bring civil proceedings. The enabling provisions to which he alluded are found in sections 9 and 25 of the Commissioners for Revenue and Customs Act 2005.[27] And one particular civil law action he mentioned that would be available to the commissioners was the action against a receiver for misfeasance in winding up proceedings. Lord Scott also rejected the claim that the 1994 Act was intended to establish a comprehensive remedial regime.[28]

Given that a majority of their Lordships saw no specific statutory obstacle to the forging of a common law remedy, the question that naturally arises is whether there is a more general objection that can be raised in relation to the courts using the economic torts as gap-fillers. By way of answer to that question, I do two things. First, I counter certain arguments that have been made by other jurists against their being used in this way. And, secondly, I consider the merits of various countervailing arguments that might be used in order *positively* to support such usage.

Adopting the view that Lords Hope and Mance were right to identify the decision in *Total Network* as an unwarranted instance of interstitial law-making, Carty considers the majority's approach to have been misguided on the footing that 'this magic "gap-filling" … [was] at odds with the abstentionist agenda set by both *Allen* and *OBG*'.[29] So saying, however, presupposes that there ever was (or could be) such an agenda. But this seems implausible. For as Lord Bingham (writing extra-judicially) has pointed out: 'a judge who works to a pre-determined agenda necessarily deprives himself of the capacity to respond to the merits of a particular

[25] *Ibid*, [188].
[26] *Ibid*, [31].
[27] *Ibid*, [106].
[28] He said: 'I can see no reason why the commissioners, the victims of a fraudulent conspiracy, should be barred from recovering damages against the principal conspirator, Total. An intention that that should be so cannot, in my opinion, be attributed to the legislature in enacting the VAT scheme': *Total Network* (n 18) [60].
[29] H Carty, 'The Tort of Conspiracy as a Can of Worms' in SGA Pitel *et al* (eds), *Tort Law: Challenging Orthodoxy* (Oxford, Hart Publishing, 2013) 405.

case as it unfolds before him'.[30] Furthermore, as explained in the previous chapter, it is far from clear that there was ever an agenda that could convincingly account for the genesis and subsequent development of the economic torts. And although Lord Hoffmann is on record as having said that, '[i]n regulating competition, the common law should be modest in its ambitions',[31] he was writing extra-judicially at the time. He certainly said nothing of this kind in *OBG* itself.

Perhaps even more important, when it comes to rebutting Carty's contention, are the following two points: first, the fact that no court exerts control over those who decide to resort to litigation (rather than settle out of court); and secondly, the fact that no appellate court can control any given litigant's preparedness to appeal a first instance decision. In combination, these observations make it extremely doubtful whether there ever could or would be an agenda of the kind Carty has in mind. No individual judge – at whatever judicial level – could realistically have good reason to think a 'suitable case', or string of cases, would be likely to come their way.

Carty's second argument against gap-filling is aimed only at the general economic torts. It rests on the idea that they are designed merely to stretch existing civil liability.[32] What she means by this is that liability on the part of D towards an intermediary, T, can be stretched so as to enable C to sue D for the loss consequentially suffered by C as a result of D's initial wrong against T. And her objection, in essence, relies on the idea that liability-stretching is a quintessential feature of the torts in question. She thinks that certain developments – ie, those that would undermine the liability-stretching nature of these torts – must be rejected because otherwise the relevant torts would lose a key part of their identity. For her, any such transformation would be a step too far.

As a general matter, Carty has a valid point. If I begin with a long, plain, wooden cane, I can legitimately work on it so that it becomes shorter, or more decorative. But what I must not do, if I want it to remain recognisably a cane, is burn it so that it becomes a pile of ash. To put it less graphically, there are limits to the ways in which torts with distinctive characteristics can be reconfigured. For our purposes, then, the key question is whether it is right to consider liability-stretching a quintessential feature of the torts in view. If it is, then this would, as Carty submits, set an important limit on what can be done with these torts by a creatively minded judge. But as it turns out I think it is wrong to regard these torts as liability-stretchers. My reason for so thinking can conveniently be explained by way of a hypothetical.

Suppose that D_1 and D_2 conspire to engineer things such that D_2 is able to kidnap C's employee, T. T's being kidnapped means that T cannot now perform

[30] T Bingham, *The Business of Judging: Selected Essays and Speeches* (Oxford, Oxford University Press, 2000) 33.

[31] Hoffmann (n 14) 114.

[32] Carty (n 19) 265: '[the cases involve] stretching existing civil liability'.

an agreed task that would have been the source of income for C. Any subsequent action brought by C against either D_1 or D_2 might conceivably be based on the unlawful means tort (or even unlawful means conspiracy). But it could not be based on false imprisonment or battery (the torts actually committed against T). Yet since *only* false imprisonment and battery would be available to T were he to sue his kidnapper, it is clearly not the case that D_1 and D_2's liability towards T is being stretched from T to C.

Of course, it could be argued that what is meant by liability-stretching is nothing so precise as the liability *for tort X* being extended from the primary victim, T, to a secondary victim, C. But this is, in fact, the way that Carty uses the phrase. She expressly borrows the concept of liability-stretching from the judgment of Cromwell J in *AI Enterprises Ltd v Bram Enterprises Ltd*.[33] And Cromwell J could scarcely have been clearer when he said:

> the preferred rationale [for the economic torts], focuses on *extending an existing right to sue* from the immediate victim of the unlawful act to another party whom the defendant intended to target with the unlawful conduct. I will call this the 'liability stretching' rationale.[34]

As we have just noted, however, no such stretching of 'an existing right to sue' occurs. His Honour was, with respect, wrong to suggest that a three-party economic tort 'does not seek to create new actionable wrongs but simply to expand the range of persons who may sue for harm intentionally caused by existing actionable wrongs to a third party'.[35] There is a separate tort being committed in such cases: the unlawful means tort. There is no doubt that it is a tort in its own right rather than just an inappropriate name to give to tortious liability for a very different tort that has simply been stretched. It follows that Carty's objection to the use of the general economic torts as gap-fillers – so far as it is premised on this misconceived idea of how they *do and must* function – also founders.

Carty's final reason for rejecting the use of the economic torts to plug lacunae within the common law relies on the twin claims that (1) 'the protection of economic interests is the prime reason for the existence and development of these torts',[36] and (2) that they should remain tethered to the 'traditional function of … protect[ing] against excessive trade competition'.[37] Again, there is *possibly* something of merit in an objection of this kind. At its heart is the idea that certain torts have a particular interest at their core which cannot be ignored without undermining something quintessential about that tort. Wrongs of this kind do exist. For example, the tort of private nuisance is tethered inextricably to the protection of certain proprietary interests. It cannot – without ceasing to be the property-based

[33] *AI Enterprises Ltd v Bram Enterprises Ltd* 2014 SCC 12, [37].
[34] *Ibid*, [37] (emphasis added).
[35] *Ibid*, [45].
[36] Carty (n 1) 1, fn 2.
[37] Carty (n 19) 265.

tort it has always been – suddenly be used to provide a remedy for personal injuries suffered by persons who have no proprietary interest in the property affected by the nuisance.[38] Using private nuisance in this way would be like eating soup with a fork.

For Carty's final objection to hold good in relation to the putative 'off-limits uses' of the economic torts, then, everything turns on the question of whether these actions are (as she asserts) inextricably tied to the protection of trade and business interests. This, however, is a belief that cannot be grounded in the law as it presents itself. In chapter three, we saw that several of the antecedent cases that were relied upon in formulating the rule in *Lumley* had nothing to do with commercial relations. The cases in question did not limit damages to the reparation of purely economic losses.[39] Over the last 100 years or so, essentially the same preparedness to allow various others of the economic torts to be invoked in non-commercial settings can also be identified. Damages for losses other than trade or business losses have been awarded in cases of two-party intimidation,[40] deceit[41] and injurious falsehood.[42] And although the early twentieth century conspiracy case of *Pratt v British Medical Association*[43] did concern the commercial matter of defendants combining unlawfully to deprive certain medical officers of their livelihoods, it was nonetheless a case in which the court was also willing to grant reparation in respect of non-economic losses. Concluding his judgment in the case, McCardie J said:

> What damages, then, should I award ? … I cannot ignore the deliberate and relentless vigour with which the defendants sought to achieve the infliction of complete ruin. I must regard *not merely the pecuniary loss* sustained by the plaintiffs, but the long period for which they respectively suffered *humiliation and menace.*[44]

It turns out, then, that Carty's opposition to these torts being used in a fashion that undermines their 'proper' confinement to the protection of purely economic interests is flatly contradicted by a number of cases, some of which are old, others of which are more recent. Indeed, the truth is that most of the torts considered in this book have already been applied in contexts other than those characterised by trade rivalry; and quite a few of them have also been used as the basis for damages intended to compensate claimants for various non-economic losses.

[38] *Hunter v Canary Wharf Ltd* [1997] AC 655 (HL).

[39] See discussion there of *Andrews v Askey* (1837) 8 Car & P 7, 9 (distress and anxiety) and *Dodd v Norris* (1814) 3 Camp 519, 520 (injury to feelings).

[40] See discussion there of *Godwin v Uzoigwe* [1993] *Fam Law* 65 (CA) (claimant used as household drudge).

[41] See discussion there of *Langridge* (n 5) and *Burrows v Rhodes* [1899] 1 QB 816 (physical injury) as well as *Mafo v Adams* [1970] 1 QB 548 (CA) (physical inconvenience) and *Shelley v Paddock* [1980] QB 348 (CA) (distress).

[42] See *Khodaparast v Shad* [2000] 1 WLR 618 (CA) (injured feelings).

[43] *Pratt v British Medical Association* [1919] 1 KB 244.

[44] *Ibid*, 282 (emphasis added).

What may be concluded from the analysis in the preceding pages is that the three general objections to using torts as gap-fillers have, at best, limited purchase in relation to the economic torts. The idea that there is an agenda that must be followed is easily rebuffed if one considers the reality concerning the way cases come before both first instance and appellate courts: the idea that any given judge could meaningfully formulate and then implement such an agenda simply cannot be grounded. At the same time, although it is true that certain aspects of torts – be they key ingredients, or an historically entrenched limitation in scope – can in theory serve to constrain the range of possible uses to which those torts may be put, one must exercise caution in identifying these aspects. Simply saying, for example, that the general economic torts are quintessentially liability-stretchers, or that they must always be confined to the protection of economic interests, is plainly not enough; not when these claims are readily contradicted by reference to the extant authorities.

I realise, of course, the limitation of pointing out the absence of sound objections to the gap-filling use of the economic torts. Showing that reason A is not a good enough reason for resisting their being used in this way is not the same thing as identifying a positive reason, B, why the courts *should* extend (or be permitted to extend), their range so as to impose civil liability in previously unexplored situations. So what, in positive terms, can be said in favour of using torts generally, and the economic torts in particular, as gap-fillers?

One powerful point that can be made in this connection is that such gap-filling is a practice that, in very general terms, has the backing of some of our most senior judges whom one would expect to have a keen appreciation of the limits of judicial power. Thus, in this respect, it is noteworthy that Lord Mance does not stand alone in thinking that judicial interstitial law-making is an appropriate task for a senior judge. The distinguished Australian judge, Sir Michael Kirby once said in a Hamlyn lecture that, '[s]o long as human language remains imprecise and human capacity to predict the future limited, it will fall to judges to fill the gaps in the law's rules'[45] since from a pragmatic point of view, the judges 'know full well, from many like cases, that nothing will be done [by the legislature] because the problem is too particular, divisive, technical or boring to merit political attention and parliamentary time'.[46] More recently, in an article devoted entirely to the subject of judicial law-making, Lord Hodge also expressed the view that although judges 'are not permitted to develop the law in a direction which is contrary to the expressed will of Parliament … [t]hey may fill in gaps left by Parliament'.[47]

In addition to these distinguished judges recognising the legitimacy of judicial gap-filling, it is also notable that many previous generations of judges have actually

[45] M Kirby, *Judicial Activism: Authority, Principle and Policy in the Judicial Method* (London, Sweet and Maxwell, 2004) 29–30.

[46] *Ibid*, 66.

[47] PS Hodge, 'The Scope of Judicial Law-making in the Common Law Tradition' (2020) 84 *Rabels Zeitschrift für ausländisches und internationales Privatrecht* 211, 226.

engaged in the practice. Thus, according to Ibbetson, in his magisterial study of the evolution of the entire common law of obligations since the Middle Ages, this is exactly what the courts have done for centuries. Summarising what he perceives to be the discernible norm, he writes:

> [l]egal change occurs through filling gaps between rules in the way that seems most convenient or most just at the time; through twisting existing rules … through inventing new rules that get tacked onto existing ones … through injecting shifting ideas of fairness or justice.[48]

B. Constraints on, and Justifications for, Judicial Innovation

The freedom that judges possess to engage in interstitial law-making is not, of course, unlimited. I have already adverted to two important constraints that apply in relation to tort law generally: these are that: (1) there is only so far that the meaning ascribed to a key ingredient of any given tort may be stretched; and (2) *some torts* cannot, by definition, be used otherwise than in connection with a particular type of interest. These, however, are not concerns that have any purchase in relation to the potential uses of the economic torts that have been advanced in this study.

The second constraint is inapplicable because, as we have seen, there is a significant body of case law that belies the descriptive accuracy of the label, 'economic torts'. The torts of deceit, intimidation, unlawful means conspiracy and injurious falsehood all permit recovery for losses of a non-economic kind. Furthermore, in relation to all but one of the remaining economic torts, there is nothing in the case law that prevents their being used in connection with non-economic losses.[49] As regards the first constraint, nothing that I have suggested concerning the use of these torts involves stretching the meaning of elements like 'intention', 'malice' or 'unlawful means' beyond points already reached in past decisions. A brief reminder of what I have said concerning potential future uses may be helpful, here.

With respect to the unlawful means tort, I paid close attention to what was actually said in *OBG* and found nothing in that case that ruled out the tort's use in relation to the protection of personal or proprietary interests. By contrast, however, I did alight upon various dicta in that case that could be invoked to support the use of this tort in cases other than those involving harm to trade or business interests.[50] A possible rejoinder to these dicta is possible. It consists in the claim that

[48] DJ Ibbetson, *A Historical Introduction to the Law of Obligations* (Oxford, Oxford University Press, 1999) 294.

[49] The possibility of the economic torts being used in connection with non-economic losses has even been recognised (obiter) by the Supreme Court: see the example given in Lord Hamblen's speech in *Secretary of State for Health v Servier Laboratories Ltd* [2021] UKSC 24 (SC), [85].

[50] And although the 'dealing requirement' laid down in *OBG* was specifically endorsed in *Servier* (*ibid*), it was at no point said in that later case that C must suffer the financial ill-effects of D's wrongful conduct towards the third party with whom C has a prior economic relationship.

the ingredients and scope of the unlawful means tort should remain inflexible for pragmatic reasons. To be clear, the claim here is not that the elements of this tort are incapable of being stretched, and nor is it that this tort is tied inextricably to the protection of economic interests (in the way that private nuisance is tied to the protection of interests in land). Rather, it is that the tort's contents and contours should be clear and inflexible in the interests of commercial certainty.

The rejoinder, however, is easily rebuffed. To begin with, it rests on an argument that has only ever been advanced in academic discourse. It has no judicial authority whatsoever to back it up. Furthermore, at its core is a claim that simply cannot be squared with the historical fact that, ever since its inception, the unlawful means tort has been dogged by uncertainty. This is an important observation to make because it is demonstrably the case that businesses and traders have managed well enough in organising their affairs *despite* the tort's key ingredients and scope having always been matters for debate. The very fact that traders have managed to do this puts paid to the notion that the elements and reach of this tort *must* be clear in the interests of commercial certainty.

As regards the other economic torts in respect of which there is no extant authority indicating that they may be used to protect non-economic interests, there is, again, nothing in the decided cases that obstructs their being used in this way. And on top of this, all of these other torts contain key ingredients that are notable for their historical, conceptual fluidity. In combination, these two observations suggest that these remaining economic torts are neither intrinsically inappropriate gap-fillers, nor a set of actions that *must* invariably be confined to the protection of only trade and business interests, and comprise elements that are, needs be, clear and precise.

When it comes to opposing the use of the economic torts as gap-fillers, the closest that any of the objections considered so far gets to having any real bite is when the tort of passing off is placed under the spotlight. It is, after all, a tort that is firmly tied to the protection of a specific economic interest, namely, goodwill. But even this point, I would submit, is not enough to prevent this tort being used more expansively or imaginatively. As we saw in chapter six, it is (and has been for years) a tort at the crossroads. Add to this the fact that the various components of the so-called classical trinity have all been subject to considerable development over the years and it becomes implausible to argue that passing off is a tort with clearly defined parameters and ingredients that must be kept this way in the interests of commercial certainty.

Leaving objections based on conceptual fluidity to one side, a slightly different argument may be proffered against using the economic torts as gap-fillers. It rests on the assertion that they were originally 'designed only to enforce basic standards of civilised behaviour in economic competition between traders or between employers and labour'.[51] But note: this is mere affirmation. Furthermore, even if it were true that these torts were originally designed to fulfil this role, it would

[51] *OBG* (n 17) [56]. Even the powerful dissentient in that case, Lord Nicholls, labelled it the tort of 'interference with a business by unlawful means': *ibid*, [139].

not, without more, follow that they cannot now be used for some other purpose. This is because the mere fact that something was *designed* for purpose X does not preclude its subsequently being used to fulfil purpose Y. Consider this example. A suit of clothes is initially designed to be worn by someone in order that they may dress smartly. When, some years later, the suit is a little the worse for wear, it is not somehow inappropriate for it to be used in, say, the construction of a scarecrow in order to protect crops.[52] The suit's usefulness *as smart attire* may well have expired, but this does not mean that *all its usefulness* has been exhausted. What is true of the suit is also potentially true of torts and other rules of law. For example, the rule developed within land law about the acquisition of a prescriptive right was not initially developed in order to ground a defence to an action based on private nuisance. But it most assuredly became one.

By far the most significant obstacle faced by judges who are minded to engage in interstitial law-making is the objectionability of retrospective law-making. If, in a given case, a court decides to develop a particular area of law, and in order to do this, reformulates some or other existing rule, this will mean that the litigants concerned have their case resolved according to a rule of law that was not in force at the time of the alleged tort. The concern, then, as Stapleton vividly puts it, is that such retroactive decision-making 'is likely to be seen, at least by the losing party, as a pernicious ambush because it fails to judge the parties according to … the state of the law at the time the parties interacted'.[53]

It is a powerful point, and it cannot be ignored by judges who are, in principle, willing to develop the law creatively. On the other hand, however, if it is taken too far, this constraint on the judges' freedom to extend the reach of an existing cause of action into previously uncharted waters threatens to ossify the law. This in turn would lead to a set of rules that, over time, would appear obviously antiquated. Accordingly, the concern about retrospective rule-making must have limits. In unearthing these limits, the first point to note – and it is one expressly recognised by an eminent judge of the 1960s – is that 'judge made law is always retrospective'.[54] Every tort case, in other words, involves a court deciding *today* on the relevant rule of law governing the parties' interaction at some time in the past. When the court spells out the relevant rule of law, it is not laying down a rule that will only be applied in the future. Quite the opposite. It is articulating the rule of law that must be applied to what took place between parties some months (or even possibly, years) ago.

The significance of this point should not be underestimated. For it illuminates the fact that retrospectivity is an unavoidable feature of *any* system of judge-made law. Accordingly, unless we abandon our commitment to the common law as a system of law, the truly pertinent questions to pose in this context are as follows.

[52] I am grateful to Roderick Bagshaw for inspiring me to give this illustration by suggesting a similar, helpful, but rather more exotic, example to me.

[53] J Stapleton, *Three Essays on Torts* (Oxford, Oxford University Press, 2021) 5.

[54] Lord Reid, 'The Judge as Law Maker' [1972] *Journal of the Society of Public Teachers of Law* 22, 23.

First, what kinds of developments will always be off limits for the courts? And secondly, what kinds of factors afford legitimacy to novel and creative uses of existing rules of law?

In relation to the kinds of decisions that are always off limits, the relevant enquiry should be as to whether the proposed innovation would be *objectionably* retrospective. To explain: since retrospectivity is unavoidable, it follows that the only valid objection from the perspective of retrospectivity is that a decision is objectionably retrospective. And determining whether a decision warrants this description will depend on two factors: first, whether the decision involves the abandonment of an established rule of law; and secondly, whether the litigants had organised their relations in accordance with that rule of law. In any such case, the losing party would be perfectly entitled to feel aggrieved by the retroactive application of the new rule of law. Happily, however, very few common law innovations – and none of those that have occurred thus far within the sphere of the economic torts – meet this description.

As observed on numerous occasions in previous chapters, recent developments in the economic torts have been generally expansionary in nature.[55] In other words, they have taken these torts into pastures new. As such, the application of tort X to novel scenario Y, has inevitably failed to meet the test of objectionably retrospective law-making. Because there has been no abandonment of an extant rule of law, the development clears the first hurdle. But it also clears the second because the novelty of applying tort X to situation Y means that the parties could not possibly have arranged their affairs in the belief that this would occur. At most, one of the parties might have *hoped* the courts would be prepared to apply tort X in such circumstances; but it is not something they could both have *known* and based their dealings upon.

In the absence of any pertinent objections to the practice, what, in more positive terms, can be said in favour of making innovative uses of existing torts (including the economic torts)? In my view, there are two points of particular note that can be invoked, here: the need for the law to keep pace with contemporary circumstances, expectations and challenges; and the need for the law to deliver patently just results.

Numerous judges have, at various different times and in different areas of law, expressed the view that the common law should keep pace with changes in societal values and expectations. For example, impressed with the notion that 'the past is a foreign country',[56] Lord Reid argued that the courts should not consider

[55] *OBG* (n 17) does not fit this description, but nor should it be seen as a case that brought about a contraction in the role of the economic torts. Lots of cases that had previously been misconceived were simply *re-packaged* in *OBG* as instances of the unlawful means tort. In truth, their Lordships removed virtually nothing from the established economic torts canon. The decision in *Millar v Bassey* [1994] EMLR 44 (CA), which was held to be wrongly decided, was the stand out exception.

[56] Opening words of LP Hartley's novel, *The Go Between* (London, Hamish Hamilton, 1953).

themselves too tightly bound by what has been laid down in previous holdings; for such laws – to continue the metaphor – are alien in nature. Judges must therefore possess the power to exercise a degree of developmental freedom since it is the exercise of this power that 'prevents precedent from being our master'.[57] Stressing the need for the law to be appropriately contemporary, he insisted that:

> the law is to develop as the needs of the time require … [So] [e]ven if we do not greatly relax the doctrine of precedent and if we do not encroach on the sphere of Parliament there is still considerable scope for judges to mould the development of the common law.[58]

More pertinently for the purposes of this study is the fact that what Lord Reid suggested in very general terms has already been accepted by the courts as an appropriate way to develop the economic torts. In *Allen v Flood*, for example, Lord Herschell was clear that, '[i]t is the function of the Courts to apply established legal principles to the changing circumstances and conditions of human life'.[59] (And the fact that this was said in so central a case as *Allen* provides yet more reason to doubt Carty's claim that their Lordships had an agenda in that case.) In the equally momentous case of *Rookes v Barnard*, Lord Evershed also recognised that the law's development in this sphere reflects the changing needs and expectations of society. He noted:

> the tort of conspiracy, as now understood, is … one of relatively modern exposition differing from the ancient tort of conspiracy … [it] has arisen out of the circumstances of modern industrial relations. So also, I consider, has the tort of intimidation.[60]

In similar vein, Lord Devlin justified the significant extension to the economic torts brought about by *Rookes* in these terms: 'I think it would be quite wrong to cripple the common law so that it cannot give relief in these circumstances. I think it would be old-fashioned and unrealistic for the law to refuse relief in such a case'.[61]

Much the same approach is in evidence in relation to the misrepresentation torts, too. In chapter six, we noted that Lord Diplock thought it appropriate for the law of passing off to develop in such a way as to align itself with the policy of consumer welfarism that underpinned various related statutes that had been introduced. And, as we also saw in that chapter, the Court of Appeal in *Kaye v Robertson*[62] was happy to stretch the concept of special damage within the tort of injurious falsehood, mindful of the modern expectation in society that an individual's privacy should be properly protected by the law. Bingham LJ made plain his being driven by this concern. He noted that the case before him, 'highlights …

[57] Reid (n 54) 25.
[58] *Ibid.*
[59] *Allen* (n 10) 127–28.
[60] *Rookes* (n 11) 1185.
[61] *Ibid*, 1219.
[62] *Kaye v Robertson* [1991] FSR 62 (CA).

the failure of both the common law of England and statute to protect in an effective way the personal privacy of individual citizens';[63] and then he duly addressed that failure.

The desire to keep the law in tune with contemporary social conditions and expectations is one thing. A concern simply to arrive at a just conclusion in a case involving obviously immoral and wrongful conduct is another. And in relation to my claim that the raw concern to do justice has equally clearly impacted the development of the economic torts, there are, again, numerous supportive judicial statements on offer. Recall, for example, the point made in *Pratt* about its being appropriate to award damages in respect of the humiliation suffered in that case. McCardie J felt he could not 'ignore the deliberate and relentless vigour with which the defendants sought to achieve the infliction of complete ruin'.[64] And in *Total Network*, conscious of the different (ie, non-*OBG*) meaning that he was giving to the phrase 'unlawful means' in that case, Lord Mance contented himself not just with the observation that 'the two torts are different in their nature', but also with the fact that 'the *interests of justice* may require their development on somewhat different bases'.[65]

One of the four main claims of this book has been that the most significant late twentieth, and early twenty-first century developments in the economic torts have, to a very significant degree, been driven by an undisguised concern to do justice, to make tortiously accountable those who have engaged in especially reprehensible conduct. In one case of injurious falsehood, the entirely malicious, and not remotely rivalrous, portrayal of the claimant by the defendant as someone who advertised telephone sex services prompted the court to extend the concept of 'special damage' so as to include injured feelings and distress.[66] In a case concerning two-party intimidation, the utterly appalling use of a woman as a household slave grounded the application of that little-used tort to a non-commercial setting.[67] In the tort of passing off, in order to impose accountability for appalling scams involving the use of other companies' trade marks,[68] the courts stretched the concept of damage to goodwill so as to hold accountable defendants who had never traded, and therefore never actually syphoned off for themselves any of the claimant's existing customers. And in the tort of unlawful means conspiracy, just as they did in *Total Network*, our most senior judges afforded salience in *JSC BTA Bank v Khrapunov* to unlawful means other than the actionable civil law wrongs

[63] *Ibid*, 70.
[64] *Pratt* (n 43) 282.
[65] *Total Network* (n 18) [123] (emphasis added).
[66] See *Khodaparast* (n 42) (discussed above at p 168).
[67] See *Godwin* (n 40); and discussed above at p 133.
[68] See *Direct Line Group Ltd v Direct Line Estate Agency Ltd* [1997] FSR 374 and *Glaxo Plc v Glaxowellcome Ltd* [1996] FSR 388] (discussed above at p 150).

to which that phrase is confined in the tort of causing loss by unlawful means. On this occasion they held a contempt of court would suffice.[69]

This brief reminder of some of the most notable modern developments in the economic torts arena amply substantiates the claim, I think, that the courts have been prepared to extend the reach of these actions – to use them as gap-fillers – where considerations of justice have demanded that this be done. It is hard to disagree with Stevens' contention that 'judge-made law is legitimately concerned with conduct in relation to others which is *malum in se*'.[70] And although it seems inapt to express the point in terms suggestive of an *obligation*, it is easy to understand why the New Zealand Court of Appeal should have declared that 'it is inevitably *the duty of the Court* to extend the scope of the common law if justice so requires'.[71]

III. Interpretivism or Wishful Thinking?

It is true to say that the economic torts vary considerably in the extent to which they are invoked in everyday litigation. Some are in fairly regular use – and there is a steady stream of reported cases that readily attests to this fact. Others generate far less work for those who compile the law reports. In particular, I have in mind here lawful means conspiracy and two-party intimidation. But the mere fact that these two torts are hardly ever relied on in day-to-day litigation should not mislead us into thinking that they are moribund or, at least, suitable candidates for abolition.[72] They remain vital in the strict sense of that word, their continued existence being not just acknowledged, but also treated as crucial to the resuscitation of unlawful means conspiracy in the *Total Network* case.

The predominant harmful purpose requirement in the tort of lawful means conspiracy naturally serves to limit the range of circumstances in which that tort might successfully be invoked.[73] But this does not mean that active steps should be taken to remove it from the tort law canon.[74] Similarly, the fact that cases of

[69] *JSC BTA Bank v Khrapunov* [2020] AC 717 (SC) respectively.

[70] R Stevens, 'The Conflict of Rights' in A Robertson and TH Wu (eds), *The Goals of Private Law* (Oxford, Hart Publishing, 2009) 145.

[71] *Burt v Governor-General of New Zealand* [1992] 3 NZLR 672, 683 (emphasis added).

[72] As O'Sullivan rightly notes, 'the economic torts are not yet ready for the scrapheap': J O'Sullivan, 'Intentional Economic Torts in the House of Lords' [2007] *CLJ* 503, 503. *Cf* Hoffmann (n 14) 114), 'in regulating industrial relations, the economic torts have run their course'; Carty (n 1) 172: 'the courts should accept a minor role in policing economic behaviour … [since] [t]he economic torts act as residual rules of the game'.

[73] Lord Hoffmann expressed the point this way: 'In the *Crofter* case in 1942, the judges drew the teeth of bad motive conspiracy by requiring disinterested malice on the part of the conspirators': Hoffmann (n 14) 111. Carty too thinks this 'tort was always seen as a damp squib, the malice spark appearing to limit the tort to extreme scenarios': Carty (n 19) 266.

[74] See further, J Murphy, 'Malice as an Ingredient of Tort Liability' [2019] *CLJ* 355, 381–82.

two-party intimidation are rare indeed, does not license the conclusion that we would be better off abolishing this valuable weapon of last resort for claimants who, by definition, have been treated in a most reprehensible way.

Although cases of injurious falsehood are by no means as rare as cases involving either lawful means conspiracy or two-party intimidation, this has not stopped some judges and jurists from suggesting that it is surplus to requirements in that it merely replicates protection offered by some other statutory or common law action. But as we saw in chapter six, such claims concerning the redundancy of injurious falsehood are ungrounded: it retains, as I demonstrated at some length, a clearly discernible, discrete role; and it remains the only available action in a wider range of circumstances than is commonly supposed.[75]

What is much more difficult to substantiate than the continued vitality of the eight torts in view, is the legitimacy of their being used in the various novel (but as yet untried) ways that I suggested in chapters three to six. The obvious objection, for anyone minded to keep these torts securely tethered to the protection of economic interests, is to say that what I proposed in relation to their future possible uses is just wishful thinking on my part, that my suggestions constitute an abandonment of this book's supposed interpretive ambitions. To put it bluntly, the objection would be that my suggestions constitute a nakedly prescriptive agenda that has *only* my personal preferences to ground it.

This is an ostensibly powerful objection, but it is nonetheless, I think, one that can be rebutted, such rebuttal coming in three stages. To begin with I would acknowledge the prescriptive dimension to my claims about what these torts can be used for. But, secondly, I would also point out that *some element* of prescription is inevitable in academic analysis of law that purports to be interpretive in nature: if the account on offer is to count for more than what might be called 'legal journalism', it must aspire to be more than merely a dull and unreflective *description* of the role of the torts in question. Mere description and academic analysis are very different beasts. Finally, I would resist the accusation that some of my arguments – albeit that they are prescriptive in nature – are driven *entirely* by my personal aspirations for these torts.

The admission that it is prescriptive on my part to claim that all but one of the torts discussed in this book can *in principle* be used to protect other interests than those that are economic in nature requires no elaboration. But the foundations for the second and third parts of my response to the objection about prescription are less obvious. It is therefore important that they be explained properly.

As to the second part of my response, it is inescapably the case that an attempt to explain the nature and contours of the law (at least when those matters are to some degree fuzzy), necessarily involves making choices and, in turn, claims of the kind, 'interpretation X is preferable to interpretation Y'. I have clearly made

[75] The terrain *uniquely* covered by this tort was sketched in detail in chapter six.

such choices and advanced such claims. But it is only to the extent that doing so is inescapable, that I have indulged in prescription. Broadly speaking, three options exist for the scholar attempting to shed light on this notoriously complex bunch of torts. The first is to take seriously what the courts have said, but where doubt exists, elect always to adopt a narrow interpretation of what these torts protect. Scholars who take this approach – such as Carty and Deakin who stick resolutely to the idea that these torts are designed to only protect trade and business interests – may be thought of as 'precedent-respecting conservatives'.

At the other extreme, there are those commentators (such as Beever and Neyers) who would simply ride rough-shod over certain landmark decisions in arriving at their respective understandings of these torts. As we saw in chapter two, they – in an attempt to prop up or fortify their respective Kantian and rights-based interpretations of the actions – simply say of certain landmark holdings that they are wrong, anomalous, mysterious etc. Their accounts purport to be interpretive in nature; and the authors would doubtless say that in arriving at their understandings they merely afford more weight to the (accepted) justification component of the interpretivist enterprise than they do to the fit component.[76] But the snag for any such accounts – which are undoubtedly prescriptive insofar as they represent the authors' conception of the best possible light in which the law might be presented – is that there is only so much of the past that can legitimately be disregarded. As Dworkin, the doyen of interpretivism, explained (in setting out his account of what the enterprise entails): 'the history or shape of a practice or object constrains the available interpretations of it'.[77] So, even when the overall aim is to present the law in its best possible light, 'fit will [still] provide a rough, threshold requirement that an[y] interpretation … must meet if it is to be eligible at all'.[78] Because Beever and Neyers are so willing to side-line what was said in even certain leading cases, I label them 'precedent-ignoring mavericks'.[79]

[76] The idea that interpretive accounts of the law possess both a justification and a fit component can be traced to the scholarship of Ronald Dworkin. For Dworkin, interpretivism involves presenting the law in its best possible light. This need not require that the explanation on offer be *entirely consistent* with all of the 'brute facts' of legal history given that this best possible light will require that the interpretation be such that the law appears justifiable: see R Dworkin, *Law's Empire* (Cambridge, Massachusetts, Belknap Press, 1996) 255. More fully: interpretivism, according to Dworkin, involves an on-going narrative which, while it needs to accommodate much of the past and be overwhelmingly consistent with it, must also aspire to be morally and politically palatable in the here and now (*ibid*, 225). In his precise words, interpretivism 'begins in the present and pursues the past *only so far as and in the way that its contemporary focus dictates*' (*ibid*, 227) (emphasis added).

[77] *Ibid*, 52.

[78] *Ibid*, 255.

[79] Recall, eg, Beever's claims that (1) 'no economic tort was committed in *Total Network*' and (2) the entire tort of inducing breach of contract is 'a mistake', an action that 'was invented out of nothing': A Beever, *A Theory of Tort Liability* (Oxford, Hart Publishing, 2016) 145. And Neyers, too, in an attempt to explain the unlawful means tort according to his 'public right theory' states (with little concern for the landmark status of one very well-known case), that 'accepting the public right theory would require the English courts to turn back the clock on the tort of unlawful interference with economic relations and to accept that the decision in *Rookes v Barnard* was a wrong turn': JW Neyers, 'The Economic Torts as Corrective Justice' (2009) 17 *Torts Law Journal* 1, 33.

My own approach steers a middle course. True: it, too, offers more than a mere description of the scope of these torts as established by the decided cases. But where I have suggested answers to various questions that have yet to come before the courts, I have done so in a way that respects fully the various principles that have been unequivocally laid down in the past. Nothing that I have proposed clashes with anything that has previously been ruled out by the courts. And nor, I should stress, have I attempted to present the law in a way that is designed to chime with some or other grand theory that I am keen to peddle. Instead, all of the suggestions have been based on one of two things, either: (1) possibilities espoused in non-binding judicial statements (ie, obiter dicta in English cases, or judicial pronouncements in other common law jurisdictions); or (2) '[t]he usual priority in the law of tort'[80] (a phrase used by one current Supreme Court judge to capture the fact that personal and proprietary interests are generally more readily protected in tort law than purely economic interests).[81] Either way, all of what I have proposed can be said to rest on things that have been said by judges. And because the developments I have suggested can be traced to such sources, I would describe the limited and unavoidable prescriptive aspect of my own analysis as being minimal: that of an 'precedent-respecting progressive'.

In order to make good the third part of my rebuttal of the accusation that my depiction of the scope of the torts discussed in this book involves wishful thinking on my part, it is perhaps helpful to provide a reminder of just what I have suggested.

In chapter three, in relation to the tort of inducing breach of contract, I argued that there was nothing in the case law that constrains the use of that action to the protection of only economic losses. I emphasised the fact that some of the cases treated as foundational to the decision in *Lumley*[82] were cases in which personal interests were protected. I showed, too, that that there was nothing in *Lumley* itself (or in the case law that followed in its wake), that could be seen as restricting the tort's relevance to contracts of a purely commercial nature. It was the absence of anything to the contrary in the law as it presents itself, combined with a recognition of the judicially recognised superiority of our personal and proprietary interests that grounded the claim that the tort should be available in relation to contracts for, say, the provision of health care or the protection of property. On top

[80] Davies and Sales (n 16) 84.

[81] It is precisely because these interests are ordinarily regarded as being the most worthy of tort's protection that renders palatable (1) deceit cases providing damages for physical injury, (2) the successful invocation of intimidation by a woman treated as a virtual slave and, (3) the lawful means conspiracy case of *Gulf Oil (GB) Ltd v Page* (1987) Ch 327 (CA) signalling a willingness to extend that tort to the protection of C's reputation.

[82] *Lumley* (n 2). It is not clear, given the cases concerning the seduction of a wife or a daughter that the court turned to in *Lumley*, why Lord Hoffmann should have written (extra-judicially) that, '[t]he original purpose of *Lumley v Gye* … was to lay down a common rule about what amounts to unfair competition': Hoffmann (n 14) 107. But even so, the fact that he spoke of 'the original purpose' arguably reveals an acceptance that the tort now does (or could) fulfil a more expansive, modern purpose.

of this, it is instructive to note that, in Canada, the courts have expressly recognised the capacity of this tort to be used to secure reparation for injured feelings and loss of reputation caused by an induced breach of contract.[83] To reiterate: all of what I suggested in relation to this tort can be traced to things judges (albeit in contexts that do not render their words binding) have said.

In chapter four, I pointed out obiter dicta suggesting that unlawful means conspiracy might potentially be used to circumvent 'the problem' of limited corporate liability in cases where the company which commits the relevant wrong was a one-person company, a company with a sole director. The idea put forward, it will be recalled, was that such a director might be treated as a co-conspirator along with his or her company. I also suggested in chapter four that, although in *OBG* Lord Hoffmann insisted that for C to be able to invoke the unlawful means tort she must have had an economic link with the third party through whom the defendant struck at C, there was nothing in his speech that confined C's recoverable losses to those of an economic variety. Nothing changed in this respect when, in 2021, the Supreme Court confirmed that Lord Hoffmann's dealing requirement had been introduced as an element of the tort.[84] In mounting the argument that other (more highly valued) interests might in principle be protected by this tort, I adapted various hypotheticals proposed by others, including one proffered by Lord Sales (extra-judicially). Here again, then, my proposals were linked to things considered by judges to fall within (rather than beyond) the compass of the two torts discussed.

In chapter five, I placed considerable weight on the fact that, in *Rookes*, there are obiter dicta that specifically endorse the idea that the tort of intimidation can be invoked in a two-party scenario. I did not ignore the fact that Lord Hoffmann appeared hostile to such two-party forms of economic tort liability in *OBG*. But I did emphasise the important point that neither he, nor any other member of the panel in that case, cast any doubt on the correctness of the decisions in the two-party cases of *Godwin v Uzoigwe*,[85] and *Newsgroup Newspapers Ltd v SOGAT '82*.[86] The significance of those cases being left unscathed in *OBG* derives from the fact that their Lordships in *OBG* made a concerted effort to tidy up this area of the law, to correct the errors of the past.[87] A reasonable inference, then, is that *Godwin* and *SOGAT '82* were not seen in *OBG* as having been wrongly decided. To this observation I added the point that the differently constituted panel that decided *Total Network* treated the vitality of two-party intimidation as important when it came

[83] *Drouillard v Cogeco Cable Inc*, 2007 ONCA 485, [42] (Rouleau JA); *Sateri (Shanghai) Management Limited v Vinall*, 2017 BCSC 491, [626] (Justice Ballance).

[84] See *Servier* (n 49). Indeed, as noted above, there was even the obiter suggestion in this case that physical injury should in principle be recoverable under the auspices of the unlawful means tort.

[85] *Godwin* (n 40).

[86] *Newsgroup Newspapers Ltd v SOGAT '82* [1987] ICR 181 (CA).

[87] See, eg, *OBG* (n 17) 42 (Lord Hoffmann): 'the majority of the Court of Appeal was wrong to have allowed the action in *Millar v Bassey*'.

to establishing the legitimacy of two-party liability for unlawful means conspiracy (an idea that has since taken root in Canada[88]). Accordingly, my defence of the continued existence of two-party intimidation can similarly be seen as having been anchored to what judges have either said, albeit not in an actual case of two-party intimidation.

In chapter six, my claim that injurious falsehood is capable of providing remedies for injured feelings and distress, even in the absence of any trade or business loss, was based on historical sources supportive of a broad conception of 'special damage', as well as some more recent obiter dicta suggesting that the tort may be used in this way. I also flagged up in chapter six the fact that there exists, here and there, some limited judicial support for the notion that passing off might conceivably develop into an action for unfair competition,[89] or one for misappropriation.[90] But I was careful to place such obiter dicta in context. Ultimately, I resisted the temptation to come to any firm conclusion on the merits of such possible developments. True: I found fault with the argument against them from the standpoint of precedent-respecting conservativism – the argument, that is, that passing off should remain true to the classical trinity *tightly construed* in the interests of commercial certainty.[91] But at the same time, I could see nothing convincing to support such developments; and I was careful to note that the dicta in question were proffered in very tentative terms.

To summarise: although I have argued throughout this book that the torts in view might sensibly be put to various as-yet-untried purposes, I at no stage abandoned my commitment to supplying a properly precedent-respecting interpretation of the law as it stands. I have explained why any account of this kind necessarily involves some measure of prescription. The law is never entirely clear, so a degree of personal preference (in selecting interpretation A over interpretation B) will inevitably feature in the analysis. Nonetheless, what I think makes the choices I have made defensible is the fact that they have been based on non-binding things said by judges in combination with the usual priority afforded to various types of interests in tort law. Other commentators stand in stark contrast, since their choices have either been rooted in precommitments to some or other grand theory of tort law, or the notion that these particular torts should be confined to a minimal – indeed, residual – role in the regulation of trade rivalry. Neither of these approaches seems to me to be defensible. Indeed, in my view, these writers get

[88] See *Gagnon v Foundation Maritime Ltd* [1961] SCR 535 (SCC).

[89] See, eg, S Deakin and Z Adams, *Markesinis and Deakin's Tort Law*, 8th edn (Oxford, Oxford University Press, 2019) 693.

[90] See, eg, J Davis, 'Why the United Kingdom Should Have a Law against Misappropriation' [2010] *CLJ* 561. *Cf* M Spence, 'Passing Off and the Misappropriation of Valuable Intangibles' (1996) 112 *LQR* 472; C Wadlow, 'Passing off at the Crossroads Again: a Review Article for Hazel Carty, *An Analysis of the Economic Torts*' (2011) 33 *European Intellectual Property Review* 447, 452–53.

[91] H Carty, 'Passing Off: Frameworks of Liability Debated' (2012) 16 *Intellectual Property Quarterly* 106, 117.

things the wrong way round. If one sets out to explain the law, then it is surely the job of the explanation to fit the law, rather than the job of the law to fit the putative explanation.

At the very least it strikes me as odd that a set of actions that has never actually been confined by the courts to the protection of economic interests should in future be so confined given that economic interests are generally regarded as the lowest ranking ones that are recognised by tort law.

IV. Conclusion

Not all of those who favour a conservative role for the economic torts would accept Lord Hoffmann's view that they are now more or less redundant.[92] Writing in 2009, for example, Deakin argued that, 'as recent cases illustrate, there are situations in which legislation cannot provide an answer, and in which the torts once again assume a decisive role'.[93] But what he underestimated was just how commonplace such cases would be after *OBG* and *Total Network*. He clearly thought there was a chance that these torts might in future be confined to (his preferred) 'residual market-protecting role'.[94] And six years later, Carty advanced a broadly similar claim.[95]

Other commentators took a different view. For instance, by O'Sullivan's reckoning, the fact 'the common law still plays an important role in this area … is seen in the recent spate of appellate decisions on the scope and elements of the various economic torts'.[96] I think the true position lies somewhere between these two poles. The idea that the economic torts are destined to play a residual, market-protecting role is clearly not borne out by the decisions in *Total Network* and *Khrapunov*,[97] for neither of the cases had anything at all to do with the protection of markets. Equally the floodgate fears that featured so prominently in the Supreme Court's reckoning in *Secretary of State for Health v Servier Laboratories Ltd*[98] are hard to reconcile with the idea that these torts are somehow withering on the vine. On the other hand, it is clearly hyperbole when O'Sullivan speaks of a 'spate' of litigation concerning the economic torts. A more modest assessment is that all of the torts discussed in chapters three to six remain vital, but with only a limited role to play in the grand scheme of tort litigation.

[92] See Hoffmann (n 14).

[93] Deakin and Randall (n 6) 532.

[94] *Ibid*, 534.

[95] Carty (n 19): 283: 'these torts should remain a modest common law contribution to policing excessive competitive behaviour and no more'.

[96] J O'Sullivan, 'Intentional Economic Torts, Commercial Transactions and Professional Liability' (2008) 24 *Professional Negligence* 164, 165.

[97] *Total Network* (n 18) and *Khrapunov* (n 69).

[98] *Servier* (n 49).

As with many areas of the law, there remain numerous unanswered questions in this sphere that will doubtless trouble the courts in years to come.[99] But for all that there is lingering conceptual uncertainty about both the ingredients and scope of the various actions discussed in this book, one thing does seem clear. This is that, as Lord Sales put it, '[t]here is "no inherent unity" amongst these torts, and grouping them together only serves to confuse'.[100] In chapter seven, I explained in some detail just how differentiated a bunch of actions they are in juridical and structural terms, while in chapter eight I endeavoured to show why this should be so, ie because no single factor can be identified that satisfactorily accounts for either the genesis or the subsequent development of the various actions. The fact that the eight torts discussed in this book were created and then subsequently remoulded, at different points in time, in response to different stimuli and at the hands of many different judges, makes it unsurprising that the economic torts remain what they have always been: a loosely affiliated bunch of actions that bear out Ibbetson's contention that '[t]here are no limits to the types of conduct that can be labelled wrongful, and no natural laws determining the ways in which they can be grouped together'.[101]

In law as in life, predicting the future is risky business. I therefore stop short of saying *exactly* what direction the various economic torts will take during the remainder of the twenty first century. I have gone no further in this book than to suggest a series of possible roles that I think they *could usefully fulfil* in the future, and I have been at pains to point out that they are all roles that are by no means obstructed (and often obliquely supported) by the authorities as they present themselves.

I will dare, however, to venture here (with a higher degree of specificity) a word on what I think these torts will *not do* in the foreseeable future. And that is become a family of actions that is strictly confined to the protection of trade or business interests. The misnomer 'the economic torts' is likely to stick; but it is notable indeed that one current Supreme Court judge, Lord Sales, is on record as saying that, so far as these torts are concerned, 'the competitive process in which these torts often operate should not confine their proper ambit'.[102] The fact that he thinks this way should render it obvious why – despite my quibbles with some of his extra-judicial analysis in this field – I considered him the best possible person to have write the foreword for this book.

[99] Two of their Lordships expressly admitted as much in *Servier* (n 49): Lord Hamblen (at [97]), and Lord Sales (at [102]).

[100] Davies and Sales (n 16) 83.

[101] Ibbetson (n 48) 201.

[102] Davies and Sales (n 16) 85. At the same time, it is also worth noting that one of Lord Sales' colleagues appears to be what I have called a precedent-respecting progressive. For, according to Lord Hodge, '[c]hanges to the law should be derived from existing legal materials by applying established principles and legal values in new contexts': Hodge (n 47) 221.

INDEX

www.ingramcontent.com/pod-product-compliance
Ingram Content Group UK Ltd.
Pitfield, Milton Keynes, MK11 3LW, UK
UKHW020241290926
15470UKWH00002B/673